After Shakespeare

After Shakespeare

AN ANTHOLOGY

EDITED BY

JOHN GROSS

OXFORD
UNIVERSITY PRESS

OXFORD
UNIVERSITY PRESS

Great Clarendon Street, Oxford OX2 6DP

Oxford University Press is a department of the University of Oxford.
It furthers the University's objective of excellence in research, scholarship,
and education by publishing worldwide in

Oxford New York

Athens Auckland Bangkok Bogotá Buenos Aires Cape Town
Chennai Dar es Salaam Delhi Florence Hong Kong Istanbul Karachi
Kolkata Kuala Lumpur Madrid Melbourne Mexico City Mumbai Nairobi
Paris São Paulo Shanghai Singapore Taipei Tokyo Toronto Warsaw
with associated companies in Berlin Ibadan

Oxford is a registered trade mark of Oxford University Press
in the UK and in certain other countries

Published in the United States
by Oxford University Press Inc., New York

Introduction and selection © John Gross 2002
Further copyright information appears on pp. 345–54

The moral rights of the author have been asserted
Database right Oxford University Press (maker)

First published 2002

British Library Cataloguing in Publication Data
Data available

Library of Congress Cataloging in Publication Data
Data available
ISBN 0–19–214268–2

1 3 5 7 9 10 8 6 4 2

Typeset in Dante MT
by RefineCatch Limited, Bungay, Suffolk
Printed in Great Britain
on acid-free paper by
T.J. International Ltd.,
Padstow, Cornwall

CONTENTS

INTRODUCTION

No writer has served as such a powerful source of inspiration for other writers as Shakespeare. (Well, Homer perhaps, if there was a Homer.) No writer has attracted such widespread and varied comment. There is a Shakespeare literature which extends far beyond formal Shakespeare criticism or Shakespeare scholarship—a literature which the present anthology sets out to represent.

That his influence should have proved as fertilizing as it has is not just a gauge of his greatness. It also reflects the particular nature of that greatness, or some of its major aspects. He wrote for a popular medium. He created strong dramatic structures. Most of his characters, whatever their internal complexities, are readily grasped in outline. His plays have a mythic quality, and more than any other form of fiction myths lend themselves to borrowing and adaptation.

There are many works which can lay some claim to being Shakespearian by virtue of taking over Shakespearian plots or motifs. Sometimes the debt is unspoken though obvious: *West Side Story* is a celebrated example. Sometimes it advertises itself, as in Turgenev's *A Lear of the Steppes* or Leskov's *Lady Macbeth of Mtsensk*. But such works are analogues rather than reworkings, and rightly or wrongly they don't fall within the scope of this anthology. The Shakespearian element in them seems to me not much more than a starting-point.

Nor, on the other hand, have I tried to display Shakespeare's influence at its deepest. Influence, in principle, is something which flows, and influences which can be demonstrated in detail are usually (though not always) influences which haven't been properly digested. Conversely, the most profound influences are commonly the most diffuse. Countless writers have been roused or liberated by Shakespeare, among them some of the greatest—Pushkin, for example, or Melville; and what they have mostly learned have been new ways of organizing their experience, of unlocking their full powers of expression, of relating public themes to the life of the individual. Such lessons are broad and general, and in the works which embody them Shakespeare tends to be everywhere and nowhere in particular.

In my choice of imaginative writing, then, I have confined myself to material which is specifically Shakespearian—which builds on individual characters and plays, or on the life and personality of

Shakespeare himself. That still leaves a great deal to be getting on with.

First, the poets. Many of them have been moved to write poems about Shakespearian characters, from Herman Melville on Falstaff to Ted Hughes on Prospero and Sycorax. Sometimes they have extended the stories of such characters backwards or forwards in time; sometimes they have offered a different view of them from the one presented in the plays; sometimes they have used them to furnish dramatic parallels—Heine on Jessica and Lorenzo—or as a vehicle for their own preoccupations. In this department, as often in the anthology, *Hamlet* predominates to what many may feel is a disproportionate degree, in literary terms, but one which accurately reflects the play's status as a cultural icon. Certainly the *Hamlet* poems are impressive both for their quality and their international range: Pasternak and Brecht on the prince himself, Rimbaud and Marina Tsvetayeva on Ophelia, Cavafy on Claudius, Miroslav Holub on Polonius, the Polish poet Zbigniew Herbert's 'Elegy of Fortinbras'.

There are also a few poems devoted to entire plays. Derek Walcott packs a good deal of feeling about *Othello* into 'Goats and Monkeys', and some of the finest verse ever inspired by Shakespeare can be found in Auden's 'commentary on *The Tempest*', *The Sea and the Mirror*. (It is represented here, inadequately of course, by his poem on Trinculo.)

Nor are poems with an admixture of Shakespeare limited to poems on Shakespearian themes. In the right context, a single borrowed phrase or allusion can set up strong reverberations—Prufrock averring that he is not Prince Hamlet, Seamus Heaney quoting Captain MacMorris; and although trying to write in 'Shakespearian' is an obvious dead end, poets as far apart as Milton and Emily Dickinson have successfully integrated Shakespearian echoes into their own work. Such echoes abound in prose, too; and the entries in John Ruskin's extraordinary 'Brantwood Diary' show how deeply they can become woven into an individual psyche.

From the eighteenth century onwards, novelists have drawn on Shakespeare in a variety of ways. They have adapted his themes, drawn parallels with him (one whole section of Dostoevsky's *The Devils* is entitled 'Prince Hal'), used him as a cultural reference-point (as in *Brave New World*), or for ironic contrast, or to create atmosphere (as in Dickens—although Dickens's Shakespearian references often have a thematic point as well). *Hamlet* hovers on the edge of the first great self-reflexive novel, *Tristram Shandy*, and provides one of the central themes in the first great *Bildungsroman*, Goethe's *Wilhelm Meister*; and at the risk of letting the same play predominate once again, I have also included extracts from two later works of fiction built around it, Jules Laforgue's *Hamlet, ou les suites de la piété filiale* and John Updike's *Gertrude and Claudius*. (Fiction can present an anthologist with problems. I would like to have found space for something from Isak Dinesen's story 'Tempests', which has many parallels with the Shakespearian *Tempest*, or from the *As You Like It* sequence in Théophile Gautier's novel *Mademoiselle de Maupin*, but neither of them lent themselves to being represented by a sufficiently short excerpt.)

In the theatre, the most notable Shakespearian offshoots have been largely negative, much more so than in poetry or the novel. This apparent paradox is easily explained. As an exemplar of dramatic art, a model of how things should be done, Shakespeare's influence has been immense, especially on foreign dramatists—on Schiller, on the Pushkin of *Boris Godunov*, on Victor Hugo, on Ibsen in his early historical plays, on scores of others. But to get too close to his actual subject-matter (or, for an anglophone playwright, his actual language) is to invite being scorched by the comparison. A few intrepid spirits have tried—the Georgian poet Gordon Bottomley in his verse-plays about King Lear's wife and the early life of Lady Macbeth, for instance—but almost the only neo-Shakespearian plays with any life in them are anti-Shakespearian in spirit, or at any rate (since they pay implicit tribute to his power) hostile to his values: *Ubu Roi*, Brecht's *Coriolan*, Aimé Césaire's *Une tempête*, Ionesco's *Macbett*, the cynical revision of *King John* by Friedrich Dürrenmatt. Tom Stoppard's *Rosencrantz and Guildenstern are Dead* stands somewhat apart, however: it is a witty interrogation of *Hamlet* rather than an outright lampoon.

Perhaps the most striking feature of the imaginative writing which derives from Shakespeare is the amount of it devoted to Shakespeare himself. Beginning with Ben Jonson's tribute in the First Folio, he has inspired a number of notable poems. The most Shakespeare-saturated of great novels, *Ulysses*, is preoccupied with the man rather than the work. Story-tellers as different as Kipling and Anthony Burgess offer us equally plausible Shakespeares; and the fascination of the portraits they paint is a tribute not only to his greatness, but also to the fact that we know so much about him (since we have the plays) and so little, that he is forever just eluding our grasp. In the most effective modern play in which he figures, Peter Whelan's *The Herbal Bed*, he establishes a forceful presence by remaining out of sight: he is the man living next door of whom we almost catch a glimpse.

Much of the comment collected in this volume could reasonably be described, though sometimes only very loosely, as criticism. There are already a great many anthologies of Shakespeare criticism, both literary and dramatic, and one of my guiding principles has been to try to avoid overlapping with them. That mainly means excluding examples of academic criticism, however helpful or illuminating it may be at its best. But anthologies of criticism also commonly feature the work of Dryden, Johnson, Coleridge, and a handful of other critics who are major literary figures in their own right. The absence of such writers, in a book like the present one, may seem a very large gap indeed. None the less, bearing in mind how readily available their work is elsewhere, and how many other authors there were clamouring for attention, I have stuck to my resolve: they have been excluded. Or very nearly. When it came to it, I couldn't bring myself to apply the ban quite as ruthlessly as I had intended, and a few examples of their writing have slipped by.

There is no virtue, needless to say, in simply pushing academic criticism to one side. The only point in doing so is to make room for alternative approaches, for the more informal or discursive or—on occasion—more inspired traditions of talking about Shakespeare which I have tried to bring to the fore.

Most of the commentators represented are celebrated writers themselves. Have the extracts from them been chosen because (in my judgement) they display greater insight into Shakespeare than the observations of more narrowly professional critics? Sometimes, yes; but the reason is at least as likely to have been that they are more eloquent, or wittier, or more vehement, or more vivid. Not that their views and the manner in which they are expressed can be kept apart. The comments of an Emerson, a Chesterton, a Virginia Woolf would be far less suggestive if we tried to rephrase them; the expositions of a Yeats, an Auden, a John Berryman would lose most of their power if we boiled them down.

The amount of light which such writers shed on Shakespeare is in any case only half the story, and sometimes less than half. D. H. Lawrence on *Hamlet* reveals a certain amount about *Hamlet*, but rather more about Lawrence. The main point of Strindberg's remarks about *Othello* is that they are exquisitely Strindbergian. And even the more detached critical comments of a creative writer will always derive much of their interest from their source: they are part of that writer's work, not simply a footnote to somebody else's.

When the writer in question is foreign, there is the further bonus, for English readers, of gaining fresh entry into his or her culture. Or into one aspect of that culture, since naturally there is no 'French Shakespeare' or 'Russian Shakespeare': there are only French Shakespeares and Russian Shakespeares. Pushkin's conception of Falstaff differs considerably from Tolstoy's or Dostoevsky's. (It is more genial.) Sartre's extended reflections on *Lear* arise out of his quarrel with Flaubert. Nor does a writer necessarily have to speak directly for his own culture in order to open doors. It is hard to imagine an Englishman writing Wole Soyinka's remarkable essay on *Antony and Cleopatra*, for instance: its foreignness is almost a condition of its breadth and originality. But Soyinka is a Nigerian, and the focus of the essay is firmly on Egypt.

While novelists, poets, and playwrights are the largest group represented in *After Shakespeare*, it is an essential part of the book's purpose to move beyond them. Heminges and Condell, in their preface to the First Folio, addressed themselves 'to the great variety of readers', and ever since (if not before) the most diverse readers, and playgoers, have recorded their reactions to Shakespeare, or felt moved to voice an opinion about him. A sampling of comment which was exclusively literary would give a very imperfect idea of what he has meant to the world.

One limitation must be noted. Among all the non-literary persons—the non-literati—from whom I have quoted, hardly any could be called ordinary people. This is a matter for some regret. It would be pleasant, and satisfyingly democratic, if Everyman and Everywoman were more adequately represented—if there were more items comparable to the poignant recollection of the Lancashire weaver's daughter Alice Foley, for instance. The main problem is that Everyman and Everywoman don't often set their views down in writing, or that they don't get published when they do. (A notable exception—I have failed to come across an English-language equivalent—is the Shakespeare journal kept by the eighteenth-century Swiss weaver Ulrich Bräker.) No doubt an extensive trawl through letters, diaries and the like would turn up items of interest. Who is to say that there aren't a few precocious pearls buried in old school essays? But such a project would be far beyond the resources of an individual anthologist.

It is possible—a consoling thought—that we may not be missing all that much. The Common Reader is an admirable and indispensable figure, but I suspect that when he picks up his pen or sits down at his word-processor he has a way of turning into the Commonplace Critic. And meanwhile, we can derive a double comfort from the fact that the philosophers, artists, statesmen, scientists, and most of the other non-literati who have been included are anything but ordinary people. Their comments are often remarkable, too; and even when they aren't, the question of who is saying something lends significance to what is being said. A hundred other commentators, if they had turned their minds to it, might have come up with the observation that there is no mention of Magna Carta in *King John*. That it should have been the great historian Leopold von Ranke who got there first is a fact of considerable interest in itself. Sir Joshua Reynolds' remarks on *Macbeth* are not in themselves very profound. It is Reynolds' personality and the cultural authority he enjoyed in his own time which give them resonance.

Some of the most stirring written reactions to Shakespeare have come from artists in other fields who have adapted his work to their own medium—Berlioz, for example, or the Russian film director Grigor Kozintsev. Among other categories, I have been especially tempted to concentrate on rulers and politicians. Not only do they offer, between them, some rich contrasts. Their involvement with Shakespeare also underlines the extent to which, over the centuries, he has continued to play an active political role—recruited by warring parties, cited by rival ideologues, sometimes transcending social divisions, sometimes reinforcing them. He has been enlisted for propaganda purposes, and used as a refuge from propaganda; and he has a knack of showing up at fateful historical moments. At the end of the nineteenth century, he was being read on Devil's Island by Alfred Dreyfus. Seventy-five years later, he was being read on Robben Island by Nelson Mandela.

There are lighter aspects. Shakespeare impinges on popular culture through films, songs, and images (the Droeshout portrait must be as familiar as Mona Lisa); through well-loved jokes (like the one about the Victorian lady who had been to see *Antony and Cleopatra*—'so very different from the home life of our own dear Queen'); through familiar quotations. He has been a recurrent target for parody and burlesque. If the section of this book called 'Early Encounters' shows how deeply he can engage young imaginations, there is also an excerpt from *Down with Skool!* to remind us that most people's first encounter with him (and sometimes their last) takes place in a dusty classroom. The Baconian theory and similar speculations couldn't be entirely ignored, either—not with someone like Henry James willing to flirt with them. And I have included a few unclassifiable items that I can only call curiosities.

There are many works, in addition to those already mentioned, which I regret having had to pass over for lack of space. I would like to have included something from Ernest Renan's drama of ideas, *Caliban*. I am sorry not to have had room for Edwin Arlington Robinson's fine dramatic monologue, *Ben Jonson Entertains a Man from Stratford*. But then comprehensiveness, in such a field, is hardly to be looked for, and I hope that my selection will at least give a fair idea of the extent to which Shakespeare has been, like Falstaff, the cause of wit in others—and not only wit, but poetry, creative fantasy, and searching reflection as well.

After Shakespeare

BY WAY OF A PROLOGUE

That Shakespearian rag,—
Most intelligent, very elegant.

> GENE BUCK and HERMAN RUBY, 'That Shakespearian Rag', popular song, 1912

After God, Shakespeare has created most.

> ALEXANDRE DUMAS *père*, 'How I Became a Playwright', 1863

In his creation of souls as he had no predecessor (with one august Exception, and even Adam and Eve are more 'types' than characters, being quite unlike Hamlet and Cleopatra), so no one ever since has been his equal.

> LOGAN PEARSALL SMITH, *On Reading Shakespeare*, 1933

If we wish to know the force of human genius, we should read Shakespeare. If we wish to see the insignificance of human learning, we may study his commentators.

> WILLIAM HAZLITT, *Table Talk*, 1821

Parts of Shakespeare are ugly, and much of him is whimsical, and some of him is perverted. But his work is all a natural product, like the silk worm's thread. One can never be quite sure that even Thersites may not show under the microscope some beautiful patterns on his back, as Caliban does.

> JOHN JAY CHAPMAN, *Greek Genius and Other Essays*, 1915

In G. B. Shaw's original assaults on Shakespeare he called his ideas 'trite'. Of course they were trite, none other are admissible in pure poetry. The muses are the daughters of memory.

> J. B. YEATS, letter to his son W. B. Yeats, 1915

Shakespeare: the rendezvous of an axe and a rose.

E. M. CIORAN, *Syllogismes de l'amertume*, 1952

Sex ran in him like the sea.

JOHN MASEFIELD, *Shakespeare*, 1911

What there was in the world to be done in Shakespearean has largely been done by Shakespeare.

GEORG CHRISTOPH LICHTENBERG, notebooks, 1765–99, tr. J. P. Stern

In an age of copyright, Shakespeare, to be able to write the plays in the form in which we have them, would have had to get licenses from the owners of copyrights on works from which he took plot details or actual language. The costs of finding and negotiating with each copyright owner might have reduced Shakespeare's output, or changed (for worse—else presumably he would have made the change on his own) his method of composition.

RICHARD A. POSNER, *Law and Literature*, 1988

Fantastic! And it was all written with a feather!

SAMUEL GOLDWYN (attrib.), on first looking into the collected works of Shakespeare

Our admiration cannot easily surpass his genius.

WILLIAM HAZLITT

THE MAN AND THE LEGEND

Everything and Nothing

There was no one inside him, nothing but a trace of chill, a dream dreamt by no one else behind the face that looks like no other face (even in the bad paintings of the period) and the abundant, whimsical, impassioned words. He started out assuming that everyone was just like him; the puzzlement of a friend to whom he had confided a little of his emptiness revealed his error and left him with the lasting impression that the individual should not diverge from the species. At one time he thought he could find a cure for his ailment in books and accordingly learned the 'small Latin and less Greek' to which a contemporary later referred. He next decided that what he was looking for might be found in the practice of one of humanity's more elemental rituals: he allowed Anne Hathaway to initiate him over the course of a long June afternoon. In his twenties he went to London. He had become instinctively adept at pretending to be somebody, so that no one would suspect he was in fact nobody. In London he discovered the profession for which he was destined, that of the actor who stands on a stage and pretends to be someone else in front of a group of people who pretend to take him for that other person. Theatrical work brought him a rare happiness, possibly the first he had ever known—but when the last line had been applauded and the last corpse removed from the stage, the odious shadow of unreality fell over him again: he ceased being Ferrex or Tamburlaine and went back to being nobody. Hard pressed, he took to making up other heroes, other tragic tales. While his body fulfilled its bodily destiny in the taverns and brothels of London, the soul inside it belonged to Caesar who paid no heed to the oracle's warnings and Juliet who hated skylarks and Macbeth in conversation, on the heath, with witches who were also the Fates. No one was as many men as this man: like the Egyptian Proteus, he used up the forms of all creatures. Every now and then he would tuck a confession into some hidden corner of his work, certain that no one would spot it. Richard states that he plays many roles in one, and Iago makes the odd claim: 'I am not what I am.'

The fundamental identity of existing, dreaming, and acting inspired him to write famous lines.

For twenty years he kept up this controlled delirium. Then one morning he was overcome by the tedium and horror of being all those kings who died by the sword and all those thwarted lovers who came together and broke apart and melodiously suffered. That very day he decided to sell his troupe. Before the week was out he had returned to his hometown: there he reclaimed the trees and the river of his youth without tying them to the other selves that his muse had sung, decked out in mythological allusion and latinate words. He had to be somebody, and so he became a retired impresario who dabbled in money-lending, lawsuits, and petty usury. It was as this character that he wrote the rather dry last will and testament with which we are familiar, having purposefully expunged from it every trace of emotion and every literary flourish. When friends visited him from London, he went back to playing the role of poet for their benefit.

The story goes that shortly before or after his death, when he found himself in the presence of God, he said: 'I who have been so many men in vain want to be one man only, myself.' The voice of God answered him out of a whirlwind: 'Neither am I what I am. I dreamed the world the way you dreamt your plays, dear Shakespeare. You are one of the shapes of my dreams: like me, you are everything and nothing.'

JORGE LUIS BORGES, from the collection *The Maker*, 1960, tr. Kenneth Krabbenhoft

This is a prose-poem. A later poem by Borges, 'Things That Might Have Been', consists of a line-by-line list of unfulfilled possibilities and historical blanks, ranging from 'The vast empire the Vikings declined to build' to 'The Unicorn's other horn'. They include 'John Donne's judgment of Shakespeare'.

Shakespeare was too wise not to know that for most of the purposes of human life stupidity is a most valuable element. He had nothing of the impatience which sharp logical narrow minds habitually feel when they come across those who do not apprehend their quick and precise deductions. No doubt he talked to the stupid players, to the stupid door-keeper, to the property man, who considers paste jewels 'very preferable, besides the expense'—talked with the stupid apprentices of stupid Fleet Street, and had much pleasure in ascertaining what was their notion of 'King Lear'. In his comprehensive mind it was enough if every man hitched well into his own place in human life. If every one were logical and literary, how would there be scavengers, or watchmen, or caulkers, or coopers? Narrow minds will be subdued to what they 'work in.' The 'dyer's hand' will not more clearly carry off its tint, nor will what is moulded more precisely indicate the confines of the mould. A patient sympathy, a kindly fellow-feeling for the narrow intelligence necessarily induced by narrow circumstances,—a narrowness which, in some degrees, seems to be inevitable, and is perhaps more serviceable than most things to the wise conduct of life—this, though quick and half-bred minds may despise it, seems to be a necessary constituent in the composition of manifold genius. 'How shall the world be served?' asks the host in Chaucer. We must have cart-horses as well as race-horses, draymen as well as poets. It is no bad thing, after all, to be a slow man and to have one idea a-year. You don't make a figure, perhaps, in argumentative society, which requires a quicker species of thought, but is that the worse?

> *Holofernes.* *Via*, Goodman Dull; thou hast spoken no word all this while.
> *Dull.* Nor understood none either, sir.
> *Hol.* *Allons, we will employ thee.*
> *Dull.* I'll make one in a dance or so, or I will play on the tabor to the worthies, and let them dance the hay.
> *Hol.* Most Dull, honest Dull, to our sport away.

And such, we believe, was the notion of Shakespeare.

WALTER BAGEHOT, 'Shakespeare the Individual', 1853

I bet that the gentle Shakespeare was not remarkable for his gravity, and I think that in his plays, he is maliciously always on the watch for grave people as if he did not like them.

J. B. YEATS, letter to his son W. B. Yeats, 1922

'We had the hell of a party here the other night,' he said. 'A crowd of senior officers as drunk as monkeys, brigadiers rooting the palms out of the pots.'

His words conjured up the scene in *Antony and Cleopatra*, when arm-in-arm the generals dance on Pompey's galley, a sequence of the play

that makes it scarcely possible to disbelieve that Shakespeare himself
served for at least a period of his life in the army.
    'With thy grapes our hairs be crowned?'°
    'Took some cleaning up after, I can tell you.'

ANTHONY POWELL, The Military Philosophers, 1968

> O and Shakespeare seized his daring in both hands
> to warn the star of the age, acclaiming but adding
> something in a Chorus of *Henry V*
> on 'favourites,
>
> made proud by Princes, that advance their pride
> against that power that bred it.'
>
> Nobody told the Earl, or if one did
> it went unheeded,—from a *poet*? words
> to menace action? O I don't think so.
> I wonder if Shakespeare trotted to the jostle of his death.

JOHN BERRYMAN, from Love & Fame, Part One, 1971

*'The Earl' is the Earl of Essex, the royal favourite saluted by Shakespeare in
Henry V (Shakespeare's patron Southampton was one of his followers) and
executed after his attempted rising against the Queen in 1601.*

Shakespeare

> A coaching yard, and, looming over the river
> In terraces, the gloomy Tower set back.
> The clanking of hoofs and the rheumy pealing
> Of Westminster, from muffled piles in black.
>
> The narrow streets. The reeking houses, crowded,
> That hoard the damp in their branching timbers,
> Morose from soot and sodden from ale;
> And crooked lanes by London fogs enshrouded.
>
> The snow falls sluggishly in darkness.
> It came tumbling at twilight, wrinkled somewhat,
> Half drowsy, like a crumpling belly band,
> And smothered each deserted sleepy lot.

With thy grapes . . . crowned] *Antony and Cleopatra*, II. vii

A small window, with bits of violet mica
In leaden rims. . . . 'Damn this weather!
We may sleep in the cold, in the open yet.
Now on to a barrel! Hey, barber, water!'

As he shaves, he cackles, holding his sides
At the wit of a jester jabbering since dinner
And straining through a pipe stuck to his lips
His tedious trifles.
                            But Shakespeare bides,
Impatient with jesting and bored by the saws.
The sonnet he wrote with not one blot,
At white heat, last night at that far table
Where curdled rennet laps at lobster claws—
The sonnet speaks to him:
                            'Sir, I acclaim
Your talents, but, O my poet and master,
Do you know—you and that dolt astride
That barrel there with soap on his mug,
I'm swifter than lightning, nobler by nature
Than mortals? In brief, that, scourged in my flame,
You begin to stink like your foul tobacco?

'Forgive me, old man, my filial skepticism,
But, Sir, my good lord, I believe we lie
At an inn. Are your cronies my kind? Your verse,
For the mob? Sir, grant me the infinite sky!

'Well, read it to him! Why not? In the name
Of all guilds and bills—in his company—
Five yards away—at billiards with him,
Do you like this sort of popularity?'

'Read to him? Are you mad?' He calls for the waiter.
And fiddling with a bunch of Malaga grapes,
He reckons: half pint, French stew. And he runs,
Flinging his napkin at the phantom shape.

                    BORIS PASTERNAK, 1919, tr. Eugene M. Kayden

The Young Man in the Sonnets

The impression we get of his friend is one of a young man who was not really very nice, very conscious of his good looks, able to switch on the charm at any moment, but essentially frivolous, cold-hearted and self-centred, aware, probably, that he had some power over Shakespeare—if he thought about it at all, no doubt he gave it a cynical explanation—but with no conception of the intensity of feelings he had, unwittingly, aroused. Somebody, in fact, rather like Bassanio in *The Merchant of Venice*.

W. H. AUDEN, 'Shakespeare's Sonnets', 1964

SHAKESPEARE (whom you and every playhouse bill
Style the divine, the matchless, what you will)
For gain, not glory, wing'd his roving flight,
And grew immortal in his own despite.

ALEXANDER POPE, *Imitations of Horace*, 1737

Everything we know about Shakespear can be got into a half-hour sketch. He was a very civil gentleman who got round men of all classes; he was extremely susceptible to word-music and to graces of speech; he picked up all sorts of odds and ends from books and from the street talk of his day and welded them into his work; he was so full of witty sallies of all kinds, decorous and indecorous, that he had to be checked even at the Mermaid suppers; he was idolized by his admirers to an extent which nauseated his most enthusiastic and affectionate friends; and he got into trouble by treating women in the way already described. Add to this that he was, like all highly intelligent and conscientious people, business-like about money and appreciative of the value of respectability and the discomfort and discredit of Bohemianism; also that he stood on his social position and desired to have it affirmed by the grant of a coat of arms, and you have all we know of Shakespear beyond what we gather from his plays. And it does not carry us to a tragedy.

BERNARD SHAW, review of *The Man Shakespeare* by Frank Harris, 1910

In Robert Browning's 'Bishop Blougram's Apology' (1855) a worldly prelate expounds his philosophy of comfortable compromise. At one point he cites Shakespeare as a witness on his behalf; in effect, as a soulmate. He acknow-

ledges the huge difference in talent between them (so why try to emulate him?), but also claims that they shared a common goal. 'We want the same things, Shakespeare and myself'—social and material success.

The Bishop's arguments are specious, and meant to be, but they are forcefully presented; and, given what we know of Shakespeare, they can't be completely disregarded.

Take another case;
Fit up the cabin yet another way.
What say you to the poets? shall we write
Hamlet, Othello—make the world our own,
Without a risk to run of either sort?
I can't!—to put the strongest reason first.
'But try,' you urge, 'the trying shall suffice;
The aim, if reached or not, makes great the life:
Try to be Shakespeare, leave the rest to fate!'
Spare my self-knowledge—there's no fooling me!
If I prefer remaining my poor self,
I say so not in self-dispraise but praise.
If I'm a Shakespeare, let the well alone;
Why should I try to be what now I am?
If I'm no Shakespeare, as too probable,—
His power and consciousness and self-delight
And all we want in common, shall I find—
Trying for ever? while on points of taste
Wherewith, to speak it humbly, he and I
Are dowered alike—I'll ask you, I or he,
Which in our two lives realizes most?
Much, he imagined—somewhat, I possess.
He had the imagination; stick to that!
Let him say, 'In the face of my soul's works
Your world is worthless and I touch it not
Lest I should wrong them'—I'll withdraw my plea.
But does he say so? look upon his life!
Himself, who only can, gives judgement there.
He leaves his towers and gorgeous palaces
To build the trimmest house in Stratford town;
Saves money, spends it, owns the worth of things,
Giulio Romano's pictures, Dowland's lute;

Enjoys a show, respects the puppets, too,
And none more, had he seen its entry once,
Than 'Pandulph, of fair Milan cardinal.'°
Why then should I who play that personage,
The very Pandulph Shakespeare's fancy made,
Be told that had the poet chanced to start
From where I stand now (some degree like mine
Being just the goal he ran his race to reach)
He would have run the whole race back, forsooth,
And left being Pandulph, to begin write plays?
Ah, the earth's best can be but the earth's best!
Did Shakespeare live, he could but sit at home
And get himself in dreams the Vatican,
Greek busts, Venetian paintings, Roman walls,
And English books, none equal to his own,
Which I read, bound in gold (he never did).
—Terni's fall, Naples' bay and Gothard's top—
Eh, friend? I could not fancy one of these;
But, as I pour this claret, there they are:
I've gained them—crossed Saint Gothard last July
With ten mules to the carriage and a bed
Slung inside; is my hap the worse for that?
We want the same things, Shakespeare and myself,
And what I want, I have: he, gifted more,
Could fancy he too had them when he liked,
But not so thoroughly that, if fate allowed,
He would not have them also in my sense.
We play one game; I send the ball aloft
No less adroitly that of fifty strokes
Scarce five go o'er the wall so wide and high
Which sends them back to me: I wish and get.
He struck balls higher and with better skill,
But at a poor fence level with his head,
And hit—his Stratford house, a coat of arms,
Successful dealings in his grain and wool,—
While I receive heaven's incense in my nose
And style myself the cousin of Queen Bess.
Ask him, if this life's all, who wins the game?

'Pandulph, of fair Milan cardinal'] the highly political papal legate in *King John*

Shakespeare's plays show this need for sanity and its political expression, justice. But how did he live? His behaviour as a property-owner made him closer to Goneril than Lear. He supported and benefited from the Goneril-society—with its prisons, workhouses, whipping, starvation, mutilation, pulpit-hysteria and all the rest of it.

An example of this is his role in the Welcombe enclosure. A large part of his income came from rents (or tithes) paid on common fields at Welcombe near Stratford. Some important landowners wanted to enclose these fields—for the reasons given in the play—and there was a risk that the enclosure would affect Shakespeare's rents. He could side either with the landowners or with the poor who would lose their land and livelihood. He sided with the landowners. They gave him a guarantee against loss—and this is not a neutral document because it implies that should the people fighting the enclosers come to him for help he would refuse it. Well, the town did write to him for help and he did nothing. The struggle is quite well documented and there's no record of opposition from Shakespeare. He may have doubted that the enclosers would succeed, but at best this means he sat at home with his guarantee while others made the resistance that was the only way to stop them. They were stopped for a time. The fields were not finally enclosed till 1775.

Lear divided up his land at the beginning of the play, when he was arbitrary and unjust—not when he was shouting out his truths on the open common.

EDWARD BOND, preface to *Bingo*, 1974

Bond's play—subtitled 'Scenes of money and death'—shows Shakespeare agreeing to the Welcombe enclosure, ill-treating his family and finally succumbing to suicidal guilt. As he lies dying he repeatedly asks, 'Was anything done?'

Had Marx and Engels been contemporaries of Shakespear they could not have written the Communist Manifesto and would probably have taken a hand, as Shakespear did, in the enclosure of common lands as a step forward in civilization.

BERNARD SHAW, preface to *Geneva*, 1938

The Shakespeare Memorial

Lord Lilac thought it rather rotten
That Shakespeare should be quite forgotten,
And therefore got on a Committee
With several chaps out of the City,
And Shorter and Sir Herbert Tree,
Lord Rothschild and Lord Rosebery,
And F C G and Comyns Carr,
Two dukes and a dramatic star,
Also a clergyman now dead;
And while the vain world careless sped
Unheeding the heroic name—
The souls most fed with Shakespeare's flame
Still sat unconquered in a ring,
Remembering him like anything.

G. K. CHESTERTON, *c.* 1915

Virginia Woolf spent a day in Stratford in May 1934, in the course of which she visited the site of New Place (the house which Shakespeare bought in 1597), Holy Trinity church, and the birthplace.

All the flowers were out in Sh[akespea]re's garden. 'That was where his study windows looked out when he wrote the Tempest' said the man. And perhaps it was true. Anyhow it was a great big house, looking straight at the large windows & the grey stone of the school chapel, & when the clock struck, that was the sound Shre heard. I cannot without more labour than my roadrunning mind can compass describe the queer impression of sunny impersonality. Yes, everything seemed to say, this was Shakespeare's, had he sat & walked; but you wont find me not exactly in the flesh. He is serenely absent-present; both at once; radiating round one; yes; in the flowers, in the old hall, in the garden; but never to be pinned down. And we went to the Church, & there was the florid foolish bust, but what I had not reckoned for was the worn simple slab, turned the wrong way, Kind Friend for Jesus' sake forbear—again he seemed to be all air & sun smiling serenely; & yet down there one foot from me lay the little bones that had spread over the world this vast illumination. Yes, & then we walked round the church, & all is simple & a little worn; the river slipping past the stone wall, with a red breadth in it from some flowering tree, & the edge of the turf unspoilt, soft & green & muddy, & two casual nonchalant swans. The church & the school & the house are all roomy spacious places, resonant, sunny today, & in & out [*illegible*]—yes, an impressive place; still living, & then the little bones lying there, which have created: to think of writing The Tempest looking out on that garden; what a rage & storm of thought to have gone over any mind; no doubt the solidity of the place was comfortable. No doubt he saw the cellars with serenity. And a few scented American girls, & a good deal of parrot prattle from old gramophone discs at the birthplace, one taking up the story from the other. But isnt it odd, the caretaker at New Place agreed, that only one genuine signature of S.'s is known; & all the rest, books, furniture pictures &c has completely vanished? Now I think Shre was very happy in this, that there was no impediment of fame, but his genius flowed out of him, & is still there, in Stratford. They were acting As you like it I think in the theatre.

Diary, 9 May 1934

Did Shakespeare Write Bacon?

Were Shakespeare and Bacon identical? A new answer was recently suggested to me by a friend, and a consideration of his hypothesis led to the discovery of such corroborative arguments that it should only require a brief exposition to secure its acceptance by some people. I may briefly recall certain well-known facts. Bacon had conceived in very early youth an ambitious plan for a great philosophical reform. He had been immediately plunged into business, and at the accession of James I, when a little over forty, had been for many years a barrister and a Member of Parliament, and had moreover taken a very active part in great affairs of State. He was already lamenting, as he continued to lament, the many distractions which had forced him to sacrifice literary and philosophical to political ambition. Now that a second Solomon was to mount the throne, he naturally wished to show that he was a profound thinker, deserving the patronage of a wise monarch. Besides merely selfish reasons he hoped that James would help him to carry out his great schemes for the promotion of scientific research. He resolved, therefore, to publish a book setting forth his new philosophic ideas. He had not as yet found time to prepare any statement of them, or even to reduce them to order. He was still immersed in business and harassed by many anxieties. Now Bacon, if there be any truth in Pope's epigram or

Macaulay's essay, was not above questionable manœuvres. If he had not time to write, he could get a book written for him. We know in fact that he afterwards employed assistants, such as Hobbes and George Herbert, in preparing some of his literary work. It is plain, however, from the full account of his early life in Spedding's volumes that he had as yet no connection with the famous men of letters of his time. Not one of them is mentioned in his letters, though at a later time he became known to Ben Jonson, who has celebrated the charms of his conversation. Jonson's friendship with Shakespeare gives some significance, as we shall see, to this circumstance. Bacon took a significant step. He had recently incurred reproach by taking part in the prosecution of his former patron, Essex. He now (1603) made conciliatory overtures to Southampton, who had not only been a friend of Essex, but had been under sentence for complicity in the rising for which Essex was beheaded. Why did Bacon approach a man so certain to be prejudiced against him? One reason suggests itself. Southampton was a patron of men of letters, and especially the one man whom we know to have been helpful to Shakespeare. If Bacon was desirous of hiring an author, Southampton would be able to recommend a competent person, and there was no one whom he was more likely to recommend than Shakespeare. Shakespeare was by this time at the height of his powers, and had shown by *Hamlet* his philosophical as well as his poetical tendencies. He was recognised as an able writer, capable of turning his hand to many employments. He could vamp old plays and presumably new philosophies. If Bacon wanted a man who should have the necessary power of writing and yet not be hampered by any such scientific doctrine of his own as would make him anxious to claim independence, he could not make a better choice. Southampton is said, on pretty good authority, to have made a present of £1,000 to Shakespeare. The story is intelligible if we suppose that he paid the money on Bacon's account, and for some service of such a nature that any trace of Bacon's interest in it was to be concealed.

At any rate somebody wrote a book. The famous *Advancement of Learning* appeared in the autumn of 1605. It is dedicated to James, and gives a general survey of the state of knowledge at the time; or, as the last paragraph states, is 'a small globe of the intellectual world.' It shows literary genius and general knowledge, but not the minute information of a specialist. Who wrote the book? I need not rely upon the probabilities already mentioned, however strong they may be, which point to Shakespeare. If Shakespeare wrote it he might naturally try to insert some intimation of the authorship to which he could appeal in case of

necessity. One of the common amusements of the time was the composition of anagrams; and I accordingly inquired whether such a thing
might be discoverable in the *Advancement*. It would most probably be at
the beginning, and I was rewarded by finding in the first two lines a
distinct claim of Shakespeare's own authorship and a repudiation of
Bacon's. Naturally, when a man is writing two sentences in one set of
letters he has to be a little obscure, and will probably employ a redun-
dant word or two to include all that are required. Shakespeare's style,
therefore, if perceptible, is partly veiled. The opening words are 'There
were under the law, excellent King, both daily sacrifices and free-will
offerings, the one pro(ceeding, &c.).' To the end of 'pro' there are
eighty-one letters. Re-arrange them and they make the following: 'Crede
Will Shakespere, green innocent reader; he was author of excellent writing; F. B. N. fifth idol, Lye." I won't try to explain why the reader should
be called green and innocent, but the meaning of the whole will be
perfectly clear when the last words are explained. F. B. N., of course,
means Francis Bacon. 'Fifth idol' refers to one of the most famous
passages in a book hitherto ascribed to Bacon. In the aphorisms prefaced
to the *Novum Organum* the causes of human error are described as
belonging to *four* classes of 'idols.' False systems of philosophy, for
example, generate what are curiously (though the word would naturally
occur to a dramatist) called 'idols of the theatre.' Of the others I need
only say that they do not include one fertile source of deception, namely,
direct lying. Shakespeare intimates that his employer was illustrating this
additional or fifth kind of idol by his false claim to the authorship. The
aphorisms, however, were for the present held back. The book was
published, we may presume, before Bacon had discovered this transparent artifice. Shakespeare would chuckle when calling his attention to it
afterwards. Bacon would be vexed, but naturally could not take public
notice of the trap in which he had been caught. His feelings may be
inferred from his later action. When Shakespeare's plays were collected
after the author's death, Bacon we know got at the printers and persuaded them to insert a cryptogram claiming the authorship for himself.
The claim was obviously preposterous, but the fact that he made it is
interesting to the moralist. It is a melancholy illustration of a familiar
truth. Bacon had probably come to believe his own lie, and to fancy that

---

' If anyone cares to verify this, he may be helped by the statement that in both cases A occurs
in four places, B in one, C in three, D in three, E in fifteen, F in four, G in two, H in four, I in six,
K in one, L in six, N in six, O in four, P in one, R in seven, S in three, T in five, U in one, W in three,
X in one, and Y in one.

he had really written the *Advancement of Learning*, or that, having bought it, he had a right to it. Then, he thought, he would make sure of a posthumous revenge should the anagram be deciphered. 'If Shakespeare succeeds in claiming my philosophy, I will take his plays in exchange.' He had become demoralised to the point at which he could cheat his conscience by such lamentable casuistry.

Meanwhile Bacon's fame was growing; and so was his immersion in business. In 1607 he became Solicitor-General and a comparatively rich man. In the next year he makes references to a proposed continuation of his great philosophical work. In other words, he was thinking of procuring its continuation. Probably there was some little difficulty in getting over the misunderstandings which would inevitably arise from these dark and dangerous dealings. The bargain might be hard to strike. In 1611, however, we know that Shakespeare gave up the stage and retired to pass the last five years of his life at Stratford. All his biographers have thought this retirement strange, and have been puzzled to account for the supposed cessation of authorship. No successful writer ever gives up writing. The explanation is now clear. Shakespeare retired because Bacon, who had grown rich, could make it worth his while to retreat to a quiet place where he would not be tempted to write plays, or drink at the 'Mermaid,' or make indiscreet revelations. If it be asked what he was doing, the answer is obvious. He was writing the *Novum Organum*. It was all but impossible for Bacon in the midst of all his astonishing political and legal activity to find time to write a philosophical work. No doubt he did something: he made notes and procured collections of various observations upon natural phenomena with which he supplied his co-operator. We may even suppose that he persuaded himself that he was thus substantially the author of the book which he prompted. Shakespeare died in 1616, leaving the work as a fragment. Bacon, who not long afterwards became Lord Chancellor, put the papers together, had them translated into Latin (which would obliterate any lurking anagram), and was able to publish the book in 1620. I leave it to critics to show the true authorship from internal evidence. It is enough here to note certain obvious characteristics. The book in the first place, as is generally admitted, shows that the author was not only an amateur in science, but curiously ignorant of what was being done in his own day. That was quite natural at Stratford-on-Avon, while Bacon in London had ample means for hearing of the achievements of leading men of science, even if he could not appreciate their work. In the next place the *Novum Organum* is the work of a poet. The scientific formulæ are given in the shape of weighty concrete maxims—'Man is the servant and interpreter of Nature,' and so forth. So in classifying the various kinds of experiments, the writer does not elaborate an abstract logical scheme, but represents each class (there are no less than twenty-seven) by some vivid concrete emblem. One class suggests the analogy of a signpost at crossroads and receives the famous name of *Instantiae crucis*, the origin of our common phrase, 'crucial experiments.' Bacon was not a poet—as anyone may see who looks at his version of the Psalms—Shakespeare certainly was.

After publishing this 'magnificent fragment,' as an accomplished critic calls it, Bacon was convicted of corrupt practices, and passed his few remaining years in trying to proceed with his philosophical work. The result was significant. He had no official duties to distract him, but also he had no Shakespeare to help him. His later publications added a little or nothing in substance. The chief of them was *De Augmentis*. This is simply an enlarged edition in Latin (the anagram of course disappearing) of the *Advancement of Learning*. The early book, as the same critic says, has an advantage over the 'more pretentious' version from the 'noble and flowing' (shall we say the Shakespearean?) 'English,' while the additions are of questionable value. I will only notice one point. The *Advancement of Learning* speaks of the state of poetry at the time. 'In poesy,' says the author, 'I can report no deficience. . . . For the expression of affections, passions, corruptions, and customs we are beholden to poets more than to the philosophers' works: and for wit and eloquence not much less than to orators' harangues.' That was a very natural opinion to be expressed by Shakespeare. In the *De Augmentis* the last sentence disappears; but a fresh paragraph is inserted upon dramatic poetry. The theatre might be useful, it says, either for corruption or for discipline; but in modern times there is plenty of corruption on the stage and no discipline.

Bacon, it may be noticed, was aiming this backhanded blow at Shakespeare in the same year in which he was inserting the cryptogram in the first folio. It may appear, at first sight, that he was inconsistent in condemning the very works which he was claiming, and it may even be said by the captious that the fact throws some doubt upon the cryptogram. A deeper insight into human nature will suggest that such an inconsistency is characteristic. Bacon wishes at once to appropriate Shakespeare's work and to depreciate it so long as it is still ascribed to Shakespeare. I omit, however, the obvious psychological reflections and will only remark that other works ascribed to this period, the *Sylva Sylvarum* and so forth, no doubt represent the collections which, as I have said, Bacon formed to be used as materials by his collaborator.

I have told my story as briefly as may be, and leave details to be filled up by anyone who pleases. Plenty of writers have insisted upon Shakespeare's logical subtlety and powers of philosophical reflection. They will be ready to believe that the author of *Hamlet* was also the author of the *Novum Organum*, and will be relieved from the necessity of accepting the old paradox that the 'wisest' was also the 'meanest' man of his time. The meanness may all be ascribed to one man, and the wisdom to the man from whom he stole it.

LESLIE STEPHEN, 1901

Old Henry James, with his odd slowness, has given me some delightful talks . . . He talked to me in the church of Stratford of the inscrutable mystery of Shakespeare: the works on the one side and, on the other, that dull face, and all the stories we know of the man: 'commonplace, commonplace; almost degrading.'

JOHN BAILEY, man of letters; diary, 1908

On one occasion James's views on the 'inscrutable mystery' led to a collision with his redoubtable old friend Rhoda Broughton:

He talks of Shakespeare—of the portent of that brilliance, that prodigality, that consummation of the mind of the greatest of ages—all emerging out of what?—out of nothing, out of darkness, out of the thick provincial mind; from which a figure steps forth, a young man of ill condition, a lout from Stratford, to reappear presently—

'A lout!' exclaimed Rhoda, 'me divine William a lout?'

'But wait, dear lady, wait—see where I'm coming out—he reappears, as I say, this lout from Stratford'——

'I *won't* have yer call me divine William a lout,' she cries; and that's flat; but still she mistakes his drift, the whole tendency of the contrast to exalt, to enhance the wonder of the transformation by which this—in short this——

You could as well resist the way of an ocean liner; Henry James, in the mighty momentum of his argument, is not to be deflected; the course of his phrase is shaped, he can't go back upon it now. 'In short, this *lout*——'

'I will *not* let yer call him a lout!' cries our dauntless, our relentless, our impossible Rhoda—who won't let go, won't see that she has missed the point, doesn't care if she has. 'Me beloved Jamie calling Shakespeare a lout!'—that's all she has to say, with a crackle of short laughter.

PERCY LUBBOCK, *Mary Cholmondeley*, 1928

In 1903 James's feelings spilled over into a long short story, The Birthplace. *After years of working in 'a grey town-library' in the North of England, the central character, Morris Gedge, is appointed custodian of the birthplace of a great poet. (No names are mentioned, but it is 'the Mecca of the English-speaking race'.) An intelligent, sensitive man, Gedge becomes convinced that the legends surrounding the shrine are all so much humbug. But he is afraid of losing his job, and he soon learns to spin the kind of tale that is required of him:*

'We stand here, you see, in the old living-room, happily still to be reconstructed in the mind's eye, in spite of the havoc of time, which we have fortunately, of late years, been able to arrest. It was of course rude and humble, but it must have been snug and quaint, and we have at least the pleasure of knowing that the tradition in respect to the features that do remain is delightfully uninterrupted. Across that threshold He habitually passed; through those low windows, in childhood, He peered out into the world that He was to make so much happier by the gift to it of His genius; over the boards of this floor—that is over *some* of them, for we mustn't be carried away!—his little feet often pattered; and the beams of this ceiling (we must really in some places take care of *our* heads!) he endeavoured, in boyish strife, to jump up and touch. It's not often that in the early home of genius and renown the whole tenor of existence is laid so bare, not often that we are able to retrace, from point to point and from step to step, its connection with objects, with influences—to build it round again with the little solid facts out of which it sprang. This, therefore, I need scarcely remind you, is what makes the small space between these walls—so modest to measurement, so insignificant of aspect—unique on all the earth. *There is nothing like it,*' Morris Gedge went on, insisting as solemnly and softly, for his bewildered hearers, as over a pulpit-edge; 'there is nothing at all like it anywhere in the world. There is nothing, only reflect, for the combination of greatness, and, as we venture to say, of intimacy. You may find elsewhere perhaps absolutely fewer changes, but where shall you find a *presence* equally diffused, uncontested and undisturbed? Where in particular shall you find, on the part of the abiding spirit, an equally towering eminence? You may find elsewhere eminence of a considerable order, but where shall you find *with* it, don't you see, changes, after all, so few, and the contemporary element caught so, as it were, in the very fact?'

Others abide our question. Thou art free.
We ask and ask—Thou smilest and art still,
Out-topping knowledge. For the loftiest hill,
Who to the stars uncrowns his majesty,

Planting his steadfast footsteps in the sea,
Making the heaven of heavens his dwelling-place,
Spares but the cloudy border of his base
To the foil'd searching of mortality;

And thou, who didst the stars and sunbeams know,
Self-school'd, self-scann'd, self-honour'd, self-secure,
Didst tread on earth unguess'd at.—Better so!

All pains the immortal spirit must endure,
All weakness which impairs, all griefs which bow,
Find their sole speech in that victorious brow.

MATTHEW ARNOLD, 'Shakespeare', 1849

THE POET

I read Shakespeare *directly* I have finished writing, when my mind is agape & red & hot. Then it is astonishing. I never yet knew how amazing his stretch & speed & word coining power is, until I felt it utterly outpace & outrace my own, seeming to start equal & then I see him draw ahead & do things I could not in my wildest tumult & utmost press of mind imagine. Even the less known & worser plays are written at a speed that is quicker than anybody else's quickest; & the words drop so fast one can't pick them up. Look at this, Upon a gather'd lily almost wither'd° (that is a pure accident: I happen to light on it.) Evidently the pliancy of his mind was so complete that he could furbish out any train of thought; &, relaxing lets fall a shower of such unregarded flowers. Why then should anyone else attempt to write. This is not 'writing' at all. Indeed, I could say that Shre surpasses literature altogether, if I knew what I meant.

VIRGINIA WOOLF, diary, 13 April 1930

The verbal poetic texture of Shakespeare is the strongest the world has known, and is immensely superior to the structure of his plays as plays. With Shakespeare it is the metaphor that is the thing, not the play.

VLADIMIR NABOKOV, *Strong Opinions*, 1973

In his plays you often find remarks doing a kitchen-hand's work in some remote corner of a sentence which would deserve pride of place in a disquisition by any other writer.

GEORG CHRISTOPH LICHTENBERG, notebooks, 1765–99

The art of writing lines, replies, which express a passion with full tone and complete imaginative intensity, and in which you can none the less

---

Upon a gather'd lily almost wither'd] *Titus Andronicus*, III. i catch the resonance of its opposite—this is an art which no poet has practiced except the unique poet: Shakespeare.

SØREN KIERKEGAARD, from the draft of *The Sickness Unto Death*, 1849, adapted from the translation by Howard V. Hong and Edna H. Hong

Rhythm is fundamental to Shakespeare's poetry. Half his thoughts, and the words that verbalised them, were prompted by metre. Rhythm is the basis of Shakespeare's texts, not a framing last touch. Some of Shakespeare's stylistic vagaries can be explained in terms of rhythmic bursts, while rhythmic flow governs the order of questions and answers in his dialogues, their speed of exchange, and the length and brevity of periods in his soliloquies.

This rhythm reflects the enviable concision of English speech, in which a single iambic line can embrace an entire thought, composed of two or more contrasting propositions. It is the rhythm of a man whose historic freedom from false idols allowed him such laconic candour.

BORIS PASTERNAK, 'Observations on Translating Shakespeare', 1939–46, tr. Ann Pasternak Slater

The confounded thing about it is that actors, whose business it is to be experts in word-music, are nearly as deaf to it as other people. At the Globe° they walk in thick darkness through Shakespear's measures. They do not even seem to know that Puck may have the vivacity of a street Arab, but not his voice: his bite, but never his bark; that Theseus should know all Gluck's operas by heart, and in their spirit deliver his noble lines; that Oberon must have no Piccadilly taint in his dialect to betray him into such utterances as

> Be it ahnce, aw cat, aw bea-ah
> Pahd, aw boa-ah, with b'istled hai-ah
> In thy eye that shall appea-ah
> When thou wak'st, it is thy dea-ah.

By this time I should be converted to the device of joining consecutive vowels with r's, if conversion were possible. I know that it is easy to say Mariar Ann, and cruelly hard to say Maria Ann. But the thing is possible with courage and devotion. When Mr Benson schools himself to say

> Not Hermia but Helena I love

the Globe] the West End theatre of Shaw's own time

instead of

> Not Hermia but Helenar I love

I shall be spared a pang when next thereafter I hear him play Lysander. Helenar sounds too like cockney for Eleanor.

BERNARD SHAW, article in The Star, 1890

Sonnet: Tidying Up

Left lying about in my mind, awaiting collection,
are the thoughts and phrases that are quite unsuitable
and often shocking to all Right-thinking people—
penetrated by a purple penis for example
(almost a line?); and how it's almost certain,
from Swift's hints, that the big sexy ladies of Brobdingnag
used Gulliver as an instrument of masturbation.
Hence a tongue-twister: *Glumdalclitch's clitoris.*

Though not always decorous, there's a lot of force in phrases.
A good many poems stem from them; they start something.
More than anything Shakespeare owes his power to them
(his *secret, black and midnight hags* and hundreds more),
they almost consoled him—though life is pretty bloody
(*the multitudinous seas incarnadine*).

GAVIN EWART, 1976

You may call him up at once in the morning, after he has left the tavern at midnight, and he will give you the speech of the innocent young girl at any desired length and of unfailing beauty.

JOHN JAY CHAPMAN, Greek Genius and Other Essays, 1915

One of the party had quoted that celebrated passage from the play of 'Henry V,' 'So work the honey-bees;' and each proceeded to pick out his 'pet plum' from that perfect piece of natural history; when Wordsworth objected to the line, 'The singing masons building roofs of gold,' because, he said, of the unpleasant repetition of '*ing*' in it! Why, where were his poetical ears and judgment? But more than once it has been said that Wordsworth had not a genuine love of Shakespeare: that, when he could, he always accompanied a '*pro*' with his '*con.*,' and, Atticus-like, would 'just hint a fault and hesitate dislike.'

CHARLES and MARY COWDEN CLARKE, Recollections of Writers, 1878

There is an analysis of the line to which Wordsworth objected in William Empson's Seven Types of Ambiguity:

Bees are not forced by law or immediate hunger to act as *masons*; 'it all comes naturally to them'; as in the Golden Age they *sing* with plenty and the apparent freedom of their social structure. On the other hand *bees* only *sing* (indeed can only sing) through the noise produced by their working; though happy they are not idle; and the human opposition between the pain of work and the waste of play has been resolved by the hive into a higher unity, as in Heaven. Milton's 'the busy hum of men' makes work seem agreeable by the same comparison in a less overt form.

    Roofs are what they are *building*; the culmination of successful work, the most airy and striking parts of it; also the Gothic tradition gave a particular exaltation to *roofs*, for instance those magnificent hammer-beam affairs which had angels with *bee*-like wings on the hammers, as if they were helping in the *singing* from a heavenly choir; and to have *masons*, building a stone *roof*, with mortar instead of nails, is at once particularly like the methods of *bees* and the most solid and wealthy form of construction. But *bees build* downwards from the *roof*, so that they are always still *building* the *roof*, in a sense; the phrase is thus particularly applicable to them, and the comparison with men makes this a reckless or impossible feat, arguing an ideal security. In the same way, both parties are given wealth and delicacy because the yellow of wax is no surface gilding, not even such as in the temple of Solomon (built without a hammer, in the best *bee* tradition, though it was) shone thickly coated upon ivory, but all throughout, as the very substance of their labours, in its own pale ethereal and delicious *gold*.

WILLIAM EMPSON, Seven Types of Ambiguity, 1930

One of the three books I have with me is *Shakespeare's Poems*: I never found so many beauties in the Sonnets; they seem to be full of fine things said unintentionally—in the intensity of working out conceits. Is this to be borne? Hark ye!

When lofty trees I see barren of leaves,
Which erst from heat did canopy the head,
And Summer's green all girded up in sheaves,
Borne on the bier with white and bristly head.

He has left nothing to say about nothing or anything: for look at snails—you know what he says about snails—you know when he talks about 'cockled snails'°—well, in one of these sonnets, he says—the chap slips into—no! I lie! this is in the 'Venus and Adonis:' the simile brought it to my mind.

As the snail, whose tender horns being hit,
Shrinks back into his shelly cave with pain,
And there all smothered up in shade doth sit,
Long after fearing to put forth again;
So at his bloody view her eyes are fled,
Into the deep dark cabins of her head.

JOHN KEATS, letter to John Hamilton Reynolds, 1817

Sonnet: Shakespeare's Universality

In one sense Shakespeare's 'universality' was accidental—
due to the fact that he wrote plays. When you have so many
   characters
you're bound to have so many views of human life.
Nobody can say 'Why are all your poems about moles?'
or tell you you're very limited in your subject matter.
A playwright's material (unless it's outrageously slanted)
usually deals with a group of opinions; people can never say
'Of course this play is entirely autobiographical.'

It's interesting that Shakespeare's Sonnets, which are
(I think we can't doubt) completely based on his life,
are by a long way his least satisfactory verse.
It's better for a writer, in most cases, to get out and about.
If he gets stuck in his own psyche for too long
he bores everybody—and that includes himself.

GAVIN EWART, 1977

'cockled snails'] *Love's Labour's Lost*, IV. iii

Whereas Petrarch makes the theme of absence memorable of and for itself

> And the light has remained impressed in my mind . . .

proof could be heaped upon proof that in Shakespeare, at least at first glance, it is not the theme of absence itself that remains with us but rather a particular circumstance: a seemingly endless journey astride a stumbling nag (Sonnet 50), or the blood brought forth from a horse by a spur gash, or (in Sonnet 51) a headlong ride reminiscent of the Arabian Nights. On the other hand the theme of absence may go so far as to waste the soul away to its very depths by dint of weeping, as we see in Sonnet 30, a gem of sadness and tenderness, anguish and limitless renunciation.

> GIUSEPPE UNGARETTI, 'Notes on Shakespeare's Art of Poetry', 1945, tr. Alfred Triolo

Ungaretti was one of the foremost poets of twentieth-century Italy. His translation of forty of the Sonnets was published in 1946.

THE MAKING OF A REPUTATION

To the Memory of My Beloved, the Author
Mr William Shakespeare: And What He Hath Left Us

To draw no envy (Shakespeare) on thy name,
Am I thus ample to thy book, and fame:
While I confess thy writings to be such,
As neither man, nor muse, can praise too much.
'Tis true, and all men's suffrage. But these ways
Were not the paths I meant unto thy praise:
For seeliest° ignorance on these may light,
Which, when it sounds at best, but echoes right;
Or blind affection, which doth ne'er advance
The truth, but gropes, and urgeth all by chance;
Or crafty malice, might pretend this praise,
And think to ruin, where it seemed to raise.
These are, as some infamous bawd, or whore,
Should praise a matron. What could hurt her more?
But thou art proof against them, and indeed
Above the ill fortune of them, or the need.
I therefore will begin. Soul of the age!
The applause, delight, the wonder of our stage!
My Shakespeare, rise; I will not lodge thee by
Chaucer, or Spenser, or bid Beaumont lie
A little further, to make thee a room:
Thou art a monument, without a tomb,
And art alive still, while thy book doth live,
And we have wits to read, and praise to give.
That I not mix thee so, my brain excuses;
I mean with great, but disproportion'd muses:
For, if I thought my judgement were of years,
I should commit thee surely with thy peers,

seeliest] blindest

And tell, how far thou didst our Lyly outshine,
Or sporting Kyd, or Marlowe's mighty line.
And though thou hadst small Latin, and less Greek,
From thence to honour thee, I would not seek
For names; but call forth thundering Aeschylus,
Euripides, and Sophocles to us,
Pacuvius, Accius, him of Cordova dead,°
To life again, to hear thy buskin tread,
And shake a stage: or, when thy socks were on,
Leave thee alone, for the comparison
Of all that insolent Greece, or haughty Rome
Sent forth, or since did from their ashes come.
Triumph, my Britain, thou hast one to show,
To whom all scenes of Europe homage owe.
He was not of an age, but for all time!
And all the muses still were in their prime,
When like Apollo he came forth to warm
Our ears, or like a Mercury to charm!
Nature herself was proud of his designs,
And joyed to wear the dressing of his lines,
Which were so richly spun, and woven so fit,
As, since, she will vouchsafe no other wit.
The merry Greek, tart Aristophanes,
Neat Terence, witty Plautus, now not please;
But antiquated, and deserted lie
As they were not of nature's family.
Yet must I not give nature all: thy art,
My gentle Shakespeare, must enjoy a part.
For though the poet's matter, nature be,
His art doth give the fashion. And, that he,
Who casts to write a living line, must sweat,
(Such as thine are) and strike the second heat
Upon the muses' anvil: turn the same,
(And himself with it) that he thinks to frame;
Or for the laurel, he may gain a scorn,
For a good poet's made, as well as born.
And such wert thou. Look how the father's face
Lives in his issue, even so, the race

him of Cordova dead] Seneca the playwright

Of Shakespeare's mind, and manners brightly shines
In his well-turned, and true-filed lines:
In each of which, he seems to shake a lance,
As brandish'd at the eyes of ignorance.
Sweet swan of Avon, what a sight it were
To see thee in our waters yet appear,
And make those flights upon the banks of Thames,
That so did take Eliza, and our James!
But stay, I see thee in the hemisphere
Advanc'd, and made a constellation there!
Shine forth, thou star of poets, and with rage,
Or influence, chide, or cheer the drooping stage;
Which, since thy flight from hence, hath mourn'd like night.
And despairs day, but for thy volume's light.

BEN JONSON, prefixed to the First Folio edition of Shakespeare's works, 1623

Ben Jonson was proud, often harsh, slow to praise others, jealous of his own reputation, and Shakespeare had been a competitor as well as a friend; but in his great tribute Jonson rises nobly to the occasion. The reservations he hints at only serve to make his praise seem more sincere.

Those reservations are spelled out more fully in the private note which was first published in his posthumous collection Timber, or Discoveries. *But even here, the predominant note is surely one of affection and admiration:*

I remember, the players have often mentioned it as an honour to Shakespeare, that in his writing (whatsoever he penned) he never blotted out line. My answer hath been, would be had blotted a thousand. Which they thought a malevolent speech. I had not told posterity this, but for their ignorance, who chose that circumstance to commend their friend by, wherein he most faulted. And to justify mine own candour (for I loved the man, and do honour his memory, on this side idolatry, as much as any). He was (indeed) honest, and of an open and free nature; had an excellent phantasy, brave notions and gentle expressions, wherein he flowed with that facility, that sometime it was necessary he should be stopped ... His wit was in his own power; would the rule of it had been so too ... But he redeemed his vices with his virtues. There was ever more in him to be praised than to be pardoned.

The other commendatory verses in the First Folio—by Hugh Holland, Leonard Digges, and the unknown 'I.M.'—are of no great interest, but the Second Folio (1632) contains a celebrated poem by John Milton.

An Epitaph on the Admirable Dramatic Poet, W. Shakespeare

What needs my Shakespeare for his honour'd bones,
The labour of an age in piled stones?
Or that his hallow'd relics should be hid
Under a star-ypointing pyramid?
Dear son of Memory, great heir of Fame,
What need'st thou such weak witness of thy name?
Thou, in our wonder and astonishment,
Hast built thyself a life-long monument.
For whilst, to the shame of slow-endeavouring art,
Thy easy numbers flow; and that each heart
Hath, from the leaves of thy unvalued book,
Those Delphic lines with deep impression took;
Then thou, our fancy of itself bereaving,
Dost make us marble with too much conceiving;
And, so sepulchr'd, in such pomp dost lie,
That kings, for such a tomb should wish to die.

That Milton's earliest published poem should have been a tribute to Shakespeare is almost too good to be true. (It was written in 1630, when he was 22.)

There is another, longer poetic tribute in the Second Folio, which is less striking than Milton's, but which has its own slow, thoughtful grandeur:

On Worthy Master Shakespeare and His Poems

A mind reflecting ages past, whose clear
And equal surface can make things appear
Distant a thousand years, and represent
Them in their lively colours' just extent.
To outrun hasty time, retrieve the fates,
Roll back the heavens, blow ope the iron gates
Of death and Lethe, where (confused) lie
Great heaps of ruinous mortality.
In that deep dusky dungeon to discern

A royal ghost from churls: by art to learn
The physiognomy of shades, and give
Them sudden birth, wond'ring how oft they live.
What story coldly tells, what poets feign
At second hand, and picture without brain
Senseless and soulless shows. To give a stage
(Ample and true with life) voice, action, age,
As Plato's year and new scene of the world
Them unto us, or us to them had hurl'd.
To raise our ancient sovereigns from their herse,
Make kings his subjects, by exchanging verse
Enlive their pale trunks, that the present age
Joys in their joy, and trembles at their rage:
Yet so to temper passion, that our ears
Take pleasure in their pain; and eyes in tears
Both weep and smile; fearful at plots so sad,
Then, laughing at our fear; abus'd, and glad
To be abus'd, affected with that truth
Which we perceive is false; pleas'd in that ruth
At which we start; and by elaborate play
Tortur'd and tickled; by a crablike way
Time past made pastime, and in ugly sort
Disgorging up his ravaine for our sport—
—While the Plebeian Imp, from lofty throne,
Creates and rules a world, and works upon
Mankind by secret engines; now to move
A chilling pity, then a rigorous love:
To strike up and stroke down, both joy and ire;
To steer th'affections; and by heavenly fire
Mould us anew. Stol'n from ourselves—
   This, and much more which cannot be express'd,
But by himself, his tongue and his own breast,
Was Shakespeare's freehold, which his cunning brain
Improv'd by favour of the ninefold train.
The buskin'd Muse, the Comic Queen, the grand
And louder tone of Clio; nimble hand,
And nimbler foot of the melodious pair,
The silver voiced Lady; the most fair
Calliope, whose speaking silence daunts,
And she whose praise the heavenly body chants.

These jointly woo'd him, envying one another
(Obey'd by all as spouse, but lov'd as brother),
And wrought a curious robe of sable grave,
Fresh green, and pleasant yellow, red most brave,
And constant blue, rich purple, guiltless white,
The lowly russet, and the scarlet bright;
Branch'd and embroider'd like the painted Spring,
Each leaf match'd with a flower, and each string
Of golden wire, each line of silk; there run
Italian works whose thread the Sisters spun;
And there did sing, or seem to sing, the choice
Birds of a foreign note and various voice.
Here hangs a mossy rock; there plays a fair
But chiding fountain purled; not the air,
Nor clouds nor thunder, but were living drawn,
Not out of common tiffany or lawn,
But fine materials, which the Muses know,
And only know the countries where they grow.
Now, when they could no longer him enjoy
In mortal garments pent, death may destroy,
They say, his body, but his verse shall live;
And more than nature takes, our hands shall give.
In a less volume, but more strongly bound,
Shakespeare shall breathe and speak, with laurel crown'd
Which never fades. Fed with Ambrosian meat,
In a well-lined vesture rich and neat.
　　So with this robe they clothe him, bid him wear it;
　　For time shall never stain, nor envy tear it.
　　　　　　　　　The friendly admirer of his Endowments,
　　　　　　　　　　　　　　　I.M.S.

'The friendly admirer' has never been identified. Coleridge suggested, not very plausibly, that the initials 'I.M.S.' stood for 'John Milton, student'. Other commentators have canvassed the claims of 'John Marston, satirist'; yet others have argued that 'I.M.S.' can be ignored (it merely stands for 'in memoriam scriptoris', 'in memory of the writer'), and that two possible candidates for the authorship of the poem are George Chapman and John Donne.

　　Leonard Digges, who wrote one of the minor poems in the First Folio, contributed some much livelier verses to the collection of Shakespeare's poems

*published in 1640. Less elevated than Milton or 'the friendly admirer', he was
more concerned with Shakespeare in performance:*

> So have I seen, when Caesar would appear,
> And on the stage at half-sword parley were
> Brutus and Cassius, oh how the audience
> Were ravished, with what wonder they went hence . . .

Or again,

> let but Falstaff come,
> Hal, Poins, the rest, you scarce shall have a room,
> All is so pester'd; let but Beatrice
> And Benedick be seen, lo in a trice
> The cockpit, galleries, boxes all are full
> To hear Malvolio, that cross-gartered gull . . .

*This is one of the last glimpses of the theatre as Shakespeare knew it. The
playhouses were closed down in 1642.*

FALSTAFF—SOME SEVENTEENTH-CENTURY ALLUSIONS

*Henry IV Part One was probably written in 1596, Henry IV Part Two in
1596 or 1597. Within a few years Falstaff had become a figure of folklore.*

A Purveyor of Tobacco

Call him a broker of tobacco, he scorns the title, he had rather be
termed a cogging° merchant. Sir John Falstaff robb'd with a bottle of
sack; so doth he take men's purses, with a wicked roll of tobacco at his
girdle.

ANON, *New and Choice Characters*, 1615

cogging] cheating

[Description of the hangman at Hamburg:] His post-like legs were answerable to the rest of the great frame which they supported, and to conclude, Sir Bevis, Gog-Magog or our English Sir John Falstaff were but shrimps to this bezzling bombard's° longitude, latitude, altitude and crassitude,° for he passes, and surpasses, the whole German multitude.

> JOHN TAYLOR the Water Poet, *Three weeks, three days and three hours observation and travel, from London to Hamburg*, 1617

Gone with a vengeance! had he twenty lives
He needs must go (they say) the Devil drives.
Nor went he hence away, like lamb so mild
Or Falstaff-wise, like any chrisom-child°
In Arthur's bosom, he's not hush, yet died
Just as he did, at turning of the tide,
But with it such a wind, the sails did swell,
Charon ne'er made a quicker pass to Hell.

> HENRY BOLD, *On the Death of the late Tyrannical Usurper, Oliver Cromwell*, c. 1665

I cannot but observe, Mr Bayes, this admirable way (like fat Sir John Falstaff's singular dexterity in sinking) that you have of answering whole books and discourses, how pithy and knotty soever, in a line or two, nay sometimes with a word.

> ANDREW MARVELL, *The Rehearsal Transprosed*, 1673

Harry,
If sack and sugar be a sin, God help the wicked, was the saying of a merry fat gentleman, who lived in days of yore, loved a glass of wine, would be merry with a friend, and sometimes had an unlucky fancy for a wench.

> JOHN WILMOT, EARL OF ROCHESTER, from a letter to Henry Savile, 1680

Solicitor General. Pray my lord, give me leave to ask him a question, which I hope may clear all this matter, for it is plain the man is mistaken. *Lord Chief Justice.* Mistaken! Yes, I assure you, very grossly. Ask him

---

bezzling bombard] hard-drinking toper   crassitude] thickness
chrisom-child] innocent babe

what questions you will; but if he should swear as long as Sir John Falstaff fought, I would never believe a word he says.

State trials, Lady Ivy's case, 1684

The Lord Chief Justice in question was George Jeffreys, the notorious Judge Jeffreys of the Bloody Assizes. In Henry IV, the Lord Chief Justice of the day is meant to counterbalance Falstaff as the representative of the rule of law.

FROM SAMUEL PEPYS'S DIARY

1600

October 11—Here, in the Park, we met with Mr Salisbury, who took Mr Creed and me to the Cockpit to see 'The Moor of Venice', which was very well done. Burt acted the Moor; by the same token, a very pretty lady that sat by me called out, to see Desdemona smothered.

1661

August 24—To the Opera, and there saw 'Hamlet, Prince of Denmark' done with scenes very well, but above all Betterton did the prince's part beyond imagination.

1662

March 1—To the Opera, and there saw 'Romeo and Juliet', the first time it was ever acted, but it is a play of itself the worst that ever I heard in my life, and the worst acted that ever I saw these people do, and I am resolved to go no more to see the first time of acting, for they were all of them out more or less.

September 29—To the King's Theatre, where we saw 'Midsummer Night's Dream', which I had never seen before, nor shall ever again, for it is the most insipid ridiculous play that ever I saw in my life.

1663

May 28—By water to the Royal Theatre; but that was so full they told us we could have no room. And so to the Duke's house; and there saw 'Hamlet' done, giving us fresh reason never to think enough of Betterton.

1666

August 20—To Deptford by water, reading 'Othello, Moor of Venice', which I ever heretofore esteemed a mighty good play, but having to lately read 'The Adventures of Five Hours', it seems a mean thing.

1667

November 2—To the King's playhouse and there saw 'Henry the Fourth'; and contrary to expectation, was pleased in nothing more than in Cartwright's speaking of Falstaff's speech about 'What is Honour?' The house full of Parliament-men, it being holiday with them; and it was observable how a gentleman of good habit, sitting just before us, eating of some fruit in the midst of the play, did drop down as dead, being choked; but with much ado Orange Moll did thrust her fingers down his throat, and brought him to life again.

November 13—To the Duke of York's house, and there saw 'The Tempest' again, which is very pleasant, and full of so good variety that I cannot be more pleased almost in a comedy, only the seamen's part a little too tedious.

These entries are only a sampling. Pepys records thirty-seven visits to the theatre to see Shakespeare, and there are a number of other references to him in the diary—none more heartfelt than a passing allusion to Hamlet *and 'To be, or not to be' in the entry for 15 August 1665:*

. . . something put my last night's dream into my head, which I think is the best that ever was dreamed—which was, that I had my Lady Castlemaine in my arms and was admitted to use all the dalliance I desired with her, and then dreamed that this could not be awake but that it was only a dream. But that since it was a dream and that I took so much real pleasure in it, what a happy thing it would be, if when we are in our graves (as Shakespeare resembles it), we could dream, and dream but such dreams as this—that then we should not need to be so fearful of death as we are in this plague-time.

One further record of a visit to the theatre by Pepys is worth noting:

'Thence to the Cockpitt Theatre,' writes Pepys in the autumn of 1667, 'to witness my dearest Mrs Knipp in the Tragedie of Macbeth, than which as I did this day say to Mr Killigrew I do know no play more diverting nor more worthie to the eye. Did secure a prime place in the pitt, whereof I was glad, being neare under my Ladie Dorset and her good husband. The latter did twice salute me with effusion, and I was pleased to note that those around me did perceive this. Methought Mrs Knipp did never play so fine, specially in the matter of the two daggers, yet without brawl or overmuch tragick gesture, the which is most wearisome, as though an actress do care more to affright us than to be approved. She was most comickal and natural when she walks forth sleeping (the which I can testify, for Mrs Pepys also walks sleeping at some times), and did most ingeniously mimick the manner of women who walk thus.'

> MAX BEERBOHM, review of Forbes Robertson and Mrs Patrick Campbell in *Macbeth*, 1898

There is no such entry in the diary: this is one of Beerbohm's parodies.

★

I cannot but conclude with Mr Rymer° that our English comedy is far beyond anything of the Ancients. And notwithstanding our irregularities, so is our tragedy. Shakespeare had a genius for it; and we know, in spite of Mr Rymer, that genius alone is a greater virtue (if I may so call it) than all other qualifications put together. You see what success this learned critic has had in the world, after his blaspheming Shakespeare. Almost all the faults which he has discovered are truly there; yet who will read Mr Rymer, or not read Shakespeare? For my own part I reverence Mr Rymer's learning, but I detest his ill nature and his arrogance. I

Mr Rymer] Thomas Rymer, author of *A Short View of Tragedy* (1692), in which *Othello* was notoriously described as 'a bloody farce, without salt or savour'

indeed, and such as I, have reason to be afraid of him, but Shakespeare has not.

JOHN DRYDEN, letter to John Dennis, 1694

When Learning's triumph o'er her barb'rous foes
First rear'd the stage, immortal Shakespeare rose;
Each change of many-coloured life he drew,
Exhausted worlds, and then imagined new:
Existence saw him spurn her bounded reign,
And panting Time toil'd after him in vain:
His powerful strokes presiding truth impress'd,
And unresisted passion storm'd the breast.

SAMUEL JOHNSON, 'Prologue spoken by Mr Garrick at the opening of the Theatre in Drury Lane', 1747

'That Shakespeare,' cries the colonel, 'was a fine fellow. He was a very pretty poet indeed. Was it not Shakespeare that wrote the play about Hotspur? You must remember these lines. I got them almost by heart at the playhouse; for I never missed that play whenever it was acted, if I was in town:—

By Heav'n it was an easy leap,
To pluck bright honour into the full moon,
Or drive into the bottomless deep.

And—and—faith, I have almost forgot them; but I know it is something about saving your honour from drowning—O! it is very fine! I say, d—n me, the man that writ those lines was the greatest poet the world ever produced. There is dignity of expression and emphasis of thinking, d—n me.'

HENRY FIELDING, *Amelia*, 1751

They would talk of nothing but high life, and high-lived company, with other fashionable topics, such as pictures, taste, Shakespeare, and the musical glasses.

OLIVER GOLDSMITH, *The Vicar of Wakefield*, 1766

A coarse and barbarous piece, which would not be tolerated by the lowest rabble of France and Italy . . . You would suppose it to be a product of the imagination of a drunken savage.

VOLTAIRE, preface to *Sémiramis*, 1749

Probably the most famous of the many hostile comments which Voltaire directed against Shakespeare. The work in question was Hamlet.

Initially, having encountered him for the first time during his exile in England, Voltaire had no difficulty acknowledging Shakespeare's genius. He even tried to imitate him; his tragedy Mahomet *(1742), for instance, contains material lifted straight from* Macbeth. *But he couldn't condone what he thought of as the Englishman's 'irregularities' or his offences against good taste. (At best, he put the blame on the barbarous age in which he had lived, rather than on the man himself.) And as he grew older, his attitude hardened. 'I do not despise Shakespeare,' he protested in a letter to Horace Walpole in 1768. But by then he had denounced him so often that it was easy to suppose he did.*

His criticisms exasperated his English readers. Dr Johnson bracketed them with those of the neo-classical critics Thomas Rymer and John Dennis as 'the petty cavils of petty minds', while the celebrated bluestocking Elizabeth Montagu was provoked into writing An Essay on the Writings and Genius of Shakespear *(1769) —a work much acclaimed in its time. At an earlier stage, Mrs Montagu's resentment took on a patriotic edge. After reading Voltaire's play* L'Orphelin de la Chine, *she told her sister that it had left her unmoved:*

When I compare this indifference with the interest, the admiration, the surprise with which I read what the saucy Frenchman calls *les farces monstrueuses* of Shakespeare, I could burn him and his tragedy . . . Oh! that we were as sure our fleets and armies could drive the French out of America as that our poets and tragedians can drive them out of Parnassus.

This letter was written in November 1755, not long before the start of the Seven Years War.

In the Revd Richard Graves's novel The Spiritual Quixote, *a strolling player defends Shakespeare against his detractors:*

'Oh! Sir, . . . I must not hear a word against our venerable Patriarch and great founder of the English Drama. I will allow every objection that you can imagine against him. I will forgive Ben Jonson his malignant wish, "that, instead of one line, he had blotted out a thousand." I will not pull Voltaire by the nose (though he deserves it), for calling his Tragedies *monstrous Farces*. I will grant the Frenchman, he has offended against the laws of Aristotle and Boileau, and slighted the unities of action, time, and place; that, upon some occasions, he abounds in mixt metaphors, and uses some harsh expressions, which the age he lived in might *tolerate*, and which are become venerable only by their antiquity. But read one act, or even one scene, in Hamlet, Othello, or Macbeth, and all these trifling criticisms disperse like mists before the orient sun.'

RICHARD GRAVES, *The Spiritual Quixote*, 1772

But Shakespeare one gets acquainted with without knowing how. It is a part of an Englishman's constitution. His thoughts and beauties are so spread abroad that one touches them every where, one is intimate with him by instinct.

JANE AUSTEN, *Mansfield Park*, 1814

The speaker is Henry Crawford, but despite his faults of character we can hardly doubt that in this instance Jane Austen agreed with him.

WORLDS ELSEWHERE

The Pilgrims came to Plymouth in 1620. The plays of Shakespeare were not published until three years later. Had they been published earlier, our forefathers, or the most poetical among them, might have stayed at home to read them.

RALPH WALDO EMERSON, lecture, 1864

> Monopolizing Britain! boast no more
> His genius to your narrow bounds confin'd;
> Shakespeare's bold spirit seeks our western shore,
> A general blessing for the world design'd,
> And emulous to form the rising age,
> The noblest Bard demands the noblest Stage.

PETER MARKOE, 'The Tragic Genius of Shakespeare: An Ode', pub. Philadelphia, 1787

There is hardly a pioneer's hut which does not contain a few odd volumes of Shakespeare. I remember reading the feudal drama of *Henry V* for the first time in a log cabin.

ALEXIS DE TOCQUEVILLE, *Democracy in America*, 1835–9

Shakspeare's creations indicate no sort of anxiety to be understood. There is the Cleopatra, an irregular, unfinished, glorious, sinful character, sink or swim—there she is—& not one in the thousand of his readers apprehends the noble dimensions of the heroine. Then Ariel, Hamlet, & all—all done in sport with the free daring pencil of a Master of the World. He leaves his children with God.

RALPH WALDO EMERSON, journal, 1832

It is the distinction of genius that it is always inconceivable—once & ever a surprise. Shakspeare we cannot account for, no history, no 'life &

times' solves the insoluble problem. I cannot slope things to him so as to make him less steep & precipitous; so as to make him one of many, so as to know how I should write the same things. Goethe, I can see, wrote things which I might & should also write, were I a little more favored, a little cleverer man. He does not astonish. But Shakspeare, as Coleridge says, is as unlike his cotemporaries as he is unlike us. His style is his own. And so is Genius ever total & not mechanically composable. It stands there a beautiful unapproachable whole like a pinetree or a straw-berry—alive, perfect, yet inimitable; nor can we find where to lay the first stone, which given, we could build the arch.

Journal, 1838

The old dramatists wrote the better for the great quantity of their writ-ing and knew not when they wrote well. The playhouse was low enough to have entire interests for them; they were proprietors; it was low & popular; and not literary. That the scholars scorned it, was its saving essence. Shakspeare & his comrades, Shakspeare evidently thought the mass of old plays or of stage plays *corpus vile*, in which any experiment might be freely tried. Had the prestige which hedges about a modern tragedy or other worthless literary work existed, nothing could have been done.

Journal, 1845

How to say it, I know not, but I know that the point of praise of Shakspeare, is, the pure poetic power: he is the chosen closet companion, who can, at any moment, by incessant surprises, work the miracle of mythologising every fact of the common life; as snow, or moonlight, or the level rays of sunrise—lend a momentary glory to every pump & woodpile.

Journal, 1864

*

Now it is that blackness in Hawthorne, of which I have spoken, that so fixes and fascinates me. It may be, nevertheless, that it is too largely developed in him. Perhaps he does not give us a ray of his light for every shade of his dark. But however this may be, this blackness it is that furnishes the infinite obscure of his back-ground,—that back-ground, against which Shakespeare plays his grandest conceits, the things that

have made for Shakespeare his loftiest, but most circumscribed
renown, as the profoundest of thinkers. For by philosophers Shakespeare is not adored as the great man, of tragedy and comedy.—'Off
with his head! so much for Buckingham!' this sort of rant, interlined
by another hand, brings down the house,—those mistaken souls, who
dream of Shakespeare as a mere man of Richard-the-Third humps, and
Macbeth daggers. But it is those deep far-away things in him; those
occasional flashings-forth of the intuitive Truth in him; those short,
quick probings at the very axis of reality;—these are the things that
make Shakespeare, Shakespeare. Through the mouths of the dark
characters of Hamlet, Timon, Lear, and Iago, he craftily says, or sometimes insinuates the things, which we feel to be so terrifically true, that
it were all but madness for any good man, in his own proper character,
to utter, or even hint of them. Tormented into desperation, Lear the
frantic King tears off the mask, and speaks the sane madness of vital
truth. But, as I before said, it is the least part of genius that attracts
admiration. And so, much of the blind, unbridled admiration that has
been heaped upon Shakespeare, has been lavished upon the least part
of him. And few of his endless commentators and critics seem to have
remembered, or even perceived, that the immediate products of a
great mind are not so great, as that undeveloped, (and sometimes
undevelopable) yet dimly-discernable greatness, to which these
immediate products are but the infallible indices. In Shakespeare's
tomb lies infinitely more than Shakespeare ever wrote. And if I mag-
nify Shakespeare, it is not so much for what he did do, as for what he
did not do, or refrained from doing. For in this world of lies, Truth is
forced to fly like a scared white doe in the woodlands; and only by
cunning glimpses will she reveal herself, as in Shakespeare and other
masters of the great Art of Telling the Truth,—even though it be
covertly, and by snatches.

But if this view of the all-popular Shakespeare be seldom taken by his
readers, and if very few who extol him, have ever read him deeply, or,
perhaps, only have seen him on the tricky stage, (which alone made, and
is still making him his mere mob renown)—if few men have time, or
patience, or palate, for the spiritual truth as it is in that great genius;—it
is, then, no matter of surprise that in a contemporaneous age, Nathaniel
Hawthorne is a man, as yet, almost utterly mistaken among men. Here
and there, in some quiet arm-chair in the noisy town, or some deep nook
among the noiseless mountains, he may be appreciated for something of
what he is. But unlike Shakespeare, who was forced to the contrary

course by circumstances, Hawthorne (either from simple disinclination, or else from inaptitude) refrains from all the popularizing noise and show of broad farce, and blood-smeared tragedy; content with the still, rich utterances of a great intellect in repose, and which sends few thoughts into circulation, except they be arterialized at his large warm lungs, and expanded in his honest heart.

Nor need you fix upon that blackness in him, if it suit you not. Nor, indeed, will all readers discern it, for it is, mostly, insinuated to those who may best understand it, and account for it; it is not obtruded upon every one alike.

Some may start to read of Shakespeare and Hawthorne on the same page. They may say, that if an illustration were needed, a lesser light might have sufficed to elucidate this Hawthorne, this small man of yesterday. But I am not, willingly, one of those, who, as touching Shakespeare at least, exemplify the maxim of Rochefoucault, that 'we exalt the reputation of some, in order to depress that of others';—who, to teach all noble-souled aspirants that there is no hope for them, pronounce Shakespeare absolutely unapproachable. But Shakespeare has been approached. There are minds that have gone as far as Shakespeare into the universe. And hardly a mortal man, who, at some time or other, has not felt as great thoughts in him as any you will find in Hamlet. We must not inferentially malign mankind for the sake of any one man, whoever he may be. This is too cheap a purchase of contentment for conscious mediocrity to make. Besides, this absolute and unconditioned adoration of Shakespeare has grown to be a part of our Anglo-Saxon superstitions. The Thirty Nine articles are now Forty. Intolerance has come to exist in this matter. You must believe in Shakespeare's unapproachability, or quit the country. But what sort of a belief is this for an American, a man who is bound to carry republican progressiveness into Literature, as well as into Life? Believe me, my friends, that Shakespeares are this day being born on the banks of the Ohio. And the day will come, when you shall say who reads a book by an Englishman that is a modern? The great mistake seems to be, that even with those Americans who look forward to the coming of a great literary genius among us, they somehow fancy he will come in the costume of Queen Elizabeth's day,—be a writer of dramas founded upon old English history, or the tales of Boccaccio. Whereas, great geniuses are parts of the times; they themselves are the times; and possess a correspondent coloring. It is of a piece with the Jews, who while their Shiloh was meekly walking in their streets, were still praying for his magnificent coming; looking for him in a chariot, who was already among them on an ass. Nor must we forget, that, in his own life-time, Shakespeare was not Shakespeare, but only Master William Shakespeare of the shrewd, thriving, business firm of Condell, Shakespeare & Co., proprietors of the Globe Theatre in London; and by a courtly author, of the name of Greene, was hooted at, as an 'upstart crow' beautified 'with other bird's feathers'. For, mark it well, imitation is often the first charge brought against real originality. Why this is so, there is not space to set forth here. You must have plenty of sea-room to tell the Truth in; especially, when it seems to have an aspect of newness, as America did in 1492, though it was then just as old, and perhaps older than Asia, only those sagacious philosophers, the common sailors, had never seen it before; swearing it was all water and moonshine there.

Now, I do not say that Nathaniel of Salem is greater than William of Avon, or as great. But the difference between the two men is by no means immeasurable. Not a very great deal more, and Nathaniel were verily William.

This, too, I mean, that if Shakespeare has not been equalled, he is sure to be surpassed, and surpassed by an American born now or yet to be born. For it will never do for us who in most other things out-do as well as out-brag the world, it will not do for us to fold our hands and say, In the highest department advance there is none. Nor will it at all do to say, that the world is getting grey and grizzled now, and has lost that fresh charm which she wore of old, and by virtue of which the great poets of past times made themselves what we esteem them to be. Not so. The world is as young today, as when it was created; and this Vermont morning dew is as wet to my feet, as Eden's dew to Adam's. Nor has Nature been all over ransacked by our progenitors, so that no new charms and mysteries remain for this latter generation to find. Far from it. The trillionth part has not yet been said; and all that has been said, but multiples the avenues, to what remains to be said. It is not so much paucity, as superabundance of material that seems to incapacitate modern authors.

HERMAN MELVILLE, 'Hawthorne and His Mosses', 1850

The inward and outward characteristics of Shakspere are his vast and rich variety of persons and themes, with his wondrous delineation of each and all—not only limitless funds of verbal and pictorial resource, but great excess, superfoetation—mannerism, like a fine, aristocratic perfume, holding a touch of musk (Euphues, his mark)—with boundless sumptuousness and adornment, real velvet and gems, not shoddy nor paste—but a good deal of bombast and fustian—(certainly some terrific mouthing in Shakspere!)

Superb and inimitable as all is, it is mostly an objective and physiological kind of power and beauty the soul finds in Shakspere—a style supremely grand of the sort, but in my opinion stopping short of the grandest sort, at any rate for fulfilling and satisfying modern and scientific and democratic American purposes. Think, not of growths as forests primeval, or Yellowstone geysers, or Colorado ravines, but of costly marble palaces, and palace rooms, and the noblest fixings and furniture, and noble owners and occupants to correspond—think of carefully built gardens from the beautiful but sophisticated gardening art at its best, with walks and bowers and artificial lakes, and appropriate statue-groups and the finest cultivated roses and lilies and japonicas in plenty—and you have the tally of Shakspere. The low characters, mechanics, even the loyal henchmen—all in themselves nothing—serve as capital foils to aristocracy. The comedies (exquisite as they certainly are) bringing in admirably portray'd common characters, have the unmistakable hue of plays, portraits, made for the divertisement only of the élite of the castle, and from its point of view. The comedies are altogether non-acceptable to America and Democracy.

But to the deepest soul, it seems a shame to pick and choose from the riches Shakspere has left us—to criticise his infinitely royal, multiform quality—to gauge, with optic glasses, the dazzle of his sun-like beams.

WALT WHITMAN, 'A Thought on Shakespere', 1886

This is Whitman writing at the age of 67. His objections to Shakespeare's 'feudalism' had taken shape early on. They were an intrinsic aspect of his literary nationalism, his conviction that American writers had to clear a space for themselves and find their own voice.

He also had strong reservations, which are worth pondering, about Shakespeare's style:

Many little things are too much over-colored in Shakespeare—far too much. The features of beloved women, compliments, the descriptions of moderately brave actions, professions of service, and hundreds more, are painted too intensely. It is no answer to this to say that a lover would so state the case about a woman he loved, or that a strong, rich nature would be apt to describe incidents in that manner; and that Shakespeare is therefore correct in so presenting them. Immensely too much is unnaturally colored—the sentiment is piled on, similes, comparisons, defiances, exaltations, immortalities, bestowed upon themes certainly not worthy the same, thus losing proportion. (Also most of the discursive speeches of the great and little characters are glaringly inappropriate, both words and sentiments such as could not have come from their mouths in real life and therefore should not in the plays.) Yet on great occasions the character and action are perfect.

'Preparatory Reading and Thought', 1857

At the same time, as the turn at the end of both these passages makes clear, Whitman needed no persuading of Shakespeare's greatness. But who was Shakespeare? Whitman drew back from the lure of outright Baconianism; but as he explained to an English admirer, he was convinced that there was a mystery—that behind William Shakespeare of Stratford there lurked a second, altogether deeper personality:

The following evening I stayed to supper with Whitman in the little kitchen of his home, in company with Mr and Mrs Lay. They seemed homely decent people, rather dull and quiet. Walt, who was dressed just in shirt and trousers—for the weather was hot—kept things going. Afterwards we sat in the front room with Folger McKinsey, a young Philadelphian of literary leanings, who had come in. Walt talked about Shakespeare, the Bacon theory, the greatness of the historical plays, the 'dragon-rancours' of the barons, King Lear &c. 'I will not be positive about Bacon's connection with the plays, but I am satisfied that behind the historical Shakespeare there is another mind, guiding, and far, far reaching, giving weight and permanent value to what would otherwise have been only two plays a year written for a witty, alert, jocose audience—chiefly of young gallants.'

EDWARD CARPENTER, 'Whitman in 1884', *Days with Walt Whitman*

*

In 1872 Bayard Taylor, best remembered as the translator of Faust, celebrated the unveiling of a statue to Shakespeare in Central Park, New York.

If, here, his image seem
Of softer scenes and grayer skies to dream,
Thatched cot and rustic tavern, ivied hall,
     The cuckoo's April call
And cowslip-meads beside the Avon stream,
He shall not fail that other home to find
     We could not leave behind!
The forms of Passion, which his fancy drew,
  In us their ancient likenesses beget:
So, from our lives for ever born anew,
  He stands amid his own creations yet!
Here comes lean Cassius, of conventions tired;
  Here, in his coach, luxurious Antony
Beside his Egypt, still of men admired;
  And Brutus plans some purer liberty!
A thousand Shylocks, Jew and Christian, pass;
  A hundred Hamlets, by their times betrayed;
And sweet Anne Page comes tripping o'er the grass,
  And awkward Falstaff pants beneath the shade.
Here toss upon the wanton summer wind
     The locks of Rosalind;
Here some gay glove the damned spot conceals
     Which Lady Macbeth feels:
His ease here smiling smooth Iago takes,
  And outcast Lear gives passage to his woe,
And here some foiled Reformer sadly breaks
     His wand of Prospero!
  In liveried splendour, side by side,
  Nick Bottom and Titania ride,
  And Portia, flushed with cheers of men,
  Disdains dear faithful Imogen;
  And Puck beside the form of Morse,°
  Stops on his forty-minutes course;
  And Ariel from his swinging bough
  A blossom casts on Bryant's brow,
Until, as summoned from his brooding brain,
  He sees his children all again,
In us, as on our lips, each fresh, immortal strain!

Morse] Samuel Morse, pioneer of the electric telegraph, also commemorated in Central Park

After long disuse of her eyes she read Shakespeare and thought why is any other book needed.

EMILY DICKINSON, as reported by Thomas Wentworth Higginson

Naturally Emily Dickinson read, and 'needed', many other books. But Shakespeare, as her biographer Richard B. Sewall says, was 'omnipresent in her life'. Even more impressive than her praise of him are the constant Shakespearian references and quotations woven into her letters. Many of them, as the following sampling makes clear, are compressed or oblique.

Egypt—thou knew'st—

To Susan Gilbert Dickinson, c. 1874

This is the entire letter. The reference is to one of Antony's speeches in Antony and Cleopatra: *'Egypt, thou knew'st too well, | My heart was to thy rudder tied by the strings . . .'*

Brabantio's resignation is the only one. 'I here do give thee that with all my heart, which, but thou hast already, with all my heart I would keep from thee.'

To Maria Whitney, 1878

A letter of consolation on the death of a friend. It also contains the reflection that 'to relieve the irreparable degrades it'.

Your little Note protected, as it always does, and the 'Whips of Time' felt a long way off.

To Mrs J. G. Holland, 1878

The phrase in quotation marks is a condensed version of Hamlet's 'The whips and scorns of time'.

I trust the 'Hand' has 'ceased from troubling'—it has saved too many to be assailed by an 'envious sliver—'

To Mrs J. G. Holland, 1880

The 'envious sliver' is from Hamlet. *In a later letter (to Abbie Farley, 1885)*
Emily Dickinson wrote: ' "An envious sliver" was a passage your uncle pecu-
liarly loved in the drowning Ophelia.'

Antony's remark to a friend, 'since Cleopatra died' is said to be the
saddest ever lain in Language—That engulfing 'Since'—

To Otis Lord, c. 1882

Mattie will hide this little flower in her friend's Hand. Should she ask
who sent it, tell her as Desdemona did when they asked who slew her,
'Nobody—I myself.'

To Sara Colton, 1885

What an Embassy—
    What an Ambassador!
    'And pays his Heart for what his Eyes eat only!'

To Ned Dickinson, 1885

This last quotation, which Emily Dickinson also uses in an earlier letter (to
Susan Gilbert Dickinson), is from Antony and Cleopatra.
    Elsewhere she expected correspondents to recognize references to 'crowner's
quest' (from Hamlet*), 'remainder biscuit' (from* As You Like It*), 'very sea-*
mark of my utmost sail' (from Othello*), 'envious worm' (from* Romeo and
Juliet*). The list could easily be extended.*
    As for her poetry, Shakespeare's influence is too profound to show on the
surface. There are very few direct borrowings—a mention of Shylock here, a
recollection of Julius Caesar *there, the echo of* The Tempest *in the poem 'A*
Route of Evanescence' (see p. 100). But as Richard B. Sewall says, 'the tone and
spirit, the exhilaration and encouragement, were everything. In Shakespeare's
robust, un-Puritan expression was a whole new world for her of feeling and
fulfilment.'
    There is one poem in which his presence is explicit, although it reaches
beyond him (its whole point) into life at large:

> Drama's Vitallest Expression is the Common Day
> That arise and set about Us—
> Other Tragedy

Perish in the Recitation—
This—the best enact
When the Audience is scattered
And the Boxes shut—

'Hamlet' to Himself were Hamlet—
Had not Shakespeare wrote,—
Though the 'Romeo' left no Record
Of his Juliet.

It were infinite enacted
In the Human Heart—
Only Theatre recorded
Owner cannot shut—

*c.*1863

The notion of ordinary men and women enacting Shakespearian roles in their own lives can also be found in a poem by another major poet, Yeats's 'Lapis Lazuli':

All perform their tragic play,
There struts Hamlet, there is Lear,
That's Ophelia, that Cordelia . . .

But in Yeats these figures remain players indeed, the 'dread' of their final scenes transfigured by 'gaiety'—the gaiety of art; the gaiety, perhaps, of the poet's belief in eternal recurrence. In Emily Dickinson, by contrast, a tragic fate, in the real world, is simply something that has to be endured.

★

Shakespeare was the cleverest of climbers and necessarily he stood cap in hand in the presence of gentlemen. The dramatist of universal human nature, the poet of all time, was eager to assert his servility by befouling all underling human nature. His draft on posterity he readily sold for present favour. The Warwickshire peasant caught the insolent class consciousness of his patron. Where in the ample pages of Shakespeare do we find the London of reality that was gathering in strength to pull down both court and courtier? He was more concerned to become the first citizen of Stratford than to hold the broadest realms of poesy in fee.

V. L. PARRINGTON, historian, 1917 (Parrington is best known as the author of *Main Currents in American Thought*, 1927)

archy confesses

coarse
jocosity
catches the crowd
shakespeare
and i
are often
low browed

the fish wife
curse
and the laugh
of the horse
shakespeare
and i
are frequently
coarse

aesthetic
excuses
in bill s behalf
are adduced
to refine
big bill s
coarse laugh

but bill
he would chuckle
to hear such guff
he pulled
rough stuff
and he liked
rough stuff

hoping you
are the same

archy

DON MARQUIS, 1927

*   *   *

Ulrich Bräker (1735–98) was born in Toggenburg in the north-east region of Switzerland. His father was a peasant farmer and charcoal burner; he himself began life as a goat-boy, served briefly in the army of Frederick the Great, and then worked as a weaver, making long journeys by foot in order to sell his yarn. In his later years he also acquired modest fame as an author, chiefly on account of an autobiography which he published in 1789, but poverty compelled him to stick to the weaving trade right to the end.

    In 1776 he joined the 'Moral Society' of a nearby town. Its library gave him access to a translation of Shakespeare, and by 1780 he had completed a notebook which he entitled Etwas über William Shakespeares Schauspiele, Von Einem Armen Ungelehrten Weltbürger, der das Glück genosz, denselben zu lesen *('A Few Words about the plays of William Shakespeare, by a poor ignorant citizen of the world who had the good fortune to read them'). It was first published in Leipzig in 1852, over fifty years after his death.*

    Bräker's comments cover virtually all the plays, in most cases running to several pages. As the following extracts indicate, he valued Shakespeare above all for his realistic portrayal of character, constantly reflecting on how much it tallied with his own experience. He also came to think of the writer as something very like a personal friend.

The Taming of the Shrew

Dear Petruchio, come and visit our country and I'll find you enough customers to set you up nicely in business. If your prescriptions work, then may I beg and beseech your help humbly and dejectedly in the name of all those who are tormented and woefully mistreated by Kates, of which I know whole legions, to whom I'll heartily recommend you— all of them formed up in companies and wearing different uniforms, each individual of which is further to be distinguished, according to the length of the leading strings he's kept in! But let us know when you're coming, and arm yourself with good credentials, for there are some amongst us who are very timorous because they've already blunted their wits, trying every shift, all to no avail, and as a result are now so timid they think it would be easier to empty the sea or move mountains than silence such a tongue. I, myself, would have grave doubts about your method, but that I saw your Kate changed into a lamb. And yet I still have my doubts as to whether your Kate is the real thing, the genuine tough article. I know someone who had a Kate who called him a 'louse' the whole time, which annoyed him so much that he tried everything to stop her. But that's the very thing she's after; 'louse' is forever on her tongue! Once, when she wouldn't stop 'lousing' him, he got terribly angry, flung his Kate into a deep well, and deep in the water, when she had to shut her mouth and hold her nose, she still kept cracking lice with thumb and finger! she still kept 'lousing' him! She's one who has what it takes!

My dear Petruchio, prepare for the worst, take up position; anything might happen. My dear Sir William, you're very lenient towards the fair sex. If your Kate corresponds to her model, then she doesn't deserve the title of shrew at all, rather that Petruchio of yours deserves the title of a coarse, uncouth boor. I wouldn't inflict such a cure even on a dog, never mind such a beautiful creature who allows herself to be pushed around by such an oaf, and then in the end reveals she has a woman's heart of gold.

No, I know, William, you could easily have produced a much more ghastly horror from your store, but I can well imagine how it is when you've got to write for an audience. Anyway what's the point of heaping shame upon the whole fair sex, so many innocent, noble hearts? You could easily upset any decent chap by selecting from our own sex really fierce monsters, beasts, savages, tigers, lions, wolves, stallions, and putting them on to the stage. It's just that I thought that people of a similar nature should share the yoke—but fate doesn't pay attention to what *I* think—I'm sure she knows better than I who belong together. The best thing would be for each partner to leave the other in peace and quietly put up with each other without making such a fuss all over the show.

Richard II

News was constantly being brought to the king, each new report upsetting him worse than the previous one. Richard's speeches and bearing from the first rumour right up to his arrest and his death strike me as very fine; they gave me much food for thought. Of course the fall is great from a throne into the mire—an insignificant citizen of the world can't fall so far—and the farther you fall, the more it hurts. But there's many a man only fallen from one mire into another and has still howled pitifully enough. O Richard, it must hurt, to fall so deep; but there's many a poor wretch who thinks himself richer than you and yet in his life falls not only once but many thousands of times from his glory into the deepest misery. And you did have the satisfaction of reading about thousands of similar cases of fallen princes. O many a worm writhing in misery would give all he had to be able to see depicted before him so many precursors! In fact this is a man's greatest torment—the belief that he's the only one from the beginning of time to whom such things have ever happened and that he has to writhe unnoticed, unpitied in his misery.

Measure for Measure

I count this play amongst the finest. I'm especially delighted with the duke's scheme for keeping an eye on his realm. That hypocrite, Angelo, how strictly he contrived to regard the laws and lead an outwardly strict life and yet was capable of being a villain. How realistically he gradually did more and more harm, the way human beings do! There's plenty of moralizing on Angelo's skill in protecting humanity and, at the same time, glossing over vice so beautifully. And Isabella's speeches are amongst the very finest; and how splendidly Lucio is portrayed, a man accustomed to speak nothing but ill of his neighbours.

But, Isabella, your speeches are particularly beautiful, and yet you made me angry, you stern sister. When your wretched brother is trembling on the point of death, you call him a cowardly, despicable, squalid monster; you refused even to kneel down to save him from death. What are you thinking of, you hard-hearted beauty? I think your brother's more humane than you; you want to be more of an angel than a human being.

King Lear

Gloster, noble Gloster, your fate moves me most deeply of all! Could you not moan about your eyes as Arthur did? O this Cornwall's a monster; he couldn't be stirred to pity as Hubert was! But I did help that honest servant to give Cornwall an extra hard thrust, causing him to bleed to death. Poor, kind Gloster, you've learned what it's like to lose a pair of kind eyes, to let a wicked devil, heedless of all the kind hospitality offered to him, trample all over you. How kind you are still, blind man!

Only when you'd lost your sight, did you see, see that you'd been betrayed, that your son, Edgar, was noble and your Edmund an unnatural villain. But you were lucky to find your way back to your Edgar again. What a scene, where he takes you up a hill and there describes that fearful abyss, a terrible pit into which you would so dearly leap! No wonder, poor, wretched man!—and we only need to get toothache and in no time we're overcome by impatience. But to have to live in the world like this—you just can't imagine it—to be robbed like this of a pair of eyes, and with the sockets still hurting—to wander about in such pitch-black darkness in a world full of such tyrants, threatening worse evil the whole time—to someone in this state such a ghastly abyss must seem a soft bed!

Tr. Derek Bowman

★

Goethe assigns Shakespeare a major role in his novel Wilhelm Meister's Apprenticeship. *When the youthful hero is persuaded by a friend to read some of the plays, he is bowled over:*

They are not literary works! You believe that you are standing before the huge, open books of fate in which the high wind of life at its most agitated storms, turning the pages back and forth rapidly and with violence. I am so astonished and disconcerted by the strength and delicacy, the violence and calm, that I can only wait with longing for the time when I shall be in a position to be able to go on reading.

Prince Hal becomes one of his role models, and life with the theatrical troupe he has joined gives him a chance to indulge his fancy:

His friend Shakespeare, whom he acknowledged with great joy as his godfather and for whose sake he was all the more willing to be called Wilhelm, had introduced him to a prince who for a period spent his time in low, indeed bad company, and for all his noble nature took pleasure in the roughness, unseemliness and silliness of such wholly sensuous fellows. The ideal situation with which he could compare his present position was most welcome to him, and self-deception, to which he was almost irresistibly drawn, became much easier for him in this way.

He now began to think about his clothes. He decided that a little waistcoat, over which in case of need a short cloak could be worn, would be very appropriate attire for a traveller. Long knitted trousers and a pair of laced boots seemed to be the true garb of a walker. Then he acquired a beautiful silk sash which he first wrapped round himself with the excuse of needing to keep his body warm; on the other hand he freed his neck from the servitude of a tie and had some strips of calico fixed on to his shirt, though they came out rather wide and looked completely like a collar of the classical period. The beautiful silk necker-chief, the memento of Mariane that he had saved, would lie lightly fastened beneath the calico ruff. A round hat with a bright ribbon and a large feather made the masquerade complete.

The ladies assured him that this outfit suited him extremely well. Philine made herself out as quite enchanted by it and asked to be given his beautiful hair, which he had cut mercilessly in order to approach the more closely to the natural ideal. She made herself quite popular by this approach, and our friend, whose generosity had given him the right to behave like Prince Hal in his manners with the others, soon acquired the taste himself for initiating and encouraging some mad tricks. They fenced and danced, made up all kinds of games, and light-heartedly they enjoyed in strong measure the tolerable wine that was available, and in the disorderliness of this manner of life Philine was lying in wait for our prim hero, and may his guardian spirit take care on his behalf!

It is Hamlet, however, who engages Wilhelm most deeply. He expounds his ideas about the prince to his fellow-actors:

'Just think of this young man, this monarch's son, in clear terms,' he cried, 'imagine his position, and then watch him when he learns that the figure of his father is to appear; stand by him in the fearful night when the venerable ghost itself is to step forth. He is seized by a monstrous terror; he speaks to the miraculous shape, sees it beckon, follows and listens. His ears resound with the most terrible accusation against his uncle, with the demand for revenge, and with the urgent, repeated request: "remember me"!

'And when the ghost has disappeared, whom do we see standing before us? A young hero breathing revenge? A born monarch who feels happy at being summoned against the usurper of his crown? No! Aston-ishment and gloom befall the solitary prince; he becomes bitter against the smiling villains, swears that he will not forget the one who has departed, and closes with the significant expression of dismay: "The time is out of joint: O cursed spite, that ever I was born to set it right!"

'It is in these words, I think, that the key to Hamlet's whole behaviour lies, and it is clear to me that what Shakespeare wanted to describe was: a great deed laid upon a person who was not equal to it. And I see the play as consistently constructed with this in mind. An oak-tree is here planted in an exquisite vessel that should only have received sweet flowers into its bosom; the roots spread, and the vessel is destroyed.

'A fine, pure, noble, most highly moral person, lacking the sensuous strength that makes a hero, collapses beneath a burden that he can neither bear nor throw off; all duty is sacred to him, but this obligation is too heavy. The impossible is being asked of him, not the impossible in itself, but what is impossible for him. How he twists and turns, fears, steps back and forth, is constantly reminded, reminds himself constantly, and in the end almost loses sight of his purpose, though without ever becoming happy again!'

Preparing to play the part, he refines his conceptions further, He also forms a strong physical image of the prince:

'The more I get into the part, the more I realize that in my whole appearance there is not a trace of the physiognomy that Shakespeare offers in his Hamlet. When I truly consider how exactly everything in the part hangs together, I scarcely trust myself to produce an effect that is tolerable.'

'You are embarking on your career with great conscientiousness,' put in Serlo. 'An actor fits into his part as best he can, and the part adjusts itself, as it must, to him. But what sort of a sketch has Shakespeare given of his Hamlet? Is he so very different from you?'

'In the first place Hamlet is blond,' Wilhelm replied.

'I call that far-fetched,' said Aurelia. 'What makes you think that?'

'As a Dane, a man from the north, he is blond from the start and has blue eyes.'

'Is Shakespeare supposed to have thought of that?'

'I can't find it specifically stated, but it seems to me to be undeniable when various references are taken together. He finds fencing hard-going, the sweat pours down off his face, and the Queen says: "He's fat and scant of breath." Can you think of him there except as blonde and portly? For dark-haired people are seldom like this when they are young.

Do not his vacillating melancholy, his gentle sadness and his busy indecisiveness fit in better with that sort of a figure than when you imagine a slim youth with dark-brown hair, from whom we expect more decisiveness and agility?'

'You are upsetting my imagination,' Aurelia exclaimed, 'Away with your fat Hamlet! We would rather be given any Tom, Dick or Harry who excites and moves us. The author's intention doesn't mean so much to us as our own pleasure, and what we require is a stimulus that is congenial to us.'

All the roles in the production are filled except for that of the Ghost. Wilhelm receives a mysterious note promising that someone will take the part when the time comes: an unknown actor duly shows up on the day of the first perform-ance, but by then Wilhelm is too busy with last-minute preparations to notice his arrival:

The whole day through Wilhelm had not had time to think of the main worry, that is, whether the Ghost really would come. Now the anxiety had completely gone, and the strangest guest-performance was to be expected. The manager came and asked about this and that; Wilhelm did not have time to look around for the Ghost, and he only hurried in order to find his place by the throne, where the King and Queen were already surrounded by their court and were resplendent in all their magnifi-cence; he only caught the last words of Horatio who spoke about the appearance of the Ghost in quite a confused manner and seemed as if he had almost forgotten his part.

The drop-curtain went up, and he saw the full house before him. After Horatio had made his speech and had been dismissed by the King, he pressed close to Hamlet and as if he were presenting himself to him, the Prince, he said: 'it's the devil who's inside that armour! He's put fear into all of us.'

In the meantime all that could be seen was two tall men in white cloaks and hoods who were standing in the wings, and Wilhelm, whose first soliloquy had been a failure, as he thought, in the distraction, unrest and confusion, came on to the stage for the terrible, dramatic winter's night in a truly uneasy mood, although vigorous applause had accom-panied him when he had gone off. However, he pulled himself together and spoke the passage, purposely with the appropriate indifference, for-got the Ghost, as did the audience, in the process, and really did take fright when Horatio exclaimed 'Look, my Lord, it comes!' He turned round with a sudden movement, and the tall, noble figure, the gentle, inaudible step, and light movement in the heavy-looking armour made so strong an impression upon him that he stood there as if petrified and could exclaim 'Angels and ministers of grace defend us!' only with half a voice. He stared at the figure, drew breath several times and delivered the address to the Ghost in so confused, fragmented and forced a manner that the greatest art could not have expressed the speech so excellently.

His translation of this passage helped him greatly. He had kept close to the original, whose word order seemed to him to present in a unique way the state of mind of someone who has been taken by surprise, terrified and seized by terror.

> Be thou a spirit of health or goblin damn'd,
> Bring with thee airs from heaven or blasts from hell,
> Be thy intents wicked or charitable,
> Thou comest in such a questionable shape
> That I will speak to thee: I'll call thee Hamlet,
> King, father, royal Dane: O answer me!

It could be sensed that there was a very great effect taking place in the audience. The Ghost beckoned, the Prince followed him amidst the loudest applause.

The scene changed, and when they came to the distant place the Ghost stopped unexpectedly and turned round; as a result Hamlet came to be standing rather too close to him. Wilhelm at once looked with desire and curiosity between the lowered visor, but could only see deep-set eyes and a well shaped nose. He stood before him peering fearfully; but when the first sounds came forth from the helmet, when a harmonious, only slightly rough voice could be heard saying 'I am thy father's spirit,' Wilhelm stepped back a few paces shuddering, and the whole audience shuddered. The voice seemed known to everybody, and Wilhelm believed he could notice a similarity with his own father's voice. Wilhelm was pulled in contrary directions by these strange feelings and memories, by the curiosity to discover who the strange friend was, by fear of offending him, and even by the impropriety of approaching him as an actor too closely in this situation. During the Ghost's long narrative he changed his position so often, and seemed so vague and embarrassed, so attentive and so distracted, that his acting aroused general admiration, just as the Ghost stirred up general terror. The latter spoke more with a deep feeling of annoyance rather than of misery, but it was a slow, unbounded, spiritual annoyance. It was the despondence of a great soul which is separated from all that is earthly and yet collapses beneath infinite sufferings. In the end the Ghost sank down, but in a strange manner: for a light, transparent, grey gauze which seemed to rise like steam from the aperture spread over him and drew him down with it.

> JOHANN WOLFGANG VON GOETHE, *Wilhelm Meister's Years of Apprenticeship* (*Wilhelm Meisters Lehrjahre*), 1796, tr. H. M. Waidson

After the performance the stranger disappears, but he leaves behind another note for Wilhelm, urging him to give up the theatre—advice which he initially ignores but eventually follows.

*

Bohemia Lies by the Sea

If the houses here are green, I'll step inside a house.
If the bridges here are strong, I'll walk on solid ground.
If love's labor is lost in every age, I'd like to lose it here.

If I'm not the one, someone is, he's just as good as I.

If a word borders on me here, I'll let it border.
If Bohemia still lies by the sea, I'll believe in the sea.
And if I believe in the sea, I can hope for land.

If I'm the one, then anyone is, he's worth as much as I.
I want nothing more for myself. Let me go under now.

Underground—that means the ocean, there I'll find Bohemia again.
From my ruins, I wake up in peace.
From deep down I know, and am not lost.

Come here, all you Bohemians, seamen, harbor whores and ships
unanchored. Don't you want to be Bohemians, all you Illyrians,
Venetians and Veronese. Play the comedies that make us laugh

to tears. And go astray a hundred times,
as I went astray and never stood the trials.
Yet I did stand them, each and every time.

As Bohemia stood them and one fine day
was pardoned to the sea and now lies by water.

I still border on a word and a different land,
I border, like little else, on everything more and more,

a man from Bohemia, a vagrant, a player
who has nothing and whom nothing holds,
granted only, by a questionable sea, to gaze at the land of my choice.

INGEBORG BACHMANN, 1964, tr. Mark Anderson

'Thou art perfect, then, our ship hath touch'd upon | The deserts of Bohemia?'—The Winter's Tale, *III. iii.*

★ ★ ★

In Henry IV Part Two, *Falstaff enters the Boar's Head tavern singing, and breaks off to order a servant to 'empty the jordan'—i.e. the chamber-pot. In* William Shakespeare *(1864),* Victor Hugo *writes*:

> Falstaff m'est proposé, je l'accepte, et j'admire le *empty the jordan.*

Hugo had first proclaimed Shakespeare's greatness in the preface to his play Cromwell *(1827).* William Shakespeare, *nearly forty years later, was originally planned as a preface to the translation of the plays by his son François-Victor, but grew into a full-length book. It is written in a high rhapsodic style, with repeated references to the handful of 'Equals' in whose company Shakespeare belonged: Isaiah, St Paul, Homer, Aeschylus, Dante, one or two other giants of the past and (by implication) Hugo himself.*

Hugo also believed that Shakespeare had spoken to him a number of times, through a planchette, at seances conducted by his son Charles:

During the *séances* when Shakespeare appeared, Hugo was not always present but it seemed to make little difference to the result. When the dramatist had first been materialised, it had struck a sceptical onlooker as strange that he should deliver his messages in French—neither Hugo nor his son knew English at that time—but, when asked for the reason of this odd behaviour, the spirit had explained that this was on account of the superiority of the French language. Apparently, with corporeal flesh, spirits slough off racial prejudices and national pride as well. The message in verse which came to Hugo said that, when one of his works blossomed on earth, Shakespeare took it in his hands and all the other authors sat round to listen. Cervantes, with raised finger, silenced Molière, and all of them exclaimed: 'Let's see what it's about!' They all listened with fixed attention and Shakespeare said that he had often seen Dante weep when Hugo had shown how love can exist even in the soul of the ugliest creature, while Aeschylus, the God of awe, used to tremble at the tremendous emotions which Hugo roused. 'Your voice is sacred!' cried Shakespeare to Hugo. 'Carry on the good work! After *Hamlet* and *Don Juan* your plays are the second wave that beats against our heavenly shores. The work of art of the world lives, and it reigns! It is man's key of love to open Heaven! Let us then heap work of art upon work of art! I, Shakespeare, today, and you, Hugo, tomorrow!'

ENID STARKIE, *Baudelaire*, 1957

When I read Shakespeare I become greater, wiser, purer. When I have reached the crest of one of his works I feel that I am high on a mountain: everything disappears, everything appears. I am no longer a man, I am an *eye*. New horizons loom, perspectives extend to infinity. I forget I have been living like other men in the barely discernible hovels below, that I've been drinking from all those distant rivers that appear smaller than brooks, that I have participated in all the confusion of the anthill.

GUSTAVE FLAUBERT, letter to Louise Colet, September 1846, tr. Francis Steegmuller

And then I was overwhelmed for two days by a scene in Shakespeare (the first scene in Act Three of *King Lear*). That man will drive me mad. More and more all the others seem like children beside him. In that scene all the characters, wretched beyond endurance and completely crazed by their sufferings, go off their heads and talk wildly. There are three different kinds of madness howling at once, while the Fool cracks jokes and rain pours down amid thunder and lightning. A young gentleman, whom we have seen rich and handsome at the beginning of the play, says this: 'Ah! I knew women, etc. I was ruined by them. Distrust the light sound of their gown and the creaking of their satin shoes, etc.' Ah! *Poésie françoyse!* How clear your waters run in comparison! When I think of how faithful we are to those busts—Racine! Corneille! And other talents just as mortally boring! It makes me groan! I long (another quotation from the Bard) to 'tread them into mortar and daub the walls of a jakes with them.' Yes, it bowled me over. I could think of nothing but that scene on the heath, where wolves are heard howling and old Lear weeps in the rain and tears his beard in the wind. It is when one contemplates such peaks that one feels small: 'Doomed to mediocrity, we are humbled by transcendent minds.'°

FLAUBERT, letter to Louise Colet, January 1854

Flaubert gets a number of things wrong in his account of the scene from Lear. *In his monumental study of the novelist, Jean-Paul Sartre subjects these mistakes and their implications to an extended analysis:*

This passage calls for a few comments. In the first place, the facts are wrong: the scene in question is not the first but a combination of the second and the fourth. This detail would be unimportant if Gustave had not just reread the play—or in any case the third act. A more serious problem is that one would be hard put to find *three* kinds of madness. I have in vain counted and recounted, and I find only two. For scene 2 takes place between Lear, the fool, and Kent, a man of good sense and a loyal subject who wants to persuade Lear to take shelter. We have here *one* madman: the old vagabond king. Yet we are willing to be indulgent, in part because the mistake was common in the Romantic period. It is true that Lear is a stubborn old idiot whose wretchedness will soon raise him to greatness and who will *subsequently* lose his mind. Then comes an interpolated scene between Gloucester and his son Edmund: an old fogey who has been duped and a traitor—that makes two normal characters. We return to Lear: scene 4 begins, the scene that overwhelms Flaubert with its beauty. Lear, Kent, and the fool are in front of a hut in which Edgar has taken refuge. He immediately emerges: he will be the second madman. Where is the third? Old Gloucester, who appears at the end, has not lost his mind in the meantime, but here is the most curious thing: Edgar's madness is *feigned*. He has earlier declared in a monologue (act 2, scene 3):

No port is free; no place
That guard and most unusual vigilance
Does not attend my taking. Whiles I may scape
I will preserve myself, and am bethought
To take the basest and most poorest shape
That ever penury, in contempt of man,
Brought near to beast.

'Doomed to mediocrity . . . minds'] a quotation from Montesquieu

We later find him quite reasonable: he *plays* the madman to protect himself—and says so: 'Bad is the trade that must play the fool to sorrow.'

Critics have recently advanced the idea that Edgar was *doubly feigning*, that the game of madness was hiding an authentic madness. This is admissible for Hamlet but not here, where the feigning is an obvious manoeuvre and double feigning perfectly useless. The important thing is only that Lear should believe that he is mad. For the central character of the scene is Lear, the king who discovers his nakedness; and what Flaubert did not see—otherwise, would he say 'three different kinds of madness howling at once'? (so many words, so many errors)—is that the fool, a professional madman, the image of a certain skeptical Reason, and the feigning Edgar are *necessary* to Lear's development. The characters, far from 'howling at once' have a strange conversation, a silent dialogue and sub-talk whose eventual result is Lear's flash of intuition: 'Unaccommodated man is no more but such a poor, bare, forked animal as thou art. Off, off, you lendings! Come, unbutton here' [act 3, scene 4]. Obviously the dialectical meaning of the scene has escaped Flaubert, although he had felt that 'all the characters were wretched beyond endurance and completely crazed by their sufferings.' But, even more striking, the very details and secondary meanings were right under his nose and went unnoticed. Edgar does not say: 'Ah! I have known women and I was ruined by them'—which would make no sense since this character feigning madness, slandered by his half-brother, has abandoned his wealth and renounced his way of life *in order to flee* prosecution by old Gloucester. The meaning of the long speech in which he cries: 'Let not the creaking of shoes nor the rustling of silks betray thy poor heart to woman' is completely different: he recalls his past life, but far from regretting it or complaining of his memories, he judges it pitilessly. In this sense he undergoes the same development as Lear, even more rapidly, and it is Edgar who leads Lear finally to cry out: 'Off, off, [you] lendings.' Under the cover of feigned madness, the outlaw offers a surprising mixture of nostalgia and self-accusation—of nostalgia defending itself against itself by denigrating the past, self-accusation surging up in each sentence as the judgment of the present on days gone by and intentionally spoiling the charm of memories. And the sentence 'Let not the creaking of shoes . . .' must not be completed by 'otherwise you will be ruined': it is in itself a categorical imperative defining the norms of life as a function of a rediscovered austerity—which is joined to Christian morality. Indeed, in an earlier line of Edgar's we find a summary of the Ten Commandments: 'Take heed o'th' foul fiend. Obey thy parents,' etc. The beauty of the scene comes from the fact that it brings a father, swindled by two of his daughters and having misunderstood the third, face to face with a son, misunderstood and hunted by his father at the instigation of his half-brother. As if Lear found himself in the presence of Cordelia who had *become other*, having changed sex, and instinctively attached himself to Edgar as a function of this resemblance.

On this level, the changing partners, the metamorphoses and the correspondences are not meant to lead to philosophical conclusions; they are not *symbols of anything* but give the whole scene an obscure, profound unity full of meaning. *That very thing* should have pleased Flaubert, for it involves an *aesthetic form* indirectly suggesting depth. He failed to sense it because between two rereadings he had forgotten the character of Edgar. Witness the vague way he presents him: 'A young gentleman, whom we have seen rich and handsome at the beginning . . .' The least one can say is that wealth and good looks are not in question: when Edgar appears for the first time, his half-brother, the bastard Edmund, has already more than half outwitted Gloucester; so we *first* see him as a sympathetic and endangered young man who in all innocence is running to his doom.

Around the same time, Flaubert manages to read the works of Bouilhet and Louise attentively and to give them good advice, and a little later he will quite effectively judge and critique the books of his contemporaries. Yet here he claims to be *overwhelmed* by a scene whose general intention and details he is not even capable of rendering with precision. It is *true* that this is a fine scene, arguably the finest in the play. Thus, paradoxically, he is right to admire it, even if for the wrong reasons. As if his *taste* could locate the rarest beauties but the young man were subsequently incapable of accounting for his choice. To tell the truth, it happens to all of us with a play, a novel, a poem: we are filled with emotion without being able to explain what has moved us. But in Flaubert's case this impotence is pushed to the extreme since he waxes enthusiastic, it seems, without understanding what he reads. And how can we allow that he is '*overwhelmed for two days*' yet is not tempted to return to what overwhelms him in order to understand its richness in greater detail, to establish precisely the relations between the characters?

The answer is that he is *dreaming*. He has remarked a number of times on the confusion of ideas into which he is plunged while reading Shakespeare: 'Everything disappears, everything appears . . .' Or else: 'This is unfathomable, infinite, manifold . . . there are dark depths, vertigo.' It seems that at some moment—perhaps during the first reading—he might have had a complete but 'inexpressible' perception of the object, of the meaning that emanates from it, and of beauty as the indirect totalization of this meaning through form. Consequently, the scene or the chapter is marked. If he then returns to it, assured of having chosen the best, he *is no longer reading, he is dreaming that he reads*; he makes the language imaginary and takes the words as pretexts, letting his imagination wander. What does he love, then, in this passage from *King Lear*? Not, perhaps, what he *loved* formerly and what he no longer remembers, having failed to refresh his memory by a brief contact with the first act, but, primarily, an audio-visual and utterly superficial totalization which gives him men and nature together: four voices (since he sees *three* madmen and a fool) distracted by unhappiness, each in his way howling the pain of men in the midst of a cosmos which manifests through rain, wind, thunder and lightning its true pantheistic essence and its radical hostility to the human race. And who knows whether deep down he does not find himself again in Edgar when he renounces life, assumes the 'basest and most poorest shape,' and takes a dive into subhumanity? Of course, Edgar's choice is deliberate, Gustave has suffered his. But it is for this reason, perhaps, that he persists in believing him to be mad, reading his own adventure in the statements made by *that other victim of the paternal curse and of a bastard unjustly preferred*. King Lear, or the fathers punished: Gloucester and the old king will repent too late, and for having misunderstood the love of Edgar and Cordelia, they will die in horror, killed by their Achilles. This eternal story—man is the son of man—which Gustave tells himself in a whisper, is here shouted out to him. Shakespeare's 'immensity' gives him a right that Gustave denies himself: the right to go 'wild.' Underwritten by this 'superhuman' genius, the young man can let himself go, secretly unify macrocosm and microcosm—the first devouring the second like an old Saturn—put the curse of Adam at the beginning and end of an oneiric cosmogony, transform the Creator into an unworthy father, and finally, taking himself for Shakespeare, raise himself up to the paroxysm of being, howling, thundering, flashing, shining, blinding, alternately or simultaneously, becoming the quartet of human suffering and the roaring choir of unleashed elements. This is reading through 'resonance,' of course, but the resonance is so profound, comes from such a distance, that he could easily convince himself of the belief, like the Pythia, that the words awakened by his imaginary reading are rising up from his own 'dreadful depths.'

In *King Lear* there is much more than this pessimistic profession of faith. Overcome by misery, Lear intuits the human condition by discovering those more miserable than himself; the strangeness of his statements is not the product of a delirium but of a lucidity too new and too powerful to be easily expressed. Hence the 'passage to the act,' the attempt—immediately aborted by his companions—to tear off the 'lend-ings,' the rags that still cover him, to abolish the last vestiges of royalty and appear as the bare animal, the starting point from which a new order may be instituted that is proper to man. As if all the effort of centuries had been to hide our needs and veil our bodies, in short, to turn our backs on the truth of the human condition. Instead, true humanism, far from masking our animality, our needs exasperated by penury, should *take these as its starting point* and never deviate from them. Hope, glimpsed too late, vanishes: Lear's authentic greatness will prevent nei-ther his madness nor his death, nor that of Cordelia. Be that as it may, man is possible; curtain. This is precisely what Flaubert cannot accept: the 'master' is charged with reflecting to the disciple the radical pessim-ism that has gradually become one of his own constitutional character-istics. For this reason, the young reader avoids looking too closely at it: he isolates the scene, severs it from its extensions, organizes it in large syncretic masses—storm, madness, etc.—objects of his meditation in which he loses himself dreaming over a word. 'The rustling of silk' and 'the creaking of shoes' have surely been—since he cites them—the occa-sion for infinite daydreams. He knows quite well, moreover, that all these hapless characters will find a ghastly death and asks no more than this: what does it matter what might have been? What counts is what *is*, failure.

JEAN-PAUL SARTRE, *The Family Idiot*, 1971–2, tr. Carol Cosman (slightly altered)

'Contemplons à loisir cette caricature
Et cette ombre d'Hamlet imitant sa posture,
Le regard indécis et les cheveux au vent.
N'est-ce pas grand' pitié de voir ce bon vivant,
Ce gueux, cet histrion en vacances, ce drôle,
Parce qu'il sait jouer artistement son rôle,
Vouloir intéresser au chant de ses douleurs
Les aigles, les grillons, les ruisseaux et les fleurs,
Et même a nous, auteurs de ces vieilles rubriques,
Réciter en hurlant ses tirades publiques?'

['Let us study at leisure this caricature, this shadow of Hamlet imitating his poses; let us contemplate his indecisive look and his dishevelled hair.

Isn't it a pity to see this fine fellow, this tramp, this unemployed actor, this clown, just because he knows how to play his part artistically, hoping to interest the eagles, the crickets, the streams and the flowers in his song of sorrows, and even reciting and howling his public tirades at us, who invented all these old tricks?']

CHARLES BAUDELAIRE, from 'La Béatrice', 1857

A pack of demons are speaking; the poet imagines them mocking him as a faux-Hamlet—like so many of his contemporaries, a mere pretender to the role.

The stage-sets were simply painted and designed, and swiftly changed between each scene. To Jacques's delight some of them depicted Scottish landscapes near Inverness, superimposing recollections of his journey on their dramatic interest.

Did the actors respect Shakespeare's original text? Did they tone down the poet's blunt realism to satisfy polite English convention or did they respect its brutal splendour? This was a difficult question to answer, but one that fascinated Jacques. On the French stage the play is always abridged and mutilated, but he had read translations of *Macbeth* and knew the play well. He therefore reminded Jonathan of the famous scene in the second act, following Duncan's murder, when Macduff asks the Porter what three things drink provokes. When the moment arrived, however, Jonathan listened hard but failed to understand. The doorkeeper's reply provoked general laughter in the audience.

'Bravo!' Jacques exclaimed. 'They are faithful to Shakespeare and put art before prudery. Bravo!'

'What would be scandalous,' Jonathan said, 'would be to amend Shakespeare instead of respecting his text. These worthy Englishmen are right. You must either be faithful to Shakespeare or leave him alone.'

JULES VERNE, *Voyage à reculons en Angleterre et en Écosse*, tr. Janice Valls-Russell

Jules Verne's 'Journey Backwards to England and Scotland' (he began by visiting Edinburgh) was his first book—written in 1859, though not published until 1989. Verne was of Scottish ancestry on his mother's side, and proud of it.

The three things which wine provokes are 'nose-painting, sleep and urine'.

I have loved Racine's lines above all other literary productions. I admire

Shakespeare tremendously; but with Racine I feel an emotion that Shakespeare never gives me: that of perfection. Jean S., in a very interesting discussion, reproaches Racine's characters with not going on living once the curtain has fallen, whereas those of Shakespeare, he says very justly, appear for a moment before the footlights, but we feel that they do not end there and we could meet them again, beyond the stage. But I happen just to like that exact limitation, that non-protruding from the frame, that sharpness of outline. Shakespeare, doubtless, is more human; but something quite different is involved here: the triumph of a sublime fitness, a delightful harmony in which everything enters in and contributes, which fully satisfies at one and the same time intelligence, heart and senses. Man and nature, in his wind-swept plays, all poetry laughs, weeps and vibrates in Shakespeare; Racine is at the summit of art.

ANDRÉ GIDE, journal, October 1933, tr. Justin O'Brien

Gide didn't only admire Shakespeare. He produced translations of two of the plays, Antony and Cleopatra *(1921) and* Hamlet *(first performed in 1946, with Jean-Louis Barrault in the title role). But Racine came first.*

★   ★   ★

Characters created by Shakespeare are not, as Molière's, types exemplifying some passion or some vice, but living beings, compacted of many passions and many vices; and circumstances unfold to the spectators their varied, many-sided personalities. Molière's Miser is miserly—and that is all; Shakespeare's Shylock is miserly, resourceful, vindictive, a fond father, witty. Molière's Hypocrite trails after his patron's wife—hypocritically; takes on the care of an estate—hypocritically; asks for a glass of water—hypocritically. Shakespeare's hypocrite pronounces judgement with proud severity but with equity; he justifies his cruelty with the thoughtful arguments of a statesman; he seduces innocence with irresistibly beguiling sophisms, and not by some ludicrous combination of piety and flirtation. Angelo is a hypocrite—because his public actions contradict his secret passions! And what depth there is in this character!

ALEXANDER PUSHKIN, 'Table Talk', 1836, tr. Tatiana Wolff

Three years earlier, in 1833, Pushkin had published Angelo, *a narrative poem based on* Measure for Measure *which concentrates on the central Angelo–Isabella theme of the play, and discards the comic and underworld elements.*

But probably Shakespeare's many-sided genius did not express itself anywhere with such variety as in Falstaff, whose vices strung together form a diverting and grotesque chain, reminiscent of some ancient Bacchanalia. Analysing Falstaff's character we see that its predominant trait is sensuality; probably from his youth, coarse and cheap flirtation had been his chief preoccupation; but now he is in his fifties, he has grown fat and senile, gluttony and wine have noticeably stolen a march on Venus. Secondly he is a coward but, spending days in the company of young rakes and being constantly subject to their jibes and pranks, he hides his cowardice under a cover of evasive and mocking bravado. He is boastful both by habit and by design.

Falstaff is not at all stupid; on the contrary. He also has some of the habits of a man who has once seen good society. He observes no rules. He is as weak as an old woman. He needs strong Spanish wine (sack), a fat dinner, and money for his mistresses; and to get these he is ready to do anything, provided there is no obvious danger involved.

In my youth chance brought me into close contact with a man in whom, it seemed, nature wishing to imitate Shakespeare, repeated his magnificent creation. X was a second Falstaff: sensual, cowardly, boastful, clever, amusing, immoral, tearful, and fat. One circumstance gave him an individual charm. He was married. Shakespeare had no time to marry off his bachelor. Falstaff died among his mistresses, not having had time to be either a cuckolded husband or the father of a family; how many scenes lost to Shakespeare's brush!

Here is a glimpse of the home life of my esteemed friend. Once in his father's absence, his four-year-old son, the image of his father, a little Falstaff III, was repeating under his breath, 'How bwave daddy is! How the Empewor loves daddy!' The boy was overheard and asked, 'Who told you this, Volodia?' 'Daddy,' replied Volodia.

ALEXANDER PUSHKIN, 'Table Talk'

Hamlet, doubting all, has no pity for himself. His spirit is too developed a thing to be content with what it discovers in self. Well aware of his own weakness he delights in self-flagellation, makes much of his faults, studies himself night and day, is for ever burrowing in his own soul, catalogues his frailties to the remotest particular, feels contempt for these frailties as he feels contempt for himself, and all the while lives on this contempt and draws nourishment therefrom. All self-awareness is a force.

IVAN TURGENEV, *Hamlet and Don Quixote*, 1860, tr. Robert Nichols

I'm delighted that you've made the acquaintance of Shakespeare, or rather that you've returned to him. He is like Nature. She sometimes wears a repulsive face (just recall one of those days on the steppes in October, damp and drizzling), but even then there is certainty and truth and (be prepared: your hair will stand on end) expediency. You must also read *Hamlet, Julius Caesar, Coriolanus, Henry IV, Macbeth* and *Othello*. Don't allow any external incongruities to put you off. Get to the heart, the core of their creation, and you will see the harmony and profound truth in their great human spirit. I can see you from here laughing at these lines, but consider that perhaps T. is right. We'll just have to wait and see.

IVAN TURGENEV, letter to Leo Tolstoy, 1857, tr. A. V. Knowles

Tolstoy's Shakespeare and the Drama *(1906) is a sustained onslaught on the poet: among other things, he is accused of failing to draw real or coherent characters. For a moment, when Tolstoy comes to Falstaff, he seems about to relent, but it soon turns out that Shakespeare's success in this case is only another stick to beat him with:*

Falstaff is really a thoroughly natural and characteristic personage, almost the only natural and characteristic one depicted by Shakespeare. And he is natural and characteristic because, of all Shakespeare's characters, he alone speaks in a way proper to himself. He speaks in a manner proper to himself because he talks just that Shakespearian language, filled with jests that lack humour and unamusing puns, which while unnatural to all Shakespeare's other characters is quite in harmony with the boastful, distorted, perverted character of the drunken Falstaff. That is the only reason why this figure really presents a definite character. Unfortunately the artistic effect of the character is spoilt by the fact that it is so repulsive in its gluttony, drunkenness, debauchery, rascality, mendacity, and cowardice, that it is difficult to share the feeling of merry humour Shakespeare adopts towards it. Such is the case with Falstaff.

tr. Aylmer Maude

Dostoevsky's view of Falstaff was almost as unfavourable as Tolstoy's—he saw him as a complete parasite—but he was fascinated rather than repelled. There are a number of references to the fat knight in his writings; in the early novel

Netochka Nezvanova *there is even a dog who is called Falstaff, 'on account of his phenomenal gluttony'.*

Then there was Falstaff's royal companion. The novelist's thoughts turned to him in creating the hero of one of his greatest works, Nicholas Stavrogin in The Possessed:

During his first two years at the lycée the young man used to come home in the holidays. When Mrs Stavrogin and Mr Verkhovensky were in Petersburg, he was present at some of the literary parties at his mother's house, watching and listening. He spoke little and was as quiet and shy as before. He still treated Mr Verkhovensky with the same tender affection, but he was somehow more reserved; he was apparently not anxious to discuss higher things or memories of his past with him. Having finished his course of studies, he applied, at his mother's wish, for a commission in the army and soon joined one of the most famous cavalry regiments of the Horse Guards. He did not come to show himself to his mother in his army uniform and wrote only rarely to her from Petersburg. Mrs Stavrogin sent him money without stint, in spite of the fact that after the agrarian reform the income from her estate had fallen so low that at first it was less than half of what it had been before. She had, however, managed to save up a considerable sum by long years of economy. She was very interested in her son's success in the highest Petersburg society. What she could never achieve, was achieved by the wealthy young officer with expectations. He renewed acquaintances she hardly dared to dream of and was received everywhere with great pleasure. But very soon strange rumours began to reach Mrs Stavrogin: the young man suddenly gave himself up to a life of mad dissipation. Not that he gambled or drank too much; but stories were told about his life of wild rioting, about people being run over by his horses, of his brutal conduct to a lady of good society with whom he had had an affair and whom he afterwards publicly insulted. There seems to have been something very nasty about that business. It was added, besides, that he had become a regular bully, who picked quarrels with people and insulted them for the mere pleasure of insulting them. Mrs Stavrogin was upset and worried. Mr Verkhovensky assured her that those were only the first violent outbursts of a too richly endowed nature, that the storm would abate, and that all this was just like young Prince Harry, who made merry with Falstaff, Poins, and Mistress Quickly, as described by Shakespeare. This time Mrs Stavrogin did not cry, 'Nonsense, nonsense!' as she was lately all too ready to shout at Mr Verkhovensky, but, on the contrary, lent a willing ear to him, asked him to explain his words to her more precisely, took down Shakespeare's works herself, and read the immortal chronicle play with great attention. But the play did not set her mind at rest, and, besides, she did not think the resemblance very striking.

The Possessed (or *The Devils*), 1871, tr. David Magarshack

Stavrogin's mother is right to query the comparison, and although it is presented satirically, her own Shakespearian analogy, made later in the book, is closer to the mark. Addressing the younger Verkhovensky, in the presence of his father, she describes her son as

a proud man, a man who has suffered humiliation early in life, a man who has reached the stage of 'mockery' to which you have so aptly referred—in short, a Prince Harry, as your father so splendidly called him at the time, which would have described him perfectly if he did not resemble Hamlet even more, in my opinion, at any rate.'

'*Et vous avez raison,*' Mr Verkhovensky senior remarked impressively and with feeling.

'Thank you, my dear Mr Verkhovensky. I thank you, too, especially for your undeviating faith in Nicholas and in the greatness of his soul and calling. This faith you even strengthened in me when I was losing heart.'

'*Chère, chère . . .* ' Mr Verkhovensky was about to step forward, but checked himself in time, having realized that it was dangerous to interrupt.

'And if there had always been near Nicholas,' Mrs Stavrogin was almost intoning now, 'some gentle Horatio, great in his humility—another beautiful expression of yours, my dear Mr Verkhovensky—he might have long ago been saved from the sad and sudden "demon of irony" who has tormented him all his life. (The Demon of Irony is another wonderful expression of yours, my dear Mr Verkhovensky.) But Nicholas has never had a Horatio, or an Ophelia. He only had a mother, and what can a mother do alone and in such circumstances, too?'

In his enigmatic qualities, his sense of alienation and his eventual tragic fate, Stavrogin is certainly more of a Prince Hamlet than a Prince Harry. To the extent that the Prince Harry comparison holds good, however, he also has his

*'Falstaff'—a much-diminished one, his seedy drinking companion and hanger-
on Captain Lebyatkin. ('What does it matter if they did call me your Falstaff
from Shakespeare? What does that matter, I say, if you meant so much in my
life?')*

Another Dostoevskyan echo of Hamlet *occurs in* The Brothers Karamazov
*(1880), where Dmitri Karamazov, having resolved to shoot himself, talks wildly
to his companion Perkhotin:*

'I love a woman, a woman! What is woman? The queen of the earth! I
feel sad, I feel sad, old man. Remember Hamlet? "Alas, poor Yorick, I
knew him, Horatio!" Perhaps Yorick, that's me. Yes, I'm Yorick now, and
a skull afterwards.'

tr. David McDuff

*Shortly before this passage, discussing Dmitri's obsession with Grushenka,
Dostoevsky draws a contrast with Othello:*

Jealousy! 'Othello is not jealous, he is trustful,' observed Pushkin, and
this remark alone testifies to the extraordinary profundity of our great
poet's mind. Othello's soul is shattered and his whole outlook on life is
confused because *his ideal has been destroyed.* But Othello would not start
hiding, spying, peeping: he is trustful. On the contrary, he had to be led
on, pushed, excited by extraordinary efforts to make him suspect infidelity. Not so the truly jealous man. It is quite impossible to imagine the
disgrace and moral degradation a jealous man is capable of putting up
with without any qualms of conscience. And it is not as though all of
them had sordid, vulgar minds. On the contrary, a man of most high-
minded sentiments, whose love is pure and full of self-sacrifice, may at
the same time hide under tables, bribe the vilest people and put up with
the nastiest filthiness of spying and eavesdropping. Othello could never
reconcile himself to infidelity—he could forgive it, but not reconcile
himself to it—though his heart was as gentle and innocent as a babe's. It
is different with a really jealous man: it is hard to imagine what some
jealous men can descend to and be reconciled to and forgive! Jealous
men are more ready to forgive than anyone else—every woman knows
that! A jealous man is capable of forgiving extraordinarily quickly (after
first making a violent scene, of course), he is capable of forgiving, for
instance, infidelity that is practically proven, the embraces and kisses he

has seen, if at the same time he could, for instance, be somehow or other convinced that it had been 'for the last time' and that his rival would vanish from that very hour, depart to the ends of the earth, or that he himself would carry her off somewhere where his terrible rival would never come. The reconciliation, of course, will be only for an hour, because even if his rival did really vanish, he would invent another one the next day, a new one, and would be jealous of him. And, one cannot help asking oneself, what is there in a love that has to be so watched over and what is a love worth that has to be so strenuously guarded? But that a truly jealous man will never understand, and yet there certainly are high-principled people with lofty hearts among them. It is remarkable, too, that though the very same high-principled people, while hiding in some cubbyhole, eavesdropping and spying, understand very well with their 'lofty hearts' how low they have sunk of their own free will, yet at that moment, at any rate, they never feel any pricks of conscience.

In Notes from Underground *(1864) there is an ironic acknowledgement of how high Shakespeare's reputation stood in Russia by the middle years of the nineteenth century. The malcontent narrator spends an evening with a group of worldly acquaintances, falls out with them, but refuses to go away. Instead, he paces up and down, following their conversation with silent scorn:*

They talked about the Caucasus, about the nature of true passion, about baccarat, about the most advantageous postings; about how much income the hussar Podkharchevsky (whom none of them knew personally) had, and how glad they were that it was so enormous; about the extraordinary beauty and grace of Princess D. (whom none of them had ever set eyes on); and finally they came to the conclusion that Shakespeare is immortal.

At this point he can contain himself no longer, and lets out 'a sudden contemptuous laugh':

It was such a vilely artificial snort that they all ceased talking at once and silently watched me for about two minutes, attentively and seriously, as I walked along the wall from the table to the stove, *without paying them the slightest attention.* But nothing happened: they did not speak to me and after two minutes they ignored me again.

tr. Jessie Coulson

There are many parallels with Hamlet *in Chekhov's* The Seagull, *and also some direct quotations. When Madame Arkadina borrows Gertrude's words—*

> Thou turn'st mine eyes into my very soul.
> And there I see such black and grained spots
> As will not leave their tinct

—her son Konstantin retorts with some of Hamlet's:

> Nay, but to live
> In the rank sweat of an enseamed bed.
> Stew'd in corruption, honeying and making love
> Over the nasty sty . . .

There is a strange piece of bowdlerizing in the earliest English translation, by Constance Garnett. She blenched at the second of these passages, and substituted some other lines from the bedroom scene instead:

> And let me wring thy heart; for so I shall,
> If it be made of penetrable stuff.

Later in The Seagull, *when his mother's lover Trigorin enters carrying a book, Konstantin compares him sarcastically to Hamlet, and adds, 'Words, words, words'.*

In The Cherry Orchard, *the self-made businessman Lopakhin taunts a young woman with another quotation, but gets the name wrong: 'Okhmeliya, get thee to a nunnery . . .'*

Hamlet

> The buzz subsides. I have come on stage.
> Leaning in an open door
> I try to detect from the echo
> What the future has in store.
>
> A thousand opera-glasses level
> The dark, point-blank, at me.
> Abba, Father, if it be possible
> Let this cup pass from me.

I love your preordained design
And am ready to play this role.
But the play being acted is not mine.
For this once let me go.

But the order of the acts is planned,
The end of the road already revealed.
Alone among the Pharisees I stand.
Life is not a stroll across a field.

                    BORIS PASTERNAK, 1946, tr. Peter France and Jon Stallworthy

This is the first of the sequence of poems which make up the final section of Doctor Zhivago. *The speaker is partly an actor playing Hamlet, partly Hamlet himself, and partly Christ. In the words of Donald Davie, 'as the actor is to Shakespeare, so Hamlet was to his father's ghost, so Christ was to his Father'.*

Pasternak enlarged on his conception of Hamlet in his notes on translating the play:

According to a long-established critical tradition, *Hamlet* is a tragedy of will. This is fair enough. And yet in what sense are we to take it? Lack of will-power wasn't a known theme in Shakespeare's time. People weren't interested in it. Hamlet's character, which Shakespeare draws so fully, is clear enough, and concepts of weak will-power don't come into it. In Shakespeare's perception, Hamlet is a prince of royal blood who doesn't for a moment forget his rights to the throne; he is the spoilt child of an ancient court, rejoicing furthermore in the self-sufficiency of his own talents. In the complex of characteristics with which his author endowed him, there is no room for feebleness. On the contrary, it is excluded, and the audience is asked, instead, to judge how great Hamlet's sacrifice must be, when he commits himself and all his great expectations to a loftier duty.

From the moment the ghost appears, Hamlet renounces himself in order to 'do the will of him who sent him'. *Hamlet* is not a drama of characterlessness, but of duty and self-sacrifice. When it transpires that an abyss separates appearance and reality, it isn't important that the reminder of the world's falsehood should come in a supernatural form and that a ghost should demand revenge of Hamlet. It is far more important that a chance occurrence turns Hamlet into the judge of his own time, and servant of the future. *Hamlet* is a drama of high calling, imposed heroism, and incontrovertible destiny.

BORIS PASTERNAK, 'Observations on Translating Shakespeare', 1939–46, tr. Ann Pasternak Slater

One period of Shakespeare's life is particularly clear to us, and that is the time of his youth.

He had, then, just come up to London, an unknown young provincial from Stratford. Probably at his arrival he stopped for a while in the suburbs, beyond the beat of town carriers and draymen, in an area comparable to the Yamskaya settlement, where urban legislation didn't apply. Because of the continual night and day traffic of people coming and going, life there must have been rather like it is round our railway stations today: rich in parks, ponds, spinneys, kitchen gardens, coaching inns, booths and sideshows. There may have been theatres. The pleasure-seeking young aristocrats from London would have come here for their amusement.

In its own way it was a world close to the Tverskaya-Yamskaya Lanes° in the fifties of the last century, when Ostrovsky° and Apollon Grigoryev,° best heirs of the Stratford provincial, lived and worked there, ringed round by the nine muses, high ideas, potboys, innkeepers, gipsy singers and educated theatre-loving merchant traders.

The young new arrival was vaguely unemployed at that time, but led by a definite star which he trusted absolutely. Only this certainty could have brought him out of country obscurity into the town. He still didn't know what role he was to play, but his sense of life whispered to him that he would fulfil it uniquely and unforgettably . . .

There must have been some company of actors, writers and their patrons, who wandered from tavern to tavern, picked quarrels with strangers, and, at a constant risk to their own necks, laughed at everything under the sun. The most desperate and invulnerable of them (everything went right for him), the most intemperate and the most sober (drunkenness never touched him), the one with the straightest face who aroused the most irrepressible laughter, was this morose youngster swiftly striding into the future in his seven-league boots.

the Tverskaya-Yamskaya Lanes] a disreputable district of Moscow from which Pasternak described himself as 'always being dragged away' when he was a child
Ostrovsky] nineteenth-century Russian playwright
Grigoriev] nineteenth-century Russian poet

Maybe there really was a fat old glutton like Falstaff in this youthful crowd. Or maybe this fictional embodiment is a later memory of that time.

It wasn't only memories of past revelry which made him dear to Shakespeare. Those were the days in which his realism was born. The world was to see this realism, not worked up in the isolation of a study, but tumbled in the morning disorder of a tavern room primed with a sense of life as explosive as gunpowder. Shakespeare's realism doesn't consist of the profundities of a reformed rake, or the respected pensées of experienced maturity. His unjoking, deeply serious, circumstantial and tragic art was born from his sense of success and strength in those frivolous early days, so full of eccentric inventiveness, cheek, enterprise and mad, mortal risks.

Boris Pasternak, 'Observations on Translating Shakespeare'

By every right the tragedy of *Macbeth* could have been called *Crime and Punishment*. I couldn't shake free of the parallel with Dostoyevsky while I was translating it.

Boris Pasternak, 'Observations on Translating Shakespeare'

★   ★   ★

There is one place in thy land, O Sasana,°
In which thy foe becomes blunt and blind,
Free from all hate—
    That is Stratford on the Avon.

O Albion,
If an enemy knock at thy door,
    Take him to Stratford on the Avon!

And from his heart shall pass
All ill will and the fever of hate,
Mindful of nought but thoughts of that Druid:
    Yea, speed him to Stratford on the Avon.

On me that Druid has worked a druidism,
Which I now set down here in my verse:

Sasana] the land of the Saxons

He has won pardon from me for his land:
I at Stratford on the Avon.

> Douglas Hyde, from 'How it fared with a Gael at Stratford-
> on-Avon', 1916, tr. from the Gaelic by the author

These are concluding stanzas of a poem largely taken up with a vision of Shakespearian scenes and characters. According to a prefatory note, the speaker is 'a great, proud, morose kerne, a Munster man, who had sorely suffered, he and his folk; hatred was in his heart. The Sasanach were to him his enemies, and lo! by chance he found himself in their land, and he came to Stratford on the Avon.'

Douglas Hyde, who had played a major role in the revival of the Irish language, served as president of Ireland from 1938 to 1945.

There are people who are only interested in *things*; and these people always give themselves airs and say 'they don't like gossip', but Shakespeare, your mother and I like to talk about people. I fancy in Elizabethan times they talked nothing but gossip when they assembled in the coffee houses—there was nothing else to talk about when there were no papers or magazines or suffragettes, or novels. To be sure they used to listen to long sermons but that was after Shakespeare's time. The sermons drove out the players and the playwrights, and England has got duller and duller ever since—and the people who could not stand the sermons migrated to Dublin.

> J. B. Yeats, letter to Ruth Hart, 1910

Edmund (sits down opposite his father—contemptuously). Yes, facts don't mean a thing, do they? What you want to believe, that's the only truth! *(derisively)* Shakespeare was an Irish Catholic, for example.
Tyrone (stubbornly). So he was. The proof is in his plays.

> Eugene O'Neill, *Long Day's Journey into Night*, 1956

MacMorris,° gallivanting
round the Globe, whinged
to courtier and groundling
who had heard tell of us

MacMorris] the Irish captain in *Henry V*

as going very bare
of learning, as wild hares,
as anatomies of death:°
'What ish my nation?'

And sensibly, though so much
later, the wandering Bloom
replied, 'Ireland,' said Bloom,
'I was born here. Ireland.'

SEAMUS HEANEY, from 'Traditions', in *Wintering Out*, 1973

⋆   ⋆   ⋆

He did not disclose his business, nor could I ask him outright. So we discussed social reform and politics. I found him an accomplished conversationalist. His mind was cultivated, his education complete, and his thought far-reaching. There being a pause in the conversation, he began to turn over *The Shakespeare Gallery*° on my table. In the meanwhile, I had a good look at him. He was a most handsome man; fair, rather short but neither stout nor lean; his eyes large, hair fine, curly and carefully arranged; he was not over-dressed but was perfectly neat; a man with an exquisite conversational style and a beautiful voice. I could plainly see that he was a sophisticated person.

Amarnath did not come to business even after the plates of *The Shakespeare Gallery* had been gone over, and began to discuss the pictures. His thesis was that it was an audacious conceit that tried to depict in a picture what was expressed in language and through action; such attempts could never be successful, nor were these pictures successful. He opened the picture of Desdemona and observed: 'You get her patience, sweetness and modesty, but where is her courage with the patience, and her pride of constancy with the modesty?' He pointed to the illustration of Juliet and said: 'You have here the figure of a beauty in the first flush of youth, but you miss youth's irrepressible restlessness.'

BANKIM CHANDRA CHATTERJI, *Rajani*, 1877, tr. Nirad C. Chaudhuri

Amarnath then goes on to discuss the classic Indian drama Śakuntalā, *Indian*

anatomies of death] a phrase used to describe the famine-stricken inhabitants of Munster, in Edmund Spenser's *A View of the Present State of Ireland*
The Shakespeare Gallery] a series of illustrations of the plays by leading painters of the day, commissioned by John Boydell in 1787 and subsequently published in the form of engravings

poetry, Tacitus, Plutarch, Herodotus, Comte, John Stuart Mill, T. H. Huxley, Darwin and Schopenhauer.

Chatterji, the father of the modern Bengali novel, was also a leading proponent of Hindu nationalism.

R. K. Narayan's Krishna is a lecturer at Albert Mission College in the southern Indian town of Malgudi:

I had four hours of teaching to do that day. *Lear* for the Junior B.A. class, a composition period for the Senior Arts; detailed prose and poetry for other classes. Four periods of continuous work and I hadn't prepared even a page of lecture.

I went five minutes late to the class, and I could dawdle over the attendance for a quarter of an hour. I picked out the attendance register and called out the first name.

'Here, sir—', 'Present', and I marked. Two boys in the front bench got up and suggested 'Sir, take the attendance at the end of the period.'

'Sit down please, can't be done. I can't encroach into the next hour's work. . . .'

A babble rose in the class, a section demanding that the attendance be taken immediately and another demanding postponement. I banged the table with my fist and shouted over the din: 'Stop this, otherwise I will mark everyone absent.'

'Attendance takes up most of our hours, sir.'

'We can't help it. Your attendance is just as important as anything else. Stop all noise and answer your names; otherwise, I will mark all of you absent. . . .' At this the boys became quiet, because I out-shouted them. The lion-tamer's touch! In a sober moment perhaps I would reflect on the question of obedience. Born in different households, perhaps petted, pampered, and bullied, by parents, uncles, brothers—all persons known to them and responsible for their growth and welfare. Who was I that they should obey my command? What tie was there between me and them? Did I absorb their personalities as did the old masters and merge them in mine? I was merely a man who had mugged earlier than they the introduction and the notes in the Verity edition of *Lear*, and guided them through the mazes of Elizabethan English. I did not do it out of love for them or for Shakespeare but only out of love for myself. If they paid me the same one hundred rupees for stringing beads together or tearing up paper bits every day for a few hours, I would perhaps be doing it with equal fervour. But such reflections do not mar our peace when we occupy the class-room chair. So that I banged the table—shouted till they were silenced, and went through the attendance; all this tittle-tattle swallowed up half an hour.

I opened my Verity. I had made a pencil mark where I had stopped on the previous day: middle of the first scene in the third act.

I began in a general way: 'You will see that I stopped last time where Lear faces the storm. This is a vital portion of this great tragedy. . . .' The words rang hollow in my ears. Some part of me was saying: 'These poor boys are now all attention, cowed by your superior force. They are ready to listen to you and write down whatever you may say. What have you to give them in return?' I noticed that some boys were already sitting up alert, ready to note down the pearls dropping from my mouth. . . . I felt like breaking out into a confession! 'My dear fellows, don't trust me so much. I am merely trying to mark time because I couldn't come sufficiently prepared, because all the morning I have . . .' But I caught myself lecturing: 'This is the very heart of the tragedy and I would like you to follow this portion with the greatest attention. . . .' I stole a look at the watch. . . . Only fifteen minutes more. 'As usual I shall read through this scene first, and then I shall take it up in detail. . . .' I looked at the page on the table—'Enter Lear and Fool. Blow winds and crack your cheeks! Rage! Blow! You cataracts and hurricanes, spout till you have drenched our steeples, drowned the cocks! . . .' As I read on I myself was moved by the force and fury of the storm compressed in these lines. The sheer poetry of it carried me on. . . .

> ' . . . And thou, all-shaking Thunder
> Strike flat the thick rotundity o' the world!'

I forgot all about the time, all about my unpreparedness.

> ' . . . Let the great gods
> That keep this dreadful pother o'er our heads,
> Find out their enemies now.'

I read on. The boys listened attentively. I passed on to the next scene without knowing it. I could not stop.

> 'Poor naked wretches, wheresoe'er you are,
> That hide the pelting of this pitiless storm,
> How shall your houseless heads and unfed sides,
>   . . . defend you
> From seasons such as these?'

At the thought of helpless humanity I nearly broke down. The bell rang, I shut my book with the greatest relief, and walked out of the class.

R. K. NARAYAN, *The English Teacher*, 1945

*   *   *

All the young students I met [at Skopje, in Macedonia, in the 1930s] were familiar with *Hamlet*. All had read the play in translation, and a number had read it in English. They appreciated it, and did not merely eat it up because it was the food set before them by their teachers. They had indeed a quite individual way of looking at it. Among these South Serbs the most dynamic relationship in the family is the tie between brother and sister, and for them Laertes and Ophelia played quite a different part in the drama than we can conceive. The scene in which Laertes takes farewell of his sister before he goes to France was charged for them with an intensity which we would find it hard to understand, and they all thought one of the chief reasons why Ophelia went mad was that her brother was away when she was assailed by tragic events.

REBECCA WEST, *The Court and the Castle*, 1958

*   *   *

Ahmad Shaqui, the poet laureate of Egypt who was hailed 'the Prince of Poets' and 'Poet of Princes' by his own peers is often credited with introducing poetry into Arabic drama. Was it just a coincidence that the play in question was *Masra' Kliyupatra* (The Fall or Death of Cleopatra), and that it was inspired unequivocally by Shakespeare's own *Antony and Cleopatra*? It is true that he used material both from Egyptian and Arab-Islamic history but he did set out, according to our sources, to rewrite Shakespeare's own play. Fired by the Egyptian struggle for independence from the British, he recreates Cleopatra as a woman torn between her love of her country and her love for a man. In the end she commits suicide. For Shaqui, Shakespeare's Cleopatra was unacceptably unpatriotic, even a traitress, since she appeared ready to sacrifice her country on the altar of love. The emendations are predictable; they are of the same political and historically conscious order as, for example, the reversal of relationships which takes place when the theme of Caliban and Ariel is handled by anyone from the colonial or slavery experience, most notably in the West Indies. The case of the Arab world is however very different, owing its primary response not simply to politics or history, but to an order of visceral participation in the humane drama of its politics and history.

When one examines the majority of Shakespeare's plays very closely, there really is not much overt respect paid to 'local colour'. If anything, the colour is not infrequently borrowed from elsewhere to establish a climate of relationships, emotions or conflicts: 'Her bed is India; there she lies, a pearl' (*Troilus and Cressida*, 1.1.99). Where we encounter a localized immediacy we are wafted instantly away on a metaphoric bark to nowhere:

> Between our Ilium and where she resides
> Let it be call'd the wild and wand'ring flood;
> Ourself the merchant, and this sailing Pandar
> Our doubtful hope, our convoy, and our bark.
>
> (1.1.100–3)

Nestor finds Achilles' brains as barren as the banks of Libya while Ulysses considers it kinder fate that he parch in Afric's sun than be withered by the arrogance in Achilles' eye. Beyond two or three boastful and mutual admiration lines from Ulysses to Hector in act 4, scene 5, however, it is remarkable that in a war no less celebrated, no less legendary than Antony's scrap with Caesar, very little of the terrain of struggle is actually conveyed in Shakespeare's lines. I do not suggest that we miss it; on the contrary. The absent hills, moats, turrets and physical *belonging* all pass unnoticed thanks to the clamour of *machismo*, the conflicts of pride, the debates of honour and schemes of war. The atmosphere is replete, nothing appears missing. In *Coriolanus* we experience the city state as a corporate entity against which one man is ranged, while the Rome of *Julius Caesar* could be anywhere, and the arguments of both, unchanged.

Compare these examples with the other remarkable exception, *Macbeth*:

> *Duncan*. This castle hath a pleasant seat, the air
> Nimbly and sweetly recommends itself
> Unto our gentle senses.
> *Banquo*.   This guest of summer,
> The temple-haunting martlet, does approve
> By his lov'd mansionry that the heaven's breath
> Smells wooingly here; no jutty, frieze,
> Buttress, nor coign of vantage, but this bird
> Hath made her pendent bed and procreant cradle.
> Where they most breed and haunt, I have observ'd,
> The air is delicate.   (1.6.1–10)

Shakespeare, drawing local colour into the service of fatal irony. The colours of *Antony and Cleopatra* belong however to a different segment of the spectrum and are applied on a more liberal canvas—after all, the whole world is up for grabs. But note that even where we encounter no more than what may be called a roll-call of names, there has been prior fleshing-out, so that the discomfiture of Octavius Caesar at the rallying of former mutual enemies behind Antony is real and problematic. It is historical personages that are summoned centre stage of the tapestry of events, not mere exotic names and shadowy figures from legend:

> He hath given his empire
> Up to a whore, who now are levying
> The kings o' th' earth for war. He hath assembled
> Bocchus, the king of Libya; Archelaus
> Of Cappadocia; Philadelphos, king
> Of Paphlagonia; the Thracian king Adallas;
> King Manchus of Arabia; King of Pont;
> Herod of Jewry; Mithradates, king
> Of Comagene; Polemon and Amyntas,
> The kings of Mede and Lycaonia, with a
> More larger list of sceptres.   (3.6.66–76)

The prior setting for what would otherwise be a mere catalogue of titles is contributive to the emergence of real figures from a mere bas-relief. For this is Caesar caught in a domestic dilemma involving his sister, using the arguments of war to get it into her head that she is neither an Emperor's wife nor an ambassador but, quite ordinarily—a rejected woman. Caesar's passion is both that of a contemned protector of a weak woman, and a contender for empire on a larger-than-historic scale. And these empires become accessible, reduced to a human scale because of what Antony has done with the accumulated panoply of power: 'He hath given his empire | Up to a whore . . .' The whore? Cleopatra. Her other names—queen, whore, gipsy, Egyptian dish, the serpent of old Nile, ribaldered nag of Egypt, etc., one whose every act, whose every caprice, every clownish or imperious gesture confirms that she deserves every one of these accolades and more. And thus the kingdoms and empires which she draws into her fatal net through Antony partake of this same personal quality and expand our realistic conception and dimension of the drama being waged for possession of the world. Not without cause does Octavius Caesar envision, when the scale of war turns firmly in his favour: 'The time of universal peace is near.'

Shakespeare's enlargements of the ridiculous through sublime prisms are deft and varied; the process happens at bewildering speed, resolving seeming improbabilities through the credible chimeric qualities of the tragic heroine of the piece. Who can quarrel with the steely patriotism of Cleopatra even in defeat? Confronted with the stark choice between death and humiliation:

> Rather a ditch in Egypt
> Be gentle grave unto me! Rather on Nilus' mud
> Lay me stark nak'd, and let the water-flies
> Blow me into abhorring! Rather make
> My country's high pyramides my gibbet,
> And hang me up in chains!   (5.2.57–62)

Ahmad Shaqui, poet and patriot, had most of his work already cut out for him; there really is not much left to do in mending whatever else appears to contradict this poise of nationalist dignity . . .

That Cleopatra should match, in her final hours, the dignified poise of humility with a final thought (and abandonment) of defiance against the jealous gods is, in my view, both dramatically expected and aesthetically satisfying:

> No more but e'en a woman, and commanded
> By such poor passion as the maid that milks
> And does the meanest chares. It were for me
> To throw my sceptre at the injurious gods;
> To tell them that this world did equal theirs
> Till they had stol'n our jewel.   (4.15.73–8)

But the awesomeness of the lines that follow can only be fully absorbed by an Egyptian, or one steeped in the esoteric cults of Egypt and allied religions, including Islam. Cleopatra is speaking figuratively here of the house of death, and then again, she is not. She is evoking the deeper mysteries of the cult of Isis and the nether kingdoms of an other-existence, and it spreads an eerie quality over the final tableau—unlike any comparable end in all of Shakespeare.

The following recites like any article of faith in the Resurrection:

I have believed in Allah, and his angels, and His books, and His messengers, and the Last Day and the decree of its good and evil from Allah-ta'alla, and in the Rising after death.   (*Islamic Book of the Dead*)

But the Arabic script that transcribes this *ayat* from the Hadith is composed like a high-prowed gondola with a crew of ritualized (hierographically speaking) rowers. What Islam in fact opposes in the 'Kafir' cults of Osiris and Isis have merely been transposed from their elaborate structures with all their sacrificial rites to a mystic opacity of liturgical language—in the Islamic exegesis of death, the kinship remains blatant. Their neighbours the pagan Greeks, who borrowed from them much of their cults and religions in any case, would have no difficulty in identifying the Osiris-prowed Hadithic boat of death with Charon's canoe, scything through the River Styx. Islamic injunctions, prayers and invocations on the theme of death more than compensate the exhortations to practical meagreness by their endless liturgy and lyrical wealth of going, and the aftermath of dissolution.

Cleopatra, whom we have watched throned as Isis, imbues the approach of death with a measured ritualism that is suffused with the palpable shadowiness of the crypt. Not just her contemporary worshippers at the shrines of Isis and Osiris, but their descendants, born into the counter-claims of Islamic religion, would therefore share more than a mere metaphor of language with Cleopatra's demand: 'Then is it sin | To rush into the secret house of death . . .?' We can hear its echo in the following lines also from the *Islamic Book of the Dead*:

> It is said that every day the graves call out five times:
> I am the house of isolation. . . .
> I am the house of darkness. . . .
> I am the house of earth. . . .
> I am the house of the questioning of Munkar and Nakir . . .

I know of no parallel echo in the Christian offices of the dead. Arabic 'classical' poetry is however full of it, and of Shakespeare's sonnets, the ones which seem to attract the finest 'classical' poets among the Arabs seem to share this preoccupation with the imagery of death as a place of physical habitation. Sometimes they are outright translations but more often they are original compositions inspired by a specific sonnet of Shakespeare. And we find a consistency in the emphasis given to one part of Shakespeare's variations on the theme of love as against the main theme itself. Comparatively underplayed is the defiant sentiment:

> Not marble nor the gilded monuments
> Of princes shall outlive this pow'rful rhyme;
> But you shall shine more bright in these contents
> Than unswept stone, besmear'd with sluttish time.
>
> (Sonnet 55)

The humanistic verses of Omar Khayyám are considered worse than irreverent—they are termed heretical and subversive; nor does the graveyard humour of an Andrew Marvell hold much appeal for the True Islamic poet:

> The grave's a fine and private place
> But none, I think, do there embrace.
> ('To His Coy Mistress')

No, it is essentially the grave as a place, an abode in time, that taxes the poetic genius of Shakespeare's adapters, not as a spur to the demands of love, presented as an end which is worse for overtaking its victim love-less, against which is held the imperishable products of the Muse or the talisman of immortality in love's offspring. Elias Abu Shabbakah's 'The Song of Death' is aptly titled, though it derives from Shakespeare's Sonnet 71, 'No longer Mourn for me when I am Dead'. The contrast, despite the opening abnegation, is revealing:

My will, which I want you to remember, is to forget me when I am dead. And, if memories move you one day and your affection chooses to remind you of me, take the guitar of my inspiration into the dark night and go to my tomb in silence, and tap the guitar once; for it will let you hear a moaning sigh such as mine.

The unearthly moisture of suicide, the aspic's trail of slime on fig-leaves transports us to this totally alien earth, and I mean alien, not from the view of Shakespeare's culture alone. This is yet another world opening inwards from the mundane one into which we have already been inducted by some of the most unnerving imageries in poetic drama: a yoking of approaching bodily corruption with the essence-draining paradox of birth and infancy closes the fatal cycle of the union of opposites that began with the aspic's slime:

> Peace, peace!
> Dost thou not see my baby at my breast
> That sucks the nurse asleep? (5.2.306–8)

In this dark ceremonial, the crown which Cleopatra dons becomes not just a prop for composing herself for death as befits a queen, nor her robe the final cover for a soon-to-be-hollowed vessel, but ritual transformation steps towards the mystic moment of transition:

> Give me my robe, put on my crown; I have
> Immortal longings in me. . . .
> I am fire and air; my other elements

I give to baser life. So, have you done?
Come then, and take the last warmth of my lips.
Farewell, kind Charmian. Iras, long farewell.
Have I the aspic in my lips? Dost fall?
If thou and nature can so gently part,
The stroke of death is as a lover's pinch,
Which hurts and is desired.
                          (5.2.278–9, 287–94)

Iras has now preceded, and in that calm recital of Cleopatra,

The stroke of death is as a lover's pinch,
Which hurts and is desired

is heard the reprise and conclusion of that death aria which we have earlier descried. It commenced in the penultimate act, 'The crown o' th' earth doth melt. . . . ' (4.15.63), and winds into the awesome darkness at the Osiric passage:

Then is it sin
To rush into the secret house of death
Ere death dare come to us? (4.15.80–2)

In sustaining its threnody through one more Act, despite the triumphant boots of Caesar and entourage, punctured by the country yokel humour of the aspic-hawking Clown, it becomes clear that our playwright has already inscribed *Finis* on the actual historic conflicts of power and passion. The crown of the earth has melted, and there is nothing left remarkable beneath the visiting moon. But in this setting, is that all? Beyond it? And beneath earth itself? The spectral power of Shakespeare's poetry remains to lead us into the 'other side' of the veil whose precedent reality, which is now seen as merely contingent, gives awesome splendour to the finale of an otherwise butterfly queen. The rest of *Antony and Cleopatra* is our excursion into that world, one which lies more innocently on the Egyptian reality of that time than on the most stoical, self-submissive will in the inherent or explicit theologies of Shakespeare's other drama:

I am dying, Egypt, dying; only
I here importune death awhile, until
Of many thousand kisses the poor last
I lay upon thy lips.   (4.15.18–21)

Contrast this with the death of the genuine Moor whose folly was of a more excusable circumstance than Antony's:

I kissed thee ere I killed thee. No way but this—
Killing myself, to die upon a kiss.

(*Othello*, 5.2.362–3)

One dirge-master is understandably Shayk al-Subair,° the other William
Shakespeare. Here most noticeably, the cadences of death in Shakespeare's tragic figures are as crucial to his poetry as his celebration of
life, even when the celebrants are flawed and their own worst enemy of
life. It is difficult to underestimate this property as one which the Egyptian dramatists identified in their own world, for in *Antony and Cleopatra*
Shakespeare's sensuous powers climaxed to evoke not merely the
humanity of actors of a particular history, but the glimpsed after-world
whose liturgy of resolution imbued them with their unearthly calm at
the hour of death.

WOLE SOYINKA, from 'Shakespeare and the Living Dramatist', 1983

Shayk al-Subair] Shakespeare's original name, according to those Arabs who believe that he
was really an Arab himself

ECHOES

At last a soft and solemn-breathing sound
Rose like a steam of rich-distilled perfumes,
And stole upon the air, that even Silence
Was took ere she was ware, and wished she might
Deny her nature, and be never more
Still to be so displaced.

John Milton, Comus, 1634

Compare—and contrast—some lines from Enobarbus's account of the first meeting of the lovers ('The barge she sat in . . .') in Antony and Cleopatra:

A strange invisible perfume hits the sense
Of the adjacent wharfs. The city cast
Her people out upon her; and Antony,
Enthron'd i' the market-place, did sit alone
Whistling to the air; which, but for vacancy,
Had gone to gaze on Cleopatra too,
And made a gap in nature.

Editors have identified thirty-two indisputable reminiscences of Shakespeare in Milton's masque. Of the fourteen plays on which he drew (along with The Rape of Lucrece)*, the one he echoed most frequently was* A Midsummer Night's Dream. *One brief passage, for example—*

I sat me down to watch upon a bank
With ivy canopied, and interwove
With flaunting honeysuckle . . .

lays under contribution Oberon's celebrated speech to Puck:

I know a bank where the wild thyme blows
Where oxlips and the nodding violet grows,
Quite over-canopied with luscious woodbine,
With sweet musk roses, and with eglantine.

'I know a bank' also lurks behind a notable passage in a poem by a later poet than Milton:

White hawthorn, and the pastoral eglantine;
Fast-fading violets covered up in leaves;
And mid-May's eldest child,
The coming musk-rose, full of dewy wine . . .

JOHN KEATS, *Ode to a Nightingale*, 1819

Keats originally wrote 'sweetest' wine, and then substituted 'dewy'. Possibly he was anxious not to imitate Shakespeare, with his 'sweet musk roses', too closely; at all events, the new word he found was more evocative, more precise.

SOME ECHOES OF *HAMLET*

Then he's *so* well-bred—*so* full of alacrity, and adulation!—and has *so much* to say for himself: in such good language, too. His physiognomy so grammatical! Then his presence is so noble! I protest, when I saw him, I thought of what Hamlet says in the play: 'Hesperian curls!—the front of Job himself!—an eye, like March, to threaten at command! a station, like Harry Mercury, new'—something about kissing—on a hill—however, the similitude struck me directly.

Mrs Malaprop in RICHARD BRINSLEY SHERIDAN, *The Rivals*, 1775

Blank misgivings of a Creature
Moving about in worlds not realised;
High instincts before which our mortal Nature
Did tremble like a guilty thing surprised . . .

WILLIAM WORDSWORTH, *Ode: Intimations of Immortality*, 1807

Behold me, for I cannot sleep,
And like a guilty thing I creep
At earliest morning to the door.

ALFRED TENNYSON, *In Memoriam*, 1850

The same phrase is put to very different use in two different contexts. Its source is the departure of the ghost in the opening scene in Hamlet: *'And then it started like a guilty thing | Upon a fearful summons.'*

... the old mole that can work in the earth so fast, that worthy pioneer—the Revolution.

KARL MARX, speech, 1856

> C'est l'automne, l'automne, l'automne,
> Le grand vent et toute sa séquelle
> De représailles! et de musiques! . . .
> Rideaux tirés, clôture annuelle,
> Chute des feuilles, des Antigones, des Philomèles:
> Mon fossoyeur, *Alas poor Yorick!*
> Les remue à la pelle! . . .

It's autumn, autumn, autumn, high winds and their aftermath of reprisals, of music! Drawn curtains, annual closure, fall of leaves, of Antigones, of Philomelas; My gravedigger, *Alas poor Yorick*, shovels them up . . .

JULES LAFORGUE, 'Dimanches', 1886

' "Yes," said I, "strictly speaking, the question is not how to get cured, but how to live."

'He approved with his head, a little sadly as it seemed. *"Ja! ja!* In general, adapting the words of your great poet: That is the question. . . ." He went on nodding sympathetically. . . . "How to be! *Ach!* How to be." '

JOSEPH CONRAD, *Lord Jim*, 1900

Birkin went home again to Gerald. He went into the room, and sat down on the bed. Dead, dead and cold!

> 'Imperial Caesar dead, and turned to clay
> Would stop a hole to keep the wind away.'

There was no response from that which had been Gerald. Strange, congealed, icy substance—no more. No more!

D. H. LAWRENCE, *Women in Love*, 1920

What's he to Hecuba?
Nothing at all.
That's why there'll be no wedding on Wednesday week,
Way down in old Bengal.

Jazz-song in ALDOUS HUXLEY, Antic Hay, 1923

What's Hicupper to hem or her to Hagaba?

JAMES JOYCE, Finnegans Wake, 1939

According to Adaline Glasheen, in A Second Census of Finnegans Wake, *'Hagaba' conflates Hecuba with the biblical Hagar, mother of Ishmael. No doubt there are other buried references as well.*

'Then you thought again,' said Ruby.
  'O yes,' said Belacqua, 'the usual pale cast.'

SAMUEL BECKETT, 'Love and Lethe', 1934

'Do you recall telling me once about someone who told somebody he could tell him something which would make him think a bit? Knitted socks and porcupines entered into it, I remember.'
  'I think you may be referring to the ghost of the father of Hamlet, Prince of Denmark, sir . . . '
  'That's right. Locks, of course, not socks. Odd that he should have said porpentine when he meant porcupine. Slip of the tongue, no doubt, as so often happens with ghosts.'

P. G. WODEHOUSE, Jeeves in the Offing, 1960

⋆   ⋆   ⋆

Don Juan arouses the fury of the Turkish princess Gulbeyaz:

A vulgar tempest 'twere to a typhoon
    To match a common fury with her rage,
And yet she did not want to reach the moon,
    Like moderate Hotspur on the immortal page.
Her anger pitched into a lower tune,
    Perhaps the fault of her soft sex and age.

Her wish was but to 'kill, kill, kill', like Lear's,
And then her thirst of blood was quenched in tears.

LORD BYRON, *Don Juan*, 1819–24

The Hotspur lines are an echo of

methinks it were an easy leap
To pluck bright honour from the pale-fac'd moon

Henry IV Part One

Ein Bild! Ein Bild! Mein Pferd für'n gutes Bild!
['An image! An image! My horse for a good image!']

HEINRICH HEINE, *Friedricke*, 1820s

Ne m'écrivez point, je ne répondrais pas. Bien moins méchant que Iago,
à ce qu'il me semble, je vais dire comme lui: *From this time forth I never
will speak word*.

STENDHAL, from Julien Sorel's farewell message to Mathilde de la Mole in
Le Rouge et le Noir, 1830

Mystery was his mental element. He lived in the midst of that visionary
world in which nothing is but what is not.

Mr Flosky (a portrait of Coleridge) in
THOMAS LOVE PEACOCK, *Nightmare Abbey*, 1818

Miss Tenorina. O how beautiful! How I should love the melody of
that miniature cascade!
Mr Milestone. Beautiful, Miss Tenorina! Hideous. Base, common, and
popular.

THOMAS LOVE PEACOCK, *Headlong Hall*, 1816

*'Art thou officer? Or art thou base, common and popular?'—Pistol's challenge
to the King when he stops him, not knowing who he is, on the eve of
Agincourt* (Henry V, IV. i). *Peacock uses the same quotation in* Nightmare
Abbey.

A Route of Evanescence
With a revolving Wheel—
A Resonance of Emerald—
A Rush of Cochineal—
And every Blossom on the Bush
Adjusts it's tumbled Head—
The mail from Tunis, probably,
An easy Morning's Ride—

EMILY DICKINSON, c. 1879

In this appropriately compact poem—it is about a hummingbird—'the mail from Tunis' refers to a passage in The Tempest *in which Antonio is speaking, with flaunting hyperbole, about Alonso's daughter Claribel,*

She that is Queen of Tunis; she that dwells
Ten leagues beyond man's life; she that from Naples
Can have no note, unless the sun were post—
The man i'th'moon's too slow—till new-born chins
Be rough and razorable . . .

What would take a man fifteen or sixteen years, in other words, is 'an easy morning's ride' for the bird. (Did 'post', one wonders, suggest 'mail'?)

Until the reference has been explained, it looks like a private association, powerful (thanks to its context) but hopelessly obscure. Once it has been explained it is plain and no less powerful.

The Captain is the central character in August Strindberg's The Father *(1887). Pleading with his wife, he slides into quoting Shakespeare—without acknowledgement, but then the lines are so famous that acknowledgement is hardly called for:*

Laura. What can I do? I swear before God and all that I hold sacred that you are Bertha's father.

Captain. What use is that, when you've already said that a mother can and should commit any crime for her child's sake? I implore you, for the sake of the past—I implore you, as a wounded man begs for the death-blow—tell me everything. Don't you see that I'm as helpless as a child? Can't you hear that I'm calling to you as if you were my mother? Won't you forget that I'm a grown man—a soldier whose word of command both men and beasts obey? I am a sick man, all I ask is pity; I surrender the symbols of my power, and pray for mercy on my life.

Laura (coming to him and laying her hand on his forehead). What's this? A man, and crying?

Captain. Yes, I'm crying, although I'm a man. Has not a man eyes? Has not a man hands, organs, dimensions, senses, affections, passions? Fed with the same food, hurt with the same weapons, warmed and cooled by the same winter and summer as a woman. If you prick us, do we not bleed; if you tickle us, do we not laugh; if you poison us, do we not die? Why shouldn't a man complain, or a soldier cry? Because it's unmanly. What makes it unmanly?

Laura. Cry then, child, and your mother will be with you again.

tr. Peter Watts

★ ★ ★

In his celebrated lecture 'The Name and Nature of Poetry' (1933), A. E. Housman describes 'Fear no more the heat o' the sun' (from Cymbeline) *and 'O mistress mine, where are you roaming?' (from* Twelfth Night) *as 'the very summits of lyrical achievement'. The first of these songs, if we are to judge from his own poetry, made a particularly strong impression on him. He borrows from it on four separate occasions, twice in* A Shropshire Lad *and twice in* Last Poems:

'Wanderers eastward, wanderers west,
Know you why you cannot rest?
'Tis that every mother's son
Travails with a skeleton.

'Lie down in the bed of dust;
Bear the fruit that bear you must;
Bring the eternal seed to light,
And morn is all the same as night.

'Rest you so from trouble sore,
Fear the heat o' the sun no more,
Nor the snowing winter wild,
Now you labour not with child.'

'The Immortal Part', A Shropshire Lad, XLIII

Dust's your wages, son of sorrow,
But men may come to worse than dust.

A Shropshire Lad, XLIV

Think I, the round world over,
What golden lads are low
With hurts not mine to mourn for
And shames I shall not know.

Last Poems, II

These, in the day when heaven was falling,
The hour when earth's foundations fled,
Followed their mercenary calling
And took their wages and are dead.

'Epitaph on an Army of Mercenaries', *Last Poems*, XXXVII

These last lines were written in response to the Kaiser's jibe that the British Expeditionary Force sent to the Continent in 1914 was 'an army of mercenaries'. The ironic acceptance of the charge gives the Shakespearian echo in 'took their wages' a new and bitter twist.

Most readers have shared Housman's high estimate of 'Fear no more'. Bernard Shaw, for example, had many hard things to say about Cymbeline, *but when he reviewed Henry Irving's production and found that Irving had cut 'the antiphonal third verse of the famous dirge', he was appalled: 'A man who would do that would do anything—cut the coda out of the first movement of Beethoven's Ninth Symphony, or shorten one of Velasquez's Philips into a kitcat to make it fit over his drawing room mantelpiece.'*

There have been dissenters, however. What has particularly put them off has been the couplet comparing golden lads and girls to chimney-sweepers who 'come to dust'. In From Dawn to Decadence, *his survey of European cultural life since 1500, Jacques Barzun singles it out as a prime example of Shakespeare's erratic taste, a piece of foolish wordplay which spoils the poem's mood. In principle Barzun is right: the image ought to be grotesque. But in practice, like so many of Shakespeare's grotesqueries, it works. The incongruities blend.*

The chimney-sweepers are replaced by members of a more appropriate calling in one of T. S. Eliot's Five-Finger Exercises, *'Lines to a Yorkshire Terrier':*

Pollicle dogs and cats all must
Jellicle cats and dogs all must
Like undertakers, come to dust.

This is a 'serious' emendation, but also of course a playful one. If the substitution were made in the Cymbeline *poem itself, it would hardly represent an improvement.*

There was never a sound beside the wood but one,
And that was my long scythe whispering to the ground.
What was it it whispered? I knew not well myself;
Perhaps it was something about the heat of the sun . . .

                              ROBERT FROST, 'Mowing'

                    ★   ★   ★

With blue smock and with gold rings in his ears,
Sometimes he is a pedlar, not too poor
To keep his wit. This is tall Tom that bore
The logs in, and with Shakespeare in the hall
Once talked, when icicles hung by the wall.
As Herne the Hunter he has known hard times.
On sleepless nights he made up weather rhymes
Which others spoilt . . .

                        EDWARD THOMAS, 'Lob', 1915

*Lob is a protean figure not unlike Puck or Robin Goodfellow. The legend of
Herne the Hunter is put to comic use in* The Merry Wives of Windsor.

When magpies sing in sky and tree
And colts like dragons snuff the air
And frosts paint hollows white till three
And lamp-lit children skip their prayer;
Then Meg and Joan at midnight lie
And quake to hear the dingoes cry
Who nightly round the white church stone
Snap at their tails and the frosty moon.

When stockmen lapped in oilskin go
And lambing ewes on hill-tops bleat
And crows are out and rain winds blow
And kettles simmer at the grate;
Then Meg and Joan at midnight lie
And quake to hear the dingoes cry
Who nightly round the white church stone
Snap at their tails and the weeping moon.

                        DAVID CAMPBELL, 'Winter', 1949

'When icicles hang by the wall' transposed to Australia. Campbell wrote a

companion-piece, 'Summer', an Australian version of 'When daisies pied'. The final couplet runs:

> Oh, tramps and fat commercial men
> Call barmaid Nell their sweetheart then.

'But you had retired, Holmes. We heard of you as living the life of a hermit among your bees and your books in a small farm upon the South Downs.'

'Exactly, Watson. Here is the fruit of my leisured ease, the *magnum opus* of my latter years!' He picked up the volume from the table and read out the whole title, '*Practical Handbook of Bee Culture, with some Observations upon the Segregation of the Queen*. Alone I did it. Behold the fruit of pensive nights and laborious days, when I watched the little working gangs as once I watched the criminal world of London.'

ARTHUR CONAN DOYLE, 'His Last Bow', 1917

'Alone I did it'—the proud boast of Coriolanus ('I flutter'd your Volscians in Corioles') might seem excessive if the handbook on bees were really all that Holmes had in mind. But he is also alluding, not so very obliquely, to the feat which he has just pulled off in 'His Last Bow', in which he vanquishes the Kaiser's master-spy on the eve of the First World War.

Holmes twice quotes or slightly misquotes 'Journeys end in lovers meeting' from Twelfth Night—*once when he takes his old antagonist Colonel Sebastian Moran by surprise (in 'The Empty House') and once when Inspector Gregson of the Yard arrives at the scene of the crime (in 'The Red Circle'). And in 'The Three Students', the great detective is not above a little facetiousness, with his allusion to* Henry V: *'By Jove! my dear fellow, it is nearly nine, and the landlady babbled of green peas at seven-thirty.'*

> Ripeness is all; her in her cooling planet
> Revere; do not presume to think her wasted . . .

WILLIAM EMPSON, 'To an Old Lady', 1928

A daring appropriation. 'Ripeness is all'—a quotation without benefit of quotation marks—is one of the most hallowed phrases in literature. And the daring seems all the greater (though in the event, justified) when one learns that the old lady of the poem was in fact Empson's mother. A child addressing his parent, he had taken over the words of another child (Edgar) addressing his parent (Gloucester).

He folded over the *Tribune* with its heavy, black, crashing sensational print and read without recognizing any of the words, for his mind was still on his father's vanity. The doctor had created his own praise. People were primed and did not know it. And what did he need praise for? In a hotel where everyone was busy and contacts were so brief and had such small weight, how could it satisfy him? He could be in people's thoughts here and there for a moment; in and then out. He could never matter much to them. Wilhelm let out a long, hard breath and raised the brows of his round and somewhat circular eyes. He stared beyond the thick borders of the paper.

> . . . love that well which thou must leave ere long.

Involuntary memory brought him this line. At first he thought it referred to his father, but then he understood that it was for himself, rather. *He* should love that well. 'This thou perceivest, which makes *thy* love more strong.'

SAUL BELLOW, *Seize the Day*, 1956

The quotation is from Sonnet 73.

★   ★   ★

Of all the echoes of Shakespeare in the work of other great writers, none are more tragic than the fragments embedded in the so-called Brantwood Diary of John Ruskin, or rather in the section of it covering the third week of February 1878. (Brantwood is the house in the Lake District where Ruskin spent his later years.)

In the first half of February Ruskin was leading a busy and apparently normal life. By the middle of the month he had begun to retreat into agitated private fantasies, in what proved to be the prelude to mental collapse. His diary entries during this period turned into a tumble of free associations, most of them centring on his obsession with Rose La Touche, and many of them drawn from Shakespeare.

He had first met Rose when she was a child, and he had proposed to her when she was 18. She asked him to wait three years, but her parents—warned against him by his former wife, Effie—had intervened and forbidden him to see her. She had died in 1875, at the age of 27.

His continuing infatuation with her was a prime cause in precipitating his breakdown. In his diary he identified her with a number of figures, but especially with St Catherine of Bologna, who had been a painter, and with Ophelia. (He sometimes referred to St Catherine as 'Beata Vigri': Vigri was her family name.)

Writing on 14 February, on the brink of his crisis, he was exultant. It was St Valentine's Day, and he had 'had the Madonna for a Valentine!—from the Beata Vigri'. According to Helen Viljoen in her 1971 edition of the diary, this is a reference to a copy of Caterina Vigri's painting of St Ursula, which a friend had sent him. At the same time, the occasion seems to have stirred memories of Ophelia's song about St Valentine's Day, and about the lover who

> Let in the maid that out a maid
> Never departed more.

Three days later, for the first time, the free associations in the diary were out of control:

FEBRUARY 17.—Sunday. Stopped upstairs behind Kate° to pray, a little— after "seeing my way" at last at ½ past three this morning—with beata Vigris help—and Ophelias.— Let in—that out— Departed, never more

☩

The devil put a verse into my head just now—"let us not be desirous of *vain* glory." I am NOT oh Devil. I want useful Glory. — "provoking one another" — Oh Devil—cunning Devil—do you think I want to provoke Beata Vigri and little Ophelia then—?

I will—pro—voke—Somebody else, God willing "to day" and to purpose.

And Bishop Laertes,—you had as lief take your fingers from my throat— The Devil will not take my soul, yet a while— Also—look you— and also looking other things may be at YOUR throat before long. (Thou pray'st not well—even by your own account and the Devil will not answer you therefore) and least said is soonest mended—for—if up when the scuffle comes—the foils should be Sheffield whettles°—it is

---

Kate] one of the servants at Brantwood   whettles] long knives

dangerous work—Laertes—'very'—as Mr Jingle° said, even the public
press & Mr Jingle will advise you of that.
    Public press   Mr Jingle, in then! and St George of England both
Advise you of that.

"Forty thousand brothers" Yes, and sisters too, and I have a few—in
Heaven—besides little Ophelia—who bewept to her grave did go, larded
all with sweet flowers . . .
 . . . I come on my mothers watch in the case I used to be so fond of.
What o clock is it?
    Six minutes to 12—and a few seconds over—as far as I can see with my
magnifying glass—my old eyes wont. — Oh yes the second-hand— —
(Second! life) twenty one seconds. — Time — Twice and a half time or
so. I'm wasting it—Devil puts me in mind of Iachimo—Imogene dear—
& the mole cinq spotted— we'll beat him, wont we?

There are at least half a dozen reminiscences of Hamlet *in this passage, most
of them drawn from the scenes which feature Ophelia or Laertes. They include
'Departed, never more', 'Forty thousand brothers', and 'sweet flowers' (from
Ophelia's song 'While his shroud as the mountain snow'), along with 'The
Devil will not take my soul' (echoing Laertes' words to Hamlet in the graveyard
scene) and 'Thou pray'st not well' (echoing Hamlet's words to Laertes). And as
Helen Viljoen points out, the phrase 'look you' occurs five times in the course of
the play, used by Hamlet in connection with his father's ghost and by both
Hamlet and Polonius when they are addressing his mother.*
    *In equating Rose La Touche with Ophelia, Ruskin was by no means seeing
her purely as a victim. On the contrary, he was upbraiding her for listening to
her parents and letting him down. Thirteen years earlier, as though by premon-
ition, he had taken a hard line with Ophelia in a book written for Rose,* Sesame
and Lilies. *At the start of the second section of that book, 'Of Queens' Gardens', there is an eloquent if sweeping account of the role of women in Shakespeare's plays. Briefly, it suggests that he was a creator of heroines rather than
heroes: 'The catastrophe of every play is caused always by the folly or fault of a
man; the redemption, if there be any, is by the wisdom and virtue of a woman.'
True, there are Lady Macbeth, Regan, and Goneril, but they are 'frightful
exceptions to the ordinary laws of life', and can be set aside. (So can Cleopatra,
whom Ruskin conveniently forgets.) For the rest, 'among all the principal figures*

Mr Jingle] character in *The Pickwick Papers* who frequently concludes his telegraphic
monologues with 'very'

in Shakespeare's plays, there is only one weak woman—Ophelia; and it is because she fails Hamlet at the critical moment, and is not, and cannot in her nature be, a guide to him when he needs her most, that all the bitter catastrophe follows'.

If Ophelia represents Rose in the diary, Ruskin himself has to be Hamlet. But then his thoughts wander towards Cymbeline, *and towards the dreadful possibility that he might also be the villainous Iachimo, spying on Imogen as she sleeps, gazing at the 'mole cinque-spotted' on her breast. It is the Devil, he claims, who has put him in mind of this hateful yet alluring scene—which is as much as to say, it is the Devil who has stirred up his own lust. But 'we'll beat him, wont we?'*

There are glancing Shakespearian allusions in the relatively brief entries for the days which followed—to Bottom and Titania, to Shylock ('Soft. No Haste. The Jew shall have all'), to Hamlet *once again. But it is not until the long entry for 22 February that Shakespeare returns in full force; and when he does, he brings further satanic associations with him:*

> Recollected all about message from Rosie to me as I was drawing on the scaffolding in St Georges Chapel— My saying I would serve her to the death—
> Tonight—(last night)—lying awake—came—Ada with the Golden Hair.
> 1 —Can the Devil *speak truth* (confer letter to Francie about her little feet.)
> and 2 If that thou beest a devil &c. connected with, (Made wanton— &c. the night with her)

'Can the Devil speak true?' is Banquo's query in Macbeth, *after the first of the witches' prophecies has been fulfilled. 'If that thou be'st a devil' is the disabused Othello addressing Iago. 'He hath not yet made wanton the night with her' is Iago working on Cassio's feelings earlier in the play.*

This tight-packed passage is followed by a long tangle of further associations—above all Venetian (though they also range from the Black Prince to William Blake). For the moment Shakespeare is lost sight of again. But a sudden recollection of Keats's Endymion *leads on in turn to the phrase 'quenched in the chaste beams' from* A Midsummer Night's Dream, *where Cupid's 'fiery shaft' is 'quench'd in the chaste beams of the watery moon'). And a renewed burst of Venetian reminiscences culminates in a single line, standing alone:*

'Send for the lady to the Sagittary.'

The lady is Desdemona, summoned by Othello to bear witness on his behalf, and—unlike Rose La Touche—ready to defy her father for the sake of love.

The 22 February entry continues a few lines further and then breaks off. Ruskin spent the night which followed wrestling, as he supposed, with the Devil; the next morning his servants found him naked and deranged. He remained in a state of what looked like hopeless madness for a month, but then began to improve; by early April, though still very weak, he had recovered.

Who can doubt that the devil with whom he had to wrestle was above all his own sexuality? After listing some of the scraps of Shakespeare which he quotes in the diary—Iago, Iachimo, Ophelia's mad song—his biographer Tim Hilton observes that they

had probably disturbed Ruskin through all his adulthood. Not for the first time in his life, he was agonised by the thought of his sexual nature. As he approached madness, Ruskin thought of physical desire and virginity, but did so through the remote hand of Shakespeare. He looked for explanations of lust in the work of a supreme poet of life.

IN THE SHADOW OF HISTORY

I am Richard II, know ye not that? . . . He that will forget God, will also forget his benefactors; this tragedy was played forty times in open streets and houses.

ELIZABETH I, as reported by William Lambarde, keeper of the records in the Tower of London, in August 1601

The tragedy in question was Shakespeare's, which had been staged at the instigation of the Essex faction the previous February, the day before Essex's attempted rising. Sir Gelly Meyrick, who had persuaded the actors to revive the play by offering them extra pay, was among the conspirators executed after the rebellion had been put down.

Elizabeth was an enthusiastic patron of the drama. Without her support, the Elizabethan theatre—given the strength of Puritan opposition—would probably not have survived. The tradition that The Merry Wives of Windsor *was written at her command (because she wanted to see a play showing Falstaff in love) first appeared in print in 1702. It may be true.*

James I became patron of Shakespeare's company, the Chamberlain's Men, shortly after his accession in 1603, and proclaimed their status in a royal patent: they became the King's Men. During the course of his reign seventeen of Shakespeare's plays were performed before him, often in the presence of his family, while it seems highly probable that Macbeth *was partly designed in his honour. (Banquo was reputedly one of his ancestors.) According to his biographer D. Harris Willson, however, his taste ran to satire and to low comedy, and 'there is little indication that he was interested in serious drama or detected the genius of Shakespeare'.*

Probably no English monarch enjoyed the drama more than Charles I. His preference was for tragi-comedies, pastorals, light plays, and masques, but Shakespeare was performed before him as well, nine times in all. One notable occasion was on 17 November 1633, when according to the Office Book of the Master of the Revels 'Richard the Third was acted by the King's Players at St

James's, when the King and Queen were present, it being the first play the Queen saw since Her Majesty's delivery of the Duke of York.'

After Charles's execution, his love of plays was cited by his enemies as evidence of his depravity. One Puritan pamphleteer exclaimed: 'Had he but studied Scripture half so much as Ben Jonson or Shakespeare . . .' And John Milton put a positively sinister gloss on the Shakespearian connection. In Eikonoklastes *(1649), his point-by-point reply to the Royalist tract* Eikon Basilike: The Portraiture of His Sacred Majesty in His Solitudes and Sufferings, *Milton insisted that 'the deepest policy of a tyrant hath been ever to counterfeit religion', and of the many sources from which Charles might have learned such a lesson, he singled out one:*

I shall not instance an abstruse author, wherein the King might be less conversant, but one whom we well know was the closet companion of these his solitudes, William Shakespeare; who introduces the person of Richard the Third, speaking in as high a strain of piety, and mortification, as is uttered in any passage in this book [*Eikon Basilike*]; and sometimes to the same sense and purpose with some words in this place. 'I intended,' saith he, 'not only to oblige my friends but mine enemies.' The like saith Richard, Act 2. Scene 1:

> I do not know that Englishman alive
> With whom my soul is any jot at odds
> More than the infant that is born tonight;
> I thank my God for my humility.

Other stuff of this sort may be read throughout the whole tragedy, wherein the poet used not much licence in departing from the truth of history, which delivers him [Richard] a deep dissembler, not of his affections only but of religion.

A far cry from 'What needs my Shakespeare for his honoured bones' or the 'sweetest Shakespeare fancy's child' of L'Allegro.

In 1754 a young Polish nobleman, Stanislaus Poniatowski, later to be the last king of Poland, visited England:

Lord Strange was the first to take me to a performance of one of Shakespeare's tragedies. I took with me a vivid memory of all the beautiful rules of the unities of place, action and time, the minute observation of which gives the French dramatists their idea of their own superiority over the English. But I must admit that the more I became acquainted with the plays of Shakespeare, the less I began to believe in this supposed superiority. I felt involved, amused and more than once even edified: and I inferred from this that I might gain pleasure and even profit from seeing a play whose action lasts longer than one day and whose setting changes from one place to another, as long as the author possesses a thorough knowledge of the customs, passions, defects and even virtues of which people are capable.

STANISLAUS II, *Mémoires*, written 1797–8

Stanislaus, who reigned from 1764 until 1795, when he was forced to abdicate, was a generous patron of the arts. He founded the Polish National Theatre and translated Julius Caesar *into French.*

Whether or not Elizabeth I commissioned The Merry Wives of Windsor, *another queen—an empress, indeed—had an undoubted fondness for the play. Catherine the Great translated it into Russian in 1786, under the title* This Is What It Means to Have a Buck-Basket and Linen. *The scene was switched to St Petersburg; the characters were given Russian names—Justice Shallow became Shalov, Mistress Ford became Fordova; Falstaff was turned into a dandy who has come back from his travels abroad and is mocked for his Frenchified ways.*

Catherine wrote some twenty other plays. One of them was an adaptation (via the German) of Timon of Athens.

To convince you how wretched is the taste which prevails even now in Germany, you have only to go to the theatre. There you will find the abominable plays of Shakespeare being presented, and audiences in transports of joy listening to these ridiculous farces, which are worthy of the savages of Canada. I call them farces because they sin against all the rules of the theatre. These rules are not arbitrary, you find them in the *Poetics* of Aristotle, where the unity of place, the unity of time, and the unity of interest are prescribed as the sole means of rendering tragedies interesting. In the English pieces the action can be spread over years. Where is the resemblance to reality? There are street-porters and diggers, too, who come on stage and speak in a manner suited to their station, and then come princes and kings. How can this grotesque mixture of baseness and grandeur, of buffoonery and tragedy, move or please? One can forgive Shakespeare these bizarre errors, for the arts never come into the world fully grown. But then a play like *Goetz von Berlichingen°* is presented, a detestable imitation of these bad English pieces, and the pit applauds and calls for more.

FREDERICK THE GREAT, *De la littérature allemande,* 1780

'Was there ever,' cried he, 'such stuff as a great part of Shakespeare? Only one must not say so! What think you?—what?—Is there not sad stuff?—what?—what?'

GEORGE III, recorded by Fanny Burney in her diary, 1785

Of the 163 quotations which Thomas Jefferson had transcribed in his Literary Commonplace Book by the time he was 20, 16 were from Shakespeare—a larger sampling than that of any other author apart from Milton (35), Pope (25), and Cicero (21). Most of the Shakespeare quotations were broadly political passages from Julius Caesar *or* Coriolanus, *but Jefferson also included, somewhat less predictably, Falstaff's speech on Honour.*

The French Revolution marked a new era in awareness of Shakespeare's polit-ics and debate about where he had stood:

Shakespear has in this play shewn himself well versed in history and state-affairs. *Coriolanus* is a store-house of political common-places. Any one who studies it may save himself the trouble of reading Burke's *Reflections*, or Paine's *Rights of Man*, or the Debates in both Houses of Parliament since the French Revolution or our own. The arguments for and against aristocracy or democracy, on the privileges of the few and the claims of the many, on liberty and slavery, power and the abuse of it, peace and war, are here very ably handled, with the spirit of a poet and the acuteness of a philosopher. Shakespear himself seems to have had a leaning to the arbitrary side of the question, perhaps from some feeling of contempt for his own origin; and to have spared no occasion of baiting the rabble. What he says of them is very true: what he says of their betters is also very true, though he dwells less upon it.

WILLIAM HAZLITT, *Characters of Shakespear's Plays,* 1817

Goetz von Berlichingen] an early work by Goethe

> Eye of STRAW and toe of CADE,
> TYLER's bow, KOSCIUSKO's blade,
> RUSSELL's liver, tongue of cur,
> NORFOLK's boldness, Fox's fur;°
> Add thereto a tiger's chauldron,
> For the ingredients of our cauldron!
> Pour in streams of Regal Blood,
> Then the charm is firm and good.

Verse accompanying 'A Charm for a Democracy', a caricature by
THOMAS ROWLANDSON in the *Anti-Jacobin Review*, February 1799

*Rowlandson's drawing shows the radical John Horne Tooke and his friends
stirring a witches' brew, with monsters and demons in attendance: the Devil
himself pronounces the final couplet of the verse.*

The character of *Caliban*, as an original and caricature of Jacobinism, so
fully illustrated at Paris during the French Revolution, he described in a
vigorous and lively manner, exciting repeated bursts of applause.

Report of a lecture by COLERIDGE in the *Courier*, 9 February 1818

Caliban is so far from being a prototype of modern Jacobinism, that
he is strictly the legitimate sovereign of the isle, and Prospero and the
rest are usurpers, who have ousted him from his hereditary jurisdic-
tion by superiority of talent and knowledge. 'This island's mine, by
Sycorax my mother;' and he complains bitterly of the artifices used by
his new friends to cajole him out of it ... Even his affront to the
daughter of that upstart philosopher Prospero, could not be brought
to bar his succession to the natural sovereignty of his dominions. His
boast that 'he had peopled else this isle with Calibans,' is very proper
and dignified in such a person; for it is evident that the right line
would be supplanted in failure of his issue; and that the superior
beauty and accomplishments of Ferdinand and Miranda could no
more be opposed to the legitimate claims of this deformed and loath-

(Jack) Straw . . . (Jack) Cade . . . (Wat) Tyler] leaders of medieval insurrections
Kosciusko] leader of the Polish national uprising of 1794
Russell (sixth Duke of Bedford)] radical sympathizer
Norfolk (the eleventh duke)] associate of the leader of the Whig opposition, Charles James
Fox

some monster, than the beauty and intellect of the Bonaparte family can be opposed to the bloated and ricketty minds and bodies of the Bourbons, cast, as they are, in the true *Jus Divinum* mould! This is gross. Why does Mr Coleridge provoke us to write as great nonsense as he talks? Why also does he not tell, in his general 'lunes and abstractions,' what to think of Prospero's brother, the Duke, who usurped his crown, and drove him into banishment; or of those finished Court-practitioners, Sebastian and Antonio, who wanted to murder the sleeping King? Were they Jacobins like Caliban, or legitimate personages, like Mr Coleridge? Did they belong to the new school or the old? That is the question; but it is a question which our lay-preacher will take care not to answer.

HAZLITT, 'Mr Coleridge's Lectures', *The Yellow Dwarf*, 14 February 1818

With what aching rage, with what disdainful irony, this Roman Tory [Coriolanus] begs the 'voices' of the good citizens whom his soul despises so deeply, but whose consent he needs to become Consul! The only difference between him and most of the English gentry is that the latter, whose scars derive from fox-hunts rather than battles, have had better lessons in dissimulation from their mothers. When they present themselves for election to parliament they do not exhibit their scorn and anger as openly as stiff-necked Coriolanus.

HEINRICH HEINE, *Shakespeare's Girls and Women*, 1838, tr. S. S. Prawer

The author of Coriolanus never believed in a mob, and did something towards preventing anyone else from doing so.

WALTER BAGEHOT, 'Shakespeare the Individual', 1853

Lord Melbourne

Spoke about Shakespeare's plays; *Hamlet, Macbeth, Lear*, etc., etc.; he thinks the 2 first named the finest; he said, 'I think German critics understand Shakespeare better than we do here'; mentioned Goethe's *Wilhelm Meister*, and Schlegel's book upon Shakespeare, which he thinks very good.

QUEEN VICTORIA, diary, 17 January 1838

In later years, Cavour had less time for introspection, but his early diary betrays the morbid self-pity of a person who, without the vivacity and verve that struck other people both earlier and later, could sometimes be morose and lethargic . . .

This was one of several moments in his life when he thought of suicide as he contemplated a future 'without purpose, without hope, without desire'. Rather than be an undistinguished younger son he would a hundred times rather be dead. Among the excerpts he copied out from *Hamlet, King John* and *Macbeth* were that life was 'weary, stale, flat and unprofitable'; it was 'as tedious as a twice-told tale', 'a tale told by an idiot, signifying nothing'. In Hamlet's speech on suicide he underlined the words 'conscience doth make cowards of us all', adding that he would copy Hamlet and not kill himself 'for the moment', yet he wished he knew how to catch some deadly disease that would cure for ever a life ruined by an excess of intelligence and vanity.

DENIS MACK SMITH, *Cavour*, 1985

At the period being described (1833–4), Cavour—the future architect of Italian unification—was in his early twenties.

You felt, no doubt, that you were a very sensible person when you beheld your cold-blooded, sceptical friend in the cloudland of superstition and interpretation of dreams. Strange enough it is, too; but who will explain the contradictions that exist in the nature of every individual? Hobbes, the materialistic atheist, could not sleep alone for fear of ghosts. Now, although I, trusting in God's supreme power and submissive to His will, am not exactly afraid of supernatural contacts and influences—at least, not more than of those which are corporeal—yet I do believe, to express it in Hamlet's hackneyed words, that there are many things between heaven and earth of which our philosophers do not dream, or, if they do *dream* of them, of which they can give no satisfactory account.

OTTO VON BISMARCK, writing to his fiancée, 1847

Bismarck frequently quoted from Shakespeare (and from Schiller, and from other poets). In a previous letter to his fiancée he explained that part of the attraction of poetry had been that it answered to the moods of melancholy from which she had rescued him:

The English poems of mortal misery trouble me no more now; that was of old, when I looked out into nothing—cold and stiff, snow-drifts in my heart. Now a black cat plays with it in the sunshine, as though with a rolling skein, and I like to see its rolling. I will give you, at the end of this letter, a few more verses belonging to that period, of which fragmentary copies are still preserved, as I see, in my portfolio. You may allow me to read them still; they harm me no more.

The examples which he transcribes at the end of the letter are some lines from Tom Moore and the 'Tomorrow and tomorrow and tomorrow' speech.

Just as all the qualitative differences between commodities are effaced in money, so money on its side, a radical leveller, effaces all distinctions.

KARL MARX, Capital, Part I, 1867, tr. Eden and Cedar Paul

Marx adds, as a footnote, a quotation from Timon of Athens:

> Gold! Yellow, glittering, precious gold! . . .
>
>   .   .   .   .
>
> Thus much of this will make black, white, foul, fair,
> Wrong, right; base, noble; old, young; coward, valiant.
>   . . . What this, you gods? Why, this
> Will lug your priests and servants from your sides,
> Pluck stout men's pillows from below their heads.
> This yellow slave
> Will knit and break religions; bless the accurs'd;
> Make the hoar leprosy ador'd; place thieves,
> And give them title, knee, and approbation,
> With senators on the bench; this is it,
> That makes the wappen'd widow wed again.
>
>   .   .   .   .
>
>   . . . Come damned earth,
> Thou common whore of mankind . . .

Marx had previously quoted this passage in the so-called Paris Manuscripts of 1844, adding that 'Shakespeare portrays admirably the power of money'. As S. S. Prawer points out, however (in Karl Marx and World Literature*), on the* *earlier occasion, when he wasn't writing for publication, he transcribed the passage in its entirety; in* Capital, *like a good Victorian, he omitted the lines elaborating on 'the wappen'd widow'—*

> She whom the spital-house and ulcerous sores
> Would cast the gorge at, this embalms and spices
> To th'April day again.

('Wappen'd' is generally glossed as 'sexually exhausted'.)

Prawer's book discusses scores of references to Shakespeare in Marx's work. In his journalism he mainly cited the plays for satirical purposes—comparing Palmerston's prevarications to Falstaff's lies, for instance, and saluting a leader in The Times *as though that paper were Snug the joiner: 'Well roared, lion!'*

The poet or the artist in his truest work always belongs to the people. Whatever he does, whatever aim and thought he may have in his work, he expresses, whether he will or not, some elements of the popular character and expresses them more profoundly and more clearly than the very history of the people. Even when renouncing everything national, the artist does not lose the chief features from which it can be recognised to what people he belongs. Both in the Greek *Iphigenia* and in the Oriental *Divan* Goethe was a German. Poets really are, as the Romans called them, prophets; only they utter not what is not and what will be by chance, but what is unrecognised, what exists in the dim consciousness of the masses, what is already slumbering in it . . .

Probably no one supposes that the England of the time of Elizabeth—particularly the majority of the people—had a precise understanding of Shakespeare; they have no precise understanding of him even now—but then they have no precise understanding of themselves either. But when an Englishman goes to the theatre he understands Shakespeare instinctively, through sympathy, of that I have no doubt. At the moment when he is listening to the play, something becomes clearer and more familiar to him.

ALEXANDER HERZEN, *My Past and Thoughts*, 1861–6, tr. Constance Garnett, revised Humphrey Higgens

Herzen was brilliant at adapting Shakespearian motifs to contemporary circumstances—in his account of Garibaldi's visit to London in 1864, for instance:

Shakespeare's day has turned into Garibaldi's day. This is a coincidence lugged in by the scruff of the neck by history, which alone is successful in achieving such improbabilities.

The people who gathered together on Primrose Hill to plant a tree in memory of the Shakespeare Tricentenary remained there to talk of Garibaldi's sudden departure. The police dispersed the crowd. Fifty thousand men (according to the police report) obeyed the orders of thirty policemen and, from profound respect for the law, half-destroyed the grand right of open-air meeting, or at any rate helped to support the illegal intervention of the authorities.

Truly, something like a Shakespearian fantasy passed before our eyes against the grey background of England with a truly Shakespearian juxtaposition of the grand and the revolting, of what rends the heart and what sets the teeth on edge: the holy simplicity of the man, the naïve simplicity of the masses, and the secret conclaves behind the scenes, the intrigues and the lies. Familiar shades flit before our eyes in other forms—from Hamlet to King Lear, from Goneril and Cordelia to *honest* Iago. The Iagos are all in miniature, but what a number of them there is, and how honest they are!

Prologue: Flourish of trumpets. The idol of the masses, the one grand popular figure of our age that has been perfected since 1848, enters in all the brilliance of its glory. Everything bows down before it, everything celebrates its triumph; this is Carlyle's hero-worship being performed before our eyes. Cannon-shots, bells ringing, pendants on the ships, and no music only because England's guest has arrived on a Sunday, and Sunday here is a lenten day . . . London stands for seven hours on its feet awaiting its guest; the triumphant ovations increase with every day; the appearance in the streets of the man in the *red shirt* calls forth an outburst of enthusiasm, crowds escort him from the opera at one o'clock in the morning and at seven in the morning the crowds meet him in front of Stafford House. Working men and dukes, lords and sempstresses, bankers and High Church clergymen; the feudal wreck, Derby, and the relic of the February Revolution, the republican of 1848; Queen Victoria's eldest son and the barefooted crossing sweeper born without father or mother, vie with one another in trying to capture a hand-shake, a glance, a word. Scotland, Newcastle upon Tyne, Glasgow, Manchester are tremulous with expectation—and he vanishes in the impenetrable fog, in the blue of the ocean.

Like the ghost of Hamlet's father, the guest stepped upon some ministerial trap-door and disappeared. Where is he? 'Tis here! 'Tis here! 'Tis gone! . . . All that is left is a point, a sail just floating out of sight.

The English people were made fools of: 'the great, stupid people', as the poet said of them. John Bull is good-natured, powerful, stubborn, but heavy, torpid and unresourceful, and one is sorry for him while one laughs! A bull with the manners of a lion, he was just shaking his mane and preening himself to greet a guest as he had never greeted any monarch still on duty or dismissed from service, and his guest was snatched from him. The lion-bull stamps with his cleft hoof, tears at the ground in his rage . . . but his guards know the subtle mechanism of the locks and bolts of *liberty* by which he is confined, babble some nonsense to him and keep the key in their pocket, while the point vanishes on the ocean.

My Past and Thoughts

Some of Shakespeare's Plays, I have never read, whilst others I have gone over perhaps as frequently as any unprofessional reader. Among the latter are Lear, Richard Third, Henry Eighth, Hamlet, and especially Macbeth. I think none equals Macbeth. It is wonderful. Unlike you gentlemen of the profession, I think the soliloquy in Hamlet commencing 'O, my offence is rank,' surpasses that commencing 'To be or not to be.' But pardon this small attempt at criticism. I should like to hear you pronounce the opening speech of Richard the Third.

ABRAHAM LINCOLN, letter to the actor James Hackett, 1863

Walt Whitman discerned Shakespearian qualities in Lincoln:

One of the best of the late commentators on Shakespere (Professor Dowden) makes the height and aggregate of his quality as a poet to be, that he thoroughly blended the ideal with the practical or the realistic. If this be so, I should say that what Shakespere did in poetic expression, Abraham Lincoln essentially did in his personal and official life.

November Boughs, 1888

More memorably, Whitman recalled the first time he had seen Lincoln, in 1861, when the newly elected President was passing through New York en route *for Washington:*

I had, I say, a capital view of it all, and especially of Mr Lincoln, his look and gait—his perfect composure and coolness—his unusual and uncouth height, his dress of complete black, stovepipe hat push'd back on the head, dark-brown complexion, seam'd and wrinkled yet canny-looking face, disproportionately long neck, and his hands held behind as he stood observing the people. He look'd with curiosity upon that immense sea of faces, and the sea of faces return'd the look with similar curiosity. In both there was dash of comedy, almost farce, such as Shakspere puts in his blackest tragedies.

Lecture on Lincoln delivered in New York, 1879

One other incident of the run of *King Lear* is, I think, worthy of record, inasmuch as it bears on the character and feeling of that great English-man, Mr Gladstone. In the second week of the run he came to see the play, occupying his usual seat on the stage on the O.P. [Opposite Prompt] corner. He seemed most interested in all that went on, but not entirely happy. At the end, after many compliments to Mr Irving and Miss Terry, he commented on the unpatriotic conduct of taking aid from the French—from any foreigner—under any circumstances whatever of domestic stress.

BRAM STOKER, *Personal Reminiscences of Henry Irving*, 1907

Alfred Dreyfus was imprisoned on Devil's Island (the smallest of the Îles du Salut, off the coast of French Guiana) for four and a half years, from 1895 to 1899. He was the island's only inmate, confined to a small stone cabin, with six guards to watch over him. Physical conditions were appalling. His wife was able to send him books, however, and in Dreyfus: A Family Affair *Michael Burns gives an account of his reading and his favourite authors:*

But above them all was Shakespeare. Not the playwright dissected by Taine in his study of English literature (and stripped, according to Drey-fus, of all grandeur), but the humorous, passionate, sympathetic Shake-speare, the prisoner 'never understood better than during this tragic epoch,' and who, like Dreyfus, may also have turned to Montaigne as a source of inspiration. Distracted and enlightened by what he called 'those most delicious comedies,' *The Merry Wives of Windsor* and *As You Like It*, Dreyfus found in *King Lear, Othello, Hamlet, Macbeth*, and *Richard III* poetic variations on the themes he had been attempting to describe in letters to his wife and family. 'Money is nothing, honor is all,' he had insisted, but Iago put it better, and in one letter Dreyfus reminded Lucie of those lines from the third act of *Othello* they had read together in French translation: 'Who steals my purse steals trash; 'tis something, nothing; | 'Twas mine, 'tis his, and has been slave to thousands; | But he that filches from me my good name | Robs me of that which not enriches him | And makes me poor indeed.' Commenting on the quote, Dreyfus told his wife: 'Yes, the wretch who stole my honor has made me poor indeed.'

Shakespeare provided a fresh vocabulary to relieve the monotony of the prisoner's prose, but more important, he introduced into the 'silence and solitude' of Devil's Island other intrigues, other stories of foul play, false hearts, and human courage, which helped Dreyfus feel less alone. The prisoner copied 'that admirable line Shakespeare put on the lips of old Polonius' ('This above all: to thine own self be true, | And it must follow, as the night the day, | Thou canst not then be false to any man'), and he learned from *Lear*—that most 'heart-rending play' that exposes all the 'steps of human misery'—the 'bitter irony of Shakespeare's moral philosophy.' For Dreyfus *Lear* was the definitive treatise on the 'weakness of the human condition,' a confirmation of how 'the wicked rarely profit from their crimes, while the good are rarely rewarded for their Virtue.' All of Shakespeare's works became a compendium of allegories of all of Dreyfus's dilemmas; ignorant of the details concerning his own tragedy, his own arrest and conviction, and desperate to make sense of his ordeal, Dreyfus cast the unknown characters of his case in Shakespearean roles—the good, evil, and indifferent players who populated the back rooms of the General Staff and plotted against France in foreign embassies. And in one sense at least, he saw himself as that ill-starred army officer, who had refused to partake in Macbeth's 'dishonorable enterprise.' Devil's Island might destroy Dreyfus in the end, but he promised his wife that the truth would out, 'because like Banquo's ghost I will emerge from the tomb in order to shout "courage, courage" to you, to everyone, with all my soul . . . and in order to remind the Fatherland that it too has a sacred duty to fulfill.'

Since the days in Santé prison, his first classroom of one, Dreyfus had been studying English to break the 'terrible monotony of waiting,' and in the hope that he could better grasp the essence of Shakespeare's plays. Functionaries who examined the prisoner's every word considered those English exercises 'insignificant,' but when rumors spread in Paris that his dictionaries and primers might be code books linking him to foreign co-conspirators, officials ordered a full-scale *fouillé*, a surprise ransacking of all his possessions. Late at night, with guns and truncheons drawn, guards stormed into his cabin, cut through his mattress, searched his laundry, tore off the heels of his shoes, and ordered him to strip. Reports filed later described Dreyfus laughing at the absurdity of it all, and when guards found no code book on his person or on his shelf, they allowed him to keep his 'insignificant' English books.

Returning to his studies, he copied English exercises for three and four hours a day. He had a gift for languages (fluent in German, he also had a good knowledge of Italian and Latin), and by his third year in exile, thanks to the popular 'Ollendorf method,' he was reading *Othello* in English and transcribing his favorite Iago speech ('He that filches from me my good name . . . '), though not without errors. In a whisper, he recited long lists of idiomatic expressions, and even the phrases he chose to memorize suggested that government officials were wrong again: For the prisoner, English provided more than an 'insignificant' distraction. 'What does that prove?' 'Can you disprove it?' began one list of fifty English phrases in his journal in 1898. 'I can prove that it is not true.' Even his grammar exercises interlaced allusions to his case, and he learned other phrases that signaled his resolve: 'At least I have my duty,' he wrote in English; and he translated the sentence 'Nothing will last forever.' One day, he hoped, after his acquittal or after his death, his wife would receive his journal, and next to the French dedication, 'Pour ma chère Lucie,' he copied, in English, the lines Hamlet, 'his hot love on the wing,' had sent Ophelia: 'Doubt thou, the stars are fire; | Doubt that the sun doth move; | Doubt truth to be a liar; | But never doubt I love!'

A disciplined officer who, in society, had always seemed rigid and sober, without lightness and without passion, Dreyfus appeared more complicated in his prison journals and in his reveries more like the French essayist he admired: 'I am by nature not melancholy,' Montaigne confessed, 'but dreamy.' Despite all the apologias for reason and rationalism that ran throughout his diaries, Dreyfus still used Shakespeare's characters to express his longings, and Shakespeare's poetry to confirm his faith in dreams.

MICHAEL BURNS, *Dreyfus: A Family Affair*, 1992

The conceptions of our own classic authors are more sober, their designs are more measured and better worked out, each scene is more scrupulously confined to the matter in hand. But if you compare Shakespeare

and Racine, and isolate a key moment in the drama, a turning-point, a
sudden surge of passion, a reversal of character, a conflict, it is Shakespeare who is the master of sobriety and restraint. He neither elaborates
nor explains. His heroes don't launch into carefully composed tirades,
into excellent but unnecessary disquisitions. A detail, a gesture, a word
are enough for him.

LÉON BLUM, review of *King Lear*, 1904

Coriolanus breathes the same scorn and the same fear in respect of the
common people as *Julius Caesar* or *The Tempest*. Let us not be too hard
on Shakespeare, however. It was difficult to be a democrat in his era. The
period in which he lived witnessed a succession of religious and political
upheavals which the people either provoked or submitted to, with a
violence in the one case which equalled their passivity in the other. In
addition Shakespeare, who came from the ranks of the people himself,
was no doubt slowly drawn away from the class into which he had been
born, if not by his genius, then at any rate by the company he kept and
the breadth of his culture; and there is nothing out of the ordinary about
intellectual parvenus conceiving a kind of physical disgust for everything
in the common people which is fickle, ignorant and crude. So Shakespeare has his excuses. And for the rest, in the conflict between Coriolanus and the people he doesn't take his hero's side. He knows that certain
virtues, when they are pushed to excess and not balanced by contrary
virtues, become defects or vices. He knows that a man with Coriolanus's
character is rightly doomed to go down to defeat and final ruin.

Review of *Coriolanus*, 1910

*Blum, leader of the French Socialist party and prime minister of France in
1936–7, 1938, and briefly in 1946–7, was also a distinguished man of letters. In
the years before 1914 he frequently reviewed plays for* Le Matin *and other
papers.*

Shakespeare provided a political script for J. R. Clynes, the son of an Irish
farm laborer, who rose from the textile mills of Oldham to become
deputy leader of the House of Commons. In his youth he drew inspiration from the 'strange truth' he discovered in *Twelfth Night*: 'Be not
afraid of greatness.' ('What a creed! How it would upset the world if
men lived up to it, I thought.') Urged on by a Co-operative society

librarian, he worked through the plays and discovered they were about people who 'had died for their beliefs. Wat Tyler and Jack Cade seemed heroes.' Reading *Julius Caesar*, 'the realisation came suddenly to me that it was a mighty political drama' about the class struggle, 'not just an entertainment.' According to his comrade Will Thorne, Clynes was 'the only man who ever settled a trade dispute by citing Shakespeare.' (Evidently, he overawed a stubborn employer by reciting an entire scene from *Julius Caesar*.) Elected to Parliament in 1906, he read *A Midsummer Night's Dream* while awaiting the returns.

JONATHAN ROSE, The Intellectual Life of the British Working Classes, 2001

During the First World War Shakespeare, like God, was enlisted by both sides. British propaganda drew on him for slogans and motifs (on recruiting posters, for example). At the same time the Germans clung firmly to the idea that he was a naturalized German; the main difference now was that they were also inclined to claim that latter-day Englishmen were unworthy of him.

A widely publicized incident took place in the autumn of 1914 at Leipzig, where a production of Twelfth Night *was preceded by a verse-prologue, written by one Ernst Hardt and spoken by the actor who played Feste. An English version appeared in* The Times *shortly afterwards:*

> Ye unto him have been until today
> His second home; his first and native home
> Was England; but this England of the present
> Is so contrarious in her acts and feelings,
> Yea, so abhorr'd of his pure majesty
> And the proud spirit of his free-born being,
> That he doth find himself quite homeless there.
> A fugitive he seeks his second home,
> This Germany, that loves him most of all,
> To whom before all others he gives thanks,
> And says: Thou wonderful and noble land,
> Remain thou Shakespeare's one and only home.

The same theme was taken up by the foremost German dramatist of the day, in an address which he gave on the tercentenary of Shakespeare's death:

Shakespeare's figures are part of our world, his soul has merged with ours; and if he was born and buried in England, it is in Germany that he truly lives.

GERHART HAUPTMANN, 'Germany and Shakespeare', 1916

David Jones's In Parenthesis *(1937) defies easy classification. It is at once a front-line soldier's memoir of the First World War, a prose poem, and a many-layered myth. The realities of the trenches are omnipresent in its pages, but so is a deep sense of history; and as Jones makes clear in his preface, that sense was an intrinsic part of his own wartime experience:*

I suppose at no time did one so much live with a consciousness of the past, the very remote, and the more immediate and trivial past, both superficially and more subtly. No one, I suppose, however much not given to association, could see infantry in tin hats, with ground-sheets over their shoulders, and sharpened pine-stakes in their hands, and not recall

> . . . or say we cram,
> Within this wooden O . . .

But there were even deeper complexities of sight and sound to make ever present

> the pibble pabble in Pompey's camp

Every man's speech and habit of mind were a perpetual showing: now of Napier's expedition, now of the Legions at the Wall, now of 'train-band captains', now of Jack Cade, of John Ball, of the commons in arms. Now of *High Germany*, of *Dolly Gray*, of Bullcalf, Wart and Poins . . .

and the list goes on, culminating in 'the Celtic cycle that lies, a subterranean influence as a deep water troubling, under every tump in this island, like Merlin complaining under his big rock'.

Shakespeare is only one element in this legacy, but one of the most import-ant. The 'wooden O' and 'pibble pabble' both come from Henry V *(from the Chorus and Fluellen respectively). Jones also evokes* Henry IV *with his mention of Bullcalf, Wart, and Poins, but it is to* Henry V *that he keeps recurring. In one of the notes at the end of* In Parenthesis *he observes that 'trench life brought that work pretty constantly to the mind', and elsewhere in his preface he considers the parallel more closely:*

Some of us ask ourselves if Mr X adjusting his box-respirator can be equated with what the poet envisaged in

I saw young Harry with his beaver on.

We are in no doubt at all but what Bardolph's marching kiss for Pistol's 'quondam Quickly' is an experience substantially the same as you and I suffered on Victoria platform.

'Young Harry with his beaver on' comes from Henry IV Part One, *but it is the future victor of Agincourt that it describes. (A 'beaver' was a helmet or face-guard.)*

David Jones was far from glorifying the 1914–18 war. He painted a detailed picture of its horrors; his sympathies lay with the much-enduring rank and file. But neither did he simply denounce the war. If his literary allusions often have an ironic edge, they also ennoble his common soldiers to the extent of giving them their place in history, linking them to tradition. Merely to ask whether Mr X could be equated with 'young Harry' was to raise the possibility that he could.

At one point in the main text of In Parenthesis *we hear about a 'beaver' again, from a young staff officer:*

Bring meats proper to great lords in harness and: I say Calthrop, have a bite of this perfectly good chocolate you can eat the stuff with your beaver up, this Jackerie knows perfectly well that organising brains must be adequately nourished.

As Jones explained many years later, this allusion was inspired by an actual incident—very different in tone—which took place while he was collecting ammunition boxes behind the lines. He had got separated from a mate; he called out to another friend who was hurrying past, 'Have you seen Harry?'; the friend called back, 'I saw young Harry with his beaver on.'

Three of the soldiers in In Parenthesis *share a name with characters in* Henry V: *Williams, Bates, and Captain Gower. There are several echoes of Fluellen and his preoccupation with 'the Excellent Disciplines of the Wars'. The second section of the book is entitled 'Chambers Go Off, Corporals Stay', which runs together a stage direction at the end of Henry V's speech outside Harfleur ('chambers' were small cannon) and the opening of the low-life scene with Corporal Bardolph and Corporal Nym which follows.*

The most powerful of the allusions to Henry V *is a dark and distorted version of the Harfleur speech. Henry exhorts his men to 'imitate the action of the tiger'—*

> Stiffen the sinews, conjure up the blood,
> Disguise fair nature with hard-favour'd rage;
> Then lend the eye a terrible aspect;
> Let it pry through the portage of the head
> Like a brass cannon . . .

And these are the thoughts of the men in In Parenthesis *as they prepare for battle:*

. . . you can count on an apocalypse, you can wait on exceptional frightfulness—it will be him and you in an open place, he will look into your face; fear will so condition you that you each will pale for the other, and in one another you will hate your own flesh. Your fair natures will be so disguised that the aspect of his eyes will pry like deep-sea horrors divers see, from the portage of his rigid type of gas-bag—but more like you'll get it in the assembly-trench—without so much as a glimpse of his port and crest.

★

Frederic Manning's Her Privates We *is arguably the finest novel in English to come out of the First World War. It has eighteen chapters; each of them is preceded by a quotation from Shakespeare, though without any indication of which play it comes from.*

The book's first Shakespearian borrowing occurs on the title-page, where Manning quotes (in a condensed version) an exchange between Hamlet and Rosencrantz and Guildenstern:

Hamlet. Good lads, how do you both?
Rosencrantz. As the indifferent children of the earth.
Guildenstern. Happy in that we are not over-happy; on Fortune's cap we are not the very button.
Hamlet. Nor the soles of her shoe?
Rosencrantz. Neither, my lord.
Hamlet. Then you live about her waist, or in the middle of her favours?
Guildenstern. Faith, her privates we.
Hamlet. In the secret parts of Fortune? O most true, she is a strumpet.

Manning's highlighting of this passage partly serves to suggest the role played by pure chance in war, especially in the front line. But as William Boyd has written, the sexual innuendoes also signal the fact that coarseness is going to be a central feature of the book itself, and one of its great assets.

Her Privates We *was first published in* 1929, *under the title* The Middle Parts of Fortune, *in a small private edition which made liberal (and liberating) use of four-letter words and other taboo terms. The following year it was revised and republished in a trade edition, under the title by which it has since been known. The new version, though still outspoken by the standards of the time, had been heavily bowdlerized, and it was not until the 1970s that the original text was restored.*

Some of the chapter-headings in the book have a direct bearing on what follows. A quotation from Henry V, *for example—*

But thy speaking of my tongue, and I thine, most truly-falsely, must needs be granted to be much at one

introduces an episode in which a comic misunderstanding arises between a local woman and a British soldier who tries to communicate with her in pidgin-French. Another quotation from the same play—

> But I had not so much of man in me,
> And all my mother came into mine eyes
> And gave me up to tears

stands at the head of a chapter in which a soldier weeps in spite of himself while describing how a friend died of his injuries. In other cases, however, the relevance of chapter-heading to chapter is less obvious; and the over-all effect— reinforced by the fact that some of the quotations aren't particularly well known—is to create the impression of a generalized Shakespearian undercurrent, a running accompaniment to the main action.

The relationship between the Shakespearian element and the here-and-now of the trenches is complicated. The quotations from the plays (one or two from as far afield as Julius Caesar *and* Antony and Cleopatra) *suggest that many of the facts of war are timeless; that the soldiers in the book are the direct heirs of the soldiers Shakespeare wrote about. But there are differences as well as parallels. When they aren't grim, the conditions described in* Her Privates We *are drab and prosaic. Shakespeare confers a certain grandeur on them, and sets them in a longer perspective. At the same time, Manning's narrative has strengths which it would be pointless to look for in the older writer, partly by virtue of his modernity, and partly by virtue of his realism. You might say the four-letter words are valuable—in this context—precisely because Shakespeare doesn't use them.*

The final chapter of the book demonstrates in a painfully direct manner just how much of a lottery war is. The epigraph Manning chose for it came from the exchange between Hamlet and Rosencrantz and Guildenstern, though the actual words had been dropped from the truncated version used on the title-page:

Fortune? O, most true; she is a strumpet.

★　★　★

Today [1919] on an immense platform which might be that of Elsinore, but runs instead from Basle to Cologne, touching the sands of Nieuport, the marshes of the Somme, the granites of Alsace, and the chalky plateaus of Champagne—the European Hamlet stares at millions of ghosts.

But he is an intellectual Hamlet. He meditates on the life and death of truths. For phantoms he has all the subjects of our controversies; for regrets he has all our titles to glory; he bows under the weight of discoveries and learning, unable to renounce and unable to resume this limitless activity. He reflects on the boredom of recommencing the past, on the folly of always striving to be original. He wavers between one abyss and the other, for two dangers still threaten the world: order and disorder.

If he takes a skull in his hands, the skull is illustrious.—'Whose was it?'—That was *Leonardo*. He invented the flying man, but the flying man has hardly fulfilled the purpose of the inventor; we know that the flying man mounted on his great swan (*il grande uccello sopra del dosso del suo magno cecero*) has other uses in our days than to go fetch snow from the mountain-tops and sprinkle it over city streets in the heat of summer. . . . And this other skull is that of *Leibnitz*, who dreamed of universal peace. And this was *Kant, Kant who begat Hegel, who begat Marx, who begat* . . .

Hamlet hardly knows what to do with all these skulls. But if he throws them away! . . . Will he then cease to be himself? His fearfully lucid mind surveys the passage from war to peace. This transition is more dangerous, more obscure than the passage from peace to war; all nations are convulsed by it. 'And I, the European intellect, what will become of me? . . . And what is peace?' he asks. '*Peace is perhaps the state of things in which the natural hostility of man toward men is manifested by creation, in place of the destruction which marks a war.* It is the period of creative competition and the struggle of inventions. But as for me, am I not weary of inventing? Have I not exhausted the desire for extreme attempts and made a vice of my skillful fabrications? Must I abandon my difficult duties and my transcendent ambitions? Should I follow the movement like Polonius, who has become the editor of a great news-paper? like Laertes, who is somewhere in the aviation? like Rosenkrantz, who does I don't know what under a Russian name?

'Phantoms, farewell! The world has no more need of you. Nor of me. The world, which has given the name of "progress" to its tendency toward a fatal precision, is seeking to unite the blessings of life with the advantages of death. A certain confusion still reigns, but yet a little while and all will be made clear; at last we shall behold the miracle of a strictly animal society, a perfect and final ant-hill.'

Paul Valéry, 'The Intellectual Crisis', 1919, tr. Malcolm Cowley

In the tragedies of Shakespeare, which would be entirely unthinkable without the Reformation, the fate of the ancients and the passions of the mediæval Christians are crowded out by individual human passions, such as love, jealousy, revengeful greediness, and spiritual dissension. But in every one of Shakespeare's dramas, the individual passion is carried to such a high degree of tension that it outgrows the individual, becomes super-personal, and is transformed into a fate of a certain kind. The jealousy of Othello, the ambition of Macbeth, the greed of Shylock, the love of Romeo and Juliet, the arrogance of Coriolanus, the spiritual wavering of Hamlet, are all of this kind. Tragedy in Shakespeare is individualistic, and in this sense has not the general significance of Œdipus Rex, which expresses the consciousness of a whole people. None the less, compared with Æschylus, Shakespeare represents a great step forward and not backward. Shakespeare's art is more human. At any rate, we shall no longer accept a tragedy in which God gives orders and man submits. Moreover, there will be no one to write such a tragedy.

Having broken up human relations into atoms, bourgeois society, during the period of its rise, had a great aim for itself. Personal emancipation was its name. Out of it grew the dramas of Shakespeare and Goethe's 'Faust'. Man placed himself in the center of the universe, and therefore in the center of art also. This theme sufficed for centuries. In reality, all modern literature has been nothing but an enlargement of this theme.

But to the degree in which the internal bankruptcy of bourgeois society was revealed as a result of its unbearable contradictions, the original purpose, the emancipation and qualification of the individual faded away and was relegated more and more into the sphere of a new mythology, without soul or spirit.

Leon Trotsky, *Literature and Revolution*, 1923, tr. Rose Strunsky

Karl Kraus (1874–1936), the Viennese satirist, was famous for his spell-binding public recitals of his own work, of poetic and dramatic classics, even of the operettas of Offenbach:

Kraus, when he reads in public, does not speak the words of Offenbach or Nestroy: they speak from him. And now and then a breathtaking, half-blank, half-glittering whoremonger's glance falls on the crowd before him, inviting them to the unholy marriage with the masks in which they do not recognize themselves, and for the last time invokes the evil privilege of ambiguity.

It is only now that the satirist's true face, or rather true mask, is revealed. It is the mask of Timon the misanthrope. 'Shakespeare had foreknowledge of everything'—yes. But above all of Kraus. Shakespeare portrays inhuman figures—Timon the most inhuman of them—and says: Nature would produce such a creature if she wished to create something befitting the world as your kind have fashioned it, something worthy of it. Such a creature is Timon; such is Kraus. Neither has, or wants, anything in common with men. 'An animal feud is on, and so we renounce humanity'; from a remote village in the Swiss mountains Kraus throws down this challenge to mankind, and Timon wants only the sea to weep at his grave.

WALTER BENJAMIN, 'Karl Kraus', 1931, tr. Edmund Jephcott

One of Kraus's most memorable readings took place after the assassination of the Austrian chancellor Engelbert Dollfuss in 1934. (Previously a man of the left, he had come out in support of Dollfuss, who was very much a man of the right, two years earlier, because he believed he was the one Austrian politician who understood the new danger presented to Austria by Germany.)

Kraus's public comment on the assassination came in a recital of readings from Shakespeare which was given in November 1934. The dark imagery of 'Macbeth', especially the scene in which the ghost of the murdered Banquo haunts the feast of his murderer, made a profound impression on the audience present on this occasion. In the speech of Ross on the situation of Scotland after Macbeth's seizure of power, there seemed to be a foreshadowing of the fate of Austria and of Europe:

Alas! poor country;
Almost afraid to know itself. It cannot
Be call'd our mother, but our grave; where nothing,
But who knows nothing, is once seen to smile;
Where sighs and groans and shrieks that rent the air
Are made, not mark'd; where violent sorrow seems
A modern ecstasy; the dead man's knell
Is there scarce ask'd for who; and good men's lives
Expire before the flowers in their caps,
Dying or ere they sicken.

FRANK FIELD, *The Last Days of Mankind: Karl Kraus and His Vienna*, 1967

After his change of allegiance, Kraus was subjected to bitter attacks by Social Democrats and Communists, without winning any new friends in government circles. 'Perhaps it was no accident', Frank Field writes, 'that two of the plays which figured most prominently in the satirist's public recitals during this last period of his life should have been King Lear *and* Timon of Athens, *which he read in his own translations.'*

Initially, some [Nazi] Party activists had sought a ban on Shakespeare. To them he was merely another foreigner depriving Germans of their place in the sun. But these attempts had met with disapproval from the highest quarters. Only months after Hitler became chancellor, the Party's education department had issued a pamphlet entitled *Shakespeare—a Germanic Writer* . . .

In 1936 it was noted with quiet satisfaction that there had been that year more productions of Shakespearean plays in Germany than in the rest of the world put together. A year later, a special Shakespeare festival was put on for the Hitler Youth in the presence of Rudolf Hess . . .

When, early in the war, members of a Berlin FLAK regiment took time off from guarding the skies over Hitler's capital, they promptly put on *A Midsummer Night's Dream* . . .

Inevitably, some of Shakespeare's plays had to be sacrificed: many of the royal epics with their 'narrow English patriotism' faded from the stage, though these were never officially banned. Other plays, too, were controversial. One of these, paradoxically, was *The Merchant of Venice*. Apart from being not nearly anti-Semitic enough—Marlowe's *Jew of Malta*, largely unknown in Germany, was suggested as a 'more powerful' alternative—there was the matter of Shylock's daughter marrying an

Aryan youth. In deference to 'contemporary sensitivities', Jessica tended either to become an adopted (Aryan) child bound for bliss in Lorenzo's arms, or stayed Jewish (and celibate).

GERWIN STROBL, 'Shakespeare and the Nazis', *History Today*, May 1997

I can't help telling you what immense pleasure I have had out of 'What Happens in Hamlet'. I had asked for it as a Christmas present, and when it duly appeared I sat up several nights into the small hours reading it (for it cannot properly be read too hastily). When I had finished it, I did what I don't think I have ever done before with any book; I immediately read it all over again! And that won't be the last time of reading, for there is much meat in it . . .

Having now expressed what I wanted to say I feel emboldened to ask a question or two.

I was a little bothered on hearing that the Ghost came from Purgatory for though I confess to a very hazy idea of what happened there I had not associated it with 'sulphurous and tormenting flames'. However the encyclopaedia tells me that according to the orthodox after Thomas Aquinas souls in Purgatory *were* tormented with fire, and as you do not allude to the passage above or to the 'fasting in fires' I presume you are not conscious of any difficulty.

The 'tables' speech or rather the passage about the tables has always bothered me, since it seems odd that a man, all by himself, should write down for his own satisfaction what he could always go on saying to himself. Bradley of course felt the difficulty and tried to account for it. I should like much to know what your view is . . .

One last question and I have done. In Act IV Scene III Hamlet calls Claudius 'dear Mother' and on correction gives his sardonic explanation. I am sure you have thought over this passage and can tell me what exactly is in Hamlet's mind in affecting to make a mistake. I am satisfied that it signifies something but I can't make up my mind what.

NEVILLE CHAMBERLAIN, from a letter to John Dover Wilson, 7 June 1936

Chamberlain was Chancellor of the Exchequer at the time. He became Prime Minister the following year. Wilson had published What Happens in Hamlet *in 1935.*

Sometimes, all three of us read bits of Shakespeare together—

particularly the speech of young Arthur's mother, who feared that in heaven she might not know her son, 'meagre as an ague's fit,' tormented by the executioner, his 'pretty looks' lost because of all his terrible sufferings. I found it astonishing that the English, after reading about young Arthur and the way he softened the hearts of his executioners, had not given up killing their fellowmen forever. Galina said that people went on slaughtering in the same old way after Shakespeare because they had simply not seen this play: for a long time Shakespeare was not read or staged. (I have often met Englishmen and Americans living in this country who laugh when they hear I am always reading Shakespeare: What do you need that old stuff for? they ask.) At nights I wept at the thought that executioners never read what might soften their hearts. It still makes me weep.

NADEZHDA MANDELSTAM, *Hope Abandoned*, 1972, tr. Max Hayward

The episode which Nadezhda Mandelstam recalls took place in 1939, when she was staying in Maly Yaroslavets, a town south-west of Moscow. Her husband, the poet Osip Mandelstam, had been arrested in May 1938, and was never seen again; by the beginning of 1939 she had concluded, correctly, that he was dead.

Mandelstam's two companions during her stay in Maly Yaroslavets were Galina von Meck and Galina's mother. Galina (a grandniece of Tchaikovsky) had been frequently imprisoned since the Revolution, and her husband, whom she had met in the camps, had recently been re-arrested. Her father, another victim of Stalin's Purges, had been shot: Mandelstam gives a harrowing glimpse of the last visit Galina's mother paid to him in prison.

The speech of 'young Arthur's mother' can be found in King John, *Act III, scene iii.*

In *Illusions perdues*, Balzac admiringly cites the saying, 'Collective crimes implicate no one.' But what crime is not collective? Even if the murderer confronts his victim alone, his accomplices among the living and the dead could readily be found. Yet only he is tried, only he pays the penalty.

History treats collective crimes the way Society treats individual murders; it requires only a few names and faces. It has charged Charles IX and Catherine de Medici with the crushing responsibility for the Saint Bartholomew's Day Massacre, a collective crime if ever there was one. A few Montagnards share with Robespierre the odium of the Terror and the decrees passed by the National Convention.

Our European war leaders are well aware of this pattern. Peace is barely restored before they publish their memoirs and, armed to the teeth, busily defend themselves and attack their fellow professionals with a vengeance. Fear of History's verdict has inspired more books than you could count. A statesman or military leader may be most firmly persuaded of his own innocence but he is no less apprehensive, and he is right. History is not impartial. Qualified witnesses, pro and con, succeed each other century after century; they besiege the bar of History, lustily exchanging blow for blow, for men's passions survive the scourge of violence they precipitate.

Curiously enough, when it occurs to a playwright (if he is called Shakespeare) to put historical characters on the stage, and if he permits his own ideas and inventiveness to control the situation, he offends Justice less than does official history. I was struck by this recently as I was re-reading, one after another, Shakespeare's Histories (all the *Henrys, Richard II* and *III, King John*). I had found them tedious before and had never really got inside them, but the drama of war that we ourselves have come through has strangely illuminated the beauty of these plays.

Shakespeare shows us that the source of all history lies in human emotions. The destiny of England has been guided by passions that he reveals to us in these plays; it has been incarnate in a few beings who belonged to the breed whose fearful secret Napoleon once let slip: 'What do a million lives mean to me?'

Shakespeare has helped me follow with my mind's eye the leading rôles played in our wars, and a few magazines have helped, too, I must admit. I remember, for example, a photograph in which Stalin, standing behind the very correct German diplomats, looked as if he had blood-smeared jaws, and another, taken in Poland, which showed Hitler and his Minister of Foreign Affairs walking along a gravelly road-bed, slightly stooped, their hands clasped behind their backs, and their feet apparently dragging an invisible ball and chain.

Shakespeare knew what the Reichschancellor said to himself when he was alone and leaned his forehead against the window-pane, or when he looked at himself in a mirror, or touched his cheek, murmuring, 'This is I, Hitler. . . . ' Or when the vision of a gutted Warsaw froze him motionless in the middle of the room. Perhaps, like Richard III in the horror of his last night, he murmured:

> What do I fear? Myself? There's none else by:
> Richard loves Richard; that is, I am I. . . .

The restlessly darting thoughts of the master of Germany, his agonies, and his suspicions—Shakespeare knew them all, as he knew all the conflicts of interest, all the stirrings of jealousy, the bitterness and fear enveloping the malefic man who, on September 1, 1939, gave the signal summoning death.

Like our human courts, like posterity, Shakespeare denounces the guilty person, the responsible individual. But by a miracle of genius he shows him to us encircled and engulfed by necessity; Shakespeare does not separate the man from the obscure forces that conjoined to culminate in a particular nature brimming with insolent guilt. In this fashion, Art prevails over History when it judges the creatures of History. To the end Shakespeare's vilest assassin preserves the excuse that at every moment of his life he is a human being caught up in a maelstrom of events that are not determined by him. His thirst to dominate does not spring from his own life; it comes from farther away.

FRANÇOIS MAURIAC, *Journal*, third series, 1940, tr. Adrienne Foulke

To the Londoners (1940)

Shakespeare's play, his twenty-fourth—
Time is writing it impassively.
By the leaden river what can we,
Who know what such feasts are,
Do, except read Hamlet, Caesar, Lear?
Or escort Juliet to her bed, and christen
Her death, poor dove, with torches and singing;
Or peep through the window at Macbeth,
Trembling with the one who kills from greed—
Only not this one, not this one, not this one,
This one we do not have the strength to read.

ANNA AKHMATOVA, tr. D. M. Thomas

We have only one misfortune—up to now we haven't found a dramatist who has tackled the history of the German kings. Schiller had to go and glorify that Swiss sniper [William Tell]. The English have their Shakespeare, but most of the figures in their history were brutes or absolute nothings.

ADOLF HITLER, *Table-Talk*, entry for 4 February 1942

'I've been reading *Hamlet* since I saw it at the Old Vic, I don't think I have read it before. No living being,' he mused, 'has been analysed like that creature of the imagination. It is a tremendous tale.'

He looked out at the fog drifting across the Horse Guards Parade.

'Bloody world,' he murmured. 'No human being would have come into it if he had known what it was like.'

LORD MORAN, *Winston Churchill: The Struggle for Survival*, 1966

Churchill was 79 at the time.

★   ★   ★

Uhuru!

'Freedom!'—the African liberation-cry, and the first word uttered by Caliban in Une tempête *(1969), the reworking of* The Tempest *by the black poet Aimé Césaire (born in Martinique in 1913). In Césaire's version, Prospero is the colonialist exploiter, obsessed by* la puissance, *Caliban is the exploited native, intent on* la liberté. *Caliban is also natural man in a far more positive sense than anything Shakespeare conceived of—natural as opposed to artificial, healthily at one with his environment. In this, too, he regards Prospero as his deadly enemy. ('Prospero, c'est l'anti-Nature. Moi je dis: A bas l'anti-Nature!')*

At the end of the play, Prospero and Caliban are left alone on the island. Rejecting Prospero's pact of friendship, Caliban tells him

> Et je sais qu'un jour
> mon poing nu, mon seul poing nu
> suffira pour écraser ton monde!

[And I know that one day my bare fist, my bare fist alone, will be enough to destroy your world.]

Prospero retorts by accusing Caliban of poisonous ingratitude, and comparing him to the opossum that bites the hand 'qui la tire de la nuit' ('which drags it out of the dark'). In the very last scene Prospero finds himself facing an invasion of actual opossums: Caliban has slipped away.

Césaire's reading of The Tempest *as a colonialist myth was anticipated by the ethnographer O. Mannoni in* Psychologie de la colonisation *(1950; pub-*

lished in English in 1956 as Prospero and Caliban), *a book partly inspired by the author's observations during the 1948 colonial uprising in what was then Madagascar.*

If the Robben Islanders had a common culture and text, it was not the Bible or the Koran, but Shakespeare. 'Somehow Shakespeare always had something to say to us,' said Kathrada, who had once tried to argue that Shakespeare was a racist, but was soon shouted down. 'We would recite long, long passages from Shakespeare,' Neville Alexander recalled. 'Usually the more militant passages: *Coriolanus, Julius Caesar*, of course, and *Henry V.*' Shakespeare's political relevance to black South Africans was clear enough: *Julius Caesar* offered a kind of textbook for revolutionary theory. But his deeper understanding of human courage, suffering and sacrifice reassured the prisoners that they were part of a universal drama.

Sonny Venkatrathnam kept a copy of Shakespeare's works on his shelf, disguised behind Indian religious pictures. 'I'm not a religious person, but I wouldn't part with this, because it gave us such joys and countless readings,' he said later. He circulated it to all the inmates of the single cells, to autograph their favourite passages, providing a unique jailbirds' anthology. Kathrada chose Henry V's 'Once more unto the breach.' Wilton Mkwayi chose Malvolio's 'Some are born great', from *Twelfth Night*. Govan Mbeki chose the opening lines of the same play: 'If music be the food of love'. Billy Nair chose Caliban's lines from *The Tempest*: 'This island's mine, by Sycorax my mother'. Sisulu chose Shylock's:

> Still have I borne it with a patient shrug,
> For suff'rance is the badge of all our tribe . . .

Neville Alexander chose the sonnet beginning:

> Like as the waves make towards the pebbled shore,
> So do our minutes hasten to their end.

Andrew Masondo chose Mark Antony's

> O! pardon me, thou bleeding piece of earth,
> That I am meek and gentle with these butchers.

Mandela also chose a passage from *Julius Caesar*, with his signature for 16 December 1977:

Cowards die many times before their deaths;
The valiant never taste of death but once.
Of all the wonders that I yet have heard,
It seems to me most strange that men should fear;
Seeing that death, a necessary end,
Will come when it will come.

ANTHONY SAMPSON, Mandela, 1999

Let me imagine, since facts are so hard to come by, what would have happened had Shakespeare had a wonderfully gifted sister, called Judith, let us say. Shakespeare himself went, very probably,—his mother was an heiress—to the grammar school, where he may have learnt Latin—Ovid, Virgil and Horace—and the elements of grammar and logic. He was, it is well known, a wild boy who poached rabbits, perhaps shot a deer, and had, rather sooner than he should have done, to marry a woman in the neighbourhood, who bore him a child rather quicker than was right. That escapade sent him to seek his fortune in London. He had, it seemed, a taste for the theatre; he began by holding horses at the stage door. Very soon he got work in the theatre, became a successful actor, and lived at the hub of the universe, meeting everybody, knowing everybody, practising his art on the boards, exercising his wits in the streets, and even getting access to the palace of the queen. Meanwhile his extraordinarily gifted sister, let us suppose, remained at home. She was as adventurous, as imaginative, as agog to see the world as he was. But she was not sent to school. She had no chance of learning grammar and logic, let alone of reading Horace and Virgil. She picked up a book now and then, one of her brother's perhaps, and read a few pages. But then her parents came in and told her to mend the stockings or mind the stew and not moon about with books and papers. They would have spoken sharply but kindly, for they were substantial people who knew the conditions of life for a woman and loved their daughter—indeed, more likely than not she was the apple of her father's eye. Perhaps she scribbled some pages up in an apple loft on the sly, but was careful to hide them or set fire to them. Soon, however, before she was out of her teens, she was to be betrothed to the son of a neighbouring wool-stapler. She cried out that marriage was hateful to her, and for that she was severely beaten by her father. Then he ceased to scold her. He begged her instead not to hurt him, not to shame him in this matter of her marriage. He would give her a chain of beads or a fine petticoat, he said; and there were tears in his eyes. How could she disobey him? How could she break his heart? The force of her own gift alone drove her to it. She made up a small parcel of her belongings, let herself down by a rope one summer's night and took the road to London. She was not seventeen. The birds that sang in the hedge were not more musical than she was. She had the quickest fancy, a gift like her brother's, for the tune of words. Like him, she had a taste for the theatre. She stood at the stage door; she wanted to act, she said. Men laughed in her face. The manager—a fat, loose-lipped man—guffawed. He bellowed something about poodles dancing and women acting—no woman, he said, could possibly be an actress. He hinted—you can imagine what. She could get no training in her craft. Could she even seek her dinner in a tavern or roam the streets at midnight? Yet her genius was for fiction and lusted to feed abundantly upon the lives of men and women and the study of their ways. At last—for she was very young, oddly like Shakespeare the poet in her face, with the same grey eyes and rounded brows—at last Nick Greene the actor-manager took pity on her; she found herself with child by that gentleman and so—who shall measure the heat and violence of the poet's heart when caught and tangled in a woman's body?—killed herself one winter's night and lies buried at some cross-roads where the omnibuses now stop outside the Elephant and Castle.

VIRGINIA WOOLF, A Room of One's Own, 1929

This excursion has become one of the classic texts of modern feminism.

Less attention has been paid to Shakespeare's actual sister, Joan. She was five years older than the poet, married William Hart, a hatter, had four children, and lived long enough to see the early stages of the Civil War, dying in 1646. In his will (she was by this time a widow) Shakespeare left her £20, his wearing apparel, and a life tenancy in the family house—the Birthplace—at a nominal rent. She was the only one of his siblings to survive him.

Shakespeare investigates society, but he does not take it for granted or move within it like a fish in water. He writes marvellously about political power, but he does not take politics for granted and he sees its place in human life as problematic. He conceives of the total breakdown of human order.

IRIS MURDOCH, 'Existentialists and Mystics', 1970

All's Well That Ends

or, Shakespeare Unmasked

I'm afraid he'll have to go.
He won't pass muster these days.

Black men he didn't like: he made them
Proud and gullible and jealous and black
(Good fighters, but otherwise out of their depth).
He didn't like women, but neither
Was he a frank and manly homosexual.
'Woman delights not me: no, nor man neither . . . '
As for Jews, his complaint was that they were
Interested in money, were not Christians, and
If you pricked them they bled all over the place.
They deserved to have their daughters make
Unsuitable marriages.

(Put like that, Jews sound like a lot of us.
I shall have to rewrite this bit.)

A very dangerous man.
Think of all the trouble caused by that
Thoroughly offensive play of his, *Coriolanus*.
One night it wounded the feelings of the fascists,
The next it wounded the feelings of the communists.

He was anti-Scottish: it took an English army
To settle the hash of that kilted butcher
Macbeth. He made jokes about the Welsh, the
French, the Danes, the Italians and the Spanish.
He accused a West Indian (or possibly Algerian)
Of trying to rape a white girl unsuccessfully.
If it wasn't a base Judean he displayed
As criminally careless with pearls, then
It was an equally base Indian. Thank God
He hadn't heard of the Australians!

To be sure, he was the servant of his public,
A rough unlettered lot, who rarely washed
And dwelt in the polluted alleys of London
Or the corners of slippery palaces. There wasn't

A drama critic of independent mind among them.
Even so, he must bear most of the blame,
He could have stayed in Stratford and led a
Quiet and useful life.

Worst of all, he believed in good and evil,
And mixed them up in a deliberately nasty
And confusing way. A shifty character,
He pictured the human condition as one of
Unending and uneasy struggle, not to be
Resolved in a *haiku* or even a television
Debate. He made difficulties, he made
Much ado about nothing.

Now that we've stripped him clean
Of his poetry, we can see him plain.
Plainly he'll have to go.

D. J. ENRIGHT, 1973

EARLY ENCOUNTERS

My first introduction to English imaginative literature was 'Nicholas Nickleby.' It is extraordinary how well Mrs Nickleby could chatter disconnectedly in Polish and the sinister Ralph rage in that language. As to the Crummles family and the family of the learned Squeers it seemed as natural to them as their native speech. It was, I have no doubt, an excellent translation. This must have been in the year '70. But I really believe that I am wrong. That book was not my first introduction to English literature. My first acquaintance was (or were) the 'Two Gentlemen of Verona,' and that in the very MS of my father's translation. It was during our exile in Russia, and it must have been less than a year after my mother's death, because I remember myself in the black blouse with a white border of my heavy mourning. We were living together, quite alone, in a small house on the outskirts of the town of T——. That afternoon, instead of going out to play in the large yard which we shared with our landlord, I had lingered in the room in which my father generally wrote. What emboldened me to clamber into his chair I am sure I don't know, but a couple of hours afterwards he discovered me kneeling in it with my elbows on the table and my head held in both hands over the MS of loose pages. I was greatly confused, expecting to get into trouble. He stood in the doorway looking at me with some surprise, but the only thing he said after a moment of silence was:

'Read the page aloud.'

Luckily the page lying before me was not overblotted with erasures and corrections, and my father's handwriting was otherwise extremely legible. When I got to the end he nodded and I flew out of doors thinking myself lucky to have escaped reproof for that piece of impulsive audacity. I have tried to discover since the reason of this mildness, and I imagine that all unknown to myself I had earned, in my father's mind, the right to some latitude in my relations with his writing-table. It was only a month before, or perhaps it was only a week before, that I had read to him aloud from beginning to end, and to his perfect satisfaction, as he lay on his bed, not being very well at the time, the proofs of his translation of Victor Hugo's 'Toilers of the Sea.' Such was my title to consideration, I believe, and also my first introduction to the sea in literature. If I do not remember where, how and when I learned to read, I am not likely to forget the process of being trained in the art of reading aloud. My poor father, an admirable reader himself, was the most exacting of masters. I reflect proudly that I must have read that page of 'Two Gentlemen of Verona' tolerably well at the age of eight. The next time I met them was in a 5s. one-volume edition of the dramatic works of William Shakespeare, read in Falmouth, at odd moments of the day, to the noisy accompaniment of caulkers' mallets driving oakum into the deck-seams of a ship in dry dock. We had run in, in a sinking condition and with the crew refusing duty after a month of weary battling with the gales of the North Atlantic. Books are an integral part of one's life and my Shakespearean associations are with that first year of our bereavement, the last I spent with my father in exile

JOSEPH CONRAD, A Personal Record (originally Some Reminiscences), 1908–9

In addition to The Two Gentlemen of Verona, *Conrad's father, Apollo Korzeniowski, translated* The Comedy of Errors *and* Much Ado About Nothing. *He also published a long essay, 'Studies in the Dramatic Element in the Plays of Shakespeare' (1868), which some critics have seen as exerting an important influence on his son's literary ideals.*

He [Dr Johnson] once told me another accident of his younger years. He was just nine years old when having got the play of *Hamlet* to read in his father's kitchen, he read on very quietly till he came to the Ghost Scene, when he hurried upstairs to the shop door that he might see folks about him.

HESTER THRALE, later Piozzi, diary, 1777

Hans Christian Andersen was born in 1805. As a child, he acted out scenes from Shakespeare's plays in his puppet theatre:

The bold descriptions, the heroic incidents, witches and ghosts were exactly to my taste. I saw Hamlet's ghost, and lived upon the heath with Lear. The more persons died in a play, the more interesting I thought it was.

The Story of My Life, 1855, tr. Horace Scudder

One day, towards the end of 1907, my father was standing in the yard of the outer house with a book in his hand and, seeing me, asked me to come up, for, he said, he wanted me to learn something new and in English. When he gave me the book I found that it was *Julius Caesar*. He pointed to a place and directed me to read, and I began: 'That you have wronged me doth appear in this . . .' That was the first passage in Shakespeare that I learned by heart. My brother was given the part of Brutus, and between us we acted nearly the whole dialogue, which did not take us long to learn. The second dialogue we did together was Cassius's instigation of Brutus (Act I, Scene 2). The next year we went on the school stage and acted one of the scenes with great spirit, I whipping out a dagger and crying:

> 'Come, Antony, and young Octavius, come,
> Revenge yourselves alone on Cassius,
> For Cassius is aweary of the world . . .'

But, always reciting the part of Cassius, I got myself a bad reputation. I was small and thin, and some clever people began to remark when they saw me: 'Yond Cassius has a lean and hungry look; he thinks too much: such men are dangerous. . . . I wish he were fatter.' And, as is proverbial, it was the enemy at home, my brother, who took the greatest and the most malicious delight in reminding me of the moral implications of my slight build in Julio-Shakespearean rhetoric.

Nirad C. Chaudhuri, The Autobiography of an Unknown Indian, 1951

At the time of his first encounter with Julius Caesar *Chaudhuri was 10 years old.*

'I recollect when I first heard of Shakespeare, when I went to school at Annan, where there was rather more acquaintance with things in general than in our house. I had never heard of Shakespeare there: my Father never, I believe, read a word of him in his life. But one day in the street of Annan I found a wandering Italian resting a board with very bad imagery—"images" (C. imitated the cry), and among them a figure leaning on a pedestal with "The Cloudcapt towers," etc. Various passers-by looked on, and a woman read aloud the verses, very badly, and then the name below, "Shankespeare," that was the way she gave it, "Shankespeare" (laughing).'

Thomas Carlyle, as reported in the diary of William Allingham, 1876

Reading M. N. D. in Form 4B

Australia, 1942

Miss Coulter rules us middle-class children
Whose fathers can't afford the best schools
With blue, small, crow-tracked, cruel eyes.
Philomel with melody—a refrain
Summoning the nightingale, the brown bird
Which could not live a summer in this heat.

Queen Titania, unaware of Oberon,
Is sleeping on a bank. Her fairy watch
Sings lullaby, sings lullaby,
The warm snake hatches out in her dream.
Miss Coulter is too fat for love,
We cannot imagine her like Miss Holliday
Booking for week-ends at the seaside
With officers on leave. This is not Athens
In the woods of Warwickshire—
Lordly the democratic sun
Rides our gross and southerly glass.
Miss Coulter sets the homework. Thirty boys
Leave the bard to tire on his morning wing;
Out on the asphalt the teams for Saturday
Wait, annunciations in purple ink,
Torments in locker rooms, nothing to hope for
But sleep, the reasonable view of magic.
We do not understand Shakespearean objects
Who must work and play: that gold stems from the sky:
It poisons 1942. To be young is to be in hell,
Miss Coulter will insulate us from this genius,
Rock the ground whereon these sleepers be.

PETER PORTER, 1964

Warwick.   Wil't please your grace to go along with us?
Prince Hal. No I will sit and watch here by the king.
                            [*Exeunt all but P. H.*
             'Why doth the crown lie there upon his pillow
             Being so troublesome a bedfellow?

Oh polished perturbation! golden care!
That keepst the ports of slumber open wide
To many a watchful night—sleep with it now!
Yet not so sound, and half so deeply sweet,
As he whose brow with homely biggin bound
Snores out the watch of night.'

King.   Harry I know not
The meaning of the word you just have used.

P.   What word, my liege?

K.   The word I mean is 'biggin.'

P.   It means a kind of woolen nightcap, sir,
With which the peasantry are wont to bind
Their wearied heads, ere that they take their rest.

K.   Thanks for your explanation, pray proceed.

P.   'Snores out the watch of night. Oh majesty!
When thou dost pinch thy bearer thou dost sit
Like a rich armour, worn in heat of day
That scalds with safety.'

K.   Scalding ne'er is safe
For it produces heat and feverishness
And blisters on the parched and troubled skin.

P.   Pray interrupt not. 'By his gates of breath
There lies a downy feather which stirs not.'

K.   I knew not that there was one, brush it off.

P.   'Did he suspire that light and weightless down
Perforce must move.'

K.   And it *hath* moved already.

P.   It hath *not* moved. 'My gracious lord! my father!
This sleep is sound indeed, this is a sleep
That from this golden rigol hath divorced
So many English—'

K.   What meaneth rigol, Harry?

P.   My liege, I know not, save that it doth enter
Most apt into the metre.

K.   True, it doth.
But wherefore use a word which hath no meaning?

P.   My lord, the word is said, for it hath passed
My lips, and all the powers upon this earth
Can not unsay it.

K.   You are right, proceed.

P.   'So many English kings; thy due from me
         Is tears and heavy sorrows of the blood
         Which nature, love, and filial tenderness,
         Shall, oh dear father, pay thee plenteously:
         My due from thee is this imperial crown
         Which as—'

K.   'Tis *not* your due, sir! I deny it!

P.   It *is*, my liege! How dare you contradict me?
         Moreover how can you, a sleeper, know
         That which another doth soliloquise?

K.   Your rhetoric is vain, for it is true:
         Therefore no arguments can prove it false.

P.   Yet sure it is not possible, my liege!

K.   Upon its possibility I dwelt not
         I merely said 'twas true.

P.   But yet, my liege,
         What is not possible can never happen,
         Therefore this cannot.

K.   Which do you deny
         That I have heard you or that I'm asleep?

P.   That you're asleep, my liege.

K.   Go on, go on,
         I see you are not fit to reason with.

P.   'Which as immediate from thy place and blood
         Derives itself to me. Lo, here it sits,—
         Which heaven itself shall guard, and put the world's
            whole strength
         Into which giant arm, it shall not force
         This lineal honour from me: this from thee
         Will I to mine leave as 'tis left to me.'

> LEWIS CARROLL (Charles Lutwidge Dodgson), 'A Quotation from
> Shakespeare with slight Improvements', 1845

Written by Carroll at the age of 13.

In 1864 Edmund Gosse, aged 14, was taken by his father to a religious confer-
ence 'held in an immense hall, somewhere in the north of London':

An elderly man, fat and greasy, with a voice like a bassoon, and an imperturbable assurance, was denouncing the spread of infidelity, and the lukewarmness of professing Christians, who refrained from battling the wickedness at their doors. They were like the Laodiceans, whom the angel of the Apocalypse spewed out of his mouth. For instance, who, the orator asked, is now rising to check the outburst of idolatry in our midst? 'At this very moment,' he went on, 'there is proceeding, unreproved, a blasphemous celebration of the birth of Shakespeare, a lost soul now suffering for his sins in hell!' My sensation was that of one who has suddenly been struck on the head; stars and sparks beat round me. If some person I loved had been grossly insulted in my presence, I could not have felt more powerless in anguish. No one in that vast audience raised a word of protest, and my spirits fell to their nadir. This, be it remarked, was the earliest intimation that had reached me of the tercentenary of the Birth at Stratford, and I had not the least idea what could have provoked the outburst of outraged godliness.

But Shakespeare was certainly in the air. When we returned to the hotel that noon, my Father of his own accord reverted to the subject. I held my breath, prepared to endure fresh torment. What he said, however, surprised and relieved me. 'Brother So-and-so,' he remarked, 'was not in my judgment justified in saying what he did. The uncovenanted mercies of God are not revealed to us. Before so rashly speaking of Shakespeare as "a lost soul in hell," he should have remembered how little we know of the poet's history. The light of salvation was widely disseminated in the land during the reign of Queen Elizabeth, and we cannot know that Shakespeare did not accept the atonement of Christ in simple faith before he came to die.' The concession will to-day seem meagre to gay and worldly spirits, but words cannot express how comfortable it was to me. I gazed at my Father with loving eyes across the cheese and celery, and if the waiter had not been present I believe I might have hugged him in my arms.

Father and Son, 1907

Ophélie

I

Sur l'onde calme et noire où dorment les étoiles
La blanche Ophélia flotte comme un grand lys,
Flotte très lentement, couchée en ses longs voiles . . .
—On entend dans les bois lointains des hallalis.

Voici plus de mille ans que la triste Ophélie
Passe, fantôme blanc, sur le long fleuve noir.
Voici plus de mille ans que sa douce folie
Murmure sa romance à la brise du soir.

Le vent baise ses seins et déploie en corolle
Ses grands voiles bercés mollement par les eaux;
Les saules frissonnants pleurent sur son épaule,
Sur son grand front rêveur s'inclinent les roseaux.

Les nénuphars froissés soupirent autour d'elle;
Elle éveille parfois, dans un aune qui dort,
Quelque nid, d'où s'échappe un petit frisson d'aile:
—Un chant mystérieux tombe des astres d'or.

2

O pâle Ophélia! belle comme la neige!
Oui, tu mourus, enfant, par un fleuve emporté!
—C'est que les vents tombant des grands monts de Norwège
T'avaient parlé tout bas de l'âpre liberté;

C'est qu'un souffle, tordant ta grande chevelure,
A ton esprit rêveur portait d'étranges bruits;
Que ton cœur écoutait le chant de la Nature
Dans les plaintes de l'arbre et les soupirs des nuits;

C'est que la voix des mers, folles, immense râle,
Brisait ton sein d'enfant, trop humain et trop doux;
C'est qu'un matin d'avril un beau cavalier pâle,
Un pauvre fou, s'assit muet à tes genoux!

Ciel! Amour! Liberté! Quel rêve, ô pauvre Folle!
Tu te fondais à lui comme une neige au feu;
Tes grandes visions étranglaient ta parole
—Et l'Infini terrible effara ton œil bleu!

3

—Et le Poète dit qu'aux rayons des étoiles
Tu viens chercher, la nuit, les fleurs que tu cueillis;
Et qu'il a vu sur l'eau, couchée en ses longs voiles,
La blanche Ophélia flotter, comme un grand lys.

[On the calm black waves where the stars sleep, white Ophelia floats by like a great lily, floats very slowly, lying in her long veils . . . You can hear the cries of huntsmen in the distant woods.

For more than a thousand years sad Ophelia has passed, a white ghost on the long black river; for more than a thousand years her sweet madness has murmured its song on the evening breeze.

The wind kisses her breast and unfolds like petals her great veils rocked gently by the water; the trembling willows weep over her shoulders and the reeds bend towards her dreaming brow.

Crushed water-lilies sigh around her; sometimes, in a sleeping alder-tree, she awakens the brief flutter of a wing in a nest. A mysterious singing drifts down from golden stars.

O pale Ophelia, fair as the snow! Yes, you perished, child, carried off by the current! It is because the winds blowing from the great mountains of Norway had whispered to you of harsh liberty.

It is because a breath, twisting your long tresses, carried strange sounds to your dreaming spirit; because your heart heard the song of nature in the lamentations of trees and the sighs of the night.

It is because the voice of the sea, an immense death-rattle, bruised your childlike breast, which was too human and too soft; it is because one April morning a handsome pale companion, a poor madman, sat silent at your knees.

Heaven! Love! Liberty! what a dream, o poor mad one! You melted into it like snow in a fire; your vast visions strangled your speech, and the dread Infinite overwhelmed your blue eyes!

And the poet says that at night, by starlight, you seek the flowers you gathered; and that he has seen in the water, lying in her long veils, white Ophelia float by, like a great lily.]

ARTHUR RIMBAUD, 1870

Written when Rimbaud was 15 years old.

Then there was Alice Foley who had to endure home performances by her father, a Bolton millhand:

I can remember the agony of having to be Desdemona. You see, he knew all the tragedies of Shakespeare and he would enact them, you see, half drunk he would enact them. And he used to go stalking round the house . . . he was a majestic man . . . giving us Hamlet's soliloquies and all these long speeches and if he took Othello he would fling me suddenly into either an armchair or on the old horsehair sofa and smother me with a cushion, you know. I can remember to this day the stuffy old cushion that he used to put over my mouth. And then just as suddenly he would fall back in his chair and he would say, 'The pity of it, Iago, the pity of it.' And it was his own soliloquy. It was the pity of it, you see, that he could do that kind of thing so magnificently, and yet . . .

JONATHAN ROSE, *The Intellectual Life of the British Working Classes*, 2001

Alice Foley was born in 1891.

Remember, when we were very young maids, one day we were discoursing about lovers, and we did enjoin each other to confess who professed to love us, and whom we loved, and I confessed I only was in love with three dead men, which were dead long before my time, the one was *Caesar*, for his valour, the second *Ovid*, for his wit, and the third was our countryman *Shakespeare*, for his comical and tragical humour; but soon after we both married two worthy men, and I will leave you to your own husband, for you know best what he is; as for my husband, I know him to have the valour of *Caesar*, the fancy and wit of *Ovid*, and the tragical, especially comical art of *Shakespeare*; in truth he is as far beyond *Shakespeare* for comical humour, as *Shakespeare* beyond an ordinary poet in that way.

MARGARET CAVENDISH, DUCHESS OF NEWCASTLE, *CCXI Sociable Letters*, 1664

A VARIETY OF VIEWS

If Shakespeare be considered as a MAN, born in a rude age, and educated in the lowest manner, without any instruction, either from the world or from books, he may be regarded as a prodigy. If represented as a POET, capable of furnishing a proper entertainment to a refined or intelligent audience, we must abate much of this eulogy. In his compositions, we regret, that many irregularities, and even absurdities, should so frequently disfigure the animated and passionate scenes intermixed with them; and at the same time, we perhaps admire the more those beauties, on account of their being surrounded with such deformities. A striking peculiarity of sentiment, adapted to a single character, he frequently hits, as it were, by inspiration; but a reasonable propriety of thought he cannot for any time uphold. Nervous and picturesque expressions as well as descriptions abound in him; but it is in vain we look either for purity or simplicity of diction. His total ignorance of all theatrical art and conduct, however material a defect, yet, as it affects the spectator rather than the reader, we can more easily excuse, than that want of taste which often prevails in his productions, and which gives way only by intervals to the irradiations of genius. A great and fertile genius he certainly possessed, and one enriched equally with a tragic and comic vein; but he ought to be cited as a proof, how dangerous it is to rely on these advantages alone for attaining an excellence in the finer arts. And there may even remain a suspicion, that we over-rate, if possible, the greatness of his genius; in the same manner as bodies often appear more gigantic, on account of their being disproportioned and misshapen. He died in 1616, aged fifty-three years.

DAVID HUME, *History of England*, 1754

Oliver Goldsmith deplores the fare offered by the theatres of the day:

We seem to be pretty much in the situation of travellers at a Scotch inn: vile entertainment is served up, complained of and sent down; up comes worse, and that also is changed; and every change makes our wretched cheer more unsavoury. What must be done? only sit down contented, cry up all that comes before us, and admire even the absurdities of Shakespeare.

Let the reader suspend his censure; I admire the beauties of this great father of our stage as much as they deserve but could wish, for the honour of our country, and for his honour too, that many of his scenes were forgotten. A man blind of one eye should always be painted in profile. Let the spectator who assists at any of these new revived pieces only ask himself whether he would approve such a performance if written by a modern poet; if he would not, then his applause proceeds merely from the sound of a name and an empty veneration for antiquity. In fact, the revival of those pieces of forced humour, far-fetch'd conceit, and unnatural hyperbole which have been ascribed to Shakespeare, is rather gibbeting than raising a statue to his memory; it is rather a trick of the actor, who thinks it safest acting in exaggerated characters, and who by out-stepping nature chuses to exhibit the ridiculous outré of an harlequin under the sanction of this venerable name.

An Enquiry into the Present State of Polite Learning in Europe, 1759

Goldsmith: 'I am afraid we will have no good plays now. The taste of the audience is spoiled by the pantomime of Shakespeare, the wonderful changes and shifting.' *Thomas Davies*: 'Nay, but you will allow that Shakespeare has great merit?' *Goldsmith*: 'No, I know Shakespeare very well.'

Here I said nothing, but thought him a most impudent puppy.

JAMES BOSWELL, *Boswell's London Journal*, entry for 25 December 1762

I cannot avoid mentioning here an instance of repose in that faithful and accurate painter of nature, Shakespeare; the short dialogue between Duncan and Banquo, whilst they are approaching the gates of Macbeth's castle. Their conversation very naturally turns upon the beauty of its situation, and the pleasantness of the air; and Banquo observing the martlets' nests in every recess of the cornice, remarks that where those birds most breed and haunt, the air is delicate. The subject of this quiet and easy conversation gives that repose so necessary to the mind, after the tumultuous bustle of the preceding scenes, and perfectly contrasts the scene of horror that so immediately succeeds. It seems as if Shakespeare asked himself, what is a Prince likely to say to his attendants on such an occasion? The modern writers seem, on the contrary, to be always searching for new thoughts, such as never could occur in the situation represented.

SIR JOSHUA REYNOLDS, Discourses on Art: Discourse VIII, 1778

He wrote an inimitable history of all the forms of derangement, in the tragedy of *King Lear*.

BENJAMIN RUSH, Medical Enquiries and Observations Upon Diseases of the Mind, 1812

Rush has often been called the father of American psychiatry. (He was also one of the signatories of the Declaration of Independence.) To illustrate his point about Lear, *he cites a number of passages, including Gloucester's lines at the end of Act IV, scene vi:*

> Better I were distract:
> So should my thoughts be sever'd from my griefs,
> And woes by wrong imagination lose
> The knowledge of themselves.

Talking of Shakespeare, Byron said, that he owed one half of his popularity to his low origin, which, like charity, covereth a multitude of sins with the multitude, and the other half, to the remoteness of the time at which he wrote from our own days. 'All his vulgarisms', continued Byron, 'are attributed to the circumstances of his birth and breeding depriving him of a good education; hence they are to be excused, and the obscurities with which his works abound are all easily explained away by the simple statement, that he wrote about 200 years ago, and that the terms then in familiar use are now become obsolete. With two such good excuses, as want of education, and having written above 200 years before our time, any writer may pass muster; and when to these is added the being a sturdy hind of low degree, which to three parts of the community in England has a peculiar attraction, one ceases to wonder at his supposed popularity; I say supposed, for who goes to see his plays, and who, except country parsons, or mouthing, stage-struck, theatrical amateurs, read them?' I told Byron what really was, and is, my impression, that he was not sincere in his depreciation of our immortal bard; and I added, that I preferred believing him insincere, than incapable of judging works, which his own writings proved he must, more than most other men, feel the beauties of. He laughed, and replied, 'That the compliment I paid to his writings was so entirely at the expense of his sincerity, that he had no cause to be flattered; but that, knowing I was one of those who worshipped Shakespeare, he forgave me, and would only bargain that I made equal allowance for his worship of Pope.'

LADY BLESSINGTON, Conversations of Lord Byron, 1834

Later in the same passage Lady Blessington adds:

I have rarely met with a person more conversant with the works of Shakespeare than was Byron. I have heard him quote passages from them repeatedly; and in a tone that marked how well he appreciated their beauty, which certainly lost nothing in his delivery of them, as few possessed a more harmonious voice or a more elegant pronunciation than did Byron. Could there be a less equivocal proof of his admiration of our immortal bard than the tenacity with which his memory retained the finest passages of all his works?

Conversations of Lord Byron

He affected to doubt whether Shakespeare was so great a genius as he has been taken for, and whether fashion had not a great deal to do with it; an extravagance, of which none but a patrician author could have been guilty.

LEIGH HUNT, Lord Byron and Some of His Contemporaries, 1828

The poet touches on parliamentary or religious questions extremely seldom; and it may be observed that in *King John* the great movements which led to Magna Carta are as good as left out of sight; on the contrary he lives and moves among the personal contrasts offered by the feudal system, its rights and duties.

LEOPOLD VON RANKE, A History of England, 1859–68, tr. C. W. Boase and
G. W. Kitchin

Shakespeare's Roman dramas had an especial attraction for Macaulay. Never was a great scholar so little of a pedant. He knew that what Shakespeare could teach him about human nature was worth more than anything he himself could have taught Shakespeare about Roman history and Roman institutions.

GEORGE OTTO TREVELYAN, Life of Lord Macaulay, 1876

I have tried lately to read Shakespeare, and found it so intolerably dull that it nauseated me.

CHARLES DARWIN, *Autobiography*, written 1876

Darwin had enjoyed Shakespeare as a schoolboy, however—the historical plays, at least—and he regretted 'the curious and lamentable loss of the higher aesthetic tastes' which overtook him in later life.

Imagine that someone with a capacity to imagine terrifying nightmares has pictured to himself some horror or other that is absolutely unbearable. Then it happens to him, this very horror happens to him. Humanly speaking, his collapse is altogether certain—and in despair his soul's despair fights to be permitted to despair, to attain, if you please, the composure to despair, to obtain the total personality's consent to despair and be in despair; consequently, there is nothing or no one he would curse more than an attempt or the person making an attempt to hinder him from despairing, as the poet's poet so splendidly and incomparably expresses it (*Richard II*, III, 3):

> *Verwünscht sei Vetter, der mich abgelenkt*
> *Von dem bequemen Wege zur Verzweiflung.*

> [Beshrew thee, cousin, which didst lead me forth
> Of that sweet way I was in to despair!]

SØREN KIERKEGAARD, *The Sickness Unto Death*, 1849, tr. Howard V. Hong and Edna H. Hong

Kierkegaard quotes from the German translation by Schlegel and Tieck.

The line Shakespeare gives to Macbeth (III, 2) is psychologically masterful: *Sündentsprossne Werke erlangen nur durch Sünde Kraft und Stärke* [Works arising in sin gain strength and power only through sin]. In other words, deep within itself sin has a consistency, and in this consistency in evil itself it also has a certain strength.

SØREN KIERKEGAARD, *The Sickness Unto Death*

Kierkegaard again quotes from the translation by Schlegel and Tieck, which is somewhat closer to his purpose than what Shakespeare actually wrote: 'Things bad begun make strong themselves by ill.'

Discussing 'the unchangeable nature of character', and the results which flow
from it, Schopenhauer takes as an example the Earl of Northumberland, as
portrayed by Shakespeare in Richard II *and* Henry IV Parts One *and* Two:
'He appears in only a few scenes that are distributed over fifteen acts; and so, if
we do not read with all our attention, we may easily lose sight of the character
that is depicted in such widely separated passages and of its moral identity.'

In fact Northumberland repeatedly reveals himself as either a rebel or an
undependable ally, but Schopenhauer also reflects on the apparent neutrality
with which Shakespeare allows him to make his case and rationalize his
decisions:

Everywhere he makes this Earl appear with noble knightly dignity and
use appropriate language, and on occasions he puts into his mouth very
fine and even sublime passages. For he is far from doing what Schiller
does, who likes to paint the devil black and whose moral approval or
disapproval of the characters portrayed sounds through their own
words. With Shakespeare, and also with Goethe, everyone is, while he is
present and speaks, perfectly right even if he were the devil himself.

ARTHUR SCHOPENHAUER, *Parerga and Paralipomena*, 1851, tr. E. F. J. Payne

Moreover, through the whole piece [*Hamlet*] something like a strong
wind seems to be blowing: a progression and a development of passions
and events which, although irregular if judged by our habit, assume a
character of unity which enthrones that virtue in our mind when we
think back to the play . . . There is a secret logic, an unperceived order in
those accumulations of details, which would seem to add up to nothing
more than a shapeless mountain, but in which one still feels distinct
parts, passages well planned to afford relief, and at all times continuity
and consistency.

EUGÈNE DELACROIX, journal, March 1855, tr. Walter Pach

Here at Baden, on the 25th of September, still considering this matter, I
notice from my window the great similarity that Shakespeare has to
external nature; I am thinking of the scenery that appears before my
eyes, for example, and I would note especially that heaping up of details,
the ensemble of which none the less contrives to suggest a unity to the
mind.

EUGÈNE DELACROIX, journal, 1855

But how is one to define that charming class of picture, such as the *Hamlet in the graveyard scene*, and the *Farewell of Romeo and Juliet*, which are so deeply moving and attractive that once it has bathed in their little worlds of melancholy, the eye can no longer escape them, and the mind is for ever in their thrall?

> *Et le tableau quitté* nous *tourmente et nous suit.*°

But this is not the Hamlet which Rouvière° showed us recently, and with such brilliant success—the sour, unhappy, violent Hamlet, driving his restlessness to the pitch of frenzy. There you have the romantic *strangeness* of the great tragedian; but Delacroix, more faithful perhaps to his text, has shown us a delicate and pallid Hamlet, a Hamlet with white, feminine hands, a refined, soft and somewhat irresolute nature, and an almost colourless eye.

CHARLES BAUDELAIRE, 'Eugène Delacroix', 1855, tr. Jonathan Mayne

Baudelaire's article was one of three he devoted to the Exposition Universelle of 1855. In an earlier passage in the piece, he discussed two of Delacroix's 'big pictures', the Justice of Trajan *and the* Taking of Constantinople by the Crusaders. *The first he described as 'a marvellously luminous picture, so airy, so full of tumult and splendour!' The second he praised for its 'tempestuous and gloomy harmony':*

What a sky, and what a sea! All is tumult and tranquillity, as in the aftermath of a great event. The city, ranged behind the Crusaders who have just passed through it, stretches back into the distance with a miraculous truth. And everywhere the fluttering and waving of flags, unfurling and snapping their bright folds in the transparent atmosphere! Everywhere the restless, stirring crowd, the tumult of arms, the ceremonial splendour of the clothes, and a rhetorical truth of gesture amid the great occasions of life! These two pictures are of an essentially Shakespearian beauty. For after Shakespeare, no one has excelled like Delacroix in fusing a mysterious unity of drama and reverie.

★

Et le tableau quitté . . .] 'And the picture we have left torments and follows us'—a line from Théophile Gautier
Rouvière] Philibert Rouvière won acclaim with his performance as Hamlet in Paris in 1847; he is shown playing the role in Manet's painting *L'Acteur Tragique*

... nor does imperial Tragedy demean herself, or fail to touch the heart, when she expresses utter bereavement by a mischance of the poultry yard:—

> He has no children. All my pretty ones?
> Did you say all?—O hell-kite! All?
> What, all my pretty chickens and their dam
> At one fell swoop?

SAMUEL PALMER (the painter), 'Some Observations on the Country and on Rural Poetry', c. 1880

The rest of the day he spent in looking for a room, which he soon found, and in familiarising himself with liberty. In the evening I took him to the Olympic, where Robson was then acting in a burlesque on Macbeth, Mrs Keeley, if I remember rightly, taking the part of Lady Macbeth. In the scene before the murder, Macbeth had said he could not kill Duncan when he saw his boots upon the landing. Lady Macbeth put a stop to her husband's hesitation by whipping him up under her arm, and carrying him off the stage, kicking and screaming. Ernest laughed till he cried. 'What rot Shakespeare is after this,' he exclaimed, involuntarily.

SAMUEL BUTLER, *The Way of All Flesh*, published 1903

Ernest Pontifex, the hero of the novel, has just been released from jail.

Thank you also very heartily for the Shakespeare. It will help me not to forget the little English I know, but above all it is so fine. I have begun to read the series of which I knew least, which formerly, distracted by other things or not having the time, I could not read; the series of the kings: I have already read *Richard II*, *Henry IV* and half of *Henry V*. I read without wondering if the ideas of the people of those times were different from our own, or what would become of them if you confronted them with republican and socialist beliefs and so on. But what touches me, as in some novelists of our day, is that the voices of these people, which in Shakespeare's case reach us from a distance of several centuries, do not seem unfamiliar to us. It is so much alive that you think you know them and see the thing.

And so what Rembrandt has alone or almost alone among painters, that tenderness of gaze which we see, whether it's in the 'Men of Emmaus' or in the 'Jewish Bride' or in some such strange angelic figure as the picture you have had the good fortune to see, that heart-broken tenderness, that glimpse of a super-human infinitude that seems so natural there—in many places you come upon it in Shake-speare too.

VINCENT VAN GOGH, letter to his brother Theo, 1889

Only one idea of general value has occurred to me. I have found love of the mother and jealousy of the father in my own case too, and now believe it to be a general phenomenon of early childhood, even if it does not always occur so early as in children who have been made hysterics. (Similarly with the 'romanticization of origins' in the case of paranoiacs—heroes, founders of religion). If that is the case, the grip-ping power of *Oedipus Rex*, in spite of all the rational objections to the inexorable fate that the story presupposes, becomes intelligible, and one can understand why later fate dramas were such failures. Our feelings rise against any arbitrary, individual fate such as shown in the *Ahnfrau*,° etc., but the Greek myth seizes on a compulsion which everyone recog-nizes because he has felt traces of it in himself. Every member of the audience was once a budding Oedipus in phantasy, and this dream-fulfilment played out in reality causes everyone to recoil in horror, with the full measure of repression which separates his infantile from his present state.

The idea has passed through my head that the same thing may lie at the root of *Hamlet*. I am not thinking of Shakespeare's conscious inten-tions, but supposing rather that he was impelled to write it by a real event because his own unconscious understood that of his hero. How can one explain the hysteric Hamlet's phrase 'So conscience doth make cowards of us all', and his hesitation to avenge his father by killing his uncle, when he himself so casually sends his courtiers to their death and despatches Laertes° so quickly? How better than by the torment roused in him by the obscure memory that he himself had meditated the same deed against his father because of passion for his mother—'use every man after his desert, and who should 'scape whipping?' His conscience is his unconscious feeling of guilt. And are not his sexual coldness when talking to Ophelia, his rejection of the instinct to beget children, and finally his transference of the deed from his father to Ophelia, typically hysterical? And does he not finally succeed, in just the same remarkable

the *Ahnfrau*] a play by Grillparzer   Laertes] presumably a slip for Polonius way as my hysterics do, in bringing down his punishment on himself and suffering the same fate as his father, being poisoned by the same rival?

SIGMUND FREUD, letter to Wilhelm Fliess, 15 October 1897,
tr. Eric Mosbacher and James Strachey

This letter is Freud's earliest account of the Oedipus complex.

The metaphysical Hamlet himself sees a 'true ghost,' but so far reverts to the positivism that underlies Shakespeare's thinking as to speak soon after of that 'undiscovered country from whose bourn no traveller returns.'

GEORGE SANTAYANA, 'The Absence of Religion in Shakespeare', 1899

Among the many reasons which make me glad to have been born in England, one of the first is that I read Shakespeare in my mother tongue. If I try to imagine myself as one who cannot know him face to face, who hears him only speaking from afar, and that in accents which only through the labouring intelligence can touch the living soul, there comes upon me a sense of chill discouragement, of dreary deprivation. I am wont to think that I can read Homer, and, assuredly, if any man enjoys him, it is I; but can I for a moment dream that Homer yields me all his music, that his word is to me as to him who walked by the Hellenic shore when Hellas lived? I know that there reaches me across the vast of time no more than a faint and broken echo; I know that it would be fainter still, but for its blending with those memories of youth which are as a glimmer of the world's primeval glory. Let every land have joy of its poet; for the poet is the land itself, all its greatness and its sweetness, all that incommunicable heritage for which men live and die.

GEORGE GISSING, *The Private Papers of Henry Ryecroft*, 1903

There is a world in each of Shakespeare's plays,—*the* world, I should say,—so felt and so seen as the world never was seen before nor could be felt and seen again, even by Shakespeare. Each play is a little local universe. His stage devices he repeats, but the atmosphere of a play is never repeated. *Twelfth Night, As You Like It*, and *The Merchant of Venice* are very unlike one another. The unity that is in each of them results from unimaginable depths of internal harmony in each. The group of persons in any play (I am speaking of the good plays) forms the unity; for the characters are psychologically interlocked with one another. Prospero implies Caliban; Toby Belch implies Malvolio; Shylock, Antonio. The effects of all imaginative art result from subtle implications and adjustments. The public recognizes these things as beauty, but cannot analyse them. To the artist, however, they have been the bricks and mortar out of which the work was builded. We feel, for instance, in the *Midsummer Night's Dream*, that the fairies are somehow correlative to the artisans. They are made out of a complementary chemical. On the other hand, Theseus and Demetrius and Hippolyta, in the same play, are lay figures which set off as with a foil both the fairies and the artisans. Theseus, Hippolyta, and Demetrius are marionettes which give intellect and importance to Bottom and Flute, and lend body and life to the tiny fairies. All this miraculous subtlety of understanding on Shakespeare's part is unconscious. He has had no recipe, no *métier*.

JOHN JAY CHAPMAN, *Greek Genius and Other Essays*, 1915

When Einstein says 'Shakespeare,' the eternal greatness seems to be inherent in the actual sound of the name. When he says 'Goethe,' we notice a slight undertone of dissonance, which may be interpreted without difficulty. He admires him with the pathos of distance, but no warmth glows through this pathos.

ALEXANDER MOSZKOWSKI, *Conversations with Einstein*, 1921, tr. Henry L. Brose

When I Read Shakespeare—

When I read Shakespeare I am struck with wonder
that such trivial people should muse and thunder
in such lovely language.

Lear, the old buffer, you wonder his daughters
didn't treat him rougher,
the old chough, the old chuffer!

And Hamlet, how boring, how boring to live with,
so mean and self-conscious, blowing and snoring
his wonderful speeches, full of other folks' whoring!

And Macbeth and his Lady, who should have been choring,
such suburban ambition, so messily goring
old Duncan with daggers!

How boring, how small Shakespeare's people are!
Yet the language so lovely! like the dyes from gas-tar.

D. H. LAWRENCE, 1929

We were just in a financial position to afford Shakespeare at the moment
when he presented himself!

JOHN MAYNARD KEYNES, *A Treatise on Money*, 1930

*Keynes had been talking about the 'sensational rise of prices' which had begun
in England around 1550 or 1560 and continued until 1650.*

I am not very receptive to The Theatre. There are very few plays I can
remember to have a very vivid recollection of them. And for plays in
verse, they give me for the most part a very depressing sense of unreality, very depressing, very painful. This is what I find with Shakespeare,
where the verse is conventional and the feeling is so warm and so human
and so disturbing. For me this is an antithesis which I do not make a
response to, except to feel distraut and ill at ease. But in Racine there is
no feeling of antithesis, the verse and the emotion are perfectly at one,
they fuse perfectly and effect the purgation which is the essence of
tragedy.

It is perhaps more in the vein of comedy the number of times in my
life I have now already read *Phèdre*, in great distress of mind for a finished
love-life. It is now very many times, and now I know this play very well
indeed, and for the tragedy and the simplicity of Phèdre I have a very
profound feeling. But oh how sure I am that it is so much better to have
love with all its pains and terrors and fanaticism than to live untouched
the life of the vegetable. But how it tears one, and how *unruhig* it is.

And now I have just been seeing *Romeo and Juliet*. But does that make
the same noble elevating and loamishly-sad feeling in me? No, it does
not. Again I am distraut and embarrassed by the complications and
maladroitness of the plot, but chiefly by its complications.

The plot of a tragedy must be bone-straight and simple. And that is
not. And the poetry is thwarted at every turn by the complications of
this plot, and even the genius of the nurse's character, and the genius of
the lines she speaks, are a distraction. And the so-famous Queen Mab
speech of Mercutio's that is a distraction and not a relief. And the play is

a very young play of Shakespeare's, and there is a great deal of *minor-elizabethanismus* in it, all the horrors and the bones and the charnel house, and Juliet's morbidity when she visualizes in such bludgeoning, strapping, head-smashing words all those things she would rather *not* do, but would rather not *not* do than lose her love. And the tomb scene itself is at once a *minorelizabethanismus*, and also a shadow of the later born Hamlet.

Are not all Shakespeare's plays really versions, schemes and ghosts of Hamlet? But here the echo from the future is so clear, the dead girl, no matter if later she rises, the dead girl and the two men at war upon her bier. It is interesting. I am glad to have seen this. But it is an evening of irritation, I feel, of exasperation, as if one were sided irrevocably with the verse, striving so hard to rise above the clash and clamour of inessentials. How often I have spoken about this with Harriet, but she is open and receptive to the genius of Shakespeare, and I am not, and it is my loss I make no mistake. But it is nothing that can be learnt or had for wishing.

STEVIE SMITH, *Novel on Yellow Paper*, 1936

Shakespeare's treatment of kingship—of authority—reflects a life-like conception, a sense for the human problematics of social relationships. Kingship has a claim to recognition. In itself the claim is absolute: rebellion is a wholly unjustifiable sin. This was the general attitude of the age; the detestation of rebellion was deeply felt. In England, a sermon 'Against Disobedience and Willful Rebellion' had been included in 1574 in the official *Book of Homilies*. But not in England alone; throughout the whole of Europe the intellectuals, even without the exhortations of religion, were keenly aware of the dangers that state and society might incur from rebellion, whether coming from the mob, from religious fanatics, or from turbulent noblemen. It is important to note—for without it Shakespeare's dramatic powers could not have attained their depth—that in Shakespeare's view the holder of regal authority was himself subject to the moral order. With all due reverence for the office, Shakespeare was nevertheless able to retain freedom of judgment with regard to the king's person and the king's actions: the law is valid for the king as well; he, too, is accountable for his misdeeds.

To realize the significance of this attitude and the wealth of dramatic tensions it released, contrast the doctrine proclaimed by Corneille—a doctrine that must have strait-jacketed his freedom of judgment. (It is Caesar speaking, but Corneille sides with him unhesitatingly.)

Of all these crimes of State committed to obtain the crown,
We are absolved by Heaven when it gives it to us,
And in the sacred rank where Heaven's favour has placed us
The past becomes guiltless and the future lawful.
He who can attain that rank cannot be guilty;
Whatever he may have done or does, he is inviolable.

A doctrine suited to tyrants; small wonder that Napoleon (as Talleyrand assures us in his memoirs) knew these lines from *Cinna* by heart and liked to quote them.

In the absolute rejection of rebellion Shakespeare was typical of the European civilization of his age—insofar as the theory of Machiavelli did not embolden people to eliminate all moral restraints from politics, which became thereby a mere game of power—but in his freedom of judgment, which in the final reckoning discerned the human being in king and rebel alike and assigned to both their places in the same order, he was a child of his own country. In England the universal triumph of state absolutism was still accompanied by a recognition of the sovereignty of law.

PIETER GEYL (1887–1966), Dutch historian, from 'Shakespeare as a Historian: A Fragment', 1944–5—written during the German occupation of the Netherlands, after Geyl's release from Buchenwald, and broken off when his work in the Resistance compelled him to go into hiding

It seems to me unnecessary (although it has frequently been done) to depict Shakespeare as a hardened aristocrat because in *Julius Caesar* he makes Caesar wrinkle his nose at the stench of the mob. It is true that the passage is not singular: Shakespeare's own sense of smell must have been keen. It is at any rate undeniable that he liked to show up men of the people in their stupidity and clumsiness. The ducal company in *Midsummer Night's Dream* makes mercilessly merry over the antics that Bottom and his fellow handicraftsmen perform in such deadly earnest. Audrey, the clumsy peasant girl in *As You Like It*, may have a touch of the pathetic in her callow innocence, but nobody, not even her creator, takes her seriously, and the last we hear about her is Touchstone's request to the Duke to be allowed to marry her—in this strain: '. . . an ill-favoured thing, sir, but mine own: a poor humour of mine, sir, to take that that no man else will.' The masterly little thumbnail sketch of the old nurse in *Romeo and Juliet* is strikingly unkind. True, over against these, characters of a different stamp can be placed. For instance, in *King Lear*, the servant who has the courage to protest when Cornwall is about to pull out Gloucester's eyes; or, in *As You Like It* once more, Adam, the old serving man, who sticks to Orlando in his misfortunes and offers him his savings; in his turn, when their journey proves too much for the feeble old man, Orlando carries him on his back. Here, of course, it should be remembered that the aristocratic code is always ready to acknowledge the virtue of faithfulness in a servant.

One hesitates what to conclude, but what must strike every reader of Shakespeare—and in my argument it has obvious significance—is his consistent lack of sympathy for popular movements or for any meddling with public affairs on the part of the multitude or even of the middle class. Anything in that line he treats with distaste and scorn.

In Dogberry and Verges, that precious pair of self-important but endlessly blundering constables of the civic guard in *Much Ado About Nothing*, ridicule is thrown not only on small-town middle-class men, but on the entire institution they represent. When, in *Richard III*, the King and his henchman Buckingham explain to the Lord Mayor of London how they were compelled to the killing of Hastings by the victim's (purely fictitious) attempts on their own lives, the crass stupidity with which the representative of burgherdom allows himself to be bamboozled is no less striking than the false scoundrelism of the highborn murderers.

The clearest evidence, however (although even this is not always interpreted alike in the countless speculations about Shakespeare's political sentiments by modern critics), is afforded by the set scenes of riotous, or at least politically excited, crowds in *Henry VI*, in *Julius Caesar*, and in *Coriolanus*. At every new reading one is amazed at the brilliant competence of those scenes. The arts of the popular orator, the reactions of the mob—how accurately have they been observed and with what faultless efficiency noted down. The historic sense is here very manifest. But to me there can be no doubt that observation and execution were inspired by hostility.

PIETER GEYL, 'Shakespeare as a Historian: A Fragment'

It is remarkable how hard we find it to believe something the truth of which we do not see for ourselves. If e.g. I hear expressions of admiration for Shakespeare made by the distinguished men of several centuries, I can never rid myself of a suspicion that praising him has been a matter of convention, even though I have to tell myself that this is not the case. I need the authority of a *Milton* to be really convinced. In his case I take it for granted that he was incorruptible.—But of course I don't mean to deny by this that an enormous amount of praise has been & still is lavished on Shakespeare without understanding & for specious reasons by a thousand professors of literature.

Shakespeare & the dream. A dream is all wrong, absurd, composite, & yet completely right: in *this* strange concoction it makes an impression. Why? I don't know. And if Shakespeare is great, as he is said to be, then we must be able to say of him: Everything is wrong, things *aren't like that*—& is all the same completely right according to a law of its own.

It could be put like this too: If Shakespeare is great, then he can be so only in the whole *corpus* of his plays, which create their *own* language & world. So he is completely unrealistic. (Like the dream.)

It is *not* as though S. portrayed human types well & were in that respect *true to life*. He is *not* true to life. But he has such a supple hand & such individual *brush strokes*, that each one of his characters looks *significant*, worth looking at.

'Beethoven's great heart'—no one could say 'Shakespeare's great heart'. 'The supple hand that created new natural forms of language' would seem to me nearer the mark.

It seems to me as though his pieces are, as it were, enormous *sketches*, not paintings; as though they were *dashed off* by someone who could permit himself *anything*, so to speak. And I understand how someone may admire this & call it *supreme* art, but I don't like it.—So I can understand someone who stands before those pieces speechless; but someone who admires him as one admires Beethoven, say, seems to me to misunderstand Shakespeare.

LUDWIG WITTGENSTEIN, *Culture and Value*, tr. Peter Winch, 1998
(comments written between 1946 and 1951)

  Shav.   You were not the first
To sing of broken hearts. I was the first
That taught your faithless Timons how to mend them.
  Shakes. Taught what you could not know. Sing if you can
My cloud capped towers, my gorgeous palaces,
My solemn temples. The great globe itself,
Yea, all which it inherit, shall dissolve—
  Shav.   —and like this foolish little show of ours
Leave not a wrack behind. So you have said.
I say the world will long outlast our day.
Tomorrow and tomorrow and tomorrow
We puppets shall replay our scene. Meanwhile,
Immortal William dead and turned to clay
May stop a hole to keep the wind away.
Oh that the earth which kept the world in awe
Should patch a wall t' expel the winter's flaw!
  Shakes. These words are mine, not thine.
  Shav.   Peace, jealous Bard:
We both are mortal. For a moment suffer
My glimmering light to shine.

 A light appears between them.

  Shakes. Out, out, brief candle! (*He puffs it out*)

Darkness. The play ends.

          BERNARD SHAW, *Shakes versus Shav*, 1949

Shakes Versus Shav *was Shaw's swansong—a puppet-play, written at the age
of 92, in which he pitted himself against Shakespeare for the last time.*

In the hall of the Limbo Rotary Club, presided over by a statue of
Shakespeare, the Committee of Six was holding its annual meeting. The
Committee consisted of: Hamlet, Lear, Macbeth, Othello, Antony, and
Romeo. All these six, while they yet lived on earth, had been psycho-
analysed by Macbeth's doctor, Dr Bombasticus. Macbeth, before the
doctor had taught him to speak ordinary English, had asked, in the
stilted language that in those days he employed, 'Canst thou not minister
to a mind diseas'd?' 'Why, yes,' replied the doctor, 'of course I can. It
is only necessary that you should lie on my sofa and talk, and I will

undertake to listen at a guinea a minute.' Macbeth at once agreed. And the other five agreed at various times.

Macbeth told how at one time he had fancies of homicide, and in a long dream saw all that Shakespeare relates. Fortunately, he met the doctor in time, who explained that he saw Duncan as a father-figure, and Lady Macbeth as a mother-ditto. The doctor, with some difficulty, persuaded him that Duncan was not really his father, so he became a loyal subject. Malcolm and Donalbain died young, and Macbeth succeeded in due course. He remained devoted to Lady Macbeth, and together they spent their days in good works. He encouraged Boy Scouts, and she opened bazaars. He lived to a great age, respected by all except the porter.

The statue, which had a gramophone in its interior, remarked at this stage: 'All our yesterdays have lighted fools the way to dusty death.'

Macbeth started, and said, 'Damn that statue. That fellow Shakespeare wrote a most libellous work about me. He only knew me when I was young, before I had met Dr Bombasticus, and he let his imagination run riot over all the crimes he hoped I should commit. I cannot see why people insist on doing honour to him. There's hardly a person in his plays that wouldn't have been the better for Dr Bombasticus.'

Lear, Othello, Romeo and Antony tell a similar story; they have all been cured by the good doctor's ministrations. Only Hamlet dissents. Then suddenly there is a strange shriek, and a voice moans from the depths:

'I am Dr Bombasticus! I am in Hell! I repent! I killed your souls . . . I have lived in Hell, but for what crime I knew not until now. I have lived in Hell for preferring subservience to glory; for thinking better of servility than of splendour; for seeking smoothness rather than the lightning-flash; for fearing thunder so much that I preferred a damp, unending drizzle . . .'

BERTRAND RUSSELL, *Nightmares of Eminent Persons*, 1954

Think how much original thought there is in Shakespeare, and how divinely inconspicuous it is.

IRIS MURDOCH, 'Literature and Philosophy', 1978

★   ★   ★

We occasionally see something on the stage that reminds us a little of Shakespeare.

WILLIAM HAZLITT, theatre review, 1814

The stage cannot be dissociated from Shakespeare, either as the poet or as the man. It was the lever with which he moved the world.

HENRY IRVING, introduction to *The Henry Irving Shakespeare*, 1888

Who could recognize in the sprawling, shouting, guffawing Mercutio at the Lyceum the airy gentleman of Shakespeare's fancy, or in the Portia at His Majesty's, with her affected grandeur, her barefaced sentimentality, and her laborious giggles, the lady whom we love?

LYTTON STRACHEY, 'Shakespeare on the Stage', 1908

If the best available actors are only Horatios, the authors will have to leave Hamlet out, and be content with Horatios for heroes. Some of the difference between Shakespear's Orlandos and Bassanios and Bertrams and his Hamlets and Macbeths must have been due not only to his development as a dramatic poet, but to the development of Burbage as an actor.

BERNARD SHAW, preface to *Great Catherine*, 1913

One never sees Shakespeare played without being reminded at some new point of his greatness.

HENRY JAMES, reviewing a production of *Romeo and Juliet*, 1876

AMONG NOVELISTS

He lies buried in a corner of his church-yard, in the parish of ———, under a plain marble slab, which his friend *Eugenius*, by leave of his executors, laid upon his grave, with no more than these three words of inscription serving both for his epitaph and elegy.

> Alas, poor YORICK!

Ten times in a day has *Yorick's* ghost the consolation to hear his monumental inscription read over with such a variety of plaintive tones, as denote a general pity and esteem for him;——a foot-way crossing the church-yard close by the side of his grave,—not a passenger goes by without stopping to cast a look upon it,——and sighing as he walks on,

Alas, poor YORICK!

LAURENCE STERNE, *Tristram Shandy*, 1760–7

This Yorick is a clergyman:

. . . the family was originally of *Danish* extraction, and had been transplanted into *England* as early as in the reign of *Horwendillus*, king of *Denmark*, in whose court it seems, an ancestor of this Mr *Yorick's*, and from whom he was lineally descended, held a considerable post to the day of his death. Of what nature this considerable post was, this record saith not; it only adds, That, for near two centuries, it had been totally abolished as altogether unnecessary, not only in that court, but in every other court in the Christian world.

Like his ancestor, Parson Yorick loves a jest. He is also an alter ego *of the Rev Laurence Sterne. He dies early on in* Tristram Shandy, *but he reappears in a number of later episodes, and he has the last word in the book:*

L——d! said my mother, what is all this story about?—A COCK and a BULL, said *Yorick*——And one of the best of its kind, I ever heard.

Sterne published two collections of sermons under the name of Mr Yorick, and revived the name for the narrator of A Sentimental Journey Through France and Italy. *In the latter book the parson, anxious to obtain a passport while in Versailles, establishes his credentials with the influential Count de B**** by means of a Shakespeare which happens to be lying on the table:*

I took up Hamlet, and turning immediately to the grave-diggers scene in the fifth act, I lay'd my finger upon *Yorick*, and advancing the book to the Count, with my finger all the way over the name—Me, *Voici!* said I.

Two hours later the Count returns with a passport. Yorick spends the interim reading Much Ado About Nothing.

★   ★   ★

The Theatre was in existence, I found, on asking the fishmonger, who had a compact show of stock in his window, consisting of a sole and a quart of shrimps—and I resolved to comfort my mind by going to look at it. Richard the Third, in a very uncomfortable cloak, had first appeared to me there, and had made my heart leap with terror by backing up against the stage-box in which I was posted, while struggling for life against the virtuous Richmond . . . Many wondrous secrets of Nature had I come to the knowledge of in that sanctuary: of which, not the least terrific were, that the witches in Macbeth bore an awful resemblance to the Thanes and other proper inhabitants of Scotland, and that the good King Duncan couldn't rest in his grave, but was constantly coming out of it, and calling himself somebody else.

CHARLES DICKENS, 'Dullborough Town', The Uncommercial Traveller, 1860

'Two Macbeths!'

—the actor William Macready (the most famous Macbeth of his time), after watching Dickens give a public reading of the murder of Nancy by Bill Sikes

Now, Mrs Curdle was supposed, by those who were best informed on such points, to possess quite the London taste in matters relating to literature and the drama; and as to Mr Curdle, he had written a pamphlet of sixty-four pages, post octavo, on the character of the Nurse's deceased husband in Romeo and Juliet, with an inquiry whether he really had been a 'merry man' in his lifetime, or whether it was merely

his widow's affectionate partiality that induced her so to report him. He
had likewise proved, that by altering the received mode of punctuation,
any one of Shakespeare's plays could be made quite different, and the
sense completely changed . . .

DICKENS, Nicholas Nickleby, 1838–9

'Slyme's biographer, sir, whoever he may be,' resumed the gentleman,
'must apply to me; or, if I am gone to that what's-his-name from which
no thingumbob comes back, he must apply to my executors for leave to
search among my papers.

DICKENS, Martin Chuzzlewit, 1843

*The 'gentleman' is the confidence trickster Montague Tigg, who has
just described his associate Chevy Slyme as 'the highest-minded, the
most independent-spirited, most original, spiritual, classical, talented, the
most thoroughly Shakespearian, if not Miltonic, and at the same time most
disgustingly-unappreciated dog I know.'*

A little later Tigg observes:

'I wish I may die, if this isn't the queerest state of existence that we find
ourselves forced into, without knowing why or wherefore, Mr Pecksniff!
Well, never mind! Moralise as we will, the world goes on. As Hamlet
says,° Hercules may lay about him with his club in every possible direction, but he can't prevent the cats from making a most intolerable row
on the roofs of the houses, or the dogs from being shot in the hot
weather if they run about the streets unmuzzled.'

DICKENS, Martin Chuzzlewit

'Please to bring the child in quick out of the air there,' whispered the
beadle, holding open the inner door of the church.

Little Paul might have asked with Hamlet 'into my grave?' so chill and
earthy was the place.

DICKENS, Dombey and Son, 1846–8

'In regard to my relative who does me the honour to have formed an

---

As Hamlet says] 'Let Hercules himself do what he may, | The cat will mew, and dog will have
his day' (v. i)

uncommonly good opinion of myself, I can assure the amiable wife of my friend Gay, that she may rely on my being, in point of fact, a father to her. And in regard to the changes of human life, and the extraordinary manner in which we are perpetually conducting ourselves, all I can say is, with my friend Shakespeare—man who wasn't for an age but for all time, and with whom my friend Gay is no doubt acquainted—that it's like the shadow of a dream.'

Cousin Feenix in Dombey and Son

'Then it was that I began, if I may so Shakespearianly express myself, to dwindle, peak, and pine.° I found that my services were constantly called into requisition for the falsification of business, and the mystification of an individual whom I shall designate as Mr W. . . . This was bad enough; but as the philosophic Dane observes, with that unusual applicability which distinguishes the illustrious ornament of the Elizabethan Era, worse remains behind!'°

Mr Micawber was so very much struck by this happy rounding off with a quotation, that he indulged himself, and us, with a second reading of the sentence under pretense of having lost his place.

DICKENS, David Copperfield, 1849–50

There are hundreds if not thousands of Shakespearian references in Dickens's work, and beyond the direct allusions there are any number of looser or less explicit recollections. The Mystery of Edwin Drood, *for example, frequently echoes* Macbeth. *The chapter before the murder takes place is entitled 'When shall these Three meet again?' In the last chapter, or the last Dickens wrote, John Jasper returns to his opium den and recalls an unspecified, much-contemplated fantasy which he has fulfilled: 'when it was really done, it seemed not worth the doing, it was done so soon.' ('If it were done, when 'tis done, then 'twere well it were done quickly.') But* Macbeth *is present in the atmosphere of the novel, too—in the night scenes, and in such images as that of 'the hoarse rooks hovering about the Cathedral tower'.*

In 1848 Dickens and his company of amateurs presented a production of The Merry Wives of Windsor *at the Theatre Royal, Haymarket. Dickens himself took the part of Justice Shallow:*

dwindle, peak, and pine] Macbeth, I. iii
worse remains behind] 'This bad begins, and worse remains behind' (Hamlet, III. iv)

His impersonation was perfect: the old, stiff limbs, the senile stoop of the shoulders, the head bent with age, the feeble step, with a certain attempted smartness of carriage characteristic of the conceited Justice of the Peace,—were all assumed and maintained with wonderful accuracy; while the articulation,—part lisp, part thickness of utterance, part a kind of impeded sibillation, like that of a voice that 'pipes and whistles in the sound' through loss of teeth—gave consummate effect to his mode of speech. The one in which Shallow says, ' 'Tis the heart, Master Page; 'tis here, 'tis here. I have seen the time with my long sword I would have made you four tall fellows skip like rats,' was delivered with a humour of expression in effete energy of action and would-be fire of spirit that marvellously imaged fourscore years in its attempt to denote vigour long since extinct.

Mark Lemon's Sir John Falstaff was a fine embodiment of rich, unctuous, enjoying raciness; no caricatured, rolling greasiness and grossness, no exaggerated vulgarization of Shakespeare's immortal 'fat knight;' but a florid, rotund, self-contented, self-indulgent voluptuary—thoroughly at his ease, thoroughly prepared to take advantage of all gratification that might come in his way; and throughout preserving the manners of a gentleman, accustomed to the companionship of a prince, 'the best king of good fellows.' John Forster's Master Ford was a carefully finished performance. John Leech's Master Slender was picturesquely true to the gawky, flabby, booby squire: hanging about in various attitudes of limp ecstasy, limp embarrassment, limp disconsolateness. His mode of sitting on the stile, with his long, ungainly legs dangling down, during the duel scene between Sir Hugh and Dr. Caius, looking vacantly out across 'the fields,' as if in vapid expectation of seeing 'Mistress Anne Page at a farm-house a-feasting,'—as promised him by that roguish wag mine Host of the Garter, ever and anon ejaculating his maudlin, cuckoo-cry of 'Oh sweet Anne Page,'—was a delectable treat. Mr G. H. Lewes's acting, and especially his dancing, as Sir Hugh Evans, were very dainty, with a peculiar drollery and quaintness, singularly befitting the peppery but kindly-natured Welsh parson. I once heard Mr Lewes wittily declare that his were not so much 'animal spirits,' as 'vegetable spirits;' and these kind of ultra light good-humours shone to great advantage in his conception and impersonation of Sir Hugh. George Cruikshank as mine Ancient Pistol, was supremely artistic in 'get up,' costume, and attitude; fantastic, spasmodic, ranting, bullying. Though taking the small part of Slender's servant, Simple, Augustus Egg was conspicuous for good judgment and good taste in his presentment of the character. Over his well-chosen suit of sober-coloured doublet and hose he wore a leather thong round his neck that hung loosely over his chest; and he told me he had added this to his dress, because inasmuch as Master Slender was addicted to sport, interested in coursing, and in Page's 'fallow greyhound,' it was likely that his retainer would carry a dog-leash about him.

CHARLES and MARY COWDEN CLARKE, Recollections of Writers, 1878

Mary Cowden Clarke, who wrote this account, played Mistress Quickly in the production. Mark Lemon was editor of Punch, *John Forster was Dickens's first biographer, Leopold Augustus Egg was a painter. It is perhaps not necessary to add that John Leech and George Cruikshank were caricaturists and illustrators, and that G. H. Lewes was an author and journalist and the companion of George Eliot.*

In 1856 Dickens purchased the house at Gadshill, near Rochester in Kent, which he had dreamed of owning as a child.

'This house, Gadshill Place, stands on the summit of Shakespeare's Gadshill, ever memorable for its association with Sir John Falstaff in his noble fancy. *But, my lads, tomorrow morning, by four o'clock, early at Gadshill! there are pilgrims going to Canterbury with rich offerings, and traders riding to London with fat purses: I have vizards for you all; you have horses for yourselves.'* Illuminated by Mr Owen Jones, and placed in a frame on the first-floor landing, these words were the greeting of the new tenant to his visitors. It was his first act of ownership.

JOHN FORSTER, The Life of Charles Dickens, 1872–4

. . . the great master, who knew everything . . .

DICKENS, 'Night Walks', The Uncommercial Traveller, 1860

('I wonder that the great master who knew everything, when he called Sleep the death of each day's life, did not call Dreams the insanity of each day's sanity.')

Dickens' Copperfield came to an end last night . . . I maintain it—a little Shakespeare—a cockney Shakespeare, if you will; but as distinct, if not so great, a piece of pure genius as was born in Stratford.

EDWARD FITZGERALD, letter to Fanny Kemble, 1879

★   ★   ★

Caroline, who, mounted on a chair, had been rummaging the bookcase, returned with a book.

'Here's Shakespeare,' she said, 'and there's "Coriolanus." Now, read, and discover by the feelings the reading will give you at once how low and how high you are.'

'Come, then, sit near me, and correct when I mispronounce.'

'I am to be the teacher, then, and you my pupil?'

'Ainsi, soit-il!'

'And Shakespeare is our science, since we are going to study?'

'It appears so.'

'And you are not going to be French, and sceptical, and sneering? You are not going to think it a sign of wisdom to refuse to admire?'

'I don't know.'

'If you do, Robert, I'll take Shakespeare away, and I'll shrivel up within myself, and put on my bonnet and go home.'

'Sit down; here I begin.'

'One minute, if you please, brother,' interrupted Mademoiselle, 'when the gentleman of a family reads, the ladies should always sew. Caroline, dear child, take your embroidery; you may get three sprigs done to-night.'

Caroline looked dismayed.

'I can't see by lamp-light; my eyes are tired, and I can't do two things well at once. If I sew, I cannot listen; if I listen, I cannot sew.'

'Fi, donc! Quel enfantillage!' began Hortense.

Mr Moore, as usual, suavely interposed.

'Permit her to neglect the embroidery for this evening. I wish her whole attention to be fixed on my accent, and to insure this, she must follow the reading with her eyes; she must look at the book.'

He placed it between them, reposed his arm on the back of Caroline's chair, and thus began to read.

The very first scene in 'Coriolanus' came with smart relish to his intellectual palate, and still as he read he warmed. He delivered the haughty speech of Caius Marcius to the starving citizens with unction; he did not say he thought his irrational pride right, but he seemed to feel it so. Caroline looked up at him with a singular smile.

'There's a vicious point hit already,' she said; 'you sympathize with that proud patrician who does not sympathize with his famished fellow-men, and insults them: there, go on.'

He proceeded. The warlike portions did not rouse him much; he said all that was out of date, or should be; the spirit displayed was barbarous,

yet the encounter single-handed between Marcius and Tullus Aufidius he
delighted in. As he advanced, he forgot to criticize; it was evident he
appreciated the power, the truth of each portion; and stepping out of the
narrow line of private prejudices, began to revel in the large picture of
human nature, to feel the reality stamped upon the characters who were
speaking from that page before him.

He did not read the comic scenes well, and Caroline, taking the book
out of his hand, read these parts for him. From her he seemed to enjoy
them, and indeed she gave them with a spirit no one could have expected
of her, with a pithy expression, with which she seemed gifted on the
spot, and for that brief moment only. It may be remarked, in passing,
that the general character of her conversation that evening, whether
serious or sprightly, grave or gay, was as of something untaught,
unstudied, intuitive, fitful; when once gone, no more to be reproduced
as it had been, than the glancing ray of the meteor, than the tints of the
dew-gem, than the colour or form of the sunset cloud, than the fleeting
and glittering ripple varying the flow of a rivulet.

Coriolanus in glory; Coriolanus in disaster; Coriolanus banished, followed like giant shades one after the other. Before the vision of the
banished man Moore's spirit seemed to pause. He stood on the hearth of
Aufidius's hall, facing the image of greatness fallen, but greater than ever
in that low estate. He saw 'the grim appearance,' the dark face 'bearing
command in it,' 'the noble vessel with its tackle torn.' With the revenge
of Caius Marcius Moore perfectly sympathized; he was not scandalized
by it; and again Caroline whispered:

'There I see another glimpse of brotherhood in error.'

The march on Rome, the mother's supplication, the long resistance,
the final yielding of bad passions to good, which ever must be the case in
a nature worthy the epithet of noble, the rage of Aufidius at what he
considered his ally's weakness, the death of Coriolanus, the final sorrow
of his great enemy—all scenes made of condensed truth and strength
came on in succession, and carried with them in their deep, fast flow the
heart and mind of reader and listener.

'Now, have you felt Shakespeare?' asked Caroline, some ten minutes
after her cousin had closed the book.

'I think so.'

'And have you felt anything in Coriolanus like you?'

'Perhaps I have.'

'Was he not faulty as well as great?'

Moore nodded.

'And what was his fault? What made him hated by the citizens? What caused him to be banished by his countrymen?'

'What do you think it was?'

'I ask again:

> "Whether was it pride,
> Which out of daily fortune ever taints
> The happy man? whether defect of judgment,
> To fail in the disposing of those chances
> Which he was lord of? or whether nature,
> Not to be other than one thing; not moving
> From the casque to the cushion, but commanding peace
> Even with the same austerity and garb
> As he controlled the war?" '

'Well, answer yourself, Sphinx.'

'It was a spice of all: and you must not be proud to your workpeople; you must not neglect chances of soothing them, and you must not be of an inflexible nature, uttering a request as austerely as if it were a command.'

'That is the moral you tack to the play. What puts such notions into your head?'

'A wish for your good, a care for your safety, dear Robert, and a fear caused by many things which I have heard lately that you will come to harm.'

'Who tells you these things?'

'I hear my uncle talk about you. He praises your hard spirit, your determined cast of mind, your scorn of low enemies, your resolution not "to truckle to the mob," as he says.'

'And would you have me truckle to them?'

'No, not for the world. I never wish you to lower yourself; but somehow I cannot help thinking it unjust to include all poor working people under the general and insulting name of "the mob," and continually to think of them and treat them haughtily.'

CHARLOTTE BRONTË, *Shirley*, 1849

Charlotte Brontë's novel is set during the Napoleonic wars, against the background of the Luddite riots. Robert Moore is a mill-owner, half-Belgian by birth; Caroline is his English cousin.

★   ★   ★

In Swann's Way *(1914), Marcel Proust's narrator recalls watching a meal being prepared when he was a child:*

I would stop by the table, where the kitchen-maid had shelled them, to inspect the platoons of peas, drawn up in ranks and numbered, like little green marbles, ready for a game; but what most enraptured me were the asparagus, tinged with ultramarine and pink which shaded off from their heads, finely stippled in mauve and azure, through a series of impercept-ible gradations to their white feet—still stained a little by the soil of their garden-bed—with an iridescence that was not of this world. I felt that these celestial hues indicated the presence of exquisite creatures who had been pleased to assume vegetable form and who, through the dis-guise of their firm, comestible flesh, allowed me to discern in this radi-ance of earliest dawn, these hinted rainbows, these blue evening shades, that precious quality which I should recognise again when, all night long after a dinner at which I had partaken of them, they played (lyrical and coarse in their jesting like one of Shakespeare's fairies) at transforming my chamber pot into a vase of aromatic perfume.

> In Search of Lost Time: Swann's Way, tr. C. K. Scott Moncrieff and
> Terence Kilmartin, revised D. J. Enright

In Proust's Time Regained *the narrator is walking along the Champs-Elysées when a cab draws up nearby. The passenger and his attendant turn out to be old acquaintances:*

A man with staring eyes and hunched figure was placed rather than seated in the back, and was making, to keep himself upright, the efforts that might have been made by a child who has been told to be good. But his straw hat failed to conceal an unruly forest of hair which was entirely white, and a white beard, like those which snow forms on the statues of river-gods in public gardens, flowed from his chin. It was—side by side with Jupien, who was unremitting in his attentions to him—M. de Char-lus, now convalescent after an attack of apoplexy of which I had had no knowledge (I had only been told that he had lost his sight, but in fact this trouble had been purely temporary and he could now see quite well again) and which, unless the truth was that hitherto he had dyed his hair and that he had now been forbidden to continue so fatiguing a practice, had had the effect, as in a sort of chemical precipitation, of rendering visible and brilliant all that saturation of metal which the locks of his hair and his beard, pure silver now, shot forth like so many geysers, so that upon the old fallen prince this latest illness had conferred the Shakespearian majesty of a King Lear.

Later, when the narrator watches his old acquaintance Bloch, now a famous author, arrive at the Princesse de Guermantes's reception, he reaches out for another Shakespearian parallel:

Bloch had come bounding into the room like a hyena. 'He is at home now,' I thought, 'in drawing-rooms into which twenty years ago he would never have been able to penetrate.' But he was also twenty years older. He was nearer to death. What did this profit him? At close quarters, in the translucency of a face in which, at a greater distance or in a bad light, I saw only youthful gaiety (whether because it survived there or because I with my recollections evoked it), I could detect another face, almost frightening, racked with anxiety, the face of an old Shylock, waiting in the wings, with his make-up prepared, for the moment when he would make his entry on to the stage and already reciting his first line under his breath.

> In Search of Lost Time: Time Regained, tr. Andreas Mayor and Terence Kilmartin, revised D. J. Enright

★   ★   ★

Shakespeare is an inescapable presence in the work of James Joyce, nowhere more so than in the 'Scylla and Charybdis' episode in Ulysses *(1922). Under the domed roof of the Irish National Library, Stephen Dedalus expounds his theory about the poet's life and work to John Eglinton and the other librarians, with mocking Buck Mulligan joining them halfway through.*

Briefly, Stephen contends that Shakespeare was seduced and snared into marriage by Anne Hathaway, and left for London and a career in the theatre after his children were born. He never recovered his confidence, however, and felt even more aggrieved after Anne was unfaithful to him with one of his brothers—a trauma which left its mark everywhere in his writing, but especially in Hamlet.

One piece of evidence which he asks his audience to consider is the use to which Shakespeare put the names of two of his brothers, Richard and Edmund:

—You will say those names were already in the chronicles from which he took the stuff of his plays. Why did he take them rather than others? Richard, a whoreson crookback, misbegotten, makes love to a widowed Ann (what's in a name?), woos and wins her, a whoreson merry widow. Richard the conqueror, third brother, came after William the conquered.° The other four acts of that play hang limply from that first. Of all his kings Richard is the only king unshielded by Shakespeare's reverence, the angel of the world. Why is the underplot of *King Lear* in which Edmund figures lifted out of Sidney's *Arcadia* and spatchcocked on to a Celtic legend older than history?

—That was Will's way, John Eglinton defended. We should not now combine a Norse saga with an excerpt from a novel by George Meredith. *Que voulez-vous?* Moore would say. He puts Bohemia on the seacoast and makes Ulysses quote Aristotle.

—Why? Stephen answered himself. Because the theme of the false or the usurping or the adulterous brother or all three in one is to Shakespeare, what the poor is not, always with him. The note of banishment, banishment from the heart, banishment from home, sounds uninterruptedly from *The Two Gentlemen of Verona* onward till Prospero breaks his staff, buries it certain fathoms in the earth and drowns his book. It doubles itself in the middle of his life, reflects itself in another, repeats itself, protasis, epitasis, catastasis, catastrophe. It repeats itself again when he is near the grave, when his married daughter Susan, chip of the old block, is accused of adultery. But it was the original sin that darkened his understanding, weakened his will and left in him a strong inclination to evil. The words are those of my lords bishops of Maynooth—an original sin and, like original sin, committed by another in whose sin he too has sinned. It is between the lines of his last written words, it is petrified on his tombstone under which her four bones are not to be laid. Age has not withered it. Beauty and peace have not done it away. It is in infinite variety everywhere in the world he has created, in *Much Ado about Nothing*, twice in *As you like It*, in *The Tempest*, in *Hamlet*, in *Measure for Measure*, and in all the other plays which I have not read.

He laughed to free his mind from his mind's bondage.

Judge Eglinton summed up.

—The truth is midway, he affirmed. He is the ghost and the prince. He is all in all.

William the conquered] a reversal of a famous anecdote according to which Richard Burbage turned up for an assignation and gave the prearranged password—'It is I, Richard the Third'—but found that Shakespeare had been there before him: 'William the Conqueror reigned before Richard the Third'

—He is, Stephen said. The boy of act one is the mature man of act five. All in all. In *Cymbeline*, in *Othello* he is bawd and cuckold. He acts and is acted on. Lover of an ideal or a perversion, like José he kills the real Carmen. His unremitting intellect is the hornmad Iago ceaselessly willing that the moor in him shall suffer.

—Cuckoo! Cuckoo! Cuck Mulligan clucked lewdly. O word of fear! Dark dome received, reverbed.

As a contribution to scholarship, Stephen's theory is full of holes; as an imaginative reconstruction, it buttresses one of the novel's major themes. Stephen, the aspiring artist, has been thinking of himself as much as of Shakespeare as he unfolds his story, but he lacks Shakespeare's humanity. Leopold Bloom, his opposite number, is nothing if not human, and he even has his Shakespearian aspects, but he lives below the level of art. If only the two of them could somehow join forces!

When they do meet up, in Bella Cohen's brothel, they look into a mirror together, and it is the face of Shakespeare that gazes back at them. A damaged Shakespeare, however, 'rigid in facial paralysis, crowned'—like a good cuckold—'by the reflection of the reindeer antlered hatrack in the hall'. A Shakespeare who is soon snarling at them 'With paralytic rage'.

Over two hundred Shakespearian quotations or near quotations are woven into the text of Ulysses: *they range from 'I'll tickle his catastrophe!' (from* Henry IV Part Two) *to the 'defunctive music' of* 'The Phoenix and Turtle'. *Some phrases are used more than once: Stephen quotes 'the beast with two backs' from* Othello *on three separate occasions. Some, especially the ones that Bloom favours, are clichés. A few are used for high if ironic poetic effect: the coda to the library episode is a noble passage from* Cymbeline:

> Laud we the gods
> And let our crooked smokes climb to their nostrils
> From our bless'd altars.

And some are jokes. As he catches the smell from Rourke's bakery, a couplet from The Merchant of Venice *pops into Bloom's head along with a pun which must have occurred to many readers and playgoers before:*

O tell me where is fancy bread? At Rourke's the baker's, it is said.

The main Shakespearian borrowings in Finnegans Wake *are structural rather than ornamental. In particular, Hamlet is used to reinforce the family patterns*

*in the book, the conflicts between parents, children and siblings. But there are
also a multitude of secondary echoes. Virtually all Shakespeare's works have
their titles transformed into Joyce's nocturnal dialect*—Miss Somer's nice
dream, All Swell That Aimswell, the Smirching of Venus, measures for
messieurs, kingly leer . . . *The Rape of Lucrece is elongated into a* ripping
rude rape in his lucreasious togery. *And most of the works yield broken or
distorted quotations. One passage conjures up a sense of desolation through its
references to* Macbeth, *for instance:*

. . . Yet's the time for being now, now, now.

   For a burning would is come to dance inane. Glamours hath moi-
dered's lieb and herefore Coldours must leap no more. Lack breath must
leap no more.

Shakespeare himself frequently appears in the pages of the Wake, *along with
the legends surrounding him. His name—whether through the circumstances of
the dream that is being narrated, or because Joyce saw him as a rival—is often
given a derisory twist. He resurfaces as 'shaggspick', 'Shikespower', 'sheep-
skeer', 'Scheekspair' (a pair of buttocks), even as 'Shopkeeper' (with a glance,
perhaps, at the nation of shopkeepers from which he sprang). But he is also,
most memorably, the godlike, world-creating 'Shapesphere'—though even here
Joyce can't resist citing him as a precedent for his own incessant wordplay: 'As
Great Shapesphere puns it.'*

★　★　★

Shakespeare plays a central role in Aldous Huxley's Brave New World *(1932).
The novel is set six hundred years in the future, in a grimly benign world state
in which humans are hatched from incubators, conditioned to accept their
preordained social roles amd kept happy with drugs and inane entertainments.
By contrast, Shakespeare comes to symbolize imagination, emotional depth and
moral choice.*

   *The controllers of the new order have permitted pockets of primitive life to
survive in sealed-off communities. A woman called Linda gets lost while visiting
one of these reservations, in New Mexico. Stranded there, she is compelled to
adopt the life of the local tribe.*

   *At the time she went missing, Linda was pregnant. Her child, John, is
brought up as a member of the tribe. But he is still made to feel an outsider
('They disliked me for my complexion,' he later explains, echoing the Prince of
Morocco in* The Merchant of Venice*), and he increasingly resents his
mother's lover, Popé.*

One day (John calculated later that it must have been soon after his twelfth birthday) he came home and found a book that he had never seen before lying on the floor in the bedroom. It was a thick book and looked very old. The binding had been eaten by mice; some of its pages were loose and crumpled. He picked it up, looked at the title-page: the book was called *The Complete Works of William Shakespeare*.

Linda was lying on the bed, sipping that horrible stinking *mescal* out of a cup. 'Popé brought it,' she said. Her voice was thick and hoarse like somebody else's voice. 'It was lying in one of the chests of the Antelope Kiva. It's supposed to have been there for hundreds of years. I expect it's true, because I looked at it, and it seemed to be full of nonsense. Uncivilized. Still, it'll be good enough for you to practise your reading on.' She took a last sip, set the cup down on the floor beside the bed, turned over on her side, hiccoughed once or twice and went to sleep.

He opened the book at random.

> Nay, but to live
> In the rank sweat of an enseamed bed,
> Stew'd in corruption, honeying and making love
> Over the nasty sty . . .

The strange words rolled through his mind; rumbled, like talking thunder; like the drums at the summer dances, if the drums could have spoken; like the men singing the Corn Song, beautiful, beautiful, so that you cried; like old Mitsima saying magic over his feathers and his carved sticks and his bits of bone and stone—*kiathla tsilu silokwe silokwe. Kiai silu silu, tsithl*—but better than Mitsima's magic, because it meant more, because it talked to *him*; talked wonderfully and only half-understandably, a terrible beautiful magic, about Linda; about Linda lying there snoring, with the empty cup on the floor beside the bed; about Linda and Popé, Linda and Popé.

He hated Popé more and more. A man can smile and smile and be a villain. Remorseless, treacherous, lecherous, kindless villain. What did the words exactly mean? He only half knew. But their magic was strong and went on rumbling in his head, and somehow it was as though he had never really hated Popé before; never really hated him because he had never been able to say how much he hated him. But now he had these words, these words like drums and singing and magic. These words and the strange story out of which they were taken (he couldn't make head or tail of it, but it was wonderful, wonderful all the same)—they gave

him a reason for hating Popé; and they made his hatred more real; they
even made Popé himself more real.

*Later John is taken to London—where he is known as 'the Savage'—by Bernard
Marx, a sardonic and detached intellectual (something went wrong with his
embryo during incubation). While he is there, he gets to know Helmholtz
Watson, who is a friend of Bernard, and almost equally disaffected. Helmholtz
lectures at the College of Emotional Engineering (Department of Writing), and
has 'the happiest knack' of turning out slogans and propaganda jingles. In an
earlier age he would have been a poet, and he has landed in trouble for reading
his students some rhymes in which he has tried to express the mysterious
feelings which overwhelm him when he is alone.*

*John introduces Helmholtz to Shakespeare—initially, by reading aloud 'The
Phoenix and Turtle'. Helmholtz is thrilled by the verbal magic, but when they
move on to Romeo and Juliet he can't respond to its dramatic substance: he is
still too much in thrall to his conditioning.*

At his third meeting with the Savage, Helmholtz recited his rhymes on
Solitude.

'What do you think of them?' he asked when he had done.

The Savage shook his head. 'Listen to *this*,' was his answer; and
unlocking the drawer in which he kept his mouse-eaten book, he opened
and read:

> 'Let the bird of loudest lay,
> On the sole Arabian tree,
> Herald sad and trumpet be . . .'

Helmholtz listened with a growing excitement. At 'sole Arabian tree'
he started; at 'thou shrieking harbinger' he smiled with sudden pleasure;
at 'every fowl of tyrant wing' the blood rushed up into his cheeks; but at
'defunctive music' he turned pale and trembled with an unprecedented
emotion. The Savage read on:

> 'Property was thus appall'd,
> That the self was not the same;
> Single nature's double name
> Neither two nor one was call'd.
>
> Reason in itself confounded
> Saw division grow together . . .'

'Orgy-porgy!'° said Bernard, interrupting the reading with a loud, unpleasant laugh. 'It's just a Solidarity Service hymn.' He was revenging himself on his two friends for liking one another more than they liked him.

In the course of their next two or three meetings he frequently repeated this little act of vengeance. It was simple and, since both Helmholtz and the Savage were dreadfully pained by the shattering and defilement of a favourite poetic crystal, extremely effective. In the end, Helmholtz threatened to kick him out of the room if he dared to interrupt again. And yet, strangely enough, the next interruption, the most disgraceful of all, came from Helmholtz himself.

The Savage was reading *Romeo and Juliet* aloud—reading (for all the time he was seeing himself as Romeo and Lenina as Juliet) with an intense and quivering passion. Helmholtz had listened to the scene of the lovers' first meeting with a puzzled interest. The scene in the orchard had delighted him with its poetry; but the sentiments expressed had made him smile. Getting into such a state about having a girl—it seemed rather ridiculous. But, taken detail by verbal detail, what a superb piece of emotional engineering! 'That old fellow,' he said, 'he makes our best propaganda technicians look absolutely silly.' The Savage smiled triumphantly and resumed his reading. All went tolerably well until, in the last scene of the third act, Capulet and Lady Capulet began to bully Juliet to marry Paris. Helmholtz had been restless throughout the entire scene; but when, pathetically mimed by the Savage, Juliet cried out:

> 'Is there no pity sitting in the clouds,
> That sees into the bottom of my grief?
> O, sweet my mother, cast me not away!
> Delay this marriage for a month, a week;
> Or, if you do not, make the bridal bed
> In that dim monument where Tybalt lies . . . '

when Juliet said this, Helmholtz broke out in an explosion of uncontrollable guffawing.

The mother and father (grotesque obscenity) forcing the daughter to have someone she didn't want! And the idiotic girl not saying that she was having someone else whom (for the moment, at any rate) she preferred! In its smutty absurdity the situation was irresistibly comical. He

Orgy-porgy] the rhyme which celebrates 'the final consummation of solidarity' in *Brave New World* is 'Orgy-porgy, Ford and fun, | Kiss the girls and make them One. | Boys at one with girls at peace; | Orgy-porgy gives release'

had managed, with a heroic effort, to hold down the mounting pressure of his hilarity; but 'sweet mother' (in the Savage's tremulous tone of anguish) and the reference to Tybalt lying dead, but evidently uncremated and wasting his phosphorus on a dim monument, were too much for him. He laughed and laughed till the tears streamed down his face—quenchlessly laughed while, pale with a sense of outrage, the Savage looked at him over the top of his book and then, as the laughter still continued, closed it indignantly, got up and, with the gesture of one who removes his pearl from before swine, locked it away in its drawer.

'And yet,' said Helmholtz when, having recovered breath enough to apologize, he had mollified the Savage into listening to his explanations, 'I know quite well that one needs ridiculous, mad situations like that; one can't write really well about anything else. Why was that old fellow such a marvellous propaganda technician? Because he had so many insane, excruciating things to get excited about. You've got to be hurt and upset; otherwise you can't think of the really good, penetrating, X-rayish phrases. But fathers and mothers!' He shook his head. 'You can't expect me to keep a straight face about fathers and mothers. And who's going to get excited about a boy having a girl or not having her?' (The Savage winced; but Helmholtz, who was staring pensively at the floor, saw nothing.) 'No,' he concluded, with a sigh, 'it won't do. We need some other kind of madness and violence. But what? What? Where can one find it?' He was silent; then, shaking his head, 'I don't know,' he said at last, 'I don't know.'

The last thing Aldous Huxley wrote, completed the day before he died (22 November 1963), was an essay on 'Shakespeare and Religion'. At the end of it he reverts to a favourite passage, which had already supplied him with the title of his 1944 novel Time Must Have a Stop.

Hotspur, as he is dying, sums up the human predicament with a few memorable words:

> *But thought's the slave of life, and life time's fool;*
> *And time, that takes survey of all the world,*
> *Must have a stop.*

We think we know who we are and what we ought to do about it, and yet our thought is conditioned and determined by the nature of our immediate experience as psycho-physical organisms on this particular planet. Thought, in other words, is Life's fool. Thought is the slave of Life, and Life obviously is Time's fool inasmuch as it is changing from instant to instant, changing the outside and the inner world so that we never remain the same two instants together.

Thought is determined by life, and life is determined by passing time. But the dominion of time is not absolute, for 'time must have a stop' in two senses, from the Christian point of view in which Shakespeare was writing. It must have a stop in the last judgment, and in the winding up of the universe. But on the way to this general consummation, it must have a stop in the individual mind, which must learn the regular cultivation of a mood of timelessness, of the sense of eternity.

(The Hotspur passage comes from Henry IV Part One, v. iv. *Huxley quotes the version of the first line in Quartos 2 to 5 and in the First Folio; most modern editors opt for the somewhat less grand reading to be found in Quarto 1—'But thoughts, the slaves of life, and life, time's fool . . .')*

★   ★   ★

Ember turns his face to the wall and bursts into tears. In order to bring things back to a less emotional level Krug tells him about a curious character with whom he once traveled in the States, a man who was fanatically eager to make a film out of *Hamlet*.

> 'We'd begin, he had said, with
> Ghostly apes swathed in sheets
> haunting the shuddering Roman streets.
> And the mobled moon . . .

Then: the ramparts and towers of Elsinore, its dragons and florid iron-works, the moon making fish scales of its shingle tiles, the integument of a mermaid multiplied by the gable roof, which shimmers in an abstract sky, and the green star of a glowworm on the platform before the dark castle. Hamlet's first soliloquy is delivered in an unweeded garden that has gone to seed. Burdock and thistle are the main invaders. A toad breathes and blinks on the late king's favorite garden seat. Somewhere the cannon booms as the new king drinks. By dream law and screen law the cannon is gently transformed into the obliquity of a rotten tree trunk in the garden. The trunk points cannonwise at the sky where for one instant the deliberate loops of canescent smoke form the floating word "self-slaughter".

'Hamlet at Wittenberg, always late, missing G. Bruno's° lectures, never using a watch, relying on Horatio's timepiece which is slow, saying he will be on the battlements between eleven and twelve and turning up after midnight.

'The moonlight following on tiptoe the Ghost in complete steel, a gleam now settling on a rounded pauldron, now stealing along the taces.°

'We shall also see Hamlet dragging the dead Ratman° from under the arras and along the floor and up the winding stairs, to stow him away in an obscure passage, with some weird light effects anon, when the torch-bearing Switzers are sent to find the body. Another thrill will be provided by Hamlet's sea-gowned figure, unhampered by the heavy seas, heedless of the spray, clambering over bales and barrels of Danish butter and creeping into the cabin where Rosenstern and Guildenkranz, those gentle interchangeable twins "who came to heal and went away to die," are snoring in their common bunk. As the sagebrush country and leopard-spotted hills sped past the window of the men's lounge, more and more pictorial possibilities were evolved. We might be shown, he said (he was a hawkfaced shabby man whose academic career had been suddenly brought to a close by an awkwardly timed love affair), R. following young L. through the Quartier Latin, Polonius in his youth acting Caesar at the University Playhouse, the skull in Hamlet's gloved hands developing the features of a live jester (with the censor's permission); perhaps even lusty old King Hamlet smiting with a poleax the Polacks skidding and sprawling on the ice. Then he produced a flask from his hip pocket and said: "take a shot." He added he had thought she was eighteen at least, judging by her bust, but, in fact, she was hardly fifteen, the little bitch. And then there was Ophelia's death. To the sounds of Liszt's *Les Funérailles* she would be shown wrestling—or, as another rivermaid's father° would have said, "wrustling"—with the willow. A lass, a salix.° He recommended here a side shot of the glassy water. To feature a phloating leaph. Then back again to her little white hand, holding a wreath, trying to reach, trying to wreathe a phallacious sliver. Now comes the difficulty of dealing in a dramatic way with what had been in prevocal

G. Bruno's] the philosopher Giordano Bruno (1548–1600) taught briefly at Wittenberg
pauldron] a shoulder-plate
taces] armour covering the thigh
Ratman] Polonius, killed like a rat behind the arras. 'Rat' also means both 'council' and 'counsel' in German
rivermaid's father] James Joyce. His 'daughter' is Anna Livia Plurabelle in *Finnegans Wake*
salix] the Latin for 'willow'

days the *pièce de résistance* of comic shorts—the getting-unexpectedly-wet stunt. The hawk-man in the toilet lounge pointed out (between cigar and cuspidor) that the difficulty might be neatly countered by showing only her shadow, her falling shadow, falling and glancing across the edge of the turfy bank amid a shower of shadowy flowers. See? Then: a garland afloat. That puritanical leather (on which they sat) was the very last remnant of a phylogenetic link between the modern highly differentiated Pullman idea and a bench in the primitive stagecoach: from oats to oil. Then—and only then—we see her, he said, on her back in the brook (which table-forks further on to form eventually the Rhine, the Dnepr and the Cottonwood Canyon or Nova Avon) in a dim ectoplastic cloud of soaked, bulging bombast-quilted° garments and dreamily droning hey non nonny nonny or any other old laud. This is transformed into a tinkling of bells, and now we are shown a liberal shepherd on marshy ground where *Orchis mascula* grows: period rags, sun-margined beard, five sheep and one cute lamb. An important point, this lamb, despite the brevity—one heartthrob—of the bucolic theme. Song moves to Queen's shepherd, lamb moves to brook.'

VLADIMIR NABOKOV, *Bend Sinister*, 1947

Bend Sinister, which is set in a fictitious police state, contains a long digression on Hamlet, *of which this is only a part. First, the views of the late Professor Hamm are expounded, with disdain, by Ember, who is literary adviser to the state theatre. According to Hamm, the play is a political allegory, and its true hero is Fortinbras. Such an interpretation is highly acceptable to the regime, and Ember has been ordered to follow it in a forthcoming production. The thought fills him with misery, and his friend the philosopher Krug tries to distract him by telling him the story of the film scenario.*

East is East and West is West. If Hamm's theory embodies the distortions of 'progressive', Soviet-style ideology, the film script enshrines the less vicious but no less ludicrous distortions of Hollywood-style materialism. Every metaphor is taken literally; every Shakespearian image is given its banal photographic equivalent.

Nabokov isn't so much making political points, however, as pursuing the themes of interpretation and translation (or misinterpretation and mistranslation) in general. Krug and Ember go on to subject Hamlet *to ingenious*

---

bombast-quilted] the original meaning of 'bombast' is cotton used for padding

etymological games, and to discuss Ember's own attempt to translate the play.

Shakespeare is a presiding presence in Nabokov's Pale Fire *(1962). To enumerate and explain the Shakespearian references in the novel (or to attempt to) would require a small book in itself; here, a mere trio of examples must serve.*

    Pale Fire *takes the form of a long poem, also called 'Pale Fire', by the late John Shade, and an extended commentary on it by Charles Kinbote. The poet and his commentator were colleagues at Wordsmith College in Appalachia, where one of the great attractions is a grove containing specimens of all the trees mentioned by Shakespeare—*

. . . that admirable colonnade of trees, which visitors from England have photographed from end to end. I can enumerate here only a few kinds of those trees: Jove's stout oak and two others: the thunder-cloven from Britain, the knotty-entrailed from a Mediterranean island; a weather-fending line (now lime), a phoenix (now date palm), a pine and a cedar (*Cedrus*), all insular; a Venetian sycamore tree (*Acer*); two willows, the green, likewise from Venice, the hoar-leaved from Denmark; a midsummer elm, its barky fingers enringed with ivy; a midsummer mulberry, its shade inviting to tarry; and a clown's sad cypress from Illyria.

[The stout oak, the knotty-entrailed oak, the line (now lime), the phoenix, the pine, and the cedar come from The Tempest; *the thunder-cloven oak comes from* King Lear; *the sycamore and the green willow come from* Othello; *the hoar-leaved willow comes from* Hamlet; *the elm and the mulberry come from* A Midsummer Night's Dream; *the cypress comes from* Twelfth Night.]*

Then there is the phrase 'Pale Fire' itself, which is borrowed from a speech in Timon of Athens:

> I'll example you with thievery:
> The sun's a thief, and with his great attraction
> Robs the vast sea; the moon's an arrant thief,
> And her pale fire she snatches from the sun;
> The sea's a thief, whose liquid surge resolves,
> The moon into salt tears . . .

In short, 'each thing's a thief'. And as Brian Boyd observes in his study Nabokov's 'Pale Fire': The Magic of Artistic Discovery, *'the title Shade*

lifts from Shakespeare puts a highly ironic twist on the whole practice of
purloining another's phrase, since it wittily steals from Timon's denunciation
against universal thievery'.

Another salute to Shakespeare—our final example—is the image which
glows in the second stanza of a short poem by Shade which Kinbote quotes in
the course of his commentary:

> The dead, the gentle dead—who knows?—
> In tungsten filaments abide,
> And on my bedside table glows
> Another man's departed bride.
>
> And maybe Shakespeare floods a whole
> Town with innumerable lights,
> And Shelley's incandescent soul
> Lures the pale moths of starless nights.
>
> Streetlamps are numbered, and maybe
> Number nine-hundred-ninety-nine
> (So brightly beaming through a tree
> So green) is an old friend of mine.
>
> And when above the livid plain
> Forked lightning plays, therein may dwell
> The torments of a Tamerlane,
> The roar of tyrants torn in hell.

It is curious, in the context of electrification, to consider a remark once made by
Thomas Edison:

'Ah, Shakespeare! He would have been an inventor, a wonderful
inventor, if he had turned his mind to it. He seemed to see the inside of
everything.'

Quoted in Paul Israel, *Edison*, 1999

PLAYS AND CHARACTERS

In the case of every suffering, it is always possible to conceive a will which exceeds it in intensity and is therefore unconquered by it. . . . Shakespeare shows us in Cardinal Beaufort [in *Henry VI Part Two*] the fearful end of a profligate, who dies full of despair, for no suffering or death can break his will, which is vehement to the extreme of wickedness.

ARTHUR SCHOPENHAUER, *The World as Will and Idea*, 1819,
tr. R. B. Haldane and J. Kemp

It [*Titus Andronicus*] shows a pitilessness, a sharp predilection for the ugly, a titanic quarrel with the gods, such as we find in the first works of the greatest poets.

HEINRICH HEINE, *Shakespeare's Girls and Women*, 1838, tr. S. S. Prawer

Many of the tragedies attributed to Shakespeare are not his, but were only touched up by him. The tragedy *Romeo and Juliet*, although differing absolutely from his usual method, so obviously belongs to his dramatic canon and bears so many marks of his free and sweeping brush-strokes, that it must be recognized as Shakespeare's work. The Italy contemporary to the poet is reflected in it, its climate, passions, festivals, voluptuousness, sonnets, its magnificent language full of scintillating concetti. That is what Shakespeare understood by dramatic local colour. After Juliet and Romeo, those two delightful creations that grace Shakespeare's art, Mercutio, the model young gentleman of the time, polished, affectionate, noble Mercutio, is the most wonderful character in the whole tragedy. The poet chose him to represent the Italian people, who were the people most in fashion in Europe, the French of the sixteenth century.

ALEXANDER PUSHKIN, 'Note on Shakespeare's
Romeo and Juliet', 1830, tr. Tatiana Wolff

A large part of this tragedy [*Romeo and Juliet*] is written in blank verse, as are all Shakespeare's plays. It is the mode used by the hero and heroine. But the metre is not emphasised and doesn't obtrude. It is not declamatory verse. A self-preening form doesn't obscure the profound modesty of the lovers' dialogue, which exemplifies poetry at its best, when it is always suffused with the simplicity and freshness of prose. Romeo and Juliet's speeches epitomise the snatched half-whispers and guarded, surreptitious colloquies of night meetings, mortal danger and anxiety, which will be the future beauty and unprecedented magic of *Victoria*° and *War and Peace*.

In this tragedy the deafening, emphatically rhythmic scenes are those crowded with people, in the streets or in the houses. Outside the windows ring the daggers of the quarrelling clans, the blood of Capulets and Montagues streams in the streets, while in the kitchens, cooks' knives clatter and scullions squabble over the endless dinners. And under the hubbub of cooking and carnage, as under the thumping beat of a noisy band, the tragedy of hushed feelings is played out in silent, conspiratorial whispers.

> BORIS PASTERNAK, 'Observations on Translating Shakespeare', 1939–46,
> tr. Ann Pasternak Slater

Shakespeare showed the best of his skill in his Mercutio, and he said himself that he was forced to kill him in the third Act, to prevent being killed by him.

> JOHN DRYDEN, 'Defence of the Epilogue', *The Conquest of Granada*, 1672

I cannot believe that Shakespeare looked on his Richard II with any but sympathetic eyes, understanding indeed how ill-fitted he was to be King, at a certain moment of history, but understanding that he was lovable and full of capricious fancy, 'a wild creature' as Pater has called him. The man on whom Shakespeare modelled him had been full of French elegancies, as he knew from Hollingshead,° and had given life a new luxury, a new splendour, and been 'too friendly' to his friends, 'too favourable' to his enemies. And certainly Shakespeare had these things in his head when he made his King fail, a little because he lacked some qualities that were doubtless common among his scullions, but more because he had certain qualities that are uncommon in all ages. To

Victoria] a novel (published 1898) by Knut Hamsun
Hollingshead] the chronicler Raphael Holinshed

suppose that Shakespeare preferred the men who deposed his King is to suppose that Shakespeare judged men with the eyes of a Municipal Councillor weighing the merits of a Town Clerk; and that had he been by when Verlaine cried out from his bed, 'Sir, you have been made by the stroke of a pen, but I have been made by the breath of God,' he would have thought the Hospital Superintendent the better man. He saw indeed, as I think, in Richard II the defeat that awaits all, whether they be Artist or Saint, who find themselves where men ask of them a rough energy and have nothing to give but some contemplative virtue, whether lyrical phantasy, or sweetness of temper, or dreamy dignity, or love of God, or love of His creatures. He saw that such a man through sheer bewilderment and impatience can become as unjust or as violent as any common man, any Bolingbroke or Prince John, and yet remain 'that sweet lovely rose.' The courtly and saintly ideals of the Middle Ages were fading, and the practical ideals of the modern age had begun to threaten the unuseful dome of the sky; Merry England was fading, and yet it was not so faded that the Poets could not watch the procession of the world with that untroubled sympathy for men as they are, as apart from all they do and seem, which is the substance of tragic irony.

Shakespeare cared little for the State, the source of all our judgments, apart from its shows and splendours, its turmoils and battles, its flamings out of the uncivilized heart. He did indeed think it wrong to overturn a King, and thereby to swamp peace in civil war, and the historical plays from *Henry IV* to *Richard III*, that monstrous birth and last sign of the wrath of Heaven, are a fulfilment of the prophecy of the Bishop of Carlisle, who was 'raised up by God' to make it; but he had no nice sense of utilities, no ready balance to measure deeds, like that fine instrument, with all the latest improvements, Gervinus° and Professor Dowden handle so skilfully. He meditated as Solomon, not as Bentham meditated, upon blind ambitions, untoward accidents, and capricious passions, and the world was almost as empty in his eyes as it must be in the eyes of God.

W. B. YEATS, from 'At Stratford-on-Avon', 1901

It is difficult to approach critically so great a figure as that of Bottom the Weaver. He is greater and more mysterious than Hamlet, because the interest of such men as Bottom consists of a rich subconsciousness, and

Gervinus] German literary scholar

that of Hamlet in the comparatively superficial matter of a rich consciousness. And it is especially difficult in the present age which has
become hag-ridden with the mere intellect. We are the victims of a
curious confusion whereby being great is supposed to have something to
do with being clever, as if there were the smallest reason to suppose that
Achilles was clever, as if there were not on the contrary a great deal of
internal evidence to indicate that he was next door to a fool. Greatness is
a certain indescribable but perfectly familiar and palpable quality of size
in the personality, of steadfastness, of strong flavour, of easy and natural
self-expression. Such a man is as firm as a tree and as unique as a
rhinoceros, and he might quite easily be as stupid as either of them.
Fully as much as the great poet towers above the small poet the great
fool towers above the small fool.

> G. K. CHESTERTON, 'A Midsummer Night's Dream',
> reprinted in *The Common Man*, 1950

My histrionic acquaintance spreads. I supped at Lady Dorothy Hotham's
with Mrs Siddons, have visited and been visited by her, and have seen
and liked her much, yes, very much, in the passionate scenes in 'Percy';
but I do not admire her in cool declamation, and find her voice very
hollow and defective. I asked her in which part she would most wish me
to see her? She named Portia in the 'Merchant of Venice'; but I begged to
be excused. With all my enthusiasm for Shakespeare, it is one of his
plays that I like the least. The story of the caskets is silly, and, except the
character of Shylock, I see nothing beyond the attainment of a mortal;
Euripides, or Racine, or Voltaire might have written all the rest.

> HORACE WALPOLE, letter to the Countess of Ossory, 1788

Bankrupt Antonio is a weak soul without energy, without strength to
hate and thus also without strength to love, a gloomy worm-heart
whose flesh really is good for nothing but 'to bait fish withal.' The
borrowed three thousand ducats, by the way, he does not dream of
returning to the swindled Jew. Nor does Bassanio give the money back;
he, in the words of an English critic is 'a genuine fortune-hunter'; he
borrows money to fix himself up sumptuously to bag a rich wife and a
fat dowry.

As for Lorenzo, he is an accessory to one of the most infamous
burglaries, and under the Prussian Criminal Code he would be

sentenced to fifteen years at hard labor, branded and pilloried—although he is not only susceptible to stolen ducats and jewels but also to the beauties of nature, moon-lit landscapes and music. As for the other noble Venetians whom we see appearing as Antonio's companions, they do not seem to despise money very much, either. And for their poor friend who has fallen upon evil days they have nothing but words, coined air. On that point, our good pietist Franz Horn° makes the following watery but wholly proper remark: 'Here one might fairly inquire: how was it possible that Antonio's troubles went so far?' All of Venice knew and esteemed him; his close acquaintances knew all about the terrible bond, and that the Jew would not permit a period of it to be stricken out. Still, they let one day after another pass, until finally the three months are gone and with them all hopes of rescue. For the good friends of whom the royal merchant seems to have an entire host about him, it ought to have been easy to raise three thousand ducats to save a life—and what a life!—but things like that are always somewhat inconvenient; and so the dear good friends, because they are only so-called friends or, if you will, half- or three-quarter friends, do nothing, nothing at all, and nothing once again. They pity the excellent merchant, who in the past gave them such beautiful feasts, immensely but with due languor; they revile Shylock to their hearts' and tongues' content, which also may be done without danger; and then, presumably, they all believe they have fulfilled the duties of friendship. Much as we must hate Shylock, we cannot blame him for despising these people a little, which he probably does.

HEINRICH HEINE, *Shakespeare's Girls and Women*, 1838, tr. E. B. Ashton

Heine, though he felt we had no choice but to hate Shylock, also regarded him as 'except for Portia, the most respectable character in the play'.

Later, in the same section of Shakespeare's Girls and Women—*on Jessica—he imagines himself (or his narrator) visiting a synagogue in contemporary Venice on Yom Kippur, the Day of Atonement:*

Though I looked all around in the synagogue of Venice, I could not see the face of Shylock anywhere. And yet it seemed to me that he must be there, hidden under one of those white robes, praying more fervently

Franz Horn] a high-minded literary historian who published a five-volume commentary on Shakespeare in the 1820s. Heine frequently made fun of him, though he quotes him with approval here

than any of his fellow believers, with stormy wildness, even with madness, to the throne of Jehovah, the stern divine monarch. I did not see
him. Towards evening, however, when, as the Jews believe, the gates of
heaven are closed and no further prayer can enter, I heard a voice in
which tears flowed that were never wept from human eyes. . . . It was a
sobbing that might have moved a stone to pity . . . These were sounds of
agony that could come only from a heart that held locked within it all
the martyrdom which a tormented people had endured for eighteen
centuries. . . . And it seemed to me that I knew this voice well; I felt as
though I had heard it long ago, when it lamented, with the same tone of
despair: 'Jessica, my child!'

tr. S. S. Prawer

*In Heine's poem 'Cold Hearts' (*Kalte Herzen*), the poet himself takes on the
persona of Lorenzo after falling in love with an actress:*

> Als ich dich zum ersten Male
> In der Welt von Pappe sah,
> Spieltest du in Gold und Seide
> Shylocks Tochter Jessica.

[When I first saw you, in the pasteboard world, you were dressed in gold
and silk, and you were playing Shylock's daughter Jessica.]

*The actress's features, like her voice, are 'cold and clear', but her identification
with Jessica bodes ill:*

> Und der Jud verlor die Tochter,
> Und der Christ nahm dich zum Weibe;
> Armer Shylock, ärmrer Lorenz!
> Und mir fror das Herz im Leibe.

[And the Jew lost his daughter, and the Christian took you to wife. Poor
Shylock, poorer Lorenzo! My heart froze in my body.]

*And although for a time the poet becomes her lover, her Lorenzo, in the end she
proves faithless: 'Jessica turned her back on me.'*

This [*Henry IV Part One*] is a play which all men admire, and which most women dislike.

ELIZABETH INCHBALD, 1808

For inimitably natural talk between husband and wife he would quote the scene between Hotspur and Lady Percy (*King Henry IV*, Pt. 1), and would exclaim: 'How deliciously playful is that—

> "In faith, I'll break thy little finger, Harry,
> An if thou wilt not tell me all things true"!'

ALFRED TENNYSON in Hallam Tennyson's memoir, 1897

Falstaff's Lament over Prince Hal Become Henry V

One that I cherisheed,
Yea, loved as a son—
Up early, up late with,
My promising one:
No use in good nurture,
None, lads, none!

Here on this settle
He wore the true crown,
King of good fellows,
And Fat Jack was one—
Now, Beadle of England
In formal array—
Best fellow alive
On a throne flung away!

Companions and cronies
Keep fast and lament;—
Come drawer, more sack here
To drown discontent;

For now intuitions
Shall wither to codes,
Pragmatical morals
Shall libel the gods.—

One I instructed,
Yea, talked to—alone:
Precept—example
Clean away thrown!

(Sorrow makes thirsty:
Sack, drawer, more sack!—)
One that I prayed for,
I, Honest Jack!—

To bring down these gray hairs—
To cut his old pal!
But, I'll be magnanimous—
Here's to thee, Hal!

HERMAN MELVILLE

Falstaff is introduced as a subordinate stage figure with no other function than to be robbed by the Prince and Poins, who was originally
meant to be the *raisonneur* of the piece, and the chief figure among the
prince's dissolute associates. But Poins soon fades into nothing, like
several characters in Dickens's early works; whilst Falstaff develops into
an enormous joke and an exquisitely mimicked human type. Only in the
end the joke withers. The question comes to Shakespear: *Is* this really a
laughing matter? Of course there can be only one answer; and Shakespear gives it as best he can by the mouth of the prince become king,
who might, one thinks, have the decency to wait until he has redeemed
his own character before assuming the right to lecture his boon companion. Falstaff, rebuked and humiliated, dies miserably. His followers
are hanged, except Pistol, whose exclamation 'Old do I wax; and from
my weary limbs honor is cudgelled' is a melancholy exordium to an old
age of beggary and imposture.

But suppose Shakespear had begun where he left off! Suppose he had
been born at a time when, as the result of a long propaganda of health
and temperance, sack had come to be called alcohol, alcohol had come
to be called poison, corpulence had come to be regarded as either a
disease or a breach of good manners, and a conviction had spread
throughout society that the practice of consuming 'a half-pennyworth
of bread to an intolerable deal of sack' was the cause of so much misery,
crime, and racial degeneration that whole States prohibited the sale of
potable spirits altogether, and even moderate drinking was more and

more regarded as a regrettable weakness! Suppose (to drive the change well home) the women in the great theatrical centres had completely lost that amused indulgence for the drunken man which still exists in some out-of-the-way places, and felt nothing but disgust and anger at the conduct and habits of Falstaff and Sir Toby Belch! Instead of Henry IV and The Merry Wives of Windsor, we should have had something like Zola's L'Assommoir. Indeed, we actually have Cassio, the last of Shakespear's gentleman-drunkards, talking like a temperance reformer, a fact which suggests that Shakespear had been roundly lectured for the offensive vulgarity of Sir Toby by some woman of refinement who refused to see the smallest fun in giving a knight such a name as Belch, with characteristics to correspond to it. Suppose, again, that the first performance of The Taming of the Shrew had led to a modern Feminist demonstration in the theatre, and forced upon Shakespear's consideration a whole century of agitatresses, from Mary Wollstonecraft to Mrs Fawcett and Mrs Pankhurst, is it not likely that the jest of Katharine and Petruchio would have become the earnest of Nora and Torvald Helmer?

BERNARD SHAW, preface to The Quintessence of Ibsenism, 1891

I could not say anything more beautiful in praise of Shakespeare *as a human being* than this: he believed in Brutus and did not cast one speck of suspicion upon this type of virtue. It was to him that he devoted his best tragedy—it is still called by the wrong name—to him and to the most awesome quintessence of a lofty morality. Independence of the soul!— that is at stake here. No sacrifice can be too great for that: one must be capable of sacrificing one's dearest friend for it, even if he should also be the most glorious human being, an ornament of the world, a genius without peer—if one loves freedom as the freedom of great souls and he threatens this kind of freedom. That is what Shakespeare must have felt. The height at which he places Caesar is the finest honor that he could bestow on Brutus: that is how he raises beyond measure Brutus's inner problem as well as the spiritual strength that was able to cut *this knot*.

Could it really have been political freedom that led this poet to sympathize with Brutus—and turned him into Brutus's accomplice? Or was political freedom only a symbol for something inexpressible? Could it be that we confront some unknown dark event and adventure in the poet's own soul of which he wants to speak only in signs? What is all of Hamlet's melancholy compared to that of Brutus? And perhaps Shakespeare knew both from firsthand experience. Perhaps he, too, had his gloomy hour and his evil angel, like Brutus.

But whatever similarities and secret relationships there may have been: before the whole figure and virtue of Brutus, Shakespeare prostrated himself, feeling unworthy and remote. His witness of this is written into the tragedy. Twice he brings in a poet, and twice he pours such an impatient and ultimate contempt over him that it sounds like a cry—the cry of self-contempt. Brutus, even Brutus, loses patience as the poet enters— conceited, pompous, obtrusive, as poets often are—apparently overflowing with possibilities of greatness, including moral greatness, although in the philosophy of his deeds and his life he rarely attains even ordinary integrity. 'I'll know his humor when he knows his time. | What should the wars do with these jigging fools? | Companion, hence!' shouts Brutus. This should be translated back into the soul of the poet who wrote it.

FRIEDRICH NIETZSCHE, *The Gay Science*, 1882, tr. Walter Kaufmann

The second poet in Julius Caesar *is Cinna, mistaken by the mob for Cinna the conspirator and then attacked 'for his bad verses'.*

King Claudius

My mind travels to far-off places.
I walk on the streets of Elsinore,
I stroll on the squares, and I recall
the most grievous history,
that unfortunate king
whom his nephew killed
because of some imagined suspicions.

In all the houses of the poor
they mourned him in secret (because they feared
Fortinbras). He was quiet
and meek; and he loved peace
(the land had suffered much
from the battles of his predecessor).
He acted courteously to everyone
great and small. He hated high-handed
acts, and he always sought
counsel on the affairs of state from
serious-minded and experienced people.

Just why his nephew killed him
they never stated with certainty.
He suspected him of murder.
The basis of his suspicion was
that one night as he was walking
on one of the ancient bastions
he thought he saw a ghost
and he made conversation with the ghost.
And presumably he learned from the ghost
some accusations against the king.

It must surely have been the excitement
of the imagination and an optical illusion.
(The prince was nervous in the extreme.
While studying at Wittenburg many
of his fellow-students took him to be maniacal.)

A few days later he went
to his mother to discuss with her
several of their family matters. And suddenly
as he was speaking, he grew excited
and he started to shout, to cry out
that the ghost had appeared before him.
But his mother saw nothing.

And the same day he killed
an old nobleman for no reason at all.
Since the prince was about to go
to England in a day or two,
the king rushed his departure
posthaste in order to save him.
But the people were so indignant
over the most horrible murder
that the insurgents rose up
and with the son of the slain man,
the noble Laertes (a brave
youth, and ambitious to boot,
they sought to break the palace gates;
in the commotion some of his friends
shouted: 'King Laertes, Zito!').

Later, when the place had quieted down
and the king was laid out in the grave,
killed by his nephew
(the prince did not go to England;
on the way he escaped from the boat),
a certain Horatio emerged in the midst
and with some tales he sought
to vindicate the prince.
He said that the trip to England
had been a secret plot and an order
had been given to kill him there.
(But this had not been clearly proven.)
He also spoke of poisoned wine,
poisoned by the king.
Laertes said this too, it is true,
But wasn't he lying? Wasn't he deceived?
And when did he say it? When wounded
he was expiring and his mind was wandering
and he appeared to be delirious.
As for the poisoned weapons,
later it appeared that the king
had not used the poison at all,
Laertes himself had used it.
But Horatio out of necessity
also made a witness of the ghost.
The ghost said this, said that!
The ghost did this and that!

Although they listened to him speak about these matters,
most of the people in their consciences
felt sorry for the good king
whom they killed unjustly
with ghosts and fairy tales, and was gone.

But Fortinbras, who profited
and who easily acquired authority,
gave much weight and close attention
to the words of Horatio.

C. P. CAVAFY, 1899, tr. from the Greek by Rae Dalven

Ophelia: in Defence of the Queen

Prince, let's have no more disturbing
   these wormy flower-beds. Look at
the living rose, and think of a woman
   snatching a single day—from the few left to her.

Prince Hamlet, you defile the Queen's
   womb. Enough. A virgin cannot
judge passion. Don't you know Phaedra
   was more guilty, yet men still sing of her,

and will go on singing. You, with your blend
   of chalk and rot, you bony
scandalmonger, how can you ever
   understand a fever in the blood?

Beware, if you continue . . . I can
   rise up through flagstones into the grand bed-chamber
of so much sweetness, I myself, to defend her.
   I myself—your own undying passion!

MARINA TSVETAYEVA, 1923, tr. Elaine Feinstein

On Shakespeare's Play Hamlet

Here is the body, puffy and inert
Where we can trace the virus of the mind.
How lost he seems among his steel-clad kind
This introspective sponger in a shirt!

Till they bring drums to wake him up again
As Fortinbras and all the fools he's found
March off to win that little patch of ground
'Which is not tomb enough . . . to hide the slain.'

At that his solid flesh starts to see red
He feels he's hesitated long enough
It's time to turn to (bloody) deeds instead.

So we can nod when the last Act is done
And they pronounce that he was of the stuff
To prove most royally, had he been put on.

BERTOLT BRECHT, *c.*1949, tr. John Willett

Polonius

Behind every arras
he does his duty
unswervingly.
Walls are his ears,
keyholes his eyes.

He slinks up the stairs,
oozes from the ceiling,
floats through the door
ready to give evidence,
prove what is proven,
stab with a needle
or pin on an order.

His poems always rhyme,
his brush is dipped in honey,
his music flutes
from marzipan and cane.

You buy him
by weight, boneless,
a pound of wax flesh,
a pound of mousy philosophy,
a pound of jellied
flunkey.

And when he's sold out
and the left-overs wrapped
in a tasselled obituary,
a paranoid funeral notice,

and when the spore-creating mould
of memory
covers him over,
when he falls
arse-first to the stars,

the whole continent will be lighter,
earth's axis straighten up
and in night's thunderous arena
a bird will chirp in gratitude.

MIROSLAV HOLUB, tr. from the Czech by Ian Milner

Elegy of Fortinbras
for C. M.

Now that we're alone we can talk prince man to man
though you lie on the stairs and see no more than a dead ant
nothing but black sun with broken rays
I could never think of your hands without smiling
and now that they lie on the stone like fallen nests
they are as defenceless as before The end is exactly this
The hands lie apart The sword lies apart The head apart
and the knight's feet in soft slippers

You will have a soldier's funeral without having been a soldier
the only ritual I am acquainted with a little
There will be no candles no singing only cannon-fuses and bursts
crepe dragged on the pavement helmets boots artillery horses drums
    drums I know nothing exquisite
those will be my manoeuvres before I start to rule
one has to take the city by the neck and shake it a bit

Anyhow you had to perish Hamlet you were not for life
you believed in crystal notions not in human clay
always twitching as if asleep you hunted chimeras
wolfishly you crunched the air only to vomit
you knew no human thing you did not know even how to breathe

Now you have peace Hamlet you accomplished what you had to
and you have peace The rest is not silence but belongs to me
you chose the easier part an elegant thrust
but what is heroic death compared with eternal watching
with a cold apple in one's hand on a narrow chair
with a view of the ant-hill and the clock's dial

Adieu prince I have tasks a sewer project
and a decree on prostitutes and beggars
I must also elaborate a better system of prisons
since as you justly said Denmark is a prison
I go to my affairs This night is born
a star named Hamlet We shall never meet
what I shall leave will not be worth a tragedy
It is not for us to greet each other or bid farewell we live on archipelagos
and that water these words what can they do what can they do prince

ZBIGNIEW HERBERT, tr. from the Polish by Czesław Miłosz

In Twilight in Italy *(1916) D. H. Lawrence describes his visits to the small theatre in Gargnano, on Lake Garda, where he had stayed in 1913. The leading actor in the local company was called Enrico Marconi (changed in Lawrence's account to 'Persevalli'). One of the plays in which he saw him perform was* Amleto:

I was late. The First Act was nearly over. The play was not yet alive, neither in the bosoms of the actors nor in the audience. I closed the door of the box softly, and came forward. The rolling Italian eyes of Hamlet glanced up at me. There came a new impulse over the Court of Denmark.

Enrico looked a sad fool in his melancholy black. The doublet sat close, making him stout and vulgar, the knee-breeches seemed to exaggerate the commonness of his thick, rather short, strutting legs. And he carried a long black rag, as a cloak, for histrionic purposes. And he had on his face a portentous grimace of melancholy and philosophic importance. His was the caricature of Hamlet's melancholy self-absorption.

I stooped to arrange my footstool and compose my countenance. I was trying not to grin. For the first time, attired in philosophic melancholy of black silk, Enrico looked a boor and a fool. His close-cropped, rather animal head was common above the effeminate doublet, his sturdy, ordinary figure looked absurd in a melancholic droop.

All the actors alike were out of their element. Their Majesties of Denmark were touching. The Queen, burly little peasant woman, was ill at ease in her pink satin. Enrico had had no mercy. He knew she loved to be the scolding servant or housekeeper, with her head tied up in a handkerchief, shrill and vulgar. Yet here she was pranked out in an expanse of satin, la Regina. Regina, indeed!

She obediently did her best to be important. Indeed, she rather fancied herself; she looked sideways at the audience, self-consciously, quite ready to be accepted as an imposing and noble person, if they would esteem her such. Her voice sounded hoarse and common, but whether it was the pink satin in contrast, or a cold, I do not know. She was almost childishly afraid to move. Before she began a speech she looked down and kicked her skirt viciously, so that she was sure it was under control. Then she let go. She was a burly, downright little body of sixty, one rather expected her to box Hamlet on the ears.

Only she liked being a queen when she sat on the throne. There she perched with great satisfaction, her train splendidly displayed down the steps. She was as proud as a child, and she looked like Queen Victoria of the Jubilee period.

The King, her noble consort, also had new honours thrust upon him, as well as new garments. His body was real enough, but it had nothing at all to do with his clothes. They established a separate identity by themselves. But wherever he went, they went with him, to the confusion of everybody.

He was a thin, rather frail-looking peasant, pathetic, and very gentle. There was something pure and fine about him, he was so exceedingly gentle and by natural breeding courteous. But he did not feel kingly, he acted the part with beautiful, simple resignation.

Enrico Persevalli had overshot himself in every direction, but worst of all in his own. He had become a hulking fellow, crawling about with his head ducked between his shoulders, pecking and poking, creeping about after other people, sniffing at them, setting traps for them, absorbed by his own self-important self-consciousness. His legs, in their black knee-breeches, had a crawling, slinking look; he always carried the black rag of a cloak, something for him to twist about as he twisted in his own soul, overwhelmed by a sort of inverted perversity.

I had always felt an aversion from Hamlet: a creeping, unclean thing he seems, on the stage, whether he is Forbes Robertson or anybody else. His nasty poking and sniffing at his mother, his setting traps for the King, his conceited perversion with Ophelia make him always intolerable. The character is repulsive in its conception, based on self-dislike and a spirit of disintegration.

There is, I think, this strain of cold dislike, or self-dislike, through much of the Renaissance art, and through all the later Shakespeare. In Shakespeare it is a kind of corruption in the flesh and a conscious revolt from this. A sense of corruption in the flesh makes Hamlet frenzied, for he will never admit that it is his own flesh. Leonardo da Vinci is the same, but Leonardo loves the corruption maliciously. Michael Angelo rejects any feeling of corruption, he stands by the flesh, the flesh only. It is the corresponding reaction, but in the opposite direction. But that is all four hundred years ago. Enrico Persevalli has just reached the position. He *is* Hamlet, and evidently he has great satisfaction in the part. He is the modern Italian, suspicious, isolated, self-nauseated, labouring in a sense of physical corruption. But he will not admit it is in himself. He creeps about in self-conceit, transforming his own self-loathing. With what satisfaction did he reveal corruption,—corruption in his neighbours he gloated in,—letting his mother know he had discovered her incest, her uncleanness, gloated in torturing the incestuous King. Of all the unclean ones, Hamlet was the uncleanest. But he accused only the others.

Except in the 'great' speeches, and there Enrico was betrayed, Hamlet suffered the extremity of physical self-loathing, loathing of his own flesh. The play is the statement of the most significant philosophic position of the Renaissance. Hamlet is far more even than Orestes, his prototype, a mental creature, anti-physical, anti-sensual. The whole drama is the tragedy of the convulsed reaction of the mind from the flesh, of the spirit from the self, the reaction from the great aristocratic to the great democratic principle.

An ordinary instinctive man, in Hamlet's position, would either have set about murdering his uncle, by reflex action, or else would have gone right away. There would have been no need for Hamlet to murder his mother. It would have been sufficient blood-vengeance if he had killed his uncle. But that is the statement according to the aristocratic principle.

Orestes was in the same position, but the same position two thousand years earlier, with two thousand years of experience wanting. So that the question was not so intricate in him as in Hamlet, he was not nearly so conscious. The whole Greek life was based on the idea of the supremacy of the self, and the self was always male. Orestes was his father's child, he would be the same whatever mother he had. The mother was but the vehicle, the soil in which the paternal seed was planted. When Clytemnestra murdered Agamemnon, it was as if a common individual murdered God, to the Greek.

But Agamemnon, King and Lord, was not infallible. He was fallible. He had sacrificed Iphigenia for the sake of glory in war, for the fulfilment of the superb idea of self, but on the other hand he had made cruel dissension for the sake of the concubines captured in war. The paternal flesh was fallible, ungodlike. It lusted after meaner pursuits than glory, war, and slaying, it was not faithful to the highest idea of the self. Orestes was driven mad by the furies of his mother, because of the justice that they represented. Nevertheless he was in the end exculpated. The third play of the trilogy is almost foolish, with its prating gods. But it means that, according to the Greek conviction, Orestes was right and Clytemnestra entirely wrong. But for all that, the infallible King, the infallible male Self, is dead in Orestes, killed by the furies of Clytemnestra. He gains his peace of mind after the revulsion from his own physical fallibility, but he will never be an unquestioned lord, as

Agamemnon was. Orestes is left at peace, neutralised. He is the beginning of non-aristocratic Christianity.

Hamlet's father, the King, is, like Agamemnon, a warrior-king. But,
unlike Agamemnon, he is blameless with regard to Gertrude. Yet
Gertrude, like Clytemnestra, is the potential murderer of her husband,
as Lady Macbeth is murderess, as the daughters of Lear. The women
murder the supreme male, the ideal Self, the King and Father.

This is the tragic position Shakespeare must dwell upon. The woman
rejects, repudiates the ideal Self which the male represents to her. The
supreme representative, King and Father, is murdered by the Wife and
the Daughters.

What is the reason? Hamlet goes mad in a revulsion of rage and
nausea. Yet the women-murderers only represent some ultimate judgment in his own soul. At the bottom of his own soul Hamlet has decided
that the Self in its supremacy, Father and King, must die. It is a suicidal
decision for his involuntary soul to have arrived at. Yet it is inevitable.
The great religious, philosophic tide, which had been swelling all
through the Middle Ages, had brought him there.

The question, to be or not to be, which Hamlet puts himself, does
not mean, to live or not to live. It is not the simple human being who
puts himself the question, it is the supreme I, King and Father. To be
or not to be King, Father, in the Self supreme? And the decision is, not
to be.

In Horatio's Version *(1972), Alethea Hayter conducts a fictional inquiry into
'what happens in* Hamlet'. *The newly enthroned King Fortinbras appoints a
royal commission, under the chairmanship of Voltimand, to investigate the
circumstances which led up to the welter of deaths at the end of the play; its
final report endorses Horatio's version of events, though he himself admits that
there is still a great deal he doesn't understand.*

*The book alternates between the proceedings of the commission and extracts,
as here, from the diary which Horatio keeps while it is in progress.*

We can make jokes about the Ghost now, but we were all afraid when
we actually saw it. It's no good thinking about that. Speculations of that
kind can do no good, they only make you morbid. It set us talking about
the old King when he was alive, though. I only saw him that once, but
the others knew him well by sight. He was splendid to look at, and they
said he could be kind and gracious, but terrible when he was angry, he'd

done some ferocious things. He was astonishingly brave, of course. When Marcellus first told me they'd seen the Ghost, I went and looked at the battle pictures of King Hamlet in the lobby. The best are the ones of his duel with old Fortinbras and of his battle with the Poles on the frozen river. A fine face, but a stern one. And yet the Prince loved him. I suppose he may have been different with his own family. He was open and unsuspicious, too, Hamlet would have liked that. Nothing like as clever as his son, though. The Prince was really more like his uncle than his father in that way—in natural power of mind, I mean, not in the use he made of it, God knows.

All's Well that End's Well falls into the list of plays that leave us sad. Melcholy moulders in the very title of it; for we feel that all is not well, nor ever has been nor can be well again.

JOHN JAY CHAPMAN, *Greek Genius and Other Essays*, 1915

The fact that of all those who are guilty only the one least guilty—chattering Lucio—is punished makes the title, *Measure for Measure*, a vivid satire.

FRANZ GRILLPARZER, Austrian dramatist, 1849, tr. LaMarr Kopp

The innocent fiery Isabella of the earlier act would never have consented to play out the licentious Italian comedy which Shakespeare casts her for in the last act. The spectator feels this, and resents the soil which Shakespeare has cast on his own creation. But for this slander, Isabella might have taken her place beside Desdemona and Imogen. But Shakespeare sometimes had bad taste; or rather, he had no taste at all; for taste is conscious art.

JOHN JAY CHAPMAN, *Greek Genius and Other Essays*, 1915

The murder of Desdemona:

I am glad I have ended my revisal of this dreadful scene. It is not to be endured.

SAMUEL JOHNSON, *The Plays of Shakespeare* (ed.), 1765

Shakespeare described the sex in Desdemona
     As very fair, but yet suspect in fame,
And to this day from Venice to Verona
     Such matters may be probably the same,
Except that since those times was never known a
     Husband whom mere suspicion could inflame
To suffocate a wife no more than twenty,
Because she had a 'cavalier servente.'

Their jealousy (if they are ever jealous)
     Is of a fair complexion altogether,
Not like that sooty devil of Othello's
     Which smothers women in a bed of feather,
But worthier of these much more jolly fellows;
     When weary of the matrimonial tether
His head for such a wife no mortal bothers,
But takes at once another, or another's.

                                        LORD BYRON, *Beppo*, 1818

A gloomy grief always comes over me when I entertain the thought that 'honest Iago' might not be altogether wrong in his malevolent glosses on Desdemona's love for the Moor. What repels me most every time are Othello's references to his wife's moist palm.

                    HEINRICH HEINE, *Shakespeare's Girls and Women*, 1838, tr. S. S. Prawer

One of the French decadents, Maizeroy, has recently written an idiotic novel in which 'she' whores *because* 'he' is jealous. The writer has of course been taken in, just like Shakespeare, who imagined Desdemona was innocent. I'm damned sure she didn't whore with Iago, but with a third person, and that's what revolts Iago.

                          AUGUST STRINDBERG, letter to Pehr Staaf, 1887

Two years later, Strindberg's thoughts about Desdemona were more complicated but hardly less misogynistic:

I believe Shakespeare was taken in by Desdemona, for in her coquetry towards Iago, she behaves like a whore. And Othello's so-called jealousy was merely the great man's concern to be able to decide his own descendants, or a certain justifiable fear of Desdemona's infidelity—unless, indeed, Desdemona wasn't trying to excite his jealousy in order to heighten her own pleasure by arousing his lust to do battle with other males.

Letter to Ola Hanson, 1889

Goats and Monkeys

. . . an old black ram
Is tupping your white ewe . . .

Othello, I. i

The owl's torches gutter. Chaos clouds the globe.
Shriek, augury! His earth bulk
buries her bosom in its slow eclipse.
His smoky hand has charred
that marble throat! Bent to her lips,
he is Africa, a vast, sidling shadow
that halves the world with doubt.
'Put out the light', and God's light is put out.

That flame extinct, she contemplates her dream
of him as huge as night, as bodiless,
as starred with medals, like the moon,
a moral of blind stone.
Dazzled by that bull's bulk against the sun
of Venice, couldn't she have known
like Pasiphae, poor girl, she'd breed him monsters,
or like Eurydice, her flesh a flare
travelling the infernal labyrinth of his kind
his soul would swallow hers?
Her white flesh rhymes with night. She climbs, secure.

Virgin and ape, maid and malignant Moor,
their elemental coupling halves our world.
He is your sacrificial beast, bellowing, goaded,
A black bull snarled in ribbons of its blood.
And yet what fury girded
on that saffron-sunset turban, moon-shaped sword
was not his racial, panther-black revenge

pulsing her chamber with raw musk, its sweat,
but horror of the moon's change,
the slow corruption of an absolute,
like a white fruit
pulped ripe by fondling but doubly sweet.

So he self-righteously arraigns the moon
for all she has beheld since time began,
for his own night-long lechery, ambition,
while innocence weeps uselessly for pardon.
And yet it is the moon, she silvers love,
limns lechery and mirrors our disgrace;
only annihilation can resolve
the pure corruption of a dreaming face.

Such bestial doubt is comic. We harden
with mockery for this blackamoor
who turns his back, who kills
what, like the clear moon could not abhor
his blackness; his grief
farcically knotted in a handkerchief,
a sybil's
prophetically stitched remembrancer
webb'd and embroidered with the zodiac,
this mythical, horned beast who's no more
monstrous for being black.

DEREK WALCOTT, 1964

The great moral lesson of the tragedy of 'Othello' is, that black and white blood cannot be intermingled in marriage without a gross outrage upon the law of Nature; and that, in such violations, Nature will vindicate her laws. The moral of Othello is not to beware of jealousy, for his jealousy is well founded in the character and conduct of his wife, though not in the fact of her infidelity with Cassio. Desdemona is not false to her husband, but she has been false to the purity and delicacy of her sex and condition when she married him; and the last words spoken by her father on parting from them, after he has forgiven her and acquiesced in the marriage, are—

Look to her, Moor; have a quick eye to see:
She has deceived her father, and may thee.

And this very idea is that by which the crafty villain Iago works up into madness the jealousy of Othello.

Whatever sympathy we feel for the sufferings of Desdemona flows from the consideration that she is innocent of the particular crime imputed to her, and that she is the victim of a treacherous and artful intriguer. But, while compassionating her melancholy fate, we cannot forget the vice of her character. Upon the stage, her fondling with Othello is disgusting. Who, in real life, would have her for his sister, daughter, or wife? She is not guilty of infidelity to her husband, but she forfeits all the affection of her father and all her own filial affection for him. When the duke proposes, on the departure of Othello for the war, that she should return during his absence to her father's house, the father, the daughter and the husband all say 'No!' She prefers following Othello, to be besieged by the Turks in the island of Cyprus.

JOHN QUINCY ADAMS, sixth President of the United States,
'Misconceptions of Shakspeare upon the Stage', 1835

Leaping Out of Shakespeare's Terror

Five Meditations on Othello

I

I haven't been able to stop thinking about *Othello* since I saw a production of the play in London's Barbican. It was the first time I had seen it performed on stage. As far as I could tell, I was the only black person in the audience. The seats beside me were occupied by three white girls. They noisily crackled their packets of sweets and giggled a lot. I wanted to tell them to be quiet. But I suspected that if I spoke faces would turn towards me. After a while I couldn't bear it any longer. When I spoke, what I feared happened. Faces turned, eyes lit up in recognition. My skin glowed. I felt myself illuminated, unable to hide.

I used to agree with C. L. R. James that *Othello* is not a play about race. The Royal Shakespeare Company thought so as well. They had Ben Kingsley play Othello in the tradition of the Arab Moor that Edmund Kean made popular in the nineteenth century. Ben Kingsley played the part lyrically, it was obvious that he had been doing some unsuccessful weight-lifting to give the character the stature it deserves, but there were times when his colour made nonsense of the role. The stage lighting often made it difficult to see the difference between his complexion and that of the other actors and actresses. The chromatic tension of the play was thereby rendered harmless. In addition, they imposed on the play a vaguely homosexual theme and a psychiatric condition, the Othello syndrome, a form of psychotic jealousy. None of these helped to make the play credible. These three elements join the long theatrical tradition of evading the terrors that are at the heart of the play.

Often, when people don't really want to face something, they become pretentious. The whole business of Othello as an Arab was popularised by Samuel Coleridge and Charles Lamb. They did not want to face the full implications of Othello's blackness. They did not want him in their dreams. They also did not want to confront the powerful sexual element in the play. If you take away Othello's colour then you don't really have the magnitude of the tragedy. A 'tawny Othello' is much more comfortable to take. If it did not begin as a play about race, then its history has made it one.

The emotional explosiveness of *Othello* depends utterly on seeing it on stage. Othello's colour is not real on the page. It can be avoided. Coleridge confessed to the 'beautiful compromise' he made in reading the play. But when he saw it on stage he was revolted by the 'wedded caresses' of Othello and Desdemona. Reducing the colour diminishes the force of the sex. Together they can be quite unbearable.

Shakespeare chose his tragic figure well, and then stacked the cards against him. Othello is the only black man in the universe of the play. He is isolated by colour. He cannot hide. And his position of great authority in society makes his isolation deeper. It is a terrifying position to be in. Honourable, trusting, and surrounded by people who might see him as their worst nightmare. The loneliness of colour made worse by the solitude of power. Trapped in a code of honour, to whom could he turn? Who could he trust? It was safer for him to trust those who seemed trustworthy. To begin to doubt would bring on insanity, for he would have to doubt everyone. And then his mortal terror would begin. He would find himself in the labyrinths of that nightmare of history from which there is no escape . . .

2

Every age presents *Othello* in relation to how they perceive *the other*. What else can explain the residual hostility of critics towards black actors playing the role? It took thirty-two years for English critics to accept Ira Aldridge in the nineteenth century. His Othello was successful everywhere else. When the celebrated Paul Robeson played the part in 1943 critics said it was like seeing the play for the first time and that Iago became 'a credible villain' when a black man acted Othello. And yet, Othello, fifty years later, continues to be white underneath.

Our perception of the other gives the measure of our humanity, our courage, and our imagination. Iago represents those who cannot accept the other. He cannot accept himself. He makes colour the victim of his failings. The imagery of black as unnatural comes from Iago. He smears it through the play. It is an extraordinary idea: Shakespeare presents this character who is black, and therefore visually alien, and then shows that he is not so alien after all, and paints his humanity right down to his jealous soul. On the other hand we have Iago, who is white, familiar, but who is actually the real alien to humanity and love . . .

Iago is a lonely and bitter man. He is the man who utterly refuses to transcend himself. He does not accept reality and he refuses to face history. And yet he is in his twisted way an intelligent man. He has not found the vocation in which to utilise his considerable imaginative gifts. He is so seemingly friendly, so seemingly on your side, he is all appearance. He is the supreme test for those who will not see clearly; who will not see deeply into people. He thinks more intensely than anyone else in the play. In fact, he has the mind of a playwright, manipulating people around his plots. When the plot gets out of hand, when the characters don't behave as expected, like a poor playwright he kills them off. Iago is the scourge of those whose thinking is muddled. He depends on their faulty vision to pervert reality.

One of the great themes of the play, for me, is the war between Appearance and Reality. Appearance strives to be, but Reality is. Appearance can command the gaze, distort things, but Reality is the eternal present. It is what things are in all their secret phases. It is what Appearance strives to become. Reality is the future of all secrets.

Othello is caught in the nightmare that history has made real. And there is something frightening about a majestic man who believes what they say about him. He believes too much in appearances. Here is a man of royal birth, who was taken as a slave, and rose to become a general. Whatever bitterness or bewilderment he might have had has been taken from him. In their place he has been fed bubbles of power. He fed them to himself.

Iago is the most perceptive person in the play: so coldly does he calculate the shallowness of Othello's rise, how much he must have paid, how much rage he must repress. And because Othello can't really release his rage, as it would hinder his rise, he can't transform his anger into something higher. He can't therefore transcend his jealousy when it swoops into his soul like a green bird of prey. All Iago has to do is get that repressed rage to turn on itself and to open up in Othello the element of self-destruction.

Othello can't really be honest to himself. He couldn't have risen that high and in such fearful isolation if he were. Unlike Iago, he accepts too much. He even wholly accepts the blind logic of the world in which he has sacrificed his history for ambition. That is why he has to be so trusting. Trapped in ambition, marked by his colour, refusing to confront his predicament, he is the authentic self-betrayer. He is the white man's myth of the black man. But he is also a negative myth for black people in the West. Signposts along roads that can lead to hell also have their own peculiar value.

3

It must be admitted that there is something unbelievably simple about Othello. He comfortably personifies jealousy, and his particular manifestation of it is taken as a quality of his otherness. But there he is, a man of royal birth, taken as a slave, and he has no bitterness. He doesn't possess an ounce of anger, or even a sense of injustice. It is difficult to believe that he has got so far as a warrior, climbed so high in office, and yet possesses no cunning and no ability to penetrate appearances. The most irritating thing of all is his nobility, which, in his predicament, is a sort of naïvety. When a black man is portrayed as noble in the West it usually means that he is neutralised. When white people speak so highly of a black man's nobility they are usually referring to his impotence. It is Othello's neutrality and social impotence that troubles me.

James Baldwin has said that people will face in your life only what they would face in theirs. But to this must first be added the condition that people accept your humanity as essentially equal to theirs. Shakespeare, as a white man of his era, could not fully concede Othello an equal status of humanity. It seems that the only way white people can see black people, and begin to accept them, without really having to face them, is by lessening their internal realities. Their external difference, their skin colour, is romanticised, taken as exotic.

And their souls are filled with blackness. This is why a lot of white people can know what black people suffer daily all over the globe and not be really bruised in their humanity: because they assume that black people are used to their pain, that they feel things differently, and that suffering is their unchanging condition. When you reduce the reality of the other there is the obvious benefit of not having to face the fullness of their being, their contradictions, their agonies.

Those who hate black people and those who romanticise them mean the same thing when one speaks of the colour as ugly and the other speaks of it as attractive. Both of them deny black its own unique condition and existence unto itself. The weirdest thing about Othello is that his colour is empty of history. It is the accepted thing to comment on Othello's jealousy, but few critics seem to realise that his colour, his otherness, must imply a specific history in white society. It seems that into the vessel of Othello's skin, Shakespeare poured whiteness. It is possible that Othello actually is a blackened white man.

He certainly is a lost man. His author cheats him of a satisfying period of sex with Desdemona. Instead of sex, Othello is allowed coitus interruptus. Instead of anger, he is given an almost idiotic naïvety. He has no real friends. In spite of his apparel of power and glory, he is a naked man, a deluded man. And why does he have to be trapped in that unending cycle of murder and suicide? Does the denial of someone's humanity inexorably lead them to murder? Or is it that in an abnormal situation only an abnormal action becomes possible? And when no human solution seems possible is suicide the inevitable consequence? Or is suicide a twisted affirmation of freedom? It is also a fantasy, a wishing away of reality: it avoids the problem of race. It is amazing that Othello's suicide is seen as an extension of his nobility, when in fact it is the inescapable logic of his impotence. The whole machinery of the play is set in motion by the presence of this lone black man. By the end he has killed himself. Iago who is responsible for so many deaths is dragged away, unrepentant. Without Othello, the universe of the play becomes homogenous, diminished. There are always alternatives. We always need the other.

4

In three centuries of Othello committing murder and suicide on the stage no significant change in attitude towards black people has occurred. I doubt that *Othello* really disturbs people as much as it should. Society has become smothered by complacency. Add to this the fact that Othello as a lone black man on the stage is not threatening. White audiences must merely look upon his phenomenon. It is a basic truth of literature that if you can't enter the centre of a work, then it can't really shake you. How can white people imagine themselves in Othello's skin? History does not support it. Othello is a character with only one road leading out of him, but none lead into him. The black person's response to Othello is more secret, and much more anguished, than can be imagined. It makes you unbearably lonely to know that you can empathise with them, but they will rarely empathise with you. It hurts to watch Othello.

Which brings me to another element. Othello is powerless, and Iago the real enemy, and yet I can't wholly blame Othello for trusting him. Of all the people in the play, with the natural exception of Desdemona, Iago is the only one who expresses what he feels for Othello. He is lying, but nonetheless he expresses. It means a lot to the isolated to have someone declare their affection. It means a lot to be loved.

Any black man who has gone out with a white woman knows that there are a lot of Iagos around. If the woman is desirable then the situation is more insidious. The question the new Iagos ask themselves is: why him and not me? Then they might put it down to the myth of the black man's sexuality—a myth invented by white people in the first place. Iago's obsession depends obviously on Othello's success. If Othello were a failure and hadn't won Desdemona's love he would not have begun to exist in Iago's hell. It is also crucial that Iago is a failed human being. He is full of self-loathing. The real jealousy at work in the play is not Othello's, but Iago's. When he speaks of jealousy as a green-eyed monster Iago knows what he is talking about. He's been there. He's stuck there. He has lived with jealousy for a long time. The fascinating and at the same time repellent thing about Iago is his refusal to confront his failure. The angle of his humanity is very thin. He is the man of short cuts. And so he becomes a specialist in the art of projecting his bitterness. And to crown all this: he has to mask his failure, mask his resentment, his self-obsession. And so he mingles with the crowd.

Iago today would not be a member of a fanatical racist group. He is not *that much* of a failure. He would attend the right marches, say the right things, and he would be unmistakably *vocal* in his objection to racism. He would be invisible because he is—almost—like everyone else. He lives in the closed universe between cynicism and hell. He is the perfect hypocrite in the sense that you would never think of applying the word to him. And he is an almost flawless actor and a superb ironist. Most of what Iago says has a sinister truth. It is the fact that he speaks from his own condition which gives his utterances their weird and elusive honesty. His smile should send shudders of terror through us. But it warms us a little, because we despise him and feel bad about it, because he too is human, and more seriously because we don't really know him. But he knows us. He has insinuated himself into our lives. And he loathes us, loathes everything. And in our midst he spins his web of hate. Iago is a more authentic creation than Othello. Wherever human beings fail to transcend aspects of themselves there lie the conditions for the birth of an Iago. He is the universal negative man, foil for heroes. There isn't one of us who hasn't glimpsed that curiously satisfying vengeance of drawing the hated world into the depths of our own hell. It is Iago's complete and secretive dedication which makes him so unique.

Othello, today, would not be a radical. He is too ambitious to let anger get in the way. He has come from nothing and has fought his way up in a new world. He wouldn't want to face the truth about himself because it would destroy him. He wouldn't want to face the falsity of his yearnings. To face his predicament would mean accepting the fact that he has become a willing victim of the dream that enslaved him in the first place. He is merely rising up the ladder available to him, not building his own.

And then there is Desdemona, innocent and sweet and passive. She and Othello are an unfortunate pair. Neither of them has any guile. She is too young to perceive the danger Othello is in. She takes too much for granted and believes too much in the simplicity of everything and everyone. They are mutually deluded. What did she see in him? She saw his nobility, rather than his vulnerability, his strength, rather than the weakness of his position. She is just the type who likes romances and is seduced by exoticism. Today she might be an ardent lover of a glamorised Africa. She would be just the kind of girl who believes that love makes everything right, and that the world would want for her what she wants for herself. She would have heard of slavery but never have thought about it. She would be shocked to hear that black people are treated badly because of their colour, that they have their homes burnt down, and are beaten up and mercilessly discriminated against. She would be shocked because she has never been allowed to confront reality, to face the Medusa-like truths of the world. The source of her delusion is ignorance. She is the redemption and the victim of her history.

5

Desdemona fell in love with Othello because of his stories. He had lived a heroic life. Her father thought Othello had used sorcery on her. There is no greater sorcery than poetry, than the imagination of the storyteller. Desdemona is a bit of a rebel and her humanity is large. But humanity without scepticism, without knowledge, is dangerous. In real terms she would not find happiness in her choice unless she became a little wise along the way, and the costliest price is always paid for wisdom:

the tearing down of as many illusions and lies as the human frame can bear. She would have to love Othello without illusions. It would be a hard kind of love, a rigorous love, that demands constant vigilance. She would have to alter the way she sees her history, and that would alter almost everything else. She would have to be strong. There would be many compensations but she would have to manage the difficulty of being both romantic and wise. And this is the crux of Desdemona's situation. The romantic reduces black people to a fantasy. And then they love the illusion they themselves have created. They do not face black people as they are, each in their own particular individuality. Othello and Desdemona are a doomed alliance: for he doesn't face her reality either. He never questions the true basis of her love, and consequently doesn't understand her illusions, her lack of cunning and fear. Neither of them knew their predicament and so they didn't stand a chance. And love alone is never enough. That is how those who remain unaware, blind to their predicament, are always betrayed. They are betrayed as much by those who don't care about them as by those who love them.

I think that the play is less about jealousy than about accepting the other, about opening the doors of consciousness to more of reality. Or having to become less. Rejecting is easy: all it takes is confusion and ignorance. But facing the complexity of others, their history, their raw humanity—that takes courage, and is rare.

Whose heart is not pierced when at the end of the play Othello asks Ludovico that in his letters telling of the tragedy he should 'speak of me as I am: nothing extenuate, Nor set down in malice. Then you must speak of one that loved not wisely, but too well'? These are the crucial lines of the play. Speak of me as I am. Don't beautify me. Don't simplify me. Don't make me less. Don't make me more either. I am not sure if Shakespeare faced up to that injunction, which is probably the most challenging to a writer. But he put the injunction there . . .

BEN OKRI, *A Way of Being Free*, 1997

I do not think him [the actor Edmund Kean] thorough-bred gentleman enough to play Othello.

SAMUEL TAYLOR COLERIDGE, *Table Talk*, 1836

Sonnet: On Sitting Down to Read King Lear Once Again

O golden tongued Romance, with serene lute!
    Fair plumed Syren, Queen of far-away!
    Leave melodizing on this wintry day,
Shut up thine olden pages, and be mute:
Adieu! for, once again, the fierce dispute
    Betwixt damnation and impassion'd clay
    Must I burn through; once more humbly assay
The bitter-sweet of this Shakespearian fruit:
Chief Poet! and ye clouds of Albion,
    Begetters of our deep eternal theme!
When through the old oak Forest I am gone,
    Let me not wander in a barren dream,
But, when I am consumed in the fire,
Give me new Phœnix wings to fly at my desire.

JOHN KEATS, 1818

Lear is not to be handled as an ex-monarch, unloved but feared, who poses certain problems of state by his continued presence on the scene. He is to be made to see himself as something much less than that—as a dirty, incontinent, drunken old fool, a domestic nuisance at a time when unhappily there was no geriatric ward to which he could be committed. Or as a dirty little boy, who has a running nose and ringworm and probably other disgusting diseases. His humiliations are to be of the grossest sort; his tormentors are to be contemptuously casual, not diabolically ingenious; his higher education is to be of the most direct and most unsubtle kind.

D. J. ENRIGHT, *Shakespeare and the Students*, 1970

I have heard Shakespeare's Blow winds & crack your cheeks, &c. & the rest, accused of false taste & bombast. I do not find this fault. And tho' I might not allow it in another, even in his mad king, yet I am not offended by this passage in Lear. For as the Romans were so idolatrous of Cato's virtue that when he had drunk wine they would rather believe that intemperance was virtue than that Cato was guilty of a vice, so I am afraid to circumscribe within rhetorical rules, the circuits of such a towering & majestic mind, and a taste the most exquisite that God ever informed among men.

RALPH WALDO EMERSON, journal, 1825 (Emerson was 22 at the time)

I imagine that the great imaginative invention of the English, the thing called Nonsense, never rose to such a height and sublimity of unreason and horror, as when the Fool juggles with time and space and tomorrow and yesterday, as he says soberly at the end of his rant: 'This prophecy Merlin shall make; for I live before his time.' This is one of the Shakespearian shocks or blows that take the breath away.

G. K. CHESTERTON, 'The Tragedy of King Lear', reprinted in *The Spice of Life*, 1964

When I saw *Lear* here, I asked myself how it was possible that the unbearably tragic character of these fools had not been obvious long ago to everyone, including myself. The tragedy is not the sentimental one it is sometimes thought to be; it is this:

There is a class of people in this world who have fallen into the lowest degree of humiliation, far below beggary, and who are deprived not only of all social consideration but also, in everybody's opinion, of the specific human dignity, reason itself—and these are the only people who, in fact, are able to tell the truth. All the others lie.

In *Lear* it is striking. Even Kent and Cordelia attenuate, mitigate, soften, and veil the truth; and unless they are forced to choose between telling it and telling a downright lie, they manoeuvre to evade it . . .

What makes the tragedy extreme is the fact that because the fools possess no academic titles or episcopal dignities and because no one is aware that their sayings deserve the slightest attention—everybody being convinced a priori of the contrary, since they are fools—their expression of the truth is not even listened to. Everybody, including Sh.'s readers and audiences for four centuries, is unaware that what they say is true. And not satirically or humorously true, but simply the truth. Pure unadulterated truth—luminous, profound, and essential.

SIMONE WEIL, letter to her parents, 1943 tr. Richard Rees

At the time she wrote this letter, Simone Weil was a patient in a sanatorium near Ashford, in Kent. She died two weeks later.

All good tragedy is anti-tragedy. *King Lear*. Lear wants to enact the false tragic, the solemn, the complete. Shakespeare forces him to enact the true tragic, the absurd, the incomplete.

IRIS MURDOCH, 'Salvation by Words', 1972

In the witches' scene that begins Act IV (Hecate's little speech and the extra witches and their song were very probably added to the play after Shakespeare's death), one of the witches says:

> By the pricking of my thumbs,
> Something wicked this way comes.

There is an allusion here to the ancient superstition 'that all sudden pains of the body, which could not naturally be accounted for, were presages of somewhat that was shortly to happen.' But she might also have said: 'It is suggested to me, by a sensation of pricking in my thumbs, that an evil man is on his way here.' The difference between Shakespeare's intense two lines and this rather general, unconcentrated alternative is, first, a difference in the quality of the sound, as there is a difference between what you hear at the beginning of Beethoven's Piano Sonata, Opus III and what you hear from a jukebox. The word 'wicked' keeps the sound of 'pricking' going; the reader's experience of the pricking of the witch's thumbs intensifies. In other ways, too, the two lines are built very closely into each other: '*Some*-thing' half rhymes with 'thumbs,' and the four short-*i* sounds that measuredly follow (-*thing, wick-, id, this*) carry on the two short-*i* sounds of 'pricking' as well as they convey powerfully the sense of movement, something coming, marching. There is an unusually intimate association between the lines, and perhaps we ought to understand the word 'by' has quite a different sense from the way we first took it (By means of this sensation, I know, etc.): In accordance with the pricking of my thumbs, something is on its way here, obedient or at any rate *consonant* to my sign. One gets an impression of a fated *assignation* entirely lacking from our paraphrase of the witch's couplet. This sense is greatly strengthened by the alliteration in the second line: 'wicked this way'—as if there were something very natural about the wicked man's coming the witches' way, as indeed there is. One thinks of the two ways, of good and of evil, of the Sermon on the Mount (Matthew 7: 13–14); and one does not think of them by accident, for the porter in II. iii winds up his hell discourse with 'I had thought to have let in some of all professions, that go the primrose way to the everlasting bonfire.' This play is certainly about Good and Evil, and we learn so partly from the aural organization of this couplet.

A second difference takes us outside the couplet—as indeed the word 'way' has taken us already. The combination of the concept 'thumb,' in this witch context, and of the particular rhyme that binds the couplet,

reminds us irresistibly, if we are careful readers, of four lines earlier in
Act I (I. iii 28–31):

> *First Witch.*   Here I have a pilot's thumb,
>   Wrack'd as homeward he did come.
> *Third Witch.*   A drum! a drum!
>   Macbeth doth come.

The same rhyme (here thrice repeated) heralds each of his interviews
with the Weird Sisters, and each time there is a thumb. Now this pilot
is the second of the adventuring figures (the first being the sleepless
sailor) in whom the dramatist is foreshadowing the fate of his hero:
Macbeth, for *his* wife's greed, is to suffer from lack of sleep, and he is
to be wrecked as he comes home, both in the literal sense home
(where he will do the murder) and in the metaphorical sense (as he
achieves the crown, what he aims at, home). The calling up in Act IV
of this foreshadowing passage, deepens the drama of the couplet, making present, for its suggestiveness, the moral wreckage that had been
foreshadowed. But in addition to this general usefulness, there are two
or three specific points that claim our attention. It is not possible to be
certain about the first one, because we do not know how clearly
Shakespeare differentiated the witches in his mind, or whether his
speech prefixes for them have been faithfully preserved. According to
those we have, it is the first witch who has a pilot's thumb and the
second whose thumbs prick; but in the light of the fact that presently
Macbeth will be saying, 'Had I three ears, I'd hear thee'—a striking
speech that will interest us again later—there is an eerie chance that
Shakespeare was thinking of *three* thumbs pricking, one of them not
joined to its body.

Macbeth is announced, at his first coming, by a military drum; it is
open, public; he is a hero, a man with a name. At his second coming he is
announced by the pricking of a witch's thumbs, his resort is secret, and
he comes not as a hero but as a tyrant; we must imagine as suggested
also a terrible diminishment, from the booming of a drum to a slight
physical manifestation, corresponding to a removal of the real scene
from the objective world to the subjective. But this is not all, or even the
main thing. It is as 'Macbeth' that he first comes, to be saluted by three
prophetic titles. It is with his three titles that he next comes, but not
called by them, or even described as a man, but only as 'something
wicked.' His nature has changed—not his characteristics merely, but his
essential nature. He has become, perhaps, a demon; and the form, and

sound, and allusive value of the couplet help to suggest this as no paraphrase could do.

JOHN BERRYMAN, 'On *Macbeth*', 1960

'Macbeth is not, as is too often represented, a noisy swash-buckler; he is a full-furnished, ambitious man. In the scene with Duncan, the excess of courtesy adds a touch to the tragedy. It is like Clytemnestra's profusion to Agamemnon; who, by the way, always strikes me as uncommonly cold and haughty to his wife whom he had not seen for years.'

ALFRED TENNYSON in Hallam Tennyson's memoir, 1897

The day before he died, though he could no longer read, Tennyson asked repeatedly for his Shakespeare: 'Where is my Shakespeare? I must have my Shakespeare.'

The next day, around four in the afternoon, he suddenly called out: 'I have opened it.' The volume of Shakespeare he was clasping was open at one of his favourite passages, the words of the reconciled Posthumus to Imogen near the end of Cymbeline:

> Hang there like fruit, my soul,
> Till the tree die.

He then spoke a farewell blessing to his wife and his son Hallam, and drifted away.

I have ruthlessly cut out the surprises that no longer surprise anybody. I really could not keep my countenance over the identification of Guiderius by the mole on his neck. That device was killed by Maddison Morton, once a famous farce writer, now forgotten by everyone save Mr Gordon Craig and myself. In Morton's masterpiece, Box and Cox, Box asks Cox whether he has a strawberry mark on his left arm. 'No' says Cox. 'Then you are my long lost brother' says Box as they fall into one another's arms and end the farce happily. One could wish that Guiderius had anticipated Cox.

BERNARD SHAW, foreword to *Cymbeline Refinished*, 1945

Autolycus

In his last phase when hardly bothering
To be a dramatist, the Master turned away
From his taut plots and complex characters
To tapestried romances, conjuring
With rainbow names and handfuls of sea-spray
And from them turned out happy Ever-afters.

Eclectic always, now extravagant,
Sighting his matter through a timeless prism
He ranged his classical bric-à-brac in grottos
Where knights of Ancient Greece had Latin mottoes
And fishermen their flapjacks—none should want
Colour for lack of an anachronism.

A gay world certainly though pocked and scored
With childish horrors and a fresh world though
Its mainsprings were old gags—babies exposed,
Identities confused and queens to be restored;
But when the cracker bursts it proves as you supposed—
Trinket and moral tumble out just so.

Such innocence—In his own words it was
Like an old tale, only that where time leaps
Between acts three and four there was something born
Which made the stock-type virgin dance like corn
In a wind that having known foul marshes, barren steeps,
Felt therefore kindly towards Marinas, Perditas . . .

Thus crystal learned to talk. But Shakespeare balanced it
With what we knew already, gabbing earth
Hot from Eastcheap—Watch your pockets when
That rogue comes round the corner, he can slit
Purse-strings as quickly as his maker's pen
Will try your heartstrings in the name of mirth.

O master pedlar with your confidence tricks,
Brooches, pomanders, broadsheets and what-have-you,
Who hawk such entertainment but rook your client
And leave him brooding, why should we forgive you

Did we not know that, though more self-reliant
Than we, you too were born and grew up in a fix?

LOUIS MACNEICE, 1945

Ariel to Miranda:—Take
This slave of music, for the sake
Of him, who is the slave of thee;
And teach it all the harmony
In which thou canst, and only thou,
Make the delighted spirit glow,
Till joy denies itself again
And, too intense, is turn'd to pain.
For by permission and command
Of thine own Prince Ferdinand,
Poor Ariel sends this silent token
Of more than ever can be spoken;
Your guardian spirit, Ariel, who
From life to life must still pursue
Your happiness, for thus alone
Can Ariel ever find his own.
From Prospero's enchanted cell,
As the mighty verses tell,
To the throne of Naples he
Lit you o'er the trackless sea,
Flitting on, your prow before,
Like a living meteor.
When you die, the silent Moon
In her interlunar swoon
Is not sadder in her cell
Than deserted Ariel.
When you live again on earth,
Like an unseen Star of birth
Ariel guides you o'er the sea
Of life from your nativity.
Many changes have been run
Since Ferdinand and you begun
Your course of love, and Ariel still
Has track'd your steps and served your will.
Now in humbler, happier lot,

This is all remember'd not;
And now, alas! the poor sprite is
Imprison'd for some fault of his
In a body like a grave—
From you he only dares to crave,
For his service and his sorrow
A smile to-day, a song to-morrow . . .

PERCY BYSSHE SHELLEY, from 'With a Guitar, to Jane', 1822

From king to beggar, men of every rank and every order of mind have spoken with his lips; he has uttered the lore of fairyland; now it pleases him to create a being neither man nor fairy [Caliban], a something between brute and human nature, and to endow its purpose with words. These words, how they smack of the moist and spawning earth, of the life of creatures that cannot rise above the soil! We do not think of it enough; we stint our wonder because we fall short in appreciation.

GEORGE GISSING, *The Private Papers of Henry Ryecroft*, 1903

Robert Browning's 'Caliban upon Setebos' (1864) is subtitled 'Natural Theology in the Island'. In The Tempest, *Setebos—the name of a Patagonian god, borrowed by Shakespeare from a travel-narrative—is worshipped by Caliban's mother, Sycorax. In Browning's poem, Caliban puzzles over the character of this vicious deity, and that of the greater god—'the Quiet'—who looms behind him. The significance of these musings has been much debated: they have been seen as an attack on Darwininism, for instance, and equally as a satire on Calvinism, or again as a critique of Rousseauism. Artistically, however, the most striking feature of the poem is its strange idiom, wonderfully redolent of Caliban's swamp-life, developed out of Shakespeare but never merely derivative.*

Browning's Caliban is more brutish than Shakespeare's, and even his moments of pathos tend to have their sinister aspect—the passage where he describes how he tried to imitate Prospero, for instance:

Himself° peeped late, eyed Prosper at his books
Careless and lofty, lord now of the isle:
Vexed, 'stitched a book of broad leaves, arrow-shaped,
Wrote thereon, he knows what, prodigious words;

Himself] Caliban, who always speaks of himself in the third person, and often omits the pronoun

Has peeled a wand and called it by a name;
Weareth at whiles for an enchanter's robe
The eyed skin of a supple oncelot;°
And hath an ounce° sleeker than youngling mole,
A four-legged serpent he makes cower and couch,
Now snarl, now hold its breath and mind his eye,
And saith she is Miranda and my wife:
'Keeps for his Ariel a tall pouch-bill crane
He bids go wade for fish and straight disgorge;
Also a sea-beast, lumpish, which he snared,
Blinded the eyes of, and brought somewhat tame,
And split its toe-webs, and now pens the drudge
In a hole o' the rock and calls him Caliban;
A bitter heart that bides its time and bites.
'Plays thus at being Prosper in a way,
Taketh his mirth with make-believes: so He.

Nothing in Prospero's Cloak

Caliban slave
instructed in human speech
waits

snout in dung
feet in paradise
he sniffs man
waits

nothing comes
nothing in Prospero's
magic robes
nothing from
streets and lips
from pulpits and towers
nothing from loudspeakers
speaks to nothing
about nothing

nothing begets nothing
nothing brings up nothing

oncelot] ocelot		ounce] wild cat

nothing awaits nothing
nothing threatens
nothing condemns
nothing pardons

TADEUSZ RÓŚEWICZ, 1962, tr. from the Polish by Adam Czerniawski

Prospero and Sycorax

She knows, like Ophelia,
The task has swallowed him.
She knows, like George's dragon,
Her screams have closed his helmet.

She knows, like Jocasta,
It is over.
He prefers
Blindness.

She knows, like Cordelia,
He is not himself now,
And what speaks through him must be discounted—
Though it will be the end of them both.

She knows, like God,
He has found
Something
Easier to live with—

His death, her death.

TED HUGHES, 1971

Trinculo

Mechanic, merchant, king,
Are warmed by the cold clown
Whose head is in the clouds
And never can get down.

Into a solitude
Undreamed of by their fat
Quick dreams have lifted me;
The north wind steals my hat.

On clear days I can see
Green acres far below,
And the red roof where I
Was Little Trinculo.

There lies that solid world
These hands can never reach;
My history, my love,
Is but a choice of speech.

A terror shakes my tree,
A flock of words fly out,
Whereat a laughter shakes
The busy and devout.

Wild images, come down
Out of your freezing sky,
That I, like shorter men,
May get my joke and die.

W. H. AUDEN, *The Sea and the Mirror*, 1944

FICTIONS · 1
TALES OF SHAKESPEARE

Never was more anxious and ready way made for 'my Lord of Leicester,' than as he passed through the crowded ante-rooms to go towards the river-side, in order to attend her Majesty to her barge—Never was the voice of the ushers louder, to 'make room—make room for the noble Earl'—Never were these signals more promptly and reverentially obeyed—Never were more anxious eyes turned on him to obtain a glance of favour, or even of mere recognition, while the heart of many a humble follower of his fortunes throbbed betwixt desire to offer his congratulations, and fear of intruding himself on the notice of one so infinitely above him. The whole court considered the issue of this day's audience, expected with so much doubt and anxiety, as a decisive triumph on the part of Leicester, and felt assured that the orb of his rival satellite, if not altogether obscured by his lustre, must revolve hereafter in a dimmer and more distant sphere. So thought the court; and courtiers, from high to low, acted accordingly.

On the other hand, never did Leicester return with such ready and condescending courtesy, or endeavour more successfully to gather (in the words of one, who at that moment stood at no great distance from him) 'golden opinions from all sorts of men.'° For all he had a bow, a smile at least, and often a kind word. Most of these were addressed to courtiers, whose names have long gone down the tide of oblivion; but some, to such as sound strangely in our ears, when connected with the ordinary matters of human life, above which the gratitude of posterity has long elevated them. A few of Leicester's interlocutory sentences ran as follows:

'Poynings, good morrow, and how does your wife and fair daughter?—why come they not to court?—Adams, your suit is naught—the Queen will grant no more monopolies—but I may serve you in another matter.—My good Alderman Aylford, the suit of the City,

'golden opinions . . . men'] *Macbeth*, I. vii

affecting Queenhithe, shall be forwarded as far as my poor interest can serve.—Master Edmund Spencer, touching your Irish petition, I would willingly aid you, from my love to the Muses; but thou hast nettled the Lord Treasurer.'

'My lord,' said the poet, 'were I permitted to explain'—

'Come to my lodging, Edmund,' answered the Earl—'not tomorrow, or next day, but soon.—Ha, Will Shakespeare—wild Will!—thou hast given my nephew, Philip Sidney, love-powder—he cannot sleep without thy Venus and Adonis under his pillow!—we will have thee hanged for the veriest wizard in Europe. Heark thee, mad wag, I have not forgotten thy matter of the patent, and of the bears.'

The Player bowed, and the Earl nodded and passed on—so that age would have told the tale—in ours, perhaps, we might say the immortal had done homage to the mortal.

WALTER SCOTT, *Kenilworth*, 1821

'The matter of the patent, and of the bears' refers to a petition brought against the players by Orson Pinnit, the (fictional) keeper of the royal bears, who claims that they are spoiling his business: 'the manly amusement of bear-baiting is falling into neglect.' In the scene which follows the Queen rejects Pinnit's plea, after she has heard Walter Raleigh repeat the lines from A Midsummer Night's Dream *about 'the fair vestal, throned in the west' ('In maiden meditation, fancy free').*

The action of Kenilworth *takes place in 1575. At the time, in reality, Shakespeare was a boy of 11.*

In 1834 Walter Savage Landor published an ironic account of the young Shakespeare being haled before Sir Thomas Lucy of Charlecote on a charge of poaching deer. Sir Thomas is represented (contrary to other versions of the legend) as being relatively benign. He delivers a long moral lecture; then, impressed by Shakespeare's apparent readiness to take it to heart, he goes on to warn him about some of his other activities.

The proceedings are supposedly recorded by Sir Thomas's clerk. The irascible Sir Silas, who chimes in from time to time, is his chaplain.

Sir Thomas. Youth! I never thought thee so staid. Thou hast, for these many months, been represented unto me as one dissolute and light, much given unto mummeries and mysteries, wakes and carousals, cudgel-fighters and mountebanks, and wanton women. They do also represent of thee (I hope it may be without foundation) that thou enactest the parts, not simply of foresters and fairies, girls in the green-sickness and friars, lawyers and outlaws, but likewise, having small reverence for station, of kings and queens, knights and privy-counsellors, in all their glory. It hath been whispered moreover, and the testimony of these two witnesses doth appear in some measure to countenance and confirm it, that thou hast at divers times this last summer been seen and heard alone, inasmuch as human eye may discover, on the narrow slip of greensward between the Avon and the chancel, distorting thy body like one possessed, and uttering strange language, like unto incantation. This however cometh not before me. Take heed! take heed unto thy ways: there are graver things in law even than homicide and deer-stealing.

Sir Silas. And strong against him. Folks have been consumed at the stake for pettier felonies and upon weaker evidence.

Sir Thomas. To that anon.

. . . William Shakespeare did hold down his head, answering nought. And Sir Thomas spake again unto him, as one mild and fatherly, if so be that such a word may be spoken of a knight and parliament-man. And these are the words he spake:

'Reason and ruminate with thyself now. To pass over and pretermit the danger of representing the actions of the others, and mainly of lawyers and churchmen, the former of whom do pardon no offences, and the latter those only against God (having no warrant for more), canst thou believe it innocent to counterfeit kings and queens? Supposest thou that if the impression of their faces on a farthing be felonious and rope-worthy, the imitation of head and body, voice and bearing, plume and strut, crown and mantle, and everything else that maketh them royal and glorious, be aught less? Perpend, young man, perpend! Consider who among inferior mortals shall imitate them becomingly? Dreamest thou they talk and act like checkmen at Banbury fair? How can thy shallow brain suffice for their vast conceptions? How darest thou say, as they do, hang this fellow, quarter that, flay, mutilate, stab, shoot, press, hook, torture, burn alive? These are royalties. Who appointed thee to such office? The Holy Ghost? He alone can confer it; but when wert thou anointed?'

William was so zealous in storing up these verities, that he looked as though he were unconscious that the pouring-out was over.

The Citation and Examination of William Shakespeare Touching Deer-Stealing

In The Portrait of Mr W. H. *Oscar Wilde puts forward the theory that Shakespeare's sonnets were inspired by his passion for a boy-actor, Willie Hughes. Or rather, he plays with the theory. The piece (first published in* Blackwood's Magazine *in 1889, and later greatly expanded) is very much a work of fiction.*

It opens over coffee and cigarettes in a 'pretty little house' in Birdcage Walk. The unnamed narrator is being entertained by an older man called Erskine, who tells him the sad story of his friend Cyril Graham. Graham had evolved the theory about Willie Hughes and the sonnets. Erskine had been unconvinced. Graham had finally committed suicide, leaving a letter in which he insisted that the theory was true, and that it was Erskine's duty to give it to the world. Erskine remained sceptical: for one thing, there was no evidence that Willie Hughes had ever existed.

The narrator is excited by the theory, however. He amasses a great deal of evidence (or what seems to him evidence) in its favour. He writes to Erskine, setting out his case, and this time Erskine is persuaded. But in the very act of making a convert, the narrator loses his own faith. 'Perhaps, by finding perfect expression for a passion, I had exhausted the passion itself.'

Two years later he receives a letter from Erskine, sent from a hotel in Cannes. By the time he reads it, Erskine tells him, 'I shall have died by my own hand for Willie Hughes's sake; for his sake, and for the sake of Cyril Graham, whom I drove to his death by my shallow scepticism and ignorant lack of faith. The truth was once revealed to you, and you rejected it. It comes to you now, stained with the blood of two lives—do not turn away from it.'

Horrified, the narrator hurries out to Cannes. By the time he gets there, it is too late. Erskine is already dead. And then, in a final twist, we learn that his death wasn't the suicide which was supposed to testify to his faith in Willie Hughes. He had actually died of consumption.

Wilde's foremost biographer, Richard Ellmann, described The Portrait of Mr W. H. *as a work that anticipates Borges. It teases the reader, sows uncertainties, constructs an elaborate little world of fiction within fiction. If Wilde had simply wanted to win acceptance for the Willie Hughes story, he chose an odd way of going about it. But though he was too astute to endorse the story, he didn't disown it, either. He was attracted by it to the point of fantasizing that it was true.*

In the most personal passage in the Portrait, he makes it clear that it was also a story which corresponded to something deep in his own nature:

We sit at the play with the woman we love, or listen to the music in some Oxford garden, or stroll with our friend through the cool galleries of the Pope's house at Rome, and suddenly we become aware that we have passions of which we have never dreamed, thoughts that make us afraid, pleasures whose secret has been denied to us, sorrows that have been hidden from our tears. The actor is unconscious of our presence: the musician is thinking of the subtlety of the fugue, of the tone of his instrument; the marble gods that smile so curiously at us are made of insensate stone. But they have given form and substance to what was within us; they have enabled us to realise our personality; and a sense of perilous joy, or some touch or thrill of pain, or that strange self-pity that man so often feels for himself, comes over us and leaves us different.

Some such impression the Sonnets of Shakespeare had certainly produced on me. As from opal dawns to sunsets of withered rose I read and re-read them in garden or chamber, it seemed to me that I was deciphering the story of a life that had once been mine, unrolling the record of a romance that, without my knowing it, had coloured the very texture of my nature, had dyed it with strange and subtle dyes. Art, as so often happens, had taken the place of personal experience. I felt as if I had been initiated into the secret of that passionate friendship, that love of beauty and beauty of love, of which Marsilio Ficino tells us, and of which the Sonnets in their noblest and purest significance, may be held to be the perfect expression.

Yes: I had lived it all. I had stood in the round theatre with its open roof and fluttering banners, had seen the stage draped with black for a tragedy, or set with gay garlands for some brighter show. The young gallants came out with their pages, and took their seats in front of the tawny curtain that hung from the satyr-carved pillars of the inner scene. They were insolent and debonair in their fantastic dresses. Some of them wore French lovelocks, and white doublets stiff with Italian embroidery of gold thread, and long hose of blue or pale yellow silk. Others were all in black, and carried huge plumed hats. These affected the Spanish fashion. As they played at cards, and blew thin wreaths of smoke from the tiny pipes that the pages lit for them, the truant prentices and idle schoolboys that thronged the yard mocked them. But they only smiled at each other. In the side boxes some masked women were sitting. One of them was waiting with hungry eyes and bitten lips for the drawing back of the curtain. As the trumpet sounded for the third time she leant forward, and I saw her olive skin and raven's-wing hair. I knew her. She had marred for a season the great friendship of my life. Yet there was something about her that fascinated me.

The play changed according to my mood. Sometimes it was 'Hamlet:' Taylor acted the Prince, and there were many who wept when Ophelia went mad. Sometimes it was 'Romeo and Juliet.' Burbage was Romeo. He hardly looked the part of the young Italian, but there was a rich music in his voice, and passionate beauty in every gesture. I saw 'As You Like It,' and 'Cymbeline,' and 'Twelfth Night,' and in each play there was some one whose life was bound up into mine, who realised for me every dream, and gave shape to every fancy. How gracefully he moved! The eyes of the audience were fixed on him.

And yet it was in this century that it had all happened. I had never seen my friend, but he had been with me for many years, and it was to his influence that I owed my passion for Greek thought and art, and indeed all my sympathy with the Hellenic spirit. (φιλοσοφεῖν μὲτ᾽ ἐρῶτος!)° How that phrase had stirred me in my Oxford days! I did not understand then why it was so. But I knew now. There had been a presence beside me always. Its silver feet had trod night's shadowy meadows, and the white hands had moved aside the trembling curtains of the dawn. It had walked with me through the grey cloisters, and when I sat reading in my room, it was there also. What though I had been unconscious of it? The soul had a life of its own, and the brain its own sphere of action. There was something within us that knew nothing of sequence or extension, and yet, like the philosopher of the Ideal City, was the spectator of all time and of all existence. It had senses that quickened, passions that came to birth, spiritual ecstasies of contemplation, ardours of fiery-coloured love. It was we who were unreal, and our conscious life was the least important part of our development. The soul, the secret soul, was the only reality.

How curiously it had all been revealed to me! A book of Sonnets, published nearly three hundred years ago, written by a dead hand and in honour of a dead youth, had suddenly explained to me the whole story of my soul's romance. I remembered how once in Egypt I had been present at the opening of a frescoed coffin that had been found in one of the basalt tombs at Thebes. Inside there was the body of a young girl swathed in tight bands of linen, and with a gilt mask over her face. As I stooped down to look at it, I had seen that one of the little withered hands held a scroll of yellow papyrus covered with strange characters. How I wished now that I had it read to me! It might have told me something more about the soul that hid within me, and had its mysteries

φιλοσοφεῖν μὲτ᾽ ἐρῶτος] to become wise through love

of passion of which I was kept in ignorance. Strange, that we knew so little about ourselves, and that our most intimate personality was concealed from us! Were we to look in tombs for our real life, and in art for the legend of our days?

The Craftsman

Once, after long-drawn revel at The Mermaid,
He to the overbearing Boanerges
Jonson, uttered (if half of it were liquor,
                Blessed be the vintage!)

Saying how, at an alehouse under Cotswold,
He had made sure of his very Cleopatra,
Drunk with enormous, salvation-contemning
                Love for a tinker.

How, while he hid from Sir Thomas's keepers,
Crouched in a ditch and drenched by the midnight
Dews, he had listened to gipsy Juliet
                Rail at the dawning.

How at Bankside, a boy drowning kittens
Winced at the business; whereupon his sister—
Lady Macbeth aged seven—thrust 'em under,
                Sombrely scornful.

How on a Sabbath, hushed and compassionate—
She being known since her birth to the townsfolk—
Stratford dredged and delivered from Avon
                Dripping Ophelia.

So, with a thin third finger marrying
Drop to wine-drop domed on the table,
Shakespeare opened his heart till the sunrise
                Entered to hear him.

London waked and he, imperturbable,
Passed from waking to hurry after shadows . . .
Busied upon shows of no earthly importance?
                Yes, but he knew it!

RUDYARD KIPLING, 1919

The title of this poem may put the emphasis on technique—and craftsmanship was one of Kipling's watchwords—but the poem itself surges with feeling.

Kipling returned to the idea of Shakespeare as a craftsman, in a somewhat narrower sense, in one of his last short stories, 'Proofs of Holy Writ'. This is less well known than it should be: first published in a magazine in 1934, it was too late for inclusion in his last regular collection of stories, Limits and Renewals, *and has only appeared in book form in the expensive limited edition of his work published in 1938, two years after his death.*

Once again, Shakespeare is shown talking with Jonson, this time in the garden of his house in Stratford. The year is 1610, and it turns out that his help has been enlisted by the Revd Miles Smith, one of the commissioners appointed to prepare the Authorized Version. (Miles Smith was a real person, though there is no evidence that he and Shakespeare ever met. As in the story, he was one of the commissioners entrusted with the translation of the Book of Isaiah.)

Kipling has taken one large historical liberty: when they were translating the Old Testament the commissioners worked from the original Hebrew rather than the Latin of the Vulgate. The punning title of the story comes from Othello.

'Proofs of Holy Writ'

They seated themselves in the heavy chairs on the pebbled floor beneath the eaves of the summerhouse by the orchard. A table between them carried wine and glasses, and a packet of papers, with pen and ink. The larger man of the two, his doublet unbuttoned, his broad face blotched and scarred, puffed a little as he came to rest. The other picked an apple from the grass, bit it, and went on with the thread of the talk that they must have carried out of doors with them.

'But why waste time fighting atomies who do not come up to your belly-button, Ben?' he asked.

'It breathes me—it breathes me, between bouts! *You*'d be better for a tussle or two.'

'But not to spend mind and verse on 'em. What was Dekker to you? Ye knew he'd strike back—and hard.'

'He and Marston had been baiting me like dogs . . . about my trade as they called it, though it was only my cursed stepfather's. "Bricks and mortar," Dekker said, and "hodman." And he mocked my face. 'Twas clean as curds in my youth. This humour has come on me since.'

'Ah! "Every man *and* his humour"? But why did ye not have at Dekker in peace—over the sack, as you do at me?'

'Because I'd have drawn on him—and he's no more worth a hanging than Gabriel.° Setting aside what he wrote of me, too, the hireling dog has merit, of a sort. His *Shoemaker's Holiday.* Hey? Though my *Bartlemy Fair*, when 'tis presented, will furnish out three of it and—'

'Ride all the easier. I have suffered two readings of it already. It creaks like an overloaded hay-wain,' the other cut in. 'You give too much.'

Ben smiled loftily, and went on. 'But I'm glad I lashed him in my *Poetaster*, for all I've worked with him since. How comes it that I've never fought with thee, Will?'

'First, Behemoth,' the other drawled, 'it needs two to engender any sort of iniquity. Second, the betterment of this present age—and the next, maybe—lies, in chief, on our four shoulders. If the Pillars of the Temple fall out, Nature, Art, and Learning come to a stand. Last, I am not yet ass enough to hawk up my private spites before the groundlings. What do the Court, citizens, or 'prentices give for thy fallings-out or fallings-in with Dekker—or the Grand Devil?'

'They should be taught, then—taught.'

'Always *that*? What's your commission to enlighten us?'

'My own learning which I have heaped up, lifelong, at my own pains. My assured knowledge, also, of my craft and art. I'll suffer no man's mock or malice on it.'

'The one sure road to mockery.'

'I deny nothing of my brain-store to my lines. I—I build up my own works throughout.'

'Yet when Dekker cries "hodman" y'are not content.'

Ben half heaved in his chair. 'I'll owe you a beating for that when I'm thinner. Meantime, here's on account. I say, *I* build upon my own foundations; devising and perfecting my own plots; adorning 'em justly as fits time, place, and action. In all of which you sin damnably. *I* set no landward principalities on sea-beaches.'

'They pay their penny for pleasure—not learning,' Will answered above the apple-core.

'Penny or tester,° you owe 'em justice. In the facture of plays—nay, listen, Will—at all points they must be dressed historically—*teres atque rotundus°*—in ornament and temper. As my *Sejanus*, of which the mob was unworthy.'

Here Will made a doleful face, and echoed, 'Unworthy! I was—what did I play, Ben, in that long weariness? Some most grievous ass.'

<hr>

Gabriel] Gabriel Spencer, the actor Jonson killed in a duel   tester] a small silver coin
teres atque rotundus] from Horace: 'polished and well-rounded'

'The part of Caius Silius,' said Ben stiffly.

Will laughed aloud. 'True. "Indeed that place *was* not my sphere."'°

It must have been a quotation, for Ben winced a little, ere he recovered himself and went on: 'Also my *Alchemist* which the world in part apprehends. The main of its learning is necessarily yet hid from 'em. To come to your works, Will—'

'I am a sinner on all sides. The drink's at your elbow.'

'Confession shall not save ye—nor bribery.' Ben filled his glass. 'Sooner than labour the right cold heat to devise your own plots you filch, botch, and clap 'em together out o' ballads, broadsheets, old wives' tales, chap-books—'

Will nodded with complete satisfaction. 'Say on,' quoth he.

''Tis so with nigh all yours. I've known honester jackdaws. And whom among the learned do ye deceive? Reckoning up those—forty, is it?— your plays you've misbegot, there's not six which have not plots common as Moorditch.'

'Ye're out, Ben. There's not one. My *Love's Labour* (how I came to write it, I know not) is nearest to lawful issue. My *Tempest* (how I came to write *that*, I know) is, in some part, my own stuff. Of the rest, I stand guilty. Bastards all!'

'And no shame?'

'None! Our business must be fitted with parts hot and hot—and the boys are more trouble than the men. Give me the bones of any stuff, I'll cover 'em as quickly as any. But to hatch new plots is to waste God's unreturning time like a—'—he chuckled—'like a hen.'

'Yet see what ye miss! Invention next to Knowledge, whence it proceeds, being the chief glory of Art—'

'Miss, say you? Dick Burbage—in my *Hamlet* that I botched for him when he had staled of our Kings? (Nobly he played it.) Was *he* a miss?'

Ere Ben could speak Will overbore him.

'And when poor Dick was at odds with the world in general and womenkind in special, I clapped him up my *Lear* for a vomit.'

'An hotch-potch of passion, outrunning reason,' was the verdict.

'Not altogether. Cast in a mould too large for any boards to bear. (My fault!) Yet Dick evened it. And when he'd come out of his whoremongering aftermaths of repentance, I served him my *Macbeth* to toughen him. Was that a miss?'

'I grant you your *Macbeth* as nearest in spirit to my *Sejanus*; showing

---

'Indeed that place . . . sphere'] a line from *Sejanus*

for example: "How fortune plies her sports when she begins To practise 'em." We'll see which of the two lives longest.'

'Amen! I'll bear no malice among the worms.'

A liveried serving-man, booted and spurred, led a saddle-horse through the gate into the orchard. At a sign from Will he tethered the beast to a tree, lurched aside and stretched on the grass. Ben, curious as a lizard, for all his bulk, wanted to know what it meant.

'There's a nosing Justice of the Peace lost in thee,' Will returned. 'Yon's a business I've neglected all this day for thy fat sake—and he by so much the drunker. . . . Patience! It's all set out on the table. Have a care with the ink!'

Ben reached unsteadily for the packet of papers and read the super-scription: ' "To William Shakespeare, Gentleman, at his house of New Place in the town of Stratford, these—with diligence from M.S." Why does the fellow withhold his name? Or is it one of your women? I'll look.'

Muzzy as he was, he opened and unfolded a mass of printed papers expertly enough.

'From the most learned divine, Miles Smith of Brazen Nose College,' Will explained. 'You know this business as well as I. The King has set all the scholars of England to make one Bible, which the Church shall be bound to, out of all the Bibles that men use.'

'I knew.' Ben could not lift his eyes from the printed page. 'I'm more about Court than you think. The learning of Oxford and Cambridge— "most noble and most equal," as I have said—and Westminster, to sit upon a clutch of Bibles. Those 'ud be Geneva (my mother read to me out of it at her knee), Douai, Rheims, Coverdale, Matthew's, the Bishops', the Great, and so forth.'

'They are all set down on the page there—text against text. And you call me a botcher of old clothes?'

'Justly. But what's your concern with this botchery? To keep peace among the Divines? There's fifty of 'em at it as I've heard.'

'I deal with but one. He came to know me when we played at Oxford—when the plague was too hot in London.'

'I remember this Miles Smith now. Son of a butcher? Hey?' Ben grunted.

'Is it so?' was the quiet answer. 'He was moved, he said, with some lines of mine in Dick's part. He said they were, to his godly apprehen-sion, a parable, as it might be, of his reverend self, going down darkling to his tomb 'twixt cliffs of ice and iron.'

'What lines? I know none of thine of that power. But in my *Sejanus*—'
'These were in my *Macbeth*. They lost nothing at Dick's mouth:—

> ' "To-morrow, and to-morrow, and to-morrow
> Creeps in this petty pace from day to day
> To the last syllable of recorded time,
> And all our yesterdays have lighted fools
> The way to dusty death—"

or something in that sort. Condell writes 'em out fair for him, and tells
him I am Justice of the Peace (wherein he lied) and *armiger*, which brings
me within the pale of God's creatures and the Church. Little and little,
then, this very reverend Miles Smith opens his mind to me. He and a
half-score others, his cloth, are cast to furbish up the Prophets—Isaiah to
Malachi. In his opinion by what he'd heard, I had some skill in words,
and he'd condescend—'
'How?' Ben barked. 'Condescend?'
'Why not? He'd condescend to inquire o' me privily, when direct
illumination lacked, for a tricking-out of his words or the turn of some
figure. For example'—Will pointed to the papers—'here be the first three
verses of the Sixtieth of Isaiah, and the nineteenth and twentieth of that
same. Miles has been at a stand over 'em a week or more.'
'They never called on *me*.' Ben caressed lovingly the hand-pressed
proofs on their lavish linen paper. 'Here's the Latin atop and'—his thick
forefinger ran down the slip—'some three—four—Englishings out of the
other Bibles. They spare 'emselves nothing. Let's to it together. Will you
have the Latin first?'
'Could I choke ye from that, Holofernes?'°
Ben rolled forth, richly: ' "*Surge, illumare, Jerusalem, quia venit lumen
tuum, et gloria Domini super te orta est. Quia ecce tenebrae operient terram et
caligo populos. Super te autem orietur Dominus, et gloria ejus in te videbitur. Et
ambulabunt gentes in lumine tuo, et reges in splendore ortus tui.*" Er-hum?
Think you to better that?'
'How have Smith's crew gone about it?'
'Thus.' Ben read from the paper. ' "Get thee up, O Jerusalem, and be
bright, for thy light is at hand, and the glory of God has risen up upon
thee." '
'Up-pup-up!' Will stuttered profanely.
Ben held on. ' "See how darkness is upon the earth and the peoples
thereof." '

Holofernes] the pedant in *Love's Labour's Lost*

'That's no great stuff to put into Isaiah's mouth. And further, Ben?'

' "But on thee God shall shew light and on—" or "in," is it?' (Ben held the proof closer to the deep furrow at the bridge of his nose.) ' "On thee shall His glory be manifest. So that all peoples shall walk in thy light and the Kings in the glory of thy morning." '

'It may be mended. Read me the Coverdale of it now. 'Tis on the same sheet—to the right, Ben.'

'Umm—umm! Coverdale saith, "And therefore get thee up betimes, for thy light cometh, and the glory of the Lord shall rise up upon thee. For lo! while the darkness and cloud covereth the earth and the people, the Lord shall shew thee light, and His glory shall be seen in thee. The Gentiles shall come to thy light, and kings to the brightness that springeth forth upon thee." But "gentes" is, for the most part, "peoples," ' Ben concluded.

'Eh?' said Will indifferently. 'Art sure?'

This loosed an avalanche of instances from Ovid, Quintilian, Terence, Columella, Seneca, and others. Will took no heed till the rush ceased, but stared into the orchard, through the September haze. 'Now give me the Douai and Geneva for this "Get thee up, O Jerusalem," ' said he at last. 'They'll be all there.'

Ben referred to the proofs. ' 'Tis "arise" in both,' said he. ' "Arise and be bright" in Geneva. In the Douai 'tis "Arise and be illuminated." '

'So? Give me the paper now.' Will took it from his companion, rose, and paced towards a tree in the orchard, turning again, when he had reached it, by a well-worn track through the grass. Ben leaned forward in his chair. The other's free hand went up warningly.

'Quiet, man!' said he. 'I wait on my Demon!' He fell into the stage-stride of his art at that time, speaking to the air.

'How shall this open? "Arise?" No! "Rise!" Yes. And we'll have no weak coupling. 'Tis a call to a City! "Rise—shine" . . . Nor yet any schoolmaster's "because"—because Isaiah is not Holofernes. *"Rise—shine; for thy light is come, and—!"* ' He refreshed himself from the apple and the proofs as he strode. ' "And—and the glory of God!"—No! "God" 's over short. We need the long roll here. *"And the glory of the Lord is risen on thee."* (Isaiah speaks the part. We'll have it from his own lips.) What's next in Smith's stuff? . . . "See how?" Oh, vile—vile! . . . And Geneva hath "Lo"? (Still, Ben! Still!) "Lo" is better by all odds: but to match the long roll of "the Lord" we'll have it "Behold." How goes it now? *For, behold, darkness clokes the earth and—*and—" What's the colour and use of this cursed *caligo*, Ben?—"*Et caligo populos.*" '

' "Mistiness" or, as in Pliny, "blindness." And further—'

'No—o . . . Maybe, though, *caligo* will piece out *tenebrae. "Quia ecce tenebrae operient terram et caligo populos."* Nay! "Shadow" and "mist" are not men enough for this work . . . Blindness, did ye say, Ben? . . . The blackness of blindness atop of mere darkness? . . . By God, I've used it in my own stuff many times! "Gross" searches it to the hilts! "Darkness covers"—no—"clokes" (short always). *"Darkness clokes the earth, and gross—gross darkness the people!"* (But Isaiah's prophesying, with the storm behind him. Can ye not *feel* it, Ben? It must be "shall")—*"Shall cloke the earth"* . . . The rest comes clearer . . . "But on thee God shall arise" . . . (Nay, that's sacrificing the Creator to the Creature!) *"But the Lord shall arise on thee,"* and—yes, we'll sound that "thee" again—"and on thee shall"—No! . . . *"And His glory shall be seen on thee."* Good!' He walked his beat a little in silence, mumbling the two verses before he mouthed them.

'I have it! Heark, Ben! *"Rise—shine; for thy light is come, and the glory of the Lord is risen on thee. For, behold, darkness shall cloke the earth, and gross darkness the people. But the Lord shall arise on thee, and His glory shall be seen upon thee."* '

'There's something not all amiss there,' Ben conceded.

'My Demon never betrayed me yet, while I trusted him. Now for the verse that runs to the blast of rams'-horns. *"Et ambulabunt gentes in lumine tuo, et reges in splendore ortus tui."* How goes that in the Smithy? "The Gentiles shall come to thy light, and kings to the brightness that springs forth upon thee?" The same in Coverdale and the Bishops'—eh? We'll keep "Gentiles," Ben, for the sake of the indraught of the last syllable. But it might be "And the Gentiles shall draw." No! The plainer the better! "The Gentiles shall come to thy light, and kings to the splendour of—" (Smith's out here! We'll need something that shall lift the trumpet anew.) "Kings shall—shall—Kings to—" (Listen, Ben, but on your life speak not!) "Gentiles shall come to thy light, and kings to thy brightness"—No! "Kings to the brightness that springeth—" Serves not! . . . One trumpet must answer another. And the blast of a trumpet is always *ai-ai*. "The brightness of"—*"Ortus"* signifies "rising," Ben—or what?'

'Ay, or "birth," or the East in general.'

'Ass! 'Tis the one word that answers to "light." "Kings to the brightness of thy rising." Look! The thing shines now within and without. God! That so much should lie on a word!' He repeated the verse—' *"And the Gentiles shall come to thy light, and kings to the brightness of thy rising."* '

He walked to the table and wrote rapidly on the proof margin all three verses as he had spoken them. 'If they hold by this,' said he, raising his head, 'they'll not go far astray. Now for the nineteenth and twentieth verses. On the other sheet, Ben. What? What? Smith says he has held back his rendering till he hath seen mine? Then we'll botch 'em as they stand. Read me first the Latin; next the Coverdale, and last the Bishops'. There's a contagion of sleep in the air.' He handed back the proofs, yawned, and took up his walk.

Obedient, Ben began: ' "*Non erit tibi amplius Sol ad lucendum per diem, nec splendor Lunae illuminabit te.*" Which Coverdale rendereth, "The Sun shall never be thy day light, and the light of the Moon shall never shine unto thee." The Bishops read: "Thy sun shall never be thy daylight and the light of the moon shall never shine on thee." '

'Coverdale is the better,' said Will, and, wrinkling his nose a little, 'The Bishops put out their lights clumsily. Have at it, Ben.'

Ben pursed his lips and knit his brow. 'The two verses are in the same mode, changing a hand's-breadth in the second. By so much, therefore, the more difficult.'

'Ye see *that*, then?' said the other, staring past him, and muttering as he paced, concerning suns and moons. Presently he took back the proof, chose him another apple, and grunted. 'Umm—umm! "Thy Sun shall never be—" No! Flat as a split viol. "*Non erit tibi amplius Sol—*" That *amplius* must give tongue. Ah! . . . "Thy Sun shall not—shall not—shall no more be thy light by day" . . . A fair entry. "Nor?"—No! Not on the heels of "day." "Neither" it must be—"Neither the Moon"—but here's *splendor* and the rams'-horns again. (Therefore—*ai*—*ai*!) "Neither for brightness shall the Moon—" (Pest! It is the Lord who is taking the Moon's place over Israel. It must be "thy Moon.") "Neither for brightness shall thy Moon light—give—make—give light unto thee." Ah! . . . Listen here! . . . "*The Sun shall no more be thy light by day: neither for brightness shall thy Moon give light unto thee.*" That serves, and more, for the first entry. What next, Ben?'

Ben nodded magisterially as Will neared him, reached out his hand for the proofs, and read: ' "*Sed erit tibi Dominus in lucem sempiternam et Deus tuus in gloriam tuam.*" Here is a jewel of Coverdale's that the Bishops have wisely stolen whole. Hear! "*But the Lord Himself shall be thy everlasting light, and thy God shall be thy glory.*" ' Ben paused. 'There's a hand's-breadth of splendour for a simple man to gather!'

'Both hands rather. He's swept the strings as divinely as David before Saul,' Will assented. 'We'll convey it whole, too. . . . What's amiss now, Holofernes?'

For Ben was regarding him with a scholar's cold pity. 'Both hands! Will, hast thou *ever* troubled to master *any* shape or sort of prosody—the mere names of the measures and pulses of strung words?'

'I beget some such stuff and send it to you to christen. What's your wisdomhood in labour of?'

'Naught. Naught. But not to know the names of the tools of his trade!' Ben half muttered and pronounced some Greek word or other which conveyed nothing to the listener, who replied: 'Pardon, then, for whatever sin it was. I do but know words for my need of 'em, Ben. Hold still awhile!'

He went back to his pacings and mutterings. ' "For the Lord Himself shall be thy—or thine?—everlasting light." Yes. We'll convey that.' He repeated it twice. 'Nay! Can be bettered. Hark ye, Ben. Here is the Sun going up to over-run and possess all Heaven for evermore. *There*fore (Still, man!) we'll harness the horses of the dawn. Hear their hooves? "The Lord Himself shall be unto thee thy everlasting light, and—" Hold again! After that climbing thunder must be some smooth check—like great wings gliding. *There*fore we'll not have "shall be thy glory," but *"And* thy God thy glory!" Ay—even as an eagle alighteth! Good—good! Now again, the sun and moon of that twentieth verse, Ben.'

Ben read: ' *"Non occidet ultra Sol tuus et Luna tua non minuetur: quia erit tibi Dominus in lucem sempiternam et complebuntur dies luctus tui."* '

Will snatched the paper and read aloud from the Coverdale version. ' "Thy Sun shall never go down, and thy Moon shall not be taken away . . ." What a plague's Coverdale doing with his blocking *ets* and *urs*, Ben? What's *minuetur*? . . . I'll have it all anon.'

'Minish—make less—appease—abate, as in—'

'So?' . . . Will threw the proofs back. 'Then "wane" should serve. "Neither shall thy moon wane" . . . "Wane" is good, but over-weak for place next to "moon" ' . . . He swore softly. 'Isaiah hath abolished both earthly sun and moon. *Exeunt ambo.* Aha! I begin to see! . . . Sol, the man, goes down—down stairs or trap—as needs be. Therefore "Go down" shall stand. "Set" would have been better—as a sword sent home in the scabbard—but it jars—it jars. Now Luna must retire herself in some simple fashion. . . . Which? Ass that I be! 'Tis common talk in all the plays. . . . "Withdrawn" . . . "Favour withdrawn" . . . "Countenance withdrawn." "The Queen withdraws herself" . . . "Withdraw," it shall be! "Neither shall thy moon withdraw herself." (Hear her silver train rasp the boards, Ben?) *"Thy sun shall no more go down—neither shall thy moon withdraw herself. For the Lord . . . "*—ay, the Lord, simple of Himself—

"shall be thine"—yes, "thine" here—*"everlasting light, and"* . . . How goes the ending, Ben?'

' *"Et complebuntur dies luctus tui,"* ' Ben read. ' "And thy sorrowful days shall be rewarded thee," says Coverdale.'

'And the Bishops?'

' "And thy sorrowful days shall be ended." '

'By no means. And Douai?'

' "Thy sorrow shall be ended." '

'And Geneva?'

' "And the days of thy mourning shall be ended." '

'The Switzers have it! Lay the tail of Geneva to the head of Coverdale and the last is without flaw.' He began to thump Ben on the shoulder. 'We have it! I have it all, Boanerges! Blessed be my Demon! Hear! *"The sun shall no more be thy light by day, neither for brightness the moon by night. But the Lord Himself shall be unto thee thy everlasting light, and thy God thy glory."* ' He drew a deep breath and went on. ' *"Thy sun shall no more go down; neither shall thy moon withdraw herself, for the Lord shall be thine everlasting light, and the days of thy mourning shall be ended."* ' The rain of triumphant blows began again. 'If those other seven devils in London let it stand on this sort, it serves. But God knows what they can *not* turn upsee-dejee!'

Ben wriggled. 'Let be!' he protested. 'Ye are more moved by this jugglery than if the Globe were burned.'

'Thatch—old thatch! And full of fleas! . . . But, Ben, ye should have heard my Ezekiel making mock of fallen Tyrus in his twenty-seventh chapter. Miles sent me the whole, for, he said, some small touches. I took it to the Bank—four o'clock of a summer morn; stretched out in one of our wherries—and watched London, Port and Town, up and down the river, waking all arrayed to heap more upon evident excess. Ay! "A merchant for the peoples of many isles" . . . "The ships of Tarshish did sing of thee in thy markets"? Yes! I saw all Tyre before me neighing her pride against lifted heaven. . . . But what will they let stand of all mine at long last? Which? I'll never know.'

He had set himself neatly and quickly to refolding and cording the packet while he talked. 'That's secret enough,' he said at the finish.

'He'll lose it by the way.' Ben pointed to the sleeper beneath the tree. 'He's owl-drunk.'

'But not his horse,' said Will. He crossed the orchard, roused the man; slid the packet into an holster which he carefully rebuckled; saw him out of the gate, and returned to his chair.

'Who will know we had part in it?' Ben asked.

'God, maybe—if He ever lay ear to earth. I've gained and lost enough—lost enough.' He lay back and sighed. There was long silence till he spoke half aloud. 'And Kit that was my master in the beginning, he died when all the world was young.'

'Knifed on a tavern reckoning—not even for a wench!' Ben nodded.

'Ay. But if he'd lived he'd have breathed me! 'Fore God, he'd have breathed me!'

'Was Marlowe, or any man, *ever* thy master, Will?'

'He alone. Very he. I envied Kit. Ye do not know that envy, Ben?'

'Not as touching my own works. When the mob is led to prefer a baser Muse, I have felt the hurt, and paid home. Ye know that—as ye know my doctrine of play-writing.'

'Nay—not wholly—tell it at large,' said Will, relaxing in his seat, for virtue had gone out of him. He put a few drowsy questions. In three minutes Ben had launched full-flood on the decayed state of the drama, which he was born to correct; on cabals and intrigues against him which he had fought without cease; and on the inveterate muddle-headedness of the mob unless duly scourged into approbation by his magisterial hand.

It was very still in the orchard now that the horse had gone. The heat of the day held though the sun sloped, and the wine had done its work. Presently, Ben's discourse was broken by a snort from the other chair.

'I was listening, Ben! Missed not a word—missed not a word.' Will sat up and rubbed his eyes. 'Ye held me throughout.' His head dropped again before he had done speaking.

Ben looked at him with a chuckle and quoted from one of his own plays:—

> ' "Mine earnest vehement botcher
> And deacon also, Will, I cannot dispute with you." '°

He drew out flint, steel and tinder, pipe and tobacco-bag from some-where round his waist, lit and puffed against the midges till he, too, dozed.

⋆   ⋆   ⋆

Shakespeare is also shown revising 'proofs of holy writ' in Inside Mrs Enderby, *Anthony Burgess's whimsical sequel (in its Shakespearian aspects)*

'Mine earnest vehement botcher . . . with you'] from *The Alchemist to his novel* Nothing Like the Sun. *In the Burgess version, a group of poets, including Jonson, are hired by the official translators to improve the text—'to tickle our sober accuracy into poetic life'. Shakespeare is not among them, but Jonson makes him the gift of 'three or four psalms in galley proof', and he proceeds to set his personal stamp on Psalm 46, changing 'tremble', the forty-sixth word from the beginning, to 'shake', and 'sword', the forty-sixth word from the end, to 'spear'. (By a happy coincidence, forty-six also happens to be his age at the time.) And when the Authorized Version appears the following year, it turns out that his alterations have been adopted—as anyone who consults a copy will find.*

In Nothing Like the Sun (1964) *Burgess identifies the 'Fair Friend' of the sonnets with Henry Wriothesley, Earl of Southampton, and shows Shakespeare (referred to throughout the novel as 'WS') being commissioned to write the opening sequence of sonnets by the Earl's mother, who was anxious for her son to marry. Hence the reference in the chapter which follows to 'earning gold through eloquent pleading'.*

'Dear my lord—'

'I will be called by my name.'

'It is not seemly that I—'

'Oh, it is for me to say what is and is not seemly. And I will say that it is not seemly for you to go moping about with this long puling face on so bright a June day. I keep my poet for my ape, not for my *memento mori*.'

WS looked at him with bitter love. The death of a poet was nothing to this lord who was as careless with his poets as with his gold (Pay thou this reckoning, Will; I have spent all I had with me.—But, my lord, I doubt that I have enough in my purse.—Aye, I forget that thou'rt but a poor crust-eating sonnet-monger.)

'I cannot be unmoved, my lord (Harry I would say), when I hear that my friend was stabbed with his own dagger and died in torment. His own dagger, straight through the eye, imagine. He screamed, they say, that all Deptford could hear it. The agony of suffering Christ could not be worse.' That news had come to WS late, cushioned as he was from the real world of ale and plays and lice by sumptuous satins and giddy perfumes. He had heard first the elation of the pious at the death of Antichrist; then the coroner's droning that Frizer had slain Marlowe in the defence and saving of his own life; last he had put together the ghastly scene in the room at Deptford Strand—Frizer, Skeres, Poley standing about, laughter then sudden rage from the poet lying on the bed, the flash of the dagger, the flash of the enemy hand snatching the dagger, and then—That line would not leave his mind, that scream of damned Faustus: 'See where Christ's blood streams in the firmament.'

'You may exult now, friend or no friend,' said his lordship Mr WH, Harry, 'that you are without peer. Now my poet is the only poet.' He was shrewd in some things, pretty pouting boy as he was. 'You may gladly lose a friend to know that.'

'He was not so close a friend. But there was no poet like him.' That was true. Still, he had seen his successor burst like a new sun in the very days of his daily summoning to the Council's inquisition about souls on the top of a pole and run God, run devil, have it who will (did you say this?), his own masterpiece unfinished.

'I should hope he was no close friend. Well, this may mean one more nail in the coffin of his upstart protector the tobacco-man. Sir Walter Stink. I cannot abide the oaf, what with his Brownists° and atheists and wenching at court. You must write a play mocking him and all his black circle.'

Why this enmity? Had Essex been squirting poison in? Oh, the intrigues, the ambages, the labyrinthine plottings. As for the School of Night, WS kept his own counsel. This was a new life, post-Marlovian (a pretty coinage), dedicated to love and advancement and poetry. 'I have here,' said WS, smiling, 'a new sonnet.' And he took it from his breast, the black ink that had flowed so confidently scarce dry. (' . . . Thy love is better than high birth to me, Richer than wealth, prouder than gar-ments' cost, Of more delight than hawks or horses be . . . ' Was it not perhaps over-forward, after but a few weeks of friendship, this harping on love? But Mr WH, Harry, had said it first.)

'Oh, I have no time now for reading sonnets,' said Harry in petulance. 'I have still to read the first you gave me. Place it in that chest there.' It was a box of carven camphorwood, cool-smelling and spicy within, brought, he had said, from the Indies by a captain that had loved him but was now cast out. Jealously, WS saw other poems than his own, but, certainly, there was that first sonnet: 'A woman's face with Nature's own hand painted . . . ' It was true, it was a woman's beauty, but there was the swooning delight of its being on no woman's body. Forward? There was not all the time in the world. He grew old, he would soon be thirty.

'Today,' said the lovely boy, 'we are to go down-river.' And the river it

Brownists] Puritan separatists, hostile to any form of church government was, in joyful sunlight, paddling softly towards Gravesend, the grave watermen in livery, the barge new-painted with cloth-of-gold canopy above, the handsome laughing young friends of his friend deferential to this sober-suited poet who had taken the Inns and the Universities with his mellifluous conceits. Wine and cold fowls and kickshawses, and then, as the sun went in a space, distaste blew into the poet's heart like a damp gust, he seeing himself again truly as an upstart, without birth or wealth, one plain ring only on his hand, his garments decent but no more, and a different distaste at the sudden sight of the open laughing mouth of this lord they called plain Jack, the teeth clogged with a powdery sweetmeat. They were idle, they were dying of *ennui* (a fine apt word from Master Florio), they hid diseased bodies under silk and brocade. Then the sun came out again and they were transformed once more to air and fire, the flower of English manhood. They were swans, but like the swans that sailed in the barge's wake, greedy and cold-eyed. And the kites that flew to and from their scavenging in the June air, the ultimate cleansers of the commonwealth, they attested the end of all noble flesh.

'When will the playhouses open again?'

'Oh, the plague-deaths are still above thirty a week.'

'I care not for plays. They are all bawdry and butchery.'

'Well, there is always Lyly and his little boys.' A coarse secret laugh. 'Lily-white boys.'

'May not a gentleman rise above carnality—blood and panting and close-stools? As for love—'

He would give them what they wished, redeeming his craft to art. He saw in his mind's eye a fair-hung stage shut in from sun or wind, fair languid creatures like these discoursing wittily, no Kemp grossness, no blood-bladders or Alleyn ranting. He would provide, he would lend words to these elegant puppets. But he sighed, knowing himself to be caught forever between worlds—earth and air, reason and belief, action and contemplation. Alone among all sorts of men, he embraced a poet's martyrdom.

'Your sonnets harp more and more on marriage. Oh, it is nothing but marriage I hear from my mother and my grandad and my noble guardian that has a bride in store for me, and now you join them. My friend and own poet makes one in a conspiracy.' He pettishly threw the poem on to the table. It fluttered in the fresh autumn breeze from the casement and planed gently down to the carpet (dryads and fauns greenly

embroidered). WS smiled, peering with eyes that were growing
near-sighted at the upside-down lines:

> From fairest creatures we desire increase,
> That thereby beauty's rose might never die . . .

He had come, he considered, delicately and discreetly to his burden.
Besides, it was by way of a commission, engineered by the subtle Italian.°
He was no lord with estates and retainers; he must earn money. Her
ladyship, the handsome ageing countess, all of forty years, had embraced
his hands painfully with hers sharp and crusty with rings. My thanks,
dear friend, my most grateful thanks. A matter of the songs of Apollo
after the words of Mercury. Carefully he said:

'A friend should speak what is in his heart, a poet even more so. It is
waste I fear. Should I die now at least I leave a son. The name Shakespeare will not die,' he said confidently. But, saying the rest, he felt the
old self-disgust of the actor; he was earning gold through eloquent
pleading. It was for lying, he saw hopelessly, that words had been made.
In the beginning was the word and the word was with the Father of Lies.
'But I am a mere nothing.' He extended his hands to show them empty.
'I fear so many things for you—death in the field, in the street. The
plague took, this last week, over a thousand. And what then, with you
gone? A few poor portraits, a sonnet or two. It is a perpetuity of flesh
and blood that we beg for.'

'Aye, the family first, as ever.' He was bitter. 'Wriothesly before Harry.
Mr WH.'

'There is nothing wrong in marriage. It is a thing a man will enter for
his name's sake. He can still be free.'

'Are you free? If a man has to run away from his wife I see not how he
can still be free. You dream in your plays of taming shrews.'

Aye, WS thought, I am always under-estimating him, *magister artium
per gratiam* at fifteen, commended by the Queen herself for wit and
beauty. It was the beauty got in the way. The Queen seemed to have
stepped into both their brains, for Harry now said:

'As for wranglings about succession and great houses in an uproar, the
Queen has set all a fine example.'

'The Queen is a woman.'

'Part a woman. If the Tudors will die out let the Wriotheslys also.' WS

the subtle Italian] John Florio, whom Burgess shows acting as a go-between for the Earl's
mother

smiled at those heavy words coming from the pouting girl's mouth. He said in banter:

'Well, they say there is no worry over the succession. All will be taken care of.' And, stepping to the window, as though to look carelessly out, he whistled a measure or two from a popular ballad. Harry knew it: 'For bonny sweet Robin is all my joy.'

'You grow too familiar.'

WS turned, surprised. 'Whistling? May I not whistle?'

'It is not the whistling. Your whole manner is become too familiar.'

'I have been schooled thereto by your lordship. I humbly cry your mercy, my lord.' He spoke mincingly and ended in a ridiculous smirking bow. It was Harry who was ridiculous; he could be as wayward and petulant as a girl in her courses. 'Dear my lord,' added WS.

Harry grinned. 'Well then, if I am dear your lord let us see more lowly abasement and fawning. First, you may pick up your sonnet from where it fell.' He could keep no mood up for long.

'The wind blew it, let the wind lift it.'

'Oh, but I cannot order the wind.'

'Nor me, my lord.'

'Ah, but I can. And if you will not obey I will have you escorted to the dungeons to live with toads and snakes and scorpions.'

'I have lived with worse.'

'So. Well, you shall be whipped. I will apply a whip to thine ancient shoulders. I will raise first cloth, then skin, then blood. Tatters of skin and cloth and flesh all delicately commingled.' Even in play he had a certain lordly cruelty. Power to hurt and he would do it.

'Oh oh, whip me not.' He wondered at himself, ancient WS. A friend, a lover, he saw himself an instant as a father; he carried on those ancient shoulders more than the weight of ten years' difference. Falling into the game, he went down to the carpet creaking, going oh oh on cracking joints, kneeling. Harry at once was there, a delicate foot in delicate kidskin placed upon the sonnet. WS saw: '. . . or else this glutton be, To eat the world's due by the grave and thee.' Suddenly he thrust his arms in a tight hug round the slim boy's calves. Harry's voice, high up there, screamed. Then WS brought him down, not hard on that deep pile showing embroidered green wantonness, his arms striving too late for balance, laughing, breathless. 'Now,' went WS in mock gruffness, 'I have thee.' They fought, and the craftsman's arms were the stronger.

'No more sonnets on marriage,' panted Harry.

'Oh no, none,' vowed that practitioner of lies.

★

He could not altogether keep his old life out of this new.

> When roasted crabs hiss in the bowl,
> Then nightly sings the staring owl:
> 'Tu-who;
> Tu-whit, to-who'—A merry note,
> While greasy Joan doth keel the pot.

He could see her clearly, cleaning the trenchers in cold water after the Christmas dinner. It should be a good one this year: he had sent home enough sonnet gold. He had not, however, as he had promised, sent home himself. He had had work to do, a resident playwright in a noble house, writing a play about lords who vowed three years' abstinence from love and the comedy of their breaking of that vow. 'How long will it be?' Harry had asked. And he had answered: 'Three ells.' And, as there was no company at all in London then (the play-houses still being shut, though the plague had much abated), it must be a matter of lords playing lords. The first day of Christmas brought My Lord Sussex's Men to the Rose (Henslowe recording a God Be Praised in his account-book), but that was too late. Lords must act even ladies' parts, all for an audience of ladies, and Master Florio must do Don Adriano de Armado, because of his foreign accent, while Holofernes the schoolmaster was none other than—

(The twins would be nine years old at Candlemas. How fast time flowed away.)

'. . . I marvel thy master hath not eaten thee for a word, for thou art not so long by the head as hon- hon- honorif-'

'Honorificabilitudinitatibus.'

'Oh, I cannot say that.' This was Sir John Gerrald, whose droll face singled him out for Costard. They were all remarking on the wit and the learning, the pedantry even, even when pedantry was not being mocked. This was what he wished, directing his lordly cast in the fine heavy gown that was a gift from his own lord, his friend. ('In your time, sir, perhaps Oxford men were less sportive?' A smile, a shrug in answer.) But, after a heavy night's feasting that he was forced into, for he could not plead a weak stomach all the time, nor say he was in pain or had work to do, he was sickened, veering from Arden to Shakespeare and in a manner envying that Friar Lawrence that had already appeared, duly set in a new lyric play, out of some remote cave of his brain. To be cut off, to live austere, an eremite: he sighed for that. But then he remembered his mission here, the restoring of honour to a name that had lost it, along with family fortune. And there was this damnable love, this ravishment of the senses, bursting into jealousy that, in the quietness of his own chamber, he must unload into verse to be torn up after (Harry laughing with Lord This or Sir Such-an-one, hand-touching, hand-holding) or flowing in compassion, the manner of a world-woe, when he saw tears brimming down the soft, faintly translucent cheeks as a consort of viols or recorders discoursed. *Lachrymae, lachrymae.*

> Music to hear, why hear'st thou music sadly?
> Sweets with sweets war not, joy delights in joy.

'There it is again,' Harry scolded, 'finding a pretext for a marriage sermon in everything.'

> Mark how one string, sweet husband to another,
> Strikes each in each by mutual . . .

'Ordering my life for me, all of you. And yet,' said the cunning boy, 'what would you say if I did now go a-courting and spend all my time with Lady Liza? I do believe you would be out of your mind with envious rage.' WS smiled uncertainly. 'Confess now', said Harry, leaping up with great nervous vigour from the couch where he had been lying. 'You shall confess that you do all this to please others and not yourself at all. Does my mother, then, come to your chamber and stand over you while you write, telling you to say this and say that, only, an't please your poetship, to use fine high phrases as befit a poet, and if you will not you shall out of this house and never see my son more, for, why, what art thou, thou art no better than a harlotry player?'

'*Harlotry* is good,' said WS, blushing.

'Well, is it true? Have I hit it?'

WS sighed. 'I have endeavoured to please all save you. I have done more sonnets on this same theme. I write many at a sitting but give you one only at a time. Well, I shall write no more.'

'Why why why? Why do you sing their tune? Nay, why do you make the tune for them to sing?'

WS extended his empty hands like, he thought, doing it, some usurious Jew. 'I did it for money. I must live.'

'For money? Oh God, for money? Do you not have everything you want? Do I not give you everything?' Harry stood, hands on hips, narrowing his eyes. 'For how much money? For thirty pieces of silver?'

'Oh, this is all nonsense. I must send money home. I have a wife if you have not and will not have. I cannot disown my wife, nor my three children.'

Harry grinned maliciously. 'Poor Will. Will the married man.'

'I have a son. My son must grow up a gentleman.'

'Poor Will. My poor, dear Will. Often I feel myself to be so very much older. I could speak to thee like thine own dad.'

'A son to grow up like you, though never to be a lord yet perhaps a knight. Sir Hamnet Shakespeare. I see in you what he may be. And often I feel that I may never live to see it, not in reality. Often I feel so tired.'

Harry came up to his chair from behind and embraced him, jewelled hands winking in the winter light as they lay crossed on the breast of his friend. WS took the right hand in his own and squeezed it. 'I shall write no more sonnets,' he said. 'You have seen through the poor trickery.'

Harry kissed his cheek lightly. 'Write me more sonnets,' he said, 'though not on that stale and profitless theme. And let us ride together ere spring comes to—to wherever it is thy wife and children are.'

'Stratford.'

'Aye, thither. And we shall take a fine present to Lord Hamnet.'

'You are kind. You are always kind.'

'But,' said Harry, breaking away and striding towards the window, 'thou shalt do something for me. Another poem. And let it be a revenge on women, the whole sex.' Rain had started to fall. It was a grey day. Bare branches tapped, tapped forlornly at the window. 'Especially on these women who are so holy on marriage and the sanctity of marriage. I wish to see another book and my name on it and to hear the congratulations of my friends.'

'What I have done is yours,' said WS. 'What I have to do is yours. But I cannot be altogether so harsh against women.'

They did not go to Stratford. Instead, WS worked at his poem of Lucrece and Tarquin, and Harry took to low company, drawn into it, in life's sly irony, by another poet. The poet was George Chapman, older by some four years than WS, and he had ventured on his first plays this rare time (rare in two years) of the Rose being open. He had done a ranting tragedy for Sussex's Men—*Artaxerxes*, in which Cyrus the Younger, second son of Darius, had raving speeches which smacked of WS's own Holofernes, though not in parody. Harry was much taken by his black-bearded loudness. Summoned to the Lord's room, as WS himself had once been, again in a frosty January, he tickled Harry by being most undeferential. . . .

'Will,' said Harry, 'I am in love.'

WS put down his pen carefully. He stared for full five seconds. 'In love? *In love?*'

Harry giggled. 'Oh, it is not marriage love, it is no great lady. It is a country Lucrece in Islington. She is the wife of the keeper of the Three Tuns.'

'In love. *In love.* Oh, God save us.'

'She knows not who I am. I have been with Chapman. She believes I too am a poet. She will have none of me.' He giggled again.

'So the seed stirs at last. Well. He is in love.' Then WS began to laugh. 'And what thinks the husband of all this?'

'Oh, he is away. His father is dying in Norfolk, and yet he will not die. It is a slow quietus. I must have her, Will, before he returns. How shall I have her?'

'I should think,' said WS slowly, 'that your new friends will help you there. The Sussex men are, I hear, a wenching crowd.'

'They are not. They are all for boys. There is a house in Islington.'

'Well. Well, well. In love.' He picked up his pen, sighing. 'I have a poem to write, a commission of your lordship's. My mind is wholly taken up with the harm that comes to those who force the chastity of noble matrons. I should think like harm will come to the authors of lowlier essays.'

'You mock me now. Write me a poem I can give to her. You have written sonnets enjoining me to love a woman, now write one that shall persuade a woman to love me.'

'Your friend Master Chapman is perhaps less busy than I that he can take you drinking to Islington. Ask him, my noble lord.'

'Will, I have no taste for this mockery. George cannot write that sort of verse. She would never understand any poem of his.'

'Can she read?'

'Oh yes, and write too. She has a good hand in making out of a reckoning. And as for George, he too is busy enough with a poem. He is lodging at Islington, at the Three Tuns, writing it. It is far out, he says, from the distraction of those who admire him.'

WS was amused; disturbed, a little jealous, but still amused. 'The distraction of his creditors, he would say. I have a mind to come out to Islington to see this innkeeper's wife who has all my lord's heart.' He had a mind too to see this Chapman.

'Ah, she has such a white skin. And a very tiny foot. She has a waist a man could span his two hands withal. She is black-haired and black-eyed.'

'She is out of the fashion, then.'

'These great ladies chase a man. She does not. She thrusts me away. She thrusts all men away.'

'Including Master Chapman?'

'George is only in love with himself. That is why he amuses me. He too is writing a poem, as I say, though not to my commission. He says he will honour me with its dedication.'

So. He had very much a mind to see this Chapman. 'Well, when shall we go thither?'

'Tonight. This night. You shall see her this very night.'

It was a fair ride out to Islington, where Canonbury Tower was being new-built by the Lord Mayor. A cold ride, too, that sharp night, the road ringing. They were both glad of the warmth of the fire of the inn.

'Is she not beautiful?'

'Hm.' Her eyes accompanied, in merry mockery, the chaff she was handing back to a table of three guzzling citizens (they had ravaged two whole fowls between them and were tearing at cheese and black bread); she was country-wholesome, a new experience for his friend. Well, he must learn that he could not have everything he wanted. 'I would say,' he said, 'that she is any man's meat. Perhaps you are somewhat too young and pretty. Perhaps she will take better to an older, uglier man.' An older, uglier man came heavily downstairs, yawning, showing stained teeth, his black hair all a tangle. Jowled face, mean eyes. This was Master Chapman. He and WS eyed each other like fighting cocks.

'Ah, Harry,' said Chapman loudly. He took a seat at the rough well-scrubbed table near the fire, yawning. 'Poetic labour is hard labour,' he said. 'I have been taking a nap.'

'*Homerus dormitat*,' giggled Harry. 'Sometimes your verse reads like hard labour.'

Chapman ignored this. To WS he said, 'When comes Alleyn back with the rest of the Strange snipperados?'

'I hear nothing. I am cut off this whole year from playhouse news.' WS grinned. 'Snipped off, let us say.'

She brought sweet wine, glowing. She was certainly pretty enough. Harry did a furnace-sigh. Well, this was new: his lordship in love with an alewife. He must be cured; a good swift cure, like a Lowestoft herring's. 'This,' said WS, 'seems a cleanly enough inn. It would be cold riding back. Let us lie here tonight.' And he closed one eye at Harry. Chapman said:

'Your Venus poem had a good epigraph.' He mouthed the Latin loud, sounding round brown vowels:

> ' "*Vilia miretur vulgus: mihi flavus Apollo*
> *Pocula Castalia plena ministret aqua." '*°

Then he belched gently though long on his first draught of wine. 'Whether a man can maintain two writing sides I know not. One will corrupt the other, doubtless.'

'Perhaps the better will corrupt the worse,' said WS. Harry's eyes could not leave her. 'Well,' to Chapman, 'I am glad you at least like the epigraph.'

'Oh, the rest was well enough. There was a sufficiency of lusty country matter in it. Each of us has his own way. One way is not another. We must do as we can, remembering the parable of the talents.' He then took a large swig and, his mouth dripping, looked Harry full in the eyes and declaimed:

> 'Presume not then, ye flesh-confounded souls,
> That cannot bear the full Castalian bowls,
> Which sever mounting spirits from their senses,
> To look in this deep fount for thy pretences.'

'You are welcome,' said WS, 'to my full Castalian bowls.'

'To Night,' said Chapman, raising his near-empty Castalian bowl. 'Night is my mistress and my muse. To her I drink.'

'To her I drink,' said Harry, flesh-confounded, languishing in ridiculous desire.

'We will go to bed soon,' promised WS, smiling.

They rode back to Holborn next morning in sharp sunlight, jewelled cobwebs on the bare branches, their breath going up, as they spoke, like the wraith of speech. 'Well,' said WS, 'I knew it would be easy for an older man. It is very much a matter of experience. Women will ever go for the experienced man. They can oft see experience in a man's eyes.'

Harry looked unbelieving, then aghast. 'But you did not. You could not. Her chamber-door was locked.' He was pale. 'No no no, you are joking.'

Vilia miretur . . . aqua] from Ovid's *Amores*: 'Let the crowd be dazzled by cheap things; for me, may golden Apollo minister full cups from the Castalian spring'

'To you it was locked, aye. I was not asleep though I snored. It was a fair counterfeit of sleep. I am, after all, a player.'

'But you could not. She would not open for any man.'

'I went out while you were sleeping fast.'

'I was not sleeping fast. I hardly slept at all. I thought you were going to the privy.'

Not the privy, not all the time. A quiet half-hour by the embers below. 'Oh, it was no trouble. I knocked and she asked who, and I said I was the Earl of Southampton, the older man who was growing bald. She opened at once. Ah, the bliss. Such warmth, such whiteness.'

'No no, you are lying!'

'As your lordship pleases. Well, I have shown you the way. All you need do now is to follow.'

That would teach the young puppy.

Mrs Shakespeare

The love that we made was not good.

This didn't surprise me, I must say.

Right from the start, even that first time at Welford by the mill-pool, it was always the imagined, the longed-for relish that enchanted Mr Shakespeare's senses.

My husband's palate when it came to the main course was what you might call watery.

He shrank from the act. He had no tongue for the nectar.

A sugarplate creature himself, he lacked thirst and bite.

All the same, my marchpane man got me pregnant with Susanna by that pool.

I was the three months gone when we were married.

'O my love,' he said. 'O my life.'
'O my life,' I said. 'O my love.'

Love?

No, it was not really love that we were making.

He could not.

And I would not.

And that's all.

My husband had always been less than a man should be in the labours of love.

I tell you the plain truth now.

The unhappy fact of the matter.

As God is my witness, our marriage bed never had been good.

No bliss, no place of sudden paradise or ease.

Not what it should have been.

Why, even that first time, in the long grass, under the catkins, when first he tickled trout then tickled me, when you would think that perhaps the novelty might have inspired him . . .

Well, it didn't.

I make no bones about it.

I'm sure the trout had a better time than I did.

Let me die if I lie.

He proved no ardent wooer that afternoon at Welford.

No great shakes, Mr Shakespeare, when it came to it.

Ha! (and Alas!)

His very name a joke.

Mine too, mind you.

Because, you may be sure, Reader, I had my way with him and of him.

I mean: It was me that did the hard work, or most of it, to untie my own unwelcome virgin knot.

(I gave him that greatest gift a girl can give.)

O he was excited all right. He was quite giddy with expectation.

But then, as I learned soon enough, there was always this impediment in him which came between desire and its performance.

How can I put it?

Mr Shakespeare was a sweet lecher but he was not a lusty man.

He lusted after sweetness, but he lacked muscle.

His function in my department was not sufficient.

And now, that night on that bed, that night before he reached his thirtieth birthday, I thought at first it would be the same as ever.

The spirit willing but the flesh too weak.

Lord, his action was no stronger than a flower.

'Anne?' he cried, anxious.

'Yes,' I lied, bored.

ROBERT NYE, *Mrs Shakespeare: The Complete Works*, 1993

(The central supposition of Nye's novel is that Anne Hathaway may have been the Dark Lady of the Sonnets.)

Shakespeare's Memory

There are devotees of Goethe, of the Eddas, of the late song of the Nibelungen; my fate has been Shakespeare. As it still is, though in a way that no one could have foreseen—no one save one man. Daniel Thorpe, who has just recently died in Pretoria. There is another man, too, whose face I have never seen.

My name is Hermann Sörgel. The curious reader may have chanced to leaf through my *Shakespeare Chronology*, which I once considered essential to a proper understanding of the text: it was translated into several languages, including Spanish. Nor is it beyond the realm of possibility that the reader will recall a protracted diatribe against an emendation inserted by Theobald into his critical edition of 1734—an emendation which became from that moment on an unquestioned part of the canon. Today I am taken a bit aback by the uncivil tone of those pages, which I might almost say were written by another man. In 1914 I drafted, but did not publish, an article on the compound words that the Hellenist and dramatist George Chapman coined for his versions of Homer; in forging these terms, Chapman did not realize that he had carried English back to its Anglo-Saxon origins, the *Ursprung* of the language. It never occurred to me that Chapman's voice, which I have now forgotten, might one day be so familiar to me. . . . A scattering of critical and philological 'notes,' as they are called, signed with my initials, complete, I believe, my literary biography. Although perhaps I might also be permitted to include an unpublished translation of *Macbeth*, which I began in order to distract my mind from the thought of the death of my brother, Otto Julius, who fell on the western front in 1917. I never finished translating the play; I came to realize that English has (to its credit) two registers—the Germanic and the Latinate—while our own German, in spite of its greater musicality, must content itself with one.

I mentioned Daniel Thorpe. I was introduced to Thorpe by Major Barclay at a Shakespeare conference. I will not say where or when; I know all too well that such specifics are in fact vaguenesses.

More important than Daniel Thorpe's face, which my partial blindness helps me to forget, was his notorious lucklessness. When a man reaches a certain age, there are many things he can feign; happiness is not one of them. Daniel Thorpe gave off an almost physical air of melancholy.

After a long session, night found us in a pub—an undistinguished place that might have been any pub in London. To make ourselves feel that we were in England (which of course we were), we drained many a ritual pewter mug of dark warm beer.

'In Punjab,' said the major in the course of our conversation, 'a fellow once pointed out a beggar to me. Islamic legend apparently has it, you know, that King Solomon owned a ring that allowed him to understand the language of the birds. And this beggar, so everyone believed, had somehow come into possession of that ring. The value of the thing was so beyond all reckoning that the poor bugger could never sell it, and he died in one of the courtyards of the mosque of Wazil Khan, in Lahore.'

It occurred to me that Chaucer must have been familiar with the tale of that miraculous ring, but mentioning it would have spoiled Barclay's anecdote.

'And what became of the ring?' I asked.

'Lost now, of course, as that sort of magical thingamajig always is. Probably in some secret hiding place in the mosque, or on the finger of some chap who's off living somewhere where there're no birds.'

'Or where there are so many,' I noted, 'that one can't make out what they're saying for the racket. Your story has something of the parable about it, Barclay.'

It was at that point that Daniel Thorpe spoke up. He spoke, somehow, impersonally, without looking at us. His English had a peculiar accent, which I attributed to a long stay in the East.

'It is not a parable,' he said. 'Or if it is, it is nonetheless a true story. There are things that have a price so high they can never be sold.'

The words I am attempting to reconstruct impressed me less than the conviction with which Daniel Thorpe spoke them. We thought he was going to say something further, but suddenly he fell mute, as though he regretted having spoken at all. Barclay said good night. Thorpe and I returned together to the hotel. It was quite late by now, but Thorpe suggested we continue our conversation in his room. After a short exchange of trivialities, he said to me:

'Would you like to own King Solomon's ring? I offer it to you. That's a metaphor, of course, but the thing the metaphor stands for is every bit as wondrous as that ring. Shakespeare's memory, from his youngest boyhood days to early April, 1616—I offer it to you.'

I could not get a single word out. It was as though I had been offered the ocean.

Thorpe went on:

'I am not an impostor. I am not insane. I beg you to suspend judgment until you hear me out. Major Barclay no doubt told you that I am, or was, a military physician. The story can be told very briefly. It begins in the East, in a field hospital, at dawn. The exact date is not important. An enlisted man named Adam Clay, who had been shot twice, offered me the precious memory almost literally with his last breath. Pain and fever, as you know, make us creative; I accepted his offer without crediting it— and besides, after a battle, nothing seems so very strange. He barely had time to explain the singular conditions of the gift: The one who possesses it must offer it aloud, and the one who is to receive it must accept it the same way. The man who gives it loses it forever.'

The name of the soldier and the pathetic scene of the bestowal struck me as 'literary' in the worst sense of the word. It all made me a bit leery.

'And you, now, possess Shakespeare's memory?'

'What I possess,' Thorpe answered, 'are still *two* memories—my own personal memory and the memory of that Shakespeare that I partially am. Or rather, two memories possess *me*. There is a place where they merge, somehow. There is a woman's face . . . I am not sure what century it belongs to.'

'And the one that was Shakespeare's—' I asked. 'What have you done with it?'

There was silence.

'I have written a fictionalized biography,' he then said at last, 'which garnered the contempt of critics but won some small commercial success in the United States and the colonies. I believe that's all. . . . I have warned you that my gift is not a sinecure. I am still waiting for your answer.'

I sat thinking. Had I not spent a lifetime, colorless yet strange, in pursuit of Shakespeare? Was it not fair that at the end of my labors I find him?

I said, carefully pronouncing each word:

'I accept Shakespeare's memory.'

Something happened; there is no doubt of that. But I did not feel it happen.

Perhaps just a slight sense of fatigue, perhaps imaginary.

I clearly recall that Thorpe did tell me:

'The memory has entered your mind, but it must be "discovered." It will emerge in dreams or when you are awake, when you turn the pages of a book or turn a corner. Don't be impatient; don't *invent* recollections. Chance in its mysterious workings may help it along, or it may hold it back. As I gradually forget, you will remember. I can't tell you how long the process will take.'

We dedicated what remained of the night to a discussion of the character of Shylock. I refrained from trying to discover whether Shakespeare had had personal dealings with Jews. I did not want Thorpe to imagine that I was putting him to some sort of test. I did discover (whether with relief or uneasiness, I cannot say) that his opinions were as academic and conventional as my own.

In spite of that long night without sleep, I hardly slept at all the following night. I found, as I had so many times before, that I was a coward. Out of fear of disappointment, I could not deliver myself up to openhanded hope. I preferred to think that Thorpe's gift was illusory. But hope did, irresistibly, come to prevail. I would possess Shakespeare, and possess him as no one had ever possessed anyone before—not in love, or friendship, or even hatred. I, in some way, would *be* Shakespeare. Not that I would write the tragedies or the intricate sonnets—but I would recall the instant at which the witches (who are also the Fates) had been revealed to me, the other instant at which I had been given the vast lines:

> And shake the yoke of inauspicious stars
> From this world-weary flesh.°

I would remember Anne Hathaway as I remembered that mature woman who taught me the ways of love in an apartment in Lübeck so many years ago. (I tried to recall that woman, but I could only recover the wall-paper, which was yellow, and the light that streamed in through the window. This first failure might have foreshadowed those to come.)

I had hypothesized that the images of that wondrous memory would be primarily visual. Such was not the case. Days later, as I was shaving, I spoke into the mirror a string of words that puzzled me; a colleague informed me that they were from Chaucer's 'A. B. C.' One afternoon, as I was leaving the British Museum, I began whistling a very simple melody that I had never heard before.

The reader will surely have noted the common thread that links these first revelations of the memory: it was, in spite of the splendor of some metaphors, a good deal more auditory than visual.

And shake the yoke] *Romeo and Juliet*, v. iii. 111–12.

De Quincey says that man's brain is a palimpsest. Every new text covers the previous one, and is in turn covered by the text that follows— but all-powerful Memory is able to exhume any impression, no matter how momentary it might have been, if given sufficient stimulus. To judge by the will he left, there had been not a single book in Shakespeare's house, not even the Bible, and yet everyone is familiar with the books he so often repaired to: Chaucer, Gower, Spenser, Christopher Marlowe, Holinshed's *Chronicle*, Florio's Montaigne, North's Plutarch. I possessed, at least potentially, the memory that had been Shakespeare's; the reading (which is to say the rereading) of those old volumes would, then, be the stimulus I sought. I also reread the sonnets, which are his work of greatest immediacy. Once in a while I came up with the explication, or with many explications. Good lines demand to be read aloud; after a few days I effortlessly recovered the harsh r's and open vowels of the sixteenth century.

In an article I published in the *Zeitschrift für germanische Philologie*, I wrote that Sonnet 127 referred to the memorable defeat of the Spanish Armada. I had forgotten that Samuel Butler had advanced that same thesis in 1899.

A visit to Stratford-on-Avon was, predictably enough, sterile.

Then came the gradual transformation of my dreams. I was to be granted neither splendid nightmares à la de Quincey nor pious allegorical visions in the manner of his master Jean Paul;° it was unknown rooms and faces that entered my nights. The first face I identified was Chapman's; later there was Ben Jonson's, and the face of one of the poet's neighbors, a person who does not figure in the biographies but whom Shakespeare often saw.

The man who acquires an encyclopedia does not thereby acquire every line, every paragraph, every page, and every illustration; he acquires the *possibility* of becoming familiar with one and another of those things. If that is the case with a concrete, and relatively simple, entity (given, I mean, the alphabetical order of its parts, etc.), then what must happen with a thing which is abstract and variable—*ondoyant et divers*? A dead man's magical memory, for example?

No one may capture in a single instant the fullness of his entire past. That gift was never granted even to Shakespeare, so far as I know, much less to me, who was but his partial heir. A man's memory is not a summation; it is a chaos of vague possibilities. St Augustine speaks, if I

Jean Paul] Jean Paul Friedrich Richter, German Romantic novelist

am not mistaken, of the palaces and the caverns of memory. That second metaphor is the more fitting one. It was into those caverns that I descended.

Like our own, Shakespeare's memory included regions, broad regions, of shadow—regions that he willfully rejected. It was not without shock that I remembered how Ben Jonson had made him recite Latin and Greek hexameters, and how his ear—the incomparable ear of Shakespeare—would go astray in many of them, to the hilarity of his fellows.

I knew states of happiness and darkness that transcend common human experience.

Without my realizing it, long and studious solitude had prepared me for the docile reception of the miracle. After some thirty days, the dead man's memory had come to animate me fully. For one curiously happy week, I almost believed myself Shakespeare. His work renewed itself for me. I know that for Shakespeare the moon was less the moon than it was Diana, and less Diana than that dark drawn-out word *moon*. I noted another discovery: Shakespeare's apparent instances of inadvertence— those *absences dans l'infini* of which Hugo apologetically speaks—were deliberate. Shakespeare tolerated them—or actually interpolated them—so that his discourse, destined for the stage, might appear to be spontaneous, and not overly polished and artificial (*nicht allzu glatt und gekünstelt*). That same goal inspired him to mix his metaphors:

> my way of life.
> Is fall'n into the sear, the yellow leaf.

One morning I perceived a sense of guilt deep within his memory. I did not try to define it; Shakespeare himself has done so for all time. Suffice it to say that the offense had nothing in common with perversion.

I realized that the three faculties of the human soul—memory, understanding, and will—are not some mere Scholastic fiction. Shakespeare's memory was able to reveal to me only the circumstances of *the man* Shakespeare. Clearly, these circumstances do not constitute the uniqueness of *the poet*; what matters is the literature the poet produced with that frail material.

I was naive enough to have contemplated a biography, just as Thorpe had. I soon discovered, however, that that literary genre requires a talent for writing that I do not possess. I do not know how to tell a story. I do not know how to tell *my own* story, which is a great deal more extraordinary than Shakespeare's. Besides, such a book would be pointless.

Chance, or fate, dealt Shakespeare those trivial terrible things that all men know; it was his gift to be able to transmute them into fables, into characters that were much more alive than the gray man who dreamed them, into verses which will never be abandoned, into verbal music. What purpose would it serve to unravel that wondrous fabric, besiege and mine the tower, reduce to the modest proportions of a documentary biography or a realistic novel the sound and fury of *Macbeth*?

Goethe, as we all know, is Germany's official religion; the worship of Shakespeare, which we profess not without nostalgia, is more private. (In England, the official religion is Shakespeare, who is so unlike the English; England's sacred book, however, is the Bible.)

Throughout the first stage of this adventure I felt the joy of being Shakespeare; throughout the last, terror and oppression. At first the waters of the two memories did not mix; in time, the great torrent of Shakespeare threatened to flood my own modest stream—and very nearly did so. I noted with some nervousness that I was gradually forgetting the language of my parents. Since personal identity is based on memory, I feared for my sanity.

My friends would visit me; I was astonished that they could not see that I was in hell.

I began not to understand the everyday world around me (*die alltägliche Umwelt*). One morning I became lost in a welter of great shapes forged in iron, wood, and glass. Shrieks and deafening noises assailed and confused me. It took me some time (it seemed an infinity) to recognize the engines and cars of the Bremen railway station.

As the years pass, every man is forced to bear the growing burden of his memory. I staggered beneath two (which sometimes mingled)—my own and the incommunicable other's.

The wish of all things, Spinoza says, is to continue to be what they are. The stone wishes to be stone, the tiger, tiger—and I wanted to be Hermann Sörgel again.

I have forgotten the date on which I decided to free myself. I hit upon the easiest way: I dialed telephone numbers at random. The voice of a child or a woman would answer; I believed it was my duty to respect their vulnerable estates. At last a man's refined voice answered.

'Do you,' I asked, 'want Shakespeare's memory? Consider well: it is a solemn thing I offer, as I can attest.'

An incredulous voice replied:

'I will take that risk. I accept Shakespeare's memory.'

I explained the conditions of the gift. Paradoxically, I felt both a *nostalgie* for the book I should have written, and now never would, and a fear that the guest, the specter, would never abandon me.

I hung up the receiver and repeated, like a wish, these resigned words:

Simply the thing I am shall make me live.°

I had invented exercises to awaken the antique memory; I had now to seek others to erase it. One of many was the study of the mythology of William Blake, that rebellious disciple of Swedenborg. I found it to be less complex than merely complicated.

That and other paths were futile; all led me to Shakespeare.

I hit at last upon the only solution that gave hope courage: strict, vast music—Bach.

P.S. (1924)—I am now a man among men. In my waking hours I am Professor Emeritus Hermann Sörgel; I putter about the card catalog and compose erudite trivialities, but at dawn I sometimes know that the person dreaming is that other man. Every so often in the evening I am unsettled by small, fleeting memories that are perhaps authentic.

JORGE LUIS BORGES, 1983, tr. Andrew Hurley

Simply the thing I am] *All's Well that Ends Well*, IV. iii.

FICTIONS · 2
TALES FROM SHAKESPEARE

The poet Jules Laforgue (1860–1887) is best known in the English-speaking world for his influence on T. S. Eliot. He was a writer much possessed by Hamlet: no fewer than thirteen of his poems are preceded by quotations from the play, and the opening poem in his collection Des Fleurs de Bonne Volonté *carries the dateline 'Copenhague, Elseneur, 1er janvier 1886'.*

Laforgue visited Elsinore while working on his long short story Hamlet, ou les suites de la piété filiale *('Hamlet, or the consequences of filial piety'). This is the most extended tribute he paid to the play, though a tribute of a decidedly ambiguous kind. Light in tone, close to outright burlesque, it makes good his promise to treat the Hamlet legend 'gaily, à la Yorick'. But it is also sharply and intricately subversive.*

Laforgue's Hamlet is a late-nineteenth-century aesthete in the tradition of Huysmans's Des Esseintes, dandified and often cruel. Laforgue mocks his pretensions, but he also uses them to parody the nobler pretensions of Shakespeare's Hamlet. The whole story, in fact, is calculated to undermine our faith in Shakespeare's version of events.

Writing the play within a play to trap his uncle, Laforgue's Hamlet discovers his vocation. He begins to see himself as an artist—more specifically, a dramatist; everything that has happened to him will be grist for the stage. At the same time he falls in love with Kate, an actress with the company of players who have come to Elsinore, and persuades her to elope with him. Had he lived, his theatrical version of his own legend would no doubt have become the one the world accepts. But Laertes kills him, and Kate goes back to the lover she was about to abandon, a fellow-actor called William who is also (we can reasonably surmise) the future author of a play called Hamlet. *Shakespeare is not so easily ousted.*

Hamlet, ou les suites de la piété filiale *is set in 1601, though it contains many anachronisms. (Hamlet smokes cigarettes, for example.) In the extract which follows, the prince has left the tower where he lives alone and is walking to the graveyard at Elsinore, hoping to observe Polonius's funeral.*

The graveyard of Elsinore covers the side of a hill off the main road twenty minutes from the city. Hamlet passes under the triple gate of the castle's encircling fortifications, where there are five or six shops patronized by the Guards, and then finds himself in the open country, which is just like the country anywhere, the sad, flat country beyond the ramparts . . .

Workmen are returning home; a wedding party stops by the road, trying to decide what entertainment the town might offer at such an hour.

Prince Hamlet is hardly ever recognized these days. The people hesitate, but do not bow. And how could they when faced with such an insignificant little character? . . . You can judge for yourself.

Having attained a rather sudden full bloom, Hamlet is of medium height; and bears, not terribly high on his body, an elongated childish head. He has reddish brown hair which tapers to a point on a perfectly saintly forehead. It is clearly parted on the right, and tumbles thin and straight over two pretty ladylike ears. His face is beardless without looking clean-shaven; it is a mask of a rather artificial but youthful pallor. His startled and candid gray-blue eyes, while often ice-cold, are sometimes heated by insomnia. (Fortunately, however, these romantically timid eyes radiate limpid and unmuddied thought; for Hamlet, who constantly lowers his gaze as if trying to touch Reality with invisible antennae, looks more like a Camaldolese monk than a crown prince of Denmark.) He has a sensual nose. His innocent mouth is usually open; but it passes quickly from an amorous half-closed position to an equivocal rooster grin, from a pout held in place by the ball and chain of the contemporary scene to the irresistible splitting laugh of a chubby fourteen-year-old urchin. The chin, alas, could hardly be called prominent; nor the angle of the lower jaw determined except on days of deathless boredom when the jawbone is thrust forward and the eyes, by the same token, recede in the vanquished brow: the entire mask is thus drawn in, aged by twenty years. He is now thirty. Hamlet has ladylike feet. His hands are firm but somewhat twisted and shriveled. On the index finger of his left hand he wears a ring set with a green enameled Egyptian scarab. He wears nothing but black, and up and down he strides, up and down, with a gait that is slow and proper, proper and slow . . .

With a gait that is slow and proper, then, Hamlet makes his way at twilight toward the graveyard.

He passes herds of proletarians, old men, women, and children, returning from their daily labors on the capitalistic chain gang, bowed by the weight of their sordid destiny.

God, thinks Hamlet. I know it as well as the next man, and probably better. The existing social order is a scandal great enough to suffocate Nature itself! And I am nothing but a feudal parasite. But what is there to get excited about? These people were born to it; it's an old story, and it won't stop them from having their honeymoons nor their fear of death; and all is well that has no end . . . Yes, indeed. Why don't you get up one fine morning and put an end to all this? Put everything to fire and sword! Crush like bedbugs castes, religions, ideas, languages! Bring back a brotherly childhood to this Earth, which is the mother of us all, and let us be put out to graze in the tropics.

> In the gardens where pure
> Instincts endure
> Let us gather
> What will cure.

Yes, and just see if they would come along! They are too unaesthetic, too fond of being tyrants in their own little houses; it will be a long time yet before they have the courage to look Infinity in the face. Let them gape in admiration at that pedestrian philanthropist, Polonius, as he cries to them: 'Go out and get rich! . . .' And to think that I had my moment of apostolic folly, like Sakyamuni, who was also the son of a king. Ho, ho, I with my unique little existence (which will be shared by a unique little woman); and to think of attaching that bell to my throat! And to hear in its tinkle the wild sonorous notes within my head! Let us not be more proletarian than the proletarians. Let us not permit Human Justice to be more just than Nature. Yes, my brothers, my friends, the historic come-what-may or the apocalyptic purgative, good old Progress or back to Nature . . . And in the meantime, good appetite and enjoy yourselves: tomorrow is Sunday.

The path to the graveyard is steep. Scowling, Hamlet crumples a few poppies between his fingers. He has arrived too late; the service for Polonius is over; the last official silhouettes can be seen departing. Hamlet crouches behind a hedge to let them pass. Someone gives an arm to Laertes, the son of the deceased, who is a sad sight to contemplate. A voice, as of one who has stood all he can, exclaims: 'When there's a lunatic loose in your house, the least you can do is lock him up.'

As he rises, Hamlet notices that he has just gravely damaged an ant-hill. 'So much for that,' he says to himself. 'And just to be sure that I put chance under obligation to me . . .' And he finishes off the said anthill with a few twists of his heel.

The mourners have gone. Hamlet finds himself alone with two gravediggers. He approaches one of them who is arranging the wreaths on Polonius' tomb.

'We won't have his bust until next month,' volunteers the gravedigger whom no one has asked.

'What did he die of? Do they know?'

'Of a stroke. He had led quite a merry life.'

Then and there, Hamlet, whose conscience, despite his soul's extreme cultivation, had not yet taken in the fact, realizes that he has most assuredly killed a man, suppressed a life, a life to which one can bear witness. The aforementioned Polonius . . . who from his squinting eye could have looked out on forty years more of life. (Polonius, who at the drop of a hat, would make you feel his iron muscles.) And lo, Hamlet, with one casual but fatal thrust, has scratched out those forty years just as one would make an erasure on some extravagant blueprint. And what can all these trifling little conflicts of phenomena mean in the next world?

Hamlet plants himself in front of the gravedigger who gazes out at him, waiting to be complimented on the arrangement of the wreaths; Hamlet looks down his nose at him and then barks in his face: 'Words, words, words! Do you hear me? Words, words, words!'

And then he walks over to the other gravedigger without hearing the first one call after him, 'On your way, you loafer!'

'And what are you doing, my good man?'

'As Your Lordship can see, I am sprucing up the old tombs. Ah, it's been a good long time since any of the old birds have moved in here. Our little cemetery has never increased in size, although the late king, through his bounteous favors, redoubled the population of his fine city.'

The gravedigger, who is slightly tipsy, tries to support himself on his spade.

'Well, what do you know, doubled the population? . . .'

'One can see that Your Lordship is not of these parts. The late king (who incidentally also died of a stroke) was quite a womanizer, and being a handsome man with a heart of gold, wherever he left offspring, he also left the stamp of his likeness in the ladies' hearts and on the coins in their purses.'

'But Prince Hamlet surely is the son of the king's wife, Gerutha, is he not?'

'Far from it! Your Lordship has probably heard of the late fool, the incomparable Yorick.'

'Yes, indeed.'

'Well, he and Prince Hamlet had the same mother.'

Hamlet the brother of a court fool; then he isn't of such pure lineage as he had thought! . . .

'And that mother, who was she?'

'Well, the mother was the most hellishly beautiful gypsy anyone, by your leave, has ever seen. With her son Yorick, she came here telling fortunes. She was retained by the Castle, and died a year later, giving birth to the noble Hamlet; when I say giving birth—she died of the Caesarean that had to be performed.'

'Ah, that fellow Hamlet was not so easily drawn into this low world then! . . .'

'Exactly. She was buried there where Your Lordship can see we've been digging lately. An order came not long ago from the Queen to exhume her remains and burn them, although the gypsy was a Christian like you and me, the proof being that the day we carried out the order we got royally soused. And now it's poor Yorick's turn; his bones are right there where your Lordship can grind them under foot.'

'I'll do no such thing.'

'And now I must get his tomb ready to receive Polonius' noble daughter, Ophelia. They've found her body, and will be bringing it here in an hour. Well, I suppose we all must die sooner or later.'

'Ah, Ophelia . . . they have found that young lady, have they? . . .'

'Near the dam, Sir. Her brother Laertes came to tell us this morning. He was a pitiful sight, the poor young man. Everybody likes him so much. He takes a great interest in the living conditions of the workers, you know. And, believe me, I could tell you about some strange things that go on.'

'And I suppose they're quite sure now that Prince Hamlet has gone mad? (Oh, my God, my God, by the dam . . .)'

'Yes, this is the end. As I have always said, we are ripe for annexation. Prince Fortinbras of Norway will see to it any day now. I've already invested my little pickings in Norwegian stocks. But all of that won't stop me from getting good and drunk tomorrow.'

'Right you are. Carry on.'

Hamlet puts a crown in the man's hand, and picks up Yorick's skull. With a slow and proper gait, he wanders off among the cypresses and mausoleums, so overwhelmed by shady destinies that he can't make out how he can with any decency resume his rôle.

Hamlet stops; he holds Yorick's skull tight against his ear, and listens, lost in thought . . .

'Alas, poor Yorick! Just as one thinks he hears within a single shell the full roar of the Ocean, so I seem to hear now the whole endless symphony of the universal soul, of which this sounding box was an echoing crossroad.

'What a sound idea that is! To have human beings like me who would not ask themselves questions but would find in the vague immortal rumor of the skull all they need know of death, all they need know of religion! Alas, poor Yorick! The little worms have tasted Yorick's intellect. He was a fellow of fairly infinite jest, my brother (for we had, after all, the same mother for nine months of our lives, if that can be said to entitle us to any special status). He was someone. How stuck up he was with his twisted and cunning little ego! And where has all that got him? No one will ever know. There's nothing now, not even the wraith of the sleepwalker; common sense leaves no traces. Once there was a tongue in this head and it would burr: *Good night, ladies; good night, sweet ladies! good night, good night!* It would sing, too; it would often sing smutty songs. Yorick looked into the future! (Hamlet swings the skull forward.) And into the past. (He brings it back.) He spoke, he blushed, he YAWNED! Horrible, horrible. I may still have twenty or thirty years to live, and then I'll go like the others. Like the others? Oh, like all things, terrible! Not to be? Ah, I'd like to start out tomorrow and look everywhere on earth for the most adamantine embalming processes. They also existed, the little people of History, learning to read, doing their nails, lighting their dirty lamps every evening, amorous, greedy, vain, delighting in compliments, handshakes and kisses, eating up the village gossip, saying: 'What will the weather be tomorrow? Now winter is coming . . . We have had no plums this year.' Ah, all is well that has no end. Forgive the Earth, O Silence! The little fool isn't any too sure what she's doing; and on the day Conscience pays its staggering bill to the Ideal, it will be set down with sad ditto marks in the column of miniature evolutions of the Unique Evolution, in the column of negligible quantities. But these are words, words, words! That will be my motto until someone has proved to me that our speech has some connection with a transcendent reality. As for me, with my genius, I might be what is commonly called a Messiah; and yet I have been too much Nature's spoiled darling for that. I understand everything, I worship everything, and I want to fertilize everything. That is why, as I have expressed it in this limping distich carved above my bed:

> My rare faculty of assimilation
> Goes counter to the course of my vocation.

Ah, how masterly is my boredom! . . . But what am I waiting for? Death! Death! Ah, have I time to think about death, such a gifted being as I? And as for dying, really! There will be time to talk about that later. Dying! One dies of course without noticing it just as one goes to sleep at night. One cannot follow the fading of one's last clear thought in sleep, in fainting, or in death. True. But not to be, not to be anywhere, not to be anyone! Not to be able to sit down some afternoon just to press the ancient sadness of a musical chord against one's human heart! My father is dead; I am the prolongation of a body that no longer exists. He is over there stretched out on his back with his hands clasped in front of him. And what can I do but lie down when my turn comes? And people will not laugh when they look at me, properly stretched out, my hands clasped in front of me! And they will wonder: Can this be the spoiled young Hamlet, who was once so bitter and gay? There he is as serious as everyone else; and he did not rebel against the crying injustice of being there, but accepted it with such quiet dignity?'

With his two hands Hamlet clasps the skull of his skeleton to be and tries to force a shiver through all his bones.

'Come, come! Let's be serious now! I must find words, words, words! But what is it that I lack, if all this leaves me cold. Let me see. When I am hungry, I have an intense vision of comestibles; when I am thirsty I have a clear sense of liquids; when I feel too celibate at heart, I have a heart-rending sense of lovely eyes and graceful epidermis. Then if the idea of death remains so remote to me, it must be because I am overflowing with life, because life has me in its grip and wants something from me. So, Life, let the two of us have it out!'

'Hey, you over there!' the second gravedigger calls out, 'here is Ophelia's funeral procession coming up.'

Pensive Hamlet's first impulse is to ape perfectly a clown awakened by a huge drumstick in his back; but he manages to restrain himself. Then he slips behind a trefoiled balustrade and gets ready to keep an eye on things.

tr. William Jay Smith

John Updike's Gertrude and Claudius (2000) is the pre-history of Hamlet. In the first of its three sections, the young Gerutha marries King Horwendil and feels drawn to his brother Feng. (The names come from the twelfth-century historian Saxo Grammaticus.) In the second section Fengon becomes Geruthe's lover. (The names now come from the sixteenth-century version of the Hamlet story by François de Belleforest.) In the third section the old King—Horvendile in de Belleforest—is dead; Fengon has succeeded to the throne under the name of Claudius, Gertrude is at his side, and Shakespeare's play is about to begin.

The murder of Horvendile takes place at the end of Part Two. Corambis—the name under which Polonius goes in the earlier sections—gives Fengon the key to a secret entrance to the King's orchard. Then Fengon rides over to his castle to collect the poison which he has concealed there.

The gallop back to Elsinore was urged to the edge of the Arabian's capacity. Fengon whipped the aging horse mercilessly, while vowing aloud, yelling crazily in the animal's uncomprehending ear—its hairy exterior perked, its interior lilylike and a tint akin to human flesh—to put him out, if his heart did not burst, to lush pasture with a herd of plump mares. Answering the watchman's shout in full stride, Fengon thundered across the moat, beneath the spiked portcullis, into the barbican and the outer bailey, which on one side accommodated the stables. No hostler was on hand: good. One less witness, if witnesses were ever sought. He stalled the horse himself. He patted the soaked black nose, the blood-spattered nostrils, and whispered to the beast, 'May I do as bravely.' Two rides of two hours each had been achieved in scarce three. Fengon's image was squat and miniature, a bearded troll, in the long-lashed orb of the horse's eye, with its purple iris.

Feeling airy and shaken again on foot, he glided unchallenged along the inner wall to the lesser hall, up wide stairs troughed with centuries of wear and through the deserted lobby to the great hall, up stairs again, more stealthily, through the audience chamber and into the King and Queen's own fir-floored suite. He heard from several rooms away a lute and the thready entwined voices of recorders—the Queen and her ladies were being entertained, while they stitched at their embroidery frames. Perhaps the King's footmen had gone to listen. With a snake's silence Fengon moved through his brother's deserted solar° and found the opening, low like the niche that holds a church's basin of holy water, which

solar] an upper chamber

led to a spiral stair. It rubbed him on all sides, so narrow it was, and lit but by one *meurtrière*° halfway down. The vertical slot of landscape—flashing moat, part of a thatched house, smoke from something being burned in a field—made his eyes wince and set a watery light on the curved wall behind him.

He descended into a well of darkness. The dry planks and rusted iron strapwork of a door met his fingertips; he stroked these mixed rough surfaces for the keyhole, as one strokes a woman's body for its secret small site of release. He found it. Corambis's key fit. The oiled works turned. The orchard outside appeared to be empty. He had arrived first. Thank—who? Not the Devil, Fengon didn't want to believe he was forever in thrall to the Devil.

Warming sunlight struck gold from the unscythed grass. Rotting apples and pears filled the air with a scent of fermentation. His boots crushed fruit, pulpy and fallen, and left telltale impressions in the tangled hay. His pounding heart kept company with the cold, abstract resolve of his will. There was no other course, improvised and chancy though this one had had to be.

He heard footsteps above, within the wall—such closeness of timing showed the hand of Heaven. He crouched behind a wagon used previously to hold the orchard's harvest of a month ago and now abandoned, with careless peasant husbandry, to the winter weather coming. He fingered the thick cross bulking in his doublet. The jade edges had been filed and the surfaces ground to the smoothness of skin and then incised in circular patterns like lace to the touch. He tried to think of fair and rosy Geruthe but his soul was narrowly, darkly intent upon the hunt, the kill.

The King emerged from the arched opening at the base of the bailey wall. His royal robes were brilliant in the low slant of sunshine. His face looked bloated and weary, naked in its ignorance of being observed. Fengon now slipped the vial from its socket and with a thumbnail worked at the stopper, a bead of glass held in place by a glue aged to the hardness of stone. Perhaps it would not come off; perhaps he must slink away, the deed undone. But away to what? Ruin, and not only for him—for one who had asked, *Protect me*. The bead of glass worked loose. Its film of liquid stung his forefinger.

From behind the abandoned, weathering wagon Fengon watched his brother shed a blue velvet robe and drape it over the foot of the pillowed

meurtrière] a loophole

couch set, as on a small roofed stage, upon the gazebo's raised floor. The King's surcoat was a golden yellow, his tunic snow-white linen. The cushions on his couch were green; he set his eight-sided jewelled crown on a pillow near his head and tugged up a blanket of dirty-gray sheep-skin. He lay staring skyward while his folded hands fiddled upon his chest, as if revolving within himself the information that he had been cuckolded and must wreak a thorough vengeance on the criminals. Or perhaps the parley with the Polacks had gone disturbingly. Fengon feared the agitated monarch might not sleep at all, and pondered the possibility of rushing forward and compelling Horvendile to drink the contents of the vial, hurling the poison down his howling red throat like molten lead into the mouth of a heretic.

But suppose the assault fell short, and the King's shouts brought help? Then a traitor's cautionary public mangling would be Fengon's fate. In Burgundy he had seen a staked plotter compelled to watch dogs gobble his unravelled intestines, there on the ground before him; the loyal crowd had thought this an excellent patriotic entertainment. In Toulouse he had been told of Cathars burned in bundles like fagots, only they burned more reluctantly, feet and ankles charring first. He understood from men who had survived torture that the spirit achieves another level, from which it looks down upon the body and its tormenters serenely, as from the lip of Heaven. In such a hovering mood he now waited, and when the sparrows and titmice above his head and about him in the twigs had ceased to mark his presence with twitters and scoldings such as would warn of a cat, he stepped forward to test if his brother's long blue eyes were still open. Had they been, he would have pretended to have come to plead, and looked for an opportunity to force the poison.

But from the King's belvedere issued, louder than the hum of wasps in the sugared grass, the rumble of snoring, of oblivious breathing. Fengon drew near, one tread at a time through the lank dying grass, with the unstoppered vial.

His brother slept in a familiar position, curled on his side, loose fist tucked against his chin, as Fengon had often observed when they shared a bed and then a doubly bedded chamber in lonely Jutland, where the winds made sleep fitful. Fengon had been, though younger, the lighter sleeper. Horvendile had daily exhausted himself in pushing ahead, in acting the elder and seizing his prerogatives in games and jousts, in exploration of the heath and the barren hilltops around them. Gerven-dile, bent upon raiding and carousing in imitation of the pagan gods, and with a wife who had withered to torpor in Jutie's ceaseless wind, let his sons run to nature. In their abandonment Horvendile did parental ser-vice, commanding but leading, rebuking but bringing his slighter, less prepossessing brother along with him, across the lag of eighteen months between their births. Across the heather, through the thickets, in pursuit of game with slingshot and longbow, sharing the sharp air, the hurrying wide sky. Had there not been love in this, from both sides? Alas, love is so pervasive, so ready to arise from our childish helplessness, that it would freeze all action, even that act needed to save a man's life and make his fortune.

As of their own volition Fengon's boots had silently slithered up the two steps to the platform where the King slept on his side, one ear up, his face slack. To pour the vial Fengon had to lift a lock of his brother's fair hair, still soft and curled low on his head, where not yet thinned by age and the pressure of the crown. His was a tidy ear, square and white and plumply lobed, with a froth of gray hairs around the waxy hole. Fengon's sucked breath caught in his teeth as he poured. His hand did not tremble. His brother's ear-hole, the hole that had taken in Sandro's° poisonous words, a whirlpool that led to the brain and to the universe the brain constructs, accepted the pale juice of hebona with some, at the last, overflowing; Horvendile in his sleep brushed clumsily at the spot, as if at a wasp tickling at a dream. Fengon stepped back, clutching the emptied vial in his fist. Who was the Hammer now? His pounding blood made his muscles jump.

He did not dare re-enter the spiral stair, so constricted and entrapping. At its head he might meet footmen, or the Queen with her ladies and musicians. Crouched low, he scuttled along the crooked bailey wall to where, as devious Corambis had promised, a stone chute emptied toward the moat but could be attained on the protuberances and chinks of the masonry and—Fengon gritting his teeth, holding his breath against the smell—mounted by pressing arms and legs outward and climbing. There was no ivy as when he had first scrambled up to Geruthe, but years of piss had eroded the mortar to create footholds; slime coated rocks in whose sunless crannies great white centipedes bred, daily supplied with noxious nutrient. The bright gap toward which Fengon squirmed upward was narrow but not narrower than Geruthe's lancet window. He had wriggled through that and now this, like fatty smoke rising in a flue, like excrement reversing its course, sweating and grunting and begging God or the Devil that no hostler or guard be

Sandro] Fengon's treacherous Italian servant

presently called by nature to this privy. If he were, Fengon's dagger would have to come into play, one murder demanding another.

But his emergence from the garderobe was unobserved. He brushed at the noxious dampness on his tunic and breeches and flitted along the bailey and barbican walls to where his black Arabian still panted. He stood next to the horse, to merge his odor with its sweat. He shouted for a groom, to make a witness that he had freshly arrived at Elsinore. The vial and jade cross he dropped at first opportunity into the moat. Though at his later leisure he was plagued by remorse and fear of God's creeping justice, Fengon felt no holy qualm just yet, in the fresh relief of his feat; his religion had become cold necessity, and his form of worship lucky acrobatics upon the bare bones of things.

The corpse was not found until another hour had passed and the unknowing Queen sent a man down to wake her husband. Horvendile's body, frozen with unseeing eyes bloodied and bulged outward, lay covered with a silvery crust, leperlike, all his smooth skin turned loathsome, all his body's liquids curdled. Fengon and Corambis, taking charge in the confusion, gave out the speculation that a venomous serpent nested in the unmown orchard grass had sunk its fangs into the fair and noble sleeper. Or else a distemper of the blood, long festering unseen, had abruptly broken out; the King had appeared joyless and brooding of late. At any event, amid this calamity the kingdom, its foreign enemies astir, must be administered, and the stricken queen comforted. Who better than the brother of the King, whose only son the Prince had been for over a decade immured in futile studies at Wittenberg?

There are anticipations of Shakespeare scattered throughout Updike's text, and in the closing pages, as novel blends into play, the characters start speaking in Shakespeare's words.

Claudius finished with Hamlet by bluntly stating—where others had been pussyfooting for years—that he did *not* want Hamlet to return to Wittenberg: 'It is most retrograde to our desire.' He relished the imperious ring of this, but softened it by beseeching his stiff nephew to bend, to stay here, in Elsinore, 'here in the cheer and comfort of our eye, our chiefest courtier, cousin, and our son.'

Gertrude played her part, adding, 'Let not thy mother lose her prayers, Hamlet: I pray thee, stay with us; go not to Wittenberg.'

Trapped by their twin professions of love, the Prince from beneath his clouded brow studied the two glowing middle-aged faces hung like lanterns before him—hateful luminaries fat with satisfaction and health and continued appetite. He tersely conceded, to shunt away the glare of their conjoined pleas, 'I shall in all my best obey you.'

'Why,' Claudius exclaimed, startled by the abrupt concession, ' 'tis a loving and a fair reply.' They had him. He was theirs. The King's imagination swayed forward to the sessions of guidance and lively parry he would enjoy with his surrogate son, his only match for cleverness in the castle, and to the credit such a family relation would win him in the heart of the boy's newly fond mother.

The era of Claudius had dawned; it would shine in Denmark's annals. He might, with moderation of his carousals, last another decade on the throne. Hamlet would be the perfect age of forty when the crown descended. He and Ophelia would have the royal heirs lined up like ducklings. Gertrude would gently fade, his saintly gray widow, into the people's remembrance. In his jubilation at these presages the King, standing to make his exit, announced boomingly that this gentle and unforced accord of Hamlet sat so smiling to his heart that, at every health he would drink today, the great cannons would tell the clouds. And his queen stood up beside him, all beaming in her rosy goodness, her face alight with pride at his performance. He took her yielding hand in his, his hard sceptre in the other. He had gotten away with it. All would be well.

A Changeable Report

Kent. 'Report is changeable'
King Lear, IV. vii

I have been dead for five years. I say dead and I am trying to be as precise as possible. I do not know how else to put it. My hand trembles as I write but it is comforting to have pen and ink and paper on which to write things down. It is as if I had forgotten how to use a pen. I have to pause before each word. Sometimes I cannot remember how the letters are formed. But it is a comfort to bend over the white page and think about these things. If I could explain what happened I might find myself alive once more. That is the most terrible thing. The thing I really hate them for. They have taken away my life, though no court of law would convict them for it. When I think about that time, what they did to me, my insides get knotted up in anger and despair and I hate them not so much for what they did to me then as for what they are doing to me now, knotting me up with anguish and hatred at the memory.

I have tried to understand what happened. I thought that if I could put it all down on paper I would finally understand and I would be free of them for ever. But when I try I cannot continue. There is a darkness all round the edges. I think that by writing I will be able to shift that darkness a little, allow light to fall on the central events at least. But it does not work like that. It is as though the light follows each letter, each word perhaps, but no more, and in so doing moves away from the previous word, which is once again swallowed up in darkness. I pinch myself to make myself concentrate. I bite my lips and try to look as steadily as possible at what has occurred, at what is occurring. But the light moves along with the pen and I can never hold more than a small sequence in my mind at any one time. So I give up and wait for a better moment. But there is no better moment. There is just the urge to seize the pen again and write.

I did not think writing was so important. Till they shut me up. There was no cause. I had been gulled. But they bundled me in and locked the door. They told me I was mad. In the dark I felt about for windows, candles, but there were none. I was afraid of suffocating. I have always been afraid of that. I used to have nightmares about being shut into a basket and forgotten. I could hear them outside, chattering and laughing. I asked for pen and paper. I had to write and tell her what they had done to me. When they finally let me do so she had me released at once. I did not think I had changed then. I did not realise what it does to you to be shut up in the dark without hope or the ability to keep track of time. I vowed revenge on the whole lot of them. As I left I heard him start to sing. I went out into the night.

I had never had much time for his songs or his silly repartees. I do not know why she put up with him. Or with any of them. I need my sleep. I did my work well. I tried to keep them under control. I asked for nothing more. The noise they made. I could not stand that noise, that drunken bawling at all hours of the day and night. I cannot stand the sight of grown men who have deliberately befuddled themselves. It is degrading. Besides, she paid me to keep order in the house and I kept order as best I could. She should never have indulged him. Why put up even with a cousin if he consistently behaves like that? Why keep a Fool just because your father kept one? A hateful habit, demeaning to both parties. Let the Spaniards retain the custom, they are little better than beasts themselves. But that she should do so! And a foolish Fool at that. A knave. As bad as the rest of them, Maria and the cousin and his idiot friend. The noise they made. The songs they sang. Obscene. Meaningless. Vapid. Why did she let them? If it had been me I would soon have sent them packing. Restored some decency to the house. And her still in mourning for her brother.

I thought she had more sense. A page. A mere boy. Get him into bed at any cost. Forget her brother. Forget the injunctions of her father. What kind of life do humans want to lead, what kind of a . . .

My stomach has knotted up again. I hate them for making me hate in this way. I hate them for doing this to me. When I walked out into the night he was singing about the wind and the rain. I thought I would be revenged on them all. My stomach was knotted with anger. I wanted to scream, to kick and punch them, him especially, the fat cousin, the . . .

I have said to myself that I will keep calm. I have promised myself that I will control myself and write it all down so that I may understand and be free of the darkness. I am a survivor. I have not survived so long without learning a little about how it is done. I have the will. I have the patience. They think only of the moment. They drink and joke and sing. They did this to me. They tried to make me mad. They tried to persuade me that I was mad. They could not bear to have me there, watching them, I

At moments, as I write, I no longer know who I am. It feels as though all this had happened to someone else and it has simply been reported to me. I see things in my head. My stomach knots in pain and anger. But I am not sure if my head and stomach belong to the same person.

Never mind. I must use what skills I have and not be deflected. I must be patient. Men have burrowed out of dungeons with nothing but a nail-file. What are five years or ten years when life itself is at stake? I have always been patient. I have my pen and paper and I can always start again. And again and again until the darkness is dispersed and I can emerge into the light once more and live.

I remember the man I was. But he is like a puppet. I do not know what kept him going. Perhaps it was nothing except a sense of duty. I see him bustle. He was a great bustler. I sometimes think I am still there. That I still work there, do what I have to do about the house, take orders from him, from the boy now, while she stands simpering by. I hate her for that, for what she let them do to me and for standing by now and doting on that boy.

But I am not there. I know I am not there. I turned my back on them forever and walked out, vowing revenge. Yet I was not interested in revenge. I only wanted to forget them. To start again elsewhere. But I could not. The song would not let me go. It was like a leash he had attached to me when he saw that I was determined to go. I sleep and it comes to me in my dreams. I wake and it creeps up on me in the daytime. I plotted revenge. I thought I would find my way back there and take up my post with them again. I would steal her handkerchief and poison his mind. He would have killed her for that. Killed her first and then himself. He was capable of it, he went for Andrew the minute he saw him, broke his head and then lamed Toby. They would have taken me back. I know how she felt about me. I would have played on those feelings. I would have made him kill her and then, in despair, he would have done away with himself.

At other moments I thought of other, sillier kinds of revenge. I would have them all on an island. I would be able to control the winds and the waves. I would wreck them on my island. The two drunken idiots would be pinched and bruised and bitten by my spirits, and the others, the others would get their deserts—the whole lot of them. I would frighten them with ghosts made of old sheets, I would lead them into swamps and then reveal myself to them—It would be the silliness of the punishments that would be the most shaming.

Idle thoughts. I am surprised that I can remember them. At moments they were there, so strong, so clearly formulated. But I do not think I ever took them seriously. Because it was as if I had lost the ability to act. As if his song had drained me of my will. When it flooded through my head I cried. I cried a lot. There was another music too, unearthly, and fragments of speeches, but not speeches in the ordinary sense, not exchanges of information between two people, but somehow as if their souls had found words. I understood what they said, but not the meaning of individual words and phrases. In such a night was the refrain. The names of Cressida and of Dido, of Thisbe and of Medea came into it. The floor of heaven thick inlaid with patens of bright gold. I remember that. It was like a music I had never heard before and never imagined could exist. And then I was in the dark but it was peaceful, quite different from that other dark, and another song, fear no more the heat of the sun, and home art gone and ta'en thy wages. It merged with the other voices, telling of Dido and Medea and Thisbe and Cressida. But when I tried to hear them more clearly, to focus on them better, they faded away and finally vanished altogether. I went out through a door and instead of the garden I had expected there was desert, dirt, an old newspaper blowing across a dirty street, decaying tenements. I turned back and there was the music again, but now the door was locked and I could not get in. Why do I know nothing about music? Why have I always feared it? Not just the drunken catches but the pure sweet music of viols, the pure sweet melancholy songs. I fear them all.

I tried to walk then but my feet kept going through the rotten planks. I put my hand up to my head and the hair came away in clumps. I knew this was not so. I knew it was only my imagination. I fought against it. They are trying to do this to me, I said to myself. They want you to think that you are mad. You will not give them that satisfaction. But I woke up dreaming that my head was made of stone and I held it in my lap, sightless eyes gazing past me into the sky. My daughter had betrayed me. She had stolen all my jewellery and absconded with a negro. There was a storm and women spoke and tempted me. I looked at my hands and they were covered with blood. The storm grew worse and I was on a deserted heath and howling. An idiot and a blind old man held on to me, trying to pull me down, uttering gibberish, but I kicked them off, and then there was that song again, about the wind and the rain. In the rain my daughter came and talked. Something terrible had happened but all was forgiven. She talked to me. She answered when I spoke to her. But I knew it would not last and it didn't, she was dead in my arms, I held her and she weighed less than a cat. I pretended she was alive but I knew she was dead. I walked again and the rotten boards gave way, one leg stuck in the ground, it grew into the ground, and all the time I knew it was not so, that if I could turn, if I could return, and it required so small an effort, so very small an effort, then it would all change, she would be with me on the island and I would rule over the wind and the waves, she had only pretended to run away, only pretended to be dead. But I also knew that I could not make that effort, that I could not go back, that the door was shut for ever, hey ho the wind and the rain. I marked the days, the years. I sat at my desk and wrote as well as I could on the white paper. I was determined that they would not make me mad.

It has been like death. Time has not moved at all. Yet it cannot be long before the real thing. I try to put it down as clearly as I can but there is darkness behind and in front. Nothing stays still. I cannot illuminate any of it. I form the letters as well as I am able, but I cannot read what I have written. It does not seem to be written in any language that I know. The more I look at it the more incomprehensible it seems to be. As though a spider had walked through the ink and then crawled across the page. As though it had crawled out of my head and on to the paper and there could never ever be any sense in the marks it had left.

Perhaps there are no marks. Perhaps I am still in the dark and calling out for pen and paper. Perhaps no time at all has passed since they shut me up. I call for pen and ink and paper but they only laugh and cry out that I am mad. I do not know who I am. Except that I am a survivor. I will go on trying to write something down. This is a pen in my hand. I hold it and write with it. This is me, writing. I will not listen to their words. I will not listen to that music. I will try to be as precise as possible. I will write it all down. Then the darkness will clear. It must clear. The music will fade. It must fade. I will be able to live again. That will be my revenge on them. That I have endured. That I have not let them make me mad.

Gabriel Josipovici, 1982

OFFSHOOTS AND ADAPTATIONS

With regard to Shakespeare my only excuse can be that he is fair game, like the Bible.

RALPH VAUGHAN WILLIAMS (on his opera Sir John in Love)

They had condescended to give us *Hamlet* as written, practically complete, a rare thing in this country, where there are so many people superior to Shakespeare that most of his plays are corrected and augmented by the Cibbers and the Drydens and other rogues who should have their bottoms publicly spanked.

HECTOR BERLIOZ, letter to Joseph-Louis Duc, 1846, tr. David Cairns

Berlioz, who was visiting London, had seen a performance of Hamlet *in which the Prince was played by the Irish actor Gustavus Brooke.*

On the dedication page of Alfred Jarry's play Ubu Roi *(1896) there is a motto in bogus Old French:*

Adonc le Père Ubu hoscha la poire, dont fut depuis nommé par les Anglois Shakespeare, et avez de lui sous ce nom maintes belles tragedies par escript.

Roughly translated this means: 'Then Père Ubu shook his pear, and he has since been called Shakespeare by the English, and you have many fine tragedies written by him under that name.'

Grotesque, scatological, anarchic, surreal, Ubu Roi is one of the foundation documents of modernism. It also abounds with distorted echoes of Shakespeare. There are parallels with Hamlet, Richard III, Julius Caesar, The Winter's Tale *(at one point Ubu is pursued by a bear) and* The Tempest. *And more significant than these, running through the entire play there is a squalid parody of* Macbeth.

The action opens with Père Ubu swearing ('Merdre!'—it's the key word of the play), Mère Ubu calling him a fat lout, Père Ubu threatening to 'do her in' and Mère Ubu retorting 'Not me, there's another you should get rid of.' Her

remark sets in motion a scheme to assassinate and replace the reigning monarch in which Ubu plays the part of a greedy, cowardly, degraded Macbeth and she proves an entirely worthy consort. The basic plot has many similarities to Shakespeare, but the details—mostly farcical, often revolting—are very different, and so is the prevailing spirit. The play is a systematic lampoon, not of Macbeth *itself, but of the traditional values on which* Macbeth *rests.*

Bertolt Brecht bent Shakespeare to his purposes on many occasions during his career, most notably in The Resistible Rise of Arturo Ui (1941) and the adaptation of Coriolanus which he worked on during the last years of his life (he died in 1956) and which was first staged by the Berliner Ensemble in 1964.

Arturo Ui *is an allegory of Nazism. Brecht's Führer-figure, Arturo, is a Chicago gangster, but there is an explicit parallel with Shakespeare as well: in the prologue an Announcer asks, 'Who can fail to think of Richard the Third?' Later in the play there is a parody of Richard's wooing of the Lady Anne over Henry VI's coffin; later still, the ghost of 'Ernesto Roma' (the murdered Brownshirt leader Ernst Roehm) rises up to warn Arturo of his doom, much as the accusing ghosts rise up on the eve of Bosworth Field. Arturo also hires a Shakespearian actor to coach him in public speaking. His lessons include a run-through of Mark Antony's funeral oration from* Julius Caesar.

In Coriolanus, *working as much through omission or shift of emphasis as through new material, Brecht turned Shakespeare's play into an unambiguous political tract. His plebeians are the proletarians of Marxist legend; his tribunes are selfless champions of Progress; his patricians are a bourgeoisie whose time is running out. The one mildly unexpected twist is that Coriolanus himself is not only the most unyielding of class warriors; he is also portrayed as the kind of specialist—in his case, needless to say, a specialist in warfare—who suffers from the illusion that his services to society are indispensable.*

In 1964 Günter Grass delivered a much-publicized lecture in which he attacked Brecht's adaptation as a betrayal of Shakespeare. Two years later he followed it up with his own play, The Plebeians Rehearse the Uprising, *in which a theatre director known as 'The Boss'—a thinly veiled Brecht—is shown preparing to mount a production of* Coriolanus *against the background of an insurrection plainly inspired by the workers' uprising in East Berlin in June 1953. Up to a point the Boss stands accused of both arrogance (he has some marked affinities with Coriolanus himself) and of complicity with an oppressive regime. But he also appears in other, more sympathetic guises: as a victim, an honest man, a melancholy intellectual, a figure on whom Grass can hang his ideas about art and reality. The play is packed with themes to the point of confusion.*

In many respects John Osborne's reworking of Coriolanus, A Place Calling Itself Rome *(1973), stands at the opposite pole to Brecht's. Osborne sides with the patricians, and broadly speaking he accepts Coriolanus's image of himself. But he also reduces Shakespeare's language to colloquial Osbornesque prose. This is part of the banishment scene:*

Mob. Do him. Do him! Kill him! Kill him! Kill, *(etc.)*

Sicinius. Enough, cowards. Enough, for we've seen enough. Haven't WE SEEN *enough* of this—MAN!

Brutus. It's true he's done some things for Rome.

Coriolanus. What do you know about it?

Brutus. I know what I'm talking about.

Coriolanus. You!

Menenius. So much for your promise to your mother.

Cominius. Now, listen a moment——

Coriolanus. I wouldn't take *their* say-so for NUPPENCE one way or the other. I wouldn't give 'em the sweat from my balls.

Sicinius. Let him go before he's killed—and it wouldn't be unjust——

Mob. Send him off! Take him off! Get lost! And for damned good and forever, *(etc)*.

Cominius. Listen!

Sicinius. You heard the verdict clear enough. Again?

(Roar).

Sicinius. Right. He's done for. No more talk. We have heard it all before from your like.

Brutus. Right. That's it then.

Mob. That's it! That's it! *(etc.)*

Coriolanus. You common cry of curs. You take up my air. Banish me? *I* banish *you!* Stay here in your slum. And strike. Communicate. Get shaken with rumours; fads; modishness; greed; fashion; your clannishness; your lives in depth. May you, but you won't, one minute of that depth, know desolation. May your enemies barter and exchange you coolly in their own better market-places . . . I have seen the *future* . . . here . . . and it doesn't work! *I* turn my back. There is a world *elsewhere!*

(He goes off, borne away by his supporters and sorely harassed escort. Coriolanus sings down at them a parody of 'The Red Flag'.)

> 'The Working Class
> Can Kiss My Arse
> And keep their Red
> Rag flying high.'

(He is swept off, pursued by the furious mob.)

Eugène Ionesco's Macbett *(1972) is a dark and semi-farcical reworking of* Macbeth, *in which Macbett is despatched by Macol (Malcolm) rather than Macduff. As soon as he has taken power, Macol makes it clear that his subjects are going to have a hard time of it. There is no question of a restoration of lost rights. All that has happened is that one tyrant has been replaced by another, who may well turn out to be even worse.*

The most disconcerting scene in Macbeth *is the one in which Malcolm tests Macduff, his fellow-refugee at the English court, by suddenly accusing himself of a multitude of vices and evil impulses. Ionesco's neatest trick is to take this confession at face value and transpose it to the end of the play, so that it becomes a full-blown royal proclamation. From 'Our country sinks beneath the yoke' to 'confound all unity on earth', Macol's final harangue follows Malcolm's speeches in* Macbeth, iv. iii, *almost word for word.*

(*Macol kills Macbett with a sword thrust in the back. Macbett collapses*)
    Macol. Remove this carcass!
(*Cheer from the invisible crowd: 'Long live Macol! Long live Macol! The tyrant is dead! Long live Macol, our well-loved Sovereign! Long live Macol!'*)
    Macol. And bring me a throne!
(*Other Guests arrive. Some of them pick up placards on which are written: 'Macol is always right.'*)
    The Guests. Long live Macol! Long live the dynasty of Banco! Long live our Lord!
(*Bells are heard.*
Macol is near the throne. From the Right arrives a Bishop or a Monk)
    Macol (to the Bishop). Is this for the sacrament?
    The Bishop. Yes, your Highness!
(*A Woman of the people comes in from the Left*)
    Woman. May your reign be a happy one!
    Another Woman (entering from the Right). Be good to the poor!
    Another Woman (entering from the Right). No more injustice!
    Another Man. Hate has destroyed our homes. Hate has poisoned our souls!
    Another Man. May your reign be one of peace, harmony and concord.
    First Woman. May your reign be sanctified.
    Another Woman. May your reign be the reign of joy.
    One of the Men. It will be the reign of love.
    Another Man. Embrace one another, brothers!
    The Bishop. Embrace one another and I will bless you.
    Macol (standing just in front of the throne). Silence!
    First Woman. He's going to speak to us!
    First Man. Our Lord will speak to us.

Second Woman. Let us hear what he has to say.

Second Man. We are listening to you, Sire, and we shall drink in your words.

Another Man. May the good Lord keep you.

The Bishop. May the good Lord keep you.

Macol. Silence, I tell you, stop talking all at once! I have a declaration to make to you. Let no-one move! Let no-one breathe! And get this well into your heads: Our country sinks beneath the yoke. And each new day a gash is added to her wounds. Yes, I have trod upon the tyrant's head and worn it on my sword.

(*A Man arrives bearing the head of Macbett on the end of a pike*)

Third Man. You got what you deserved.

Second Woman. You got what you deserved.

Fourth Man. May Heaven never forgive him.

First Woman. May he be damned eternally!

First Man. Let him burn in Hell!

Second Man. Let him be tortured!

Third Man. Let him never be granted a moment's peace.

Fourth Man. Let him be converted in the flames and let the good Lord refuse his conversion.

First Woman. Let his tongue be ripped out, to grow and be ripped out again, twenty times a day.

Second Man. Let him be skewered! Let him be impaled! And let him bear witness to our joy. Let our peals of laughter rend his ears!

Second Woman. Here are my knitting needles! Put his eyes out with them!

(*Placards*)

Macol. If you are not silent this instant, I shall unleash my soldiers and my dogs on you.

(*Numerous guillotines appear at the Rear, as in the first scene*)

Now that the tyrant is dead and curses his mother for his birth, I can tell you this: my poor country shall have more vices than it had before; more suffer, and in more sundry ways than ever, by him that shall succeed.

(*While Macol is making his declaration, murmurs of reprobation, of despair and stupefaction can be heard. At the end of this speech no-one at all will be left round Macol*)

It is myself I mean: in whom I know all the particulars of vice so grafted, that, when they shall be opened, Black Macbett will seem as pure as snow; and the poor state esteem him as a lamb, being compared with my confineless harms. Macbett was bloody, luxurious, avaricious, false, deceitful, sudden, malicious, smacking of every sin that has a name. But there's no bottom, none in my voluptuousness: your wives, your daughters, your matrons, and your maids, could not fill up the cistern of my lust; and my desire all continent impediments would o'erbear, that did oppose my will. Better Macbett than such a one to reign. With this, there grows, in my most ill-composed affection, such a staunchless avarice, that, were I king, I should cut off the nobles for their lands;

desire his jewels, and this other's house: and my more-having would be as a sauce to make me hunger more; that I should forge quarrels unjust against the good and loyal, destroying them for wealth. The king-becoming graces, as justice, verity, temperance, stableness, bounty, perseverance, mercy, lowliness, devotion, patience, courage, fortitude, I have no relish of them; but abound in the division of each several crime, acting it many ways.

(*The Bishop, who was the last to stay with Macol, goes out, depressed, on the Right*)

Yes, now I have the power, I shall pour the sweet milk of concord into Hell, uproot the universal peace, confound all unity on earth! Let us, to start with, make of this Archduchy a Kingdom—of which I am King. An Empire, of which I am Emperor. A Super-Highness, Super-Sire, Super-Majesty, Emperor of all the Emperors.

(*He disappears into the mist . . .*)

tr. Donald Watson

Tom Stoppard's Rosencrantz and Guildenstern are Dead *(1966) raises philosophical issues well beyond anything in W. S. Gilbert's farce about the same characters (see p. 303), but it contains a strong element of burlesque, too. Towards the end of the play, on board ship for England, 'Ros' and 'Guil' open Claudius's sealed letter and read his instructions for Hamlet to be beheaded:*

> *Ros.* The sun's going down. It will be dark soon.
> *Guil.* Do you think so?
> *Ros.* I was just making conversation. (*Pause.*) We're his *friends.*
> *Guil.* How do you know?
> *Ros.* From our young days brought up with him.
> *Guil.* You've only got their word for it.
> *Ros.* But that's what we depend on.
> *Guil.* Well, yes, and then again no. (*Airily.*) Let us keep things in proportion.

Assume, if you like, that they're going to kill him. Well, he is a man, he is mortal, death comes to us all, etcetera, and consequently he would have died anyway, sooner or later. Or to look at it from the social point of view—he's just one man among many, the loss would be well within reason and convenience. And then again, what is so terrible about death? As Socrates so philosophically put it, since we don't know what death is, it is illogical to fear it. It might be . . . very nice. Certainly it is a release from the burden of life, and, for the godly, a haven and a reward. Or to look at it another way—we are little men, we don't know the ins and outs of the matter, there are wheels within wheels, etcetera— it would be presumptuous of us to interfere with the designs of fate or even of kings. All in all, I think we'd be well advised to leave well alone. Tie up the letter—there—neatly—like that—They won't notice the broken seal, assuming you were in character.

Ros. But what's the point?

Guil. Don't apply logic.

Ros. He's done nothing to us.

Guil. Or justice.

Ros. It's awful.

Guil. But it could have been worse. I was beginning to think it was. (*And his relief comes out in a laugh.*)

Stoppard returns to Shakespeare in Dogg's Hamlet, *in which the characters perform 'the fifteen-minute* Hamlet' *and then race through an even more reduced version by way of an encore:*

Encore signs appear above each screen. Flourish of trumpets, crown hinges up. Enter Claudius and Gertrude.

    Claudius. Our sometime sister, now our Queen,
           (*Enter Hamlet.*)
           Have we taken to wife.
           (*Crown hinges down.*)

    Hamlet. That it should come to this!
           (*Exit Claudius and Gertrude. Wind noise. Moon hinges up. Enter Horatio above.*)

    Horatio. My lord, I saw him yesternight—
           The King, your father.

    Hamlet. Angels and ministers of grace defend us!
           (*Exit, running, through rest of speech.*)
           Something is rotten in the state of Denmark.
           (*Enter Ghost above.*)

    Ghost. I am thy father's spirit.
           The serpent that did sting thy father's life
           (*Enter Hamlet above.*)
           Now wears his crown.

    Hamlet. O my prophetic soul!
           Hereafter I shall think meet
           To put an antic disposition on.
           (*Moon hinges down. Exeunt.*
           Short flourish of trumpets. Enter Polonius below, running. Crown hinges up.)

    Polonius. Look where sadly the poor wretch comes.
           (*Exit Polonius, running. Enter Hamlet.*)

Hamlet.   I have heard that guilty creatures sitting at a play
          Have by the very cunning of the scene been struck.
          (*Enter Claudius, Gertrude, Ophelia, Marcellus and
          Horatio joking. All sit to watch imaginary play,
          puppets appear above screen.*)
          If he but blench, I know my course.
          (*Masque music. Claudius rises.*)
          The King rises!
All.   Give o'er the play!
          (*Exeunt all except Gertrude and Hamlet. Crown
          hinges down.*)
Hamlet.   I'll take the ghost's word for a thousand pounds.
          (*Enter Polonius, goes behind arras. Short flourish of
          trumpets.*)
          Mother, you have my father much offended.
Gertrude. Help!
Polonius. Help, Ho!
Hamlet.   (*Stabs Polonius.*) Dead for a ducat, dead!
          (*Polonius falls dead off-stage. Exit Gertrude and
          Hamlet. Short flourish of trumpets. Enter Claudius
          followed by Hamlet.*)
Claudius. Hamlet, this deed must send thee hence
          (*Exit Hamlet.*)
          Do it, England.
          (*Exit Claudius. Enter Ophelia, falls to ground. Rises
          and pulls gravestone to cover herself. Bell tolls twice.
          Enter Gravedigger and Hamlet.*)
Hamlet.   A pirate gave us chase. I alone became their prisoner.
          (*Takes skull from Gravedigger.*)
          Alas poor Yorick—but soft (*Returns skull to
              Gravedigger.*)—This is I,
          Hamlet the Dane!
          (*Exit Gravedigger. Enter Laertes.*)
Laertes. The devil take thy soul!
          (*They grapple, then break. Enter Osric between them
          with swords. They draw. Crown hinges up. Enter
          Claudius and Gertrude with goblets.*)
Hamlet.   Come on, Sir!
          (*Laertes and Hamlet fight.*)
Osric.   A hit, a very palpable hit!

Claudius. Give him the cup. Gertrude, do not drink!
Gertrude. I am poisoned! (*Dies*)
Laertes. Hamlet, thou art slain! (*Dies*)
Hamlet. Then venom to thy work! (*Kills Claudius.*
            Crown hinges down.)
            The rest is silence. (*Dies*)
            (*Two shots off-stage. End*)

                                    Dogg's Hamlet, Cahoot's Macbeth, 1980

In Wilhelm Meister's Years of Apprenticeship, *Goethe's hero makes some drastic cuts in his adaptation of* Hamlet, *but there is one piece of compression at which he draws the line:*

Wilhelm had kept the two parts of Rosencrantz and Guildenstern in his play. 'Why haven't you joined these two together?' Serlo asked; 'after all, it's an abbreviation that can be effected so easily.'

'God preserve me from such curtailments which would do away with both the meaning and the effect!' Wilhelm replied. 'What these two men are and what they do can't be presented by *one* person. It is in such details that Shakespeare's greatness shows itself. This cautious way of proceeding, this perpetual climbing down, this yes-manship, this fondling and flattering, this adroitness, this fawning, this allness and emptiness, this legally proper villainy, this incapacity—how can it be expressed by means of *one* character? There should be at least a dozen of them, if they could be had; for they are something only in society, they are society, and Shakespeare was very modest and wise in only allowing two such representatives to appear in the play. Besides, I need them in my version as a couple, in contrast to the *one* good, first-rate Horatio.'

W. S. Gilbert's burlesque Rosencrantz and Guildenstern *was prompted by the success of Henry Irving's* Hamlet *at the Lyceum, and first published in the magazine* Fun *in 1874. It opens with Claudius revealing his guilty secret to Gertrude. As a headstrong youth, he had written a five-act tragedy which was laughed off the stage. He is still brooding over his failure (even mentioning it is punishable by death), but the Queen succeeds in changing the subject:*

Queen. Think on't no more, my lord. Now, mark me well:
To cheer our son, whose solitary tastes
And tendency to long soliloquy
Have much alarmed us, I, unknown to thee,
Have sent for Rosencrantz and Guildenstern—
Two merry knaves, kin to Polonius,
Who will devise such revels in our court—
Such antic schemes of harmless merriment—
As shall abstract his meditative mind
From sad employment. Claudius, who can tell
But that they may divert my lord as well?
Ah, they are here!
   (Enter Guildenstern.)
   Guild.   My homage to the Queen!
   (Enter Rosencrantz.)
   Ros (kneeling). In hot obedience to the royal hest
We have arrived, prepared to do our best.
   Queen. We welcome you to court. Our Chamberlain
Shall see that you are suitably disposed.
Here is his daughter. She will hear your will
And see that it receives fair countenance.
   (Exeunt King and Queen, lovingly.)
   (Enter Ophelia.)
   Ros. Ophelia!
   (Both embrace her.)
   Oph (delighted and surprised). Rosencrantz and Guildenstern!
This meeting likes me much. We have not met
Since we were babies!
   Ros.   The Queen hath summoned us,
And I have come in a half-hearted hope
That I may claim once more my baby-love!
   Oph. Alas, I am betrothed!
   Ros.   Betrothed! To whom?
   Oph. To Hamlet!
   Ros.   Oh, incomprehensible!
Thou lovest Hamlet?
   Oph (demurely).   Nay, I said not so—
I said we were betrothed.
   Guild.   And what's he like?
   Oph. Alike for no two seasons at a time.

Sometimes he's tall—sometimes he's very short—
Now with black hair—now with a flaxen wig—
Sometimes an English accent—then a French—
Then English with a strong provincial 'burr'.
Once an American, and once a Jew—
But Danish never, take him how you will!
And strange to say, whate'er his tongue may be,
Whether he's dark or flaxen—English—French—
Though we're in Denmark, AD, ten—six—two—
He always dresses as King James the First!

    Guild. Oh, he is surely mad!

    Oph.   Well, there again
Opinion is divided. Some men hold
That he's the sanest, far, of all sane men—
Some that he's really sane, but shamming mad—
Some that he's really mad, but shamming sane—
Some that he will be mad, some that he *was*—
Some that he couldn't be. But on the whole
(As far as I can make out what they mean)
The favourite theory's somewhat like this:
Hamlet is idiotically sane
With lucid intervals of lunacy.

    Ros. We must devise some plan to stop this match!

    Guild. Stay! Many years ago, King Claudius
Was guilty of a five-act tragedy.
The play was damned, and none may mention it
Under the pain of death. We might contrive
To make him play this piece before the King,
And take the consequences.

    Ros.   Impossible!
For every copy was destroyed.

    Oph.   But one—
My father's!

    Ros.   Eh?

    Oph.   In his capacity
As our Lord Chamberlain he has *one* copy. I
This night, when all the court is drowned in sleep,
Will creep with stealthy foot into his den
And there abstract the precious manuscript!

    Guild. The plan is well conceived. But take good heed,

Your father may detect you.
   Oph.   Oh, dear, no.
My father spends his long official days
In reading all the rubbishing new plays.
From ten to four at work he may be found:
And then—my father sleeps exceeding sound! . . .

Gilbert told a friend that he thought Shakespeare a very obscure writer. 'What do you think of this passage?' he asked. ' "I would as lief be thrust through a thicket hedge as cry Pooh to a callow throstle".' 'That is perfectly plain,' the friend replied. 'A great lover of feathered songsters, rather than disturb the little warbler, would prefer to go through a thorny hedge. But I can't for the moment recall the passage. Where does it come from?'

'I have just invented it,' said Gilbert, 'and jolly good Shakespeare it is, too.'

The curious thing is that he really did believe it was 'jolly good Shakespeare,' and he never tired of girding at the poet whenever he could seize an opportunity.

HESKETH PEARSON, Gilbert and Sullivan, 1935

★   ★   ★

In *The Merry Wives*, Act I, Scene iii, occurs the following dialogue:

Falstaff. His filching was like an unskilful singer,—he kept not time.
Nym. The good humour is to steal at a minim's rest.

The word minim was apparently misheard by the reporters who took down the play, and they wrote 'minute's'. The eighteenth-century wiseacres, knowing nothing of music, except as an expensive noise, failed to understand the joke implied in the word minim and stuck to the nonsensical word, minute. This reading persisted right into the nineteenth century.

Why could Shakespeare make a joke about a minim's rest and be sure of his laugh, while the eighteenth century did not even know the musical term? Because, under Elizabeth, music was a living thing to old and young, rich and poor. At one end of the scale comes Morley's pupil who was ashamed because he could not take his part in a madrigal after supper, and at the other the 'groundlings' who did not misunderstand when Shakespeare called one of his most beautiful songs silly sooth, old and plain, sung by the spinsters and knitters in the sun. They knew that Shakespeare realized the beauty of their 'old plain' ballads; is he not always quoting them?

RALPH VAUGHAN WILLIAMS, 'A Minim's Rest', 1947

Only Mozart is worthy of Shakespeare!

OTTO NICOLAI

Nicolai was replying to the suggestion that he write a Shakespearian opera. He went on, despite his misgivings, to compose The Merry Wives of Windsor *(1849).*

Mozart's only known comment on Shakespeare occurs in a letter to his father, in which he argued—with reference to a scene in Idomeneo*—that audiences soon grow tired of a disembodied voice. He had seen a production of* Hamlet *in Salzburg, and he thought that the Ghost's speech went on far too long.*

It has been reported, and may well be the case, that shortly before his death Mozart agreed to write the music for a libretto based (very loosely) on The Tempest. *This must surely rank as the most tantalizing might-have-been among Shakespearian operas, though there are one or two others which run it close—Verdi's long-contemplated* King Lear, *for example, or Debussy's unrealized* As You Like It.

At the end of his memoirs Hector Berlioz expressed his regret at never having known Shakespeare, 'who might perhaps have loved me'. Certainly Berlioz loved Shakespeare. From 1827, when he saw an English company perform Hamlet *and* Romeo *in Paris, he was to remain deep under the poet's spell. (He also fell in love with the company's Ophelia and Juliet, Harriet Smithson, whom he eventually married.)*

The first major work which Berlioz published—his Opus One—was Eight Scenes from Faust *(1829). His main literary inspiration came, naturally, from Goethe, but he took the opportunity to pay homage to Shakespeare as well:*

The published score was a milestone in his progress; it was a grand stocktaking (including a dedication to the Vicomte de La Rochefoucauld in tactful tribute to his helpful acts of patronage) and a declaration of Romanticism: in addition to the printing of short passages from Gérard's°

Gérard] the translator of *Faust*; he subsequently adopted the pseudonym 'de Nerval'

translation, introducing and linking the separate scenes, each number carried an epigraph in English from *Hamlet* or *Romeo and Juliet*. The Concert de sylphes was headed by Mercutio's 'I talk of dreams', the Song of the Flea by Hamlet's 'Miching mallecho: it means mischief', Mephisto's Serenade by 'It is a damned ghost', the Romance by Romeo's 'Ah me, sad hours seem long', the Easter Hymn by Ophelia's 'Heavenly powers, restore him', and the ballad by her, 'He is dead and gone; at his head a grass green turf, at his heels a stone.'

DAVID CAIRNS, Berlioz: The Making of an Artist, 1989

In 1831, while visiting Italy, Berlioz attended a performance of I Montecchi ed i Capuleti, *Bellini's operatic version of* Romeo and Juliet. *He was deeply disappointed—and not only because Bellini had followed Italian tradition in having Romeo played by a woman:*

. . . in the libretto, no ball at the Capulets', no trace of Mercutio, no garrulous nurse, no grave and tranquil hermit, no balcony scene, no sublime soliloquy for Juliet as she takes the hermit's phial, no duet in the cell between the banished Romeo and the disconsolate friar, no Shakespeare, nothing—a botched piece of work, mangled, disfigured, *arranged*. And in the music, where was the double chorus of Montagues and Capulets, where the passion of the two lovers, the great orchestral outbursts, the vivid instrumental patterns, the new and searching melodies, the bold progressions lending colour to the scene, the unexpected modulations? Where was the musical drama, the dramatic music, that such poetry should give birth to?

From an article written in 1832. Quoted in DAVID CAIRNS, Berlioz:
The Making of an Artist

The experience, as David Cairns explains, set Berlioz thinking again of the possibility of a dramatic composition based on Romeo and Juliet, *which he had first discussed with the play's French translator two years before, and 'of the elements for which such a work must find musical expression and form':*

At the name of 'Romeo', breathed out faintly from the lips of the reviving Juliet, the young Montague stands motionless, riveted. As the voice calls a second time, more tenderly, he turns towards the tomb. He gazes at her: there is movement. He can no longer doubt it—she is living. He flings himself on the funeral couch, snatches up the beloved body, tearing away veils and shrouds, carries it to the front of the stage and holds it upright in his arms. Juliet looks dully about her from sleep-drugged eyes. Romeo calls her name; he clasps her in a desperate embrace, parts the hair hiding her pale forehead, covers her face with kisses, laughing convulsively. In his heart-rending delight he has forgotten that he is dying. Juliet breathes deeply. Juliet! Juliet! But a stab of agony recalls him: the poison is at work, devouring his vitals. 'O potent poison! Capulet, Capulet, forbear!' He crawls on his knees. Delirious, he imagines he sees Juliet's father come once more to take her from him.

During the same visit to Italy Berlioz also read King Lear *for the first time. A few weeks later he transmuted his experience of the play into the* King Lear *overture:*

The 'noble and indignant' phrases for the lower strings, beginning in proud strength but dwindling to an abstracted mutter, are clearly inspired by the stubborn, once masterful old king (as well as by the example of the instrumental recitatives in the finale of Beethoven's Ninth Symphony). So is the angry, obsessive first theme of the allegro— just as the pure, artless oboe melody of the introduction has its origin in the character of Cordelia.

DAVID CAIRNS, *Berlioz: The Making of an Artist*

The eventual outcome of the composer's reflections on Romeo and Juliet *was the dramatic symphony of that name (1839). Later works by him with a powerful Shakespearian inspiration include* The Trojans *(completed in 1858) and, more obviously,* Beatrice and Benedick *(1862).*

I have just finished the third act of my poem [*The Trojans*], and yesterday, as well, I wrote both words and music of the big duet in Act 4, a scene stolen from Shakespeare and Virgilianized which reduces me to the most absurd state. I've had to do no more than transcribe that immortal love babble which makes the last act of *The Merchant of Venice* a worthy pendant of *Romeo and Juliet*. Shakespeare is the real author of the words and the music. Strange that he should intervene—he, the poet of the north —in the great work of the poet of Rome. Virgil left out the scene. What singers, those two!

HECTOR BERLIOZ, letter to Toussaint Bennet, 1856, tr. David Cairns

I am quite transported by some words of Father Nestor's in Shakespeare's *Troilus and Cressida*. I've just reread that amazing parody of the *Iliad*, where Shakespeare none the less made Hector greater even than Homer did. Nestor, paying tribute to the sublime generosity of Troy's defender, says he has seen him many times in the midst of battle thunder past in his chariot with his sword uplifted, so as to spare the trembling ranks of Greeks. 'Lo, Jupiter is yonder, dealing life.' What a picture I should make of that, were I a great painter. God in heaven, but it's beautiful, Nestor: 'Lo, Jupiter is yonder, dealing life.' I feel as if my heart will burst when I come upon phrases like that.

BERLIOZ, letter to Princess Carolyne Sayn-Wittgenstein, 1856, tr. David Cairns

Where the opera [*Beatrice and Benedick*] adds material it takes its cue from the play. Beatrice's protest at the banal rhymes in the chorus's rejoicing—*gloire/victoire, guerriers/lauriers*—derives from Benedick's wry admission, in the play, that when he tries to fashion a sonnet in praise of Beatrice he cannot rhyme as a poet should. In the avowal of deep feeling that Berlioz's Beatrice makes during their courtship—a more open avowal than Benedick's—she parallels Shakespeare's. Even the one major addition to *Much Ado*, the foolish, fond old *maître de chapelle* Somarone (literally 'great donkey'—hence the braying motif in the Sicilienne) has its source in the play, in the very precise musician Balthazar. Somarone's 'grotesque epithalamium' comes at the same point in the action as Balthazar's 'Sigh no more, ladies' (prompting Benedick to the almost identical comment that 'if my dogs had howled thus, I would have hanged them').

DAVID CAIRNS, *Berlioz: Servitude and Greatness*, 1999

Berlioz's son Louis inherited his father's passion for Shakespeare, and something of his ability to relate the plays to his own life:

Reading *Henry IV, Part 1*, he was struck by 'the passage, very powerful for me, where the king reproaches his son. You too have had the same fears, and have had to reproach me, you too have suffered from the heedless, rash, violent, exasperated character of your adored son. As for me, I know now what Henry V felt, but unlike him I have no power or ambition to leave my rut and like a meteor astonish the world, which means so little to me—though I should like to astonish my father!'

> Louis Berlioz to Hector Berlioz, 1865, quoted in David Cairns, *Berlioz: Servitude and Greatness*, 1999

Louis and Hector had had a troubled relationship, but by the mid-1860s they were permanently reconciled. Louis became an officer in the merchant marine, and rose to command his own ship; he died of yellow fever at Havana in 1867, at the age of 32.

★

In 1843 Felix Mendelssohn's sister Fanny wrote to another sister, Rebecca, describing the first performance of the incidental music for A Midsummer Night's Dream. *The occasion was a production of the play at the New Palace, Potsdam:*

The performance was almost too much for my nerves, for I have hardly ever known our mother so vividly present to my mind—I kept fancying I could hear her laugh. I missed you also very much. The only thing I did not like in the performance was the dresses, which Tieck obstinately insisted on having in the Spanish style of the seventeenth century, which disturbed me more than I could have believed possible; whereas the clowns were for the most part excellent, and even Gern, who to the terror of the fairies played the part of Bottom, was better than I had expected. The fairies, about thirty children from the school of dancing, were charming; and when they trooped into the theatre to the strain of that lovely march, the effect was quite magical. But the most beautiful part of the whole piece, and the only thing which I never thought much of in reading the play, is the last scene, where the court goes off in procession to the splendid wedding-march, and you hear the music gradually dying away in the distance, till suddenly it breaks into the theme of the overture, and Puck and the fairies reappear on the empty stage. I assure you it is enough to make one cry. The interludes are real masterpieces, and were performed to perfection. Never did I hear an orchestra play so *pianissimo*. The three middle acts are separated by music alone, the curtain not falling at all; after the second comes a wonderful piece, representing Hermia seeking Lysander, which suddenly changes to a mad burlesque at the moment that the clowns appear in the forest expressing their delight at the beauty of the scene by comical gestures. It is irresistibly ludicrous. How delighted all the children of Berlin will be with this piece, for the lion and the ass are splendid. The ass opens its mouth wide and puts out its tongue, and when pretty Peasblossom in a little red cap and tiny Mustard-seed set to work to scratch its head, I can assure you, Walter, it is fine! But I must describe the Lion's costume. His jacket and trousers are of yellow-gray felt, his wig, made of shavings, bangs down to the ground, and his tail is an enormously long wisp of straw fastened on in an almost indecorously natural manner. Thisbe's attire is rather too extravagant for my taste: one of her stockings is hanging down, and she pulls it up when one of the courtiers remarks that Pyramus might hang himself with her garter; she has nothing womanly about her except a towel arranged as drapery. The dead-march for her and Pyramus is really stupendous; I could scarcely believe up to the last that Felix would have the impudence to bring it before the public, for it is exactly like the mock preludes he plays when you cannot get him to be serious.

Tr. Carl Klingemann

Fanny goes on to recall 'what an important part A Midsummer Night's Dream *has always played in our family, how we went through all the parts at different ages, from Peasblossom to Hermia and Helena'—'and now it has come to such a glorious ending'.*

★

Giuseppe Verdi writes to his librettist Francesco Piave:

Here is a scenario of *Macbeth.* This tragedy is one of the greatest creations of mankind! If we can't make something great with it, let's try at least to make something out of the ordinary.

1846

Tr. Charles Osborne

Verdi writes to his publisher, Ricordi, while working on Otello:

If I were an actor, and had to play Iago, I would rather have a long, thin face, thin lips, small eyes close to the nose like a monkey, a high, receding forehead, the head well developed at the back. An absent-minded air, nonchalant, indifferent to everything, sceptical, a cutting manner, speaking good and evil lightly as though he were thinking of something else, so that, if anyone were to say to him, in reproof: 'What you say, what you propose, is monstrous,' he could reply: 'Really . . . I didn't think so . . . Let's talk no more of it.' Someone like that could deceive everybody, even, up to a point, his own wife. But a malicious little fellow puts everyone on his guard, and deceives no one!

1881

tr. Charles Osborne

The composition of Otello was a much less Shakespearean feat; for the truth is that instead of Otello being an Italian opera written in the style of Shakespear, Othello is a play written by Shakespear in the style of Italian opera. It is quite peculiar among his works in this aspect. Its characters are monsters: Desdemona is a prima donna, with handkerchief, confidant, and vocal solo all complete; and Iago, though certainly more anthropomorphic than the Count di Luna, is only so when he slips out of his stage villain's part. Othello's transports are conveyed by a magnificent but senseless music which rages from the Propontick to the Hellespont in an orgy of thundering sound and bounding rhythm; and the plot is a pure farce plot: that is to say, it is supported on an artificially manufactured and desperately precarious trick with a handkerchief which a chance word might upset at any moment. With such a libretto, Verdi was quite at home: his success with it proves, not that he could occupy Shakespear's plane, but that Shakespear could on occasion occupy his, which is a very different matter.

BERNARD SHAW, article on Verdi in the *Anglo-Saxon Review*, 1901

For ninety-nine Italians out of a hundred, Othello is the name borne by a tenor for three hours on the stage. The Moor's name is associated with those of singers such as Tamagno and Marconi much more often than with that of Shakespeare. Thus it is to Boito's libretto that we must turn to understand the view of the above average Italian.

This libretto has had much greater literary stamina than almost all the others used by Verdi. That goes without saying but does not prevent it from being fundamentally wrong, for it first mutilates and then deforms the whole play. It completely mutilates the first act in which Shakespeare (who was a more acute gentleman than **Boito**) prepares all the circumstances from which the tragedy unfolds, it mutilates the crucial scenes of Iago's jealousy and above all it omits Brabantio's warning which does so much to stimulate Othello's anger, 'She has deceiv'd her father, and may thee'.

Boito, who was the quintessence of romanticism, was delighted to abandon himself entirely to the hypothesis of Iago-Satan . . . And since he found nothing in Shakespeare's text which could justify such an apocalyptic vision of Iago's character, he set himself to invent this Satan and produced the famous 'Credo' which is as unShakespearian, as unlike Iago—and as unlifelike—as a romantic fifty years after his time could conceive.

Such is the power exerted by operatic melodrama on Italian heart-strings that nowadays even Shakespeare's play is performed in our country without its first act, and the actors, unable to yell 'I believe in a cruel god' to the audience, try to give an equivalent impression by means of satanic leers and monstrous disguises. When I went to see Orson Welles's *Othello*, I heard people behind me complaining that the director had added his own beginning to the film by inserting the Venetian scenes. For the Italians the tragedy *Othello* has been killed by the opera *Otello*.

The truth is that Iago is nothing but a second-rate malefactor, similar to dozens one finds in every type of organisation, public and private, the sort of people who write anonymous letters to superiors who have not promoted them. His wickedness is on such a parsimonious scale that he does not expect (or intend) blood to flow nor the great calamity to take place. As he puts it, he simply wants to 'untune'—to destroy—the harmony existing between Othello and Desdemona. The tragedy is entirely caused by Othello's temperament, by the ease with which he becomes totally unbalanced. He is the tragic figure. Iago is merely the contemptible fuse which explodes the mine.

GIUSEPPE TOMASI DI LAMPEDUSA, 'Opera and *Othello*', tr. David Gilmour

Arrigo Boito writes to Verdi in 1889 about the difficulties of starting work on the libretto of Falstaff:

In the first few days I was in despair. To sketch the characters with a few strokes, to set the intrigue in motion, to extract all of the juice from that great Shakespearean orange without letting the useless pips slip into the little glass, to write with color, clarity, and brevity, to delineate the musical plan of the scenario so that an organic unity results that is a *piece of music* and yet at the same time is not one, to make the joyous comedy live from top to bottom, to make it live with a natural and engaging gaiety, is difficult, difficult, difficult, and yet one must make it all seem easy, easy, easy. *Corragio e avanti.*

Quoted by GARY SCHMIDGALL in Shakespeare & Opera, 1990

In September, Verdi sent off to Ricordi the third and final act of *Falstaff*, accompanied by a note of affectionate farewell to the character of Falstaff scribbled on the manuscript, paraphrasing a passage in Boito's libretto:

> *Tutto è finito.*
> *Va, va vecchio John.*
> *Cammina per la tua via*
> *Fin che tu puoi.*
> *Divertente tipo di briccone*
> *Eternamente vero sotto*
> *Maschera diversa in ogni*
> *Tempo, in ogni luogo.*
> *Va, va,*
> *Cammina, cammina,*
> *Addio.*

[It's all finished. Go, go, old John. Go on your way for as long as you can. Amusing rogue, forever true beneath the masks you wear in different times and places. Go, go, on your way. Farewell.]

CHARLES OSBORNE, Verdi: A Life in the Theatre, 1987

★

The Czech composer Bedrich Smetana was an ardent admirer of Shakespeare. His works include the symphonic poem Richard III *(1858) and a vigorous piano piece, 'Macbeth and the Three Witches'.*

Among the Czechs, as elsewhere in Central and Eastern Europe in the nineteenth century, enthusiasm for Shakespeare was often bound up with the revival of national culture and national pride:

In 1864, Smetana became the central figure in the Prague tercentenary celebrations of Shakespeare's birth. Preceded by a cycle of five Shakespearian performances, the Jubilee itself was conceived as a composite work of art, consisting of music, poetry, singing, acting, painting, and sculpture. It took place in the largest theatre hall in central Prague and was opened by Berlioz's *Romeo and Juliet* conducted by Smetana. A poetic prologue was recited by a famous actor dressed as Prospero. Six *tableaux vivants* with background music represented scenes from all of Shakespeare's dramatic genres: one comedy, one history, two tragedies, and two romances. The climax was reached when Smetana's heroic *Shakespearian March*, freshly composed for the occasion, accompanied the procession of almost 250 characters from Shakespeare's plays dressed in historical costumes and slowly passing under a large bust of the poet created by the most promising young Czech sculptor of the day. The characters were represented not only by actors, some performing short scenes, but also by prominent patriotic citizens (Falstaff was impersonated by Prague's stoutest butcher). Finally the procession settled around Shakespeare's bust to listen to the poetic epilogue of the alleged Bohemian shepherdess Perdita from the *Winter's Tale*. Represented by a popular actress, she embodied both Shakespeare's 'fair Bohemia' and Bohemian art (Perdita Ars Bohemica) which was lost after the Habsburg victory over the Bohemian estates in 1618 but was revived and fully restored now to become an equal partner of all European nations.

ZDENEK STRIBRNY, *Shakespeare and Eastern Europe*, 2000

Benjamin Britten's A Midsummer Night's Dream *(1960) is generally reckoned to be the most successful Shakespeare opera since Verdi. One of the many gifts it displays is a marked gift for parody:*

'Pyramus and Thisby' is a mere 124 lines in all, and Britten knew precisely what to do with Shakespeare's miniature send-up of Elizabethan drama: transform it into a miniature send-up of 'number' opera. He made his satirical intentions clear by switching from English to melodramatic Italian directions when the rustic actors enter Theseus' palace. Thus, Wall discharges his lugubrious part in a *lento lamentoso* and Bottom's suicidal 'passion' is an *allegro disperato*. That Britten's parody of opera should fit Shakepeare's parody of his own dramatic methods reiterates the theme of synonymy in 'Shakespearean' and 'operatic.'

The average opera's running time, we have seen, is about 140 minutes (Britten's score says the first production lasted 144 minutes), with about 18 numbers, which last, on average, a little over seven minutes each.

Britten's Lilliputian opera-within-an-opera is perfectly in scale: it lasts 17 minutes and consists of 14 numbers that last about 75 seconds each. The music of his prologue, with its rapid-fire semiquavers on the same note, proves the rustics haven't a clue what melody or 'phrasing' means, let alone the niceties of iambic pentameter. It has already been hinted by the composer that the rustics don't have the operatic knack, for in the rehearsal scene, words like 'love' and 'lofty' are given very low rather than high notes. The word-setting of their play shows such ineptitude on numerous occasions. But what is most vividly caricatured is the progression from aria to aria, with chit-chat and brickbats from the aristocratic audience in between. Wall gets his all-too-earthy entrance aria (in Schoenbergian *Sprechgesang* and notation, a wicked bit of Britten satire), then comes Bottom with a recitative ('O grim-look'd night,' marked *moderato ma tenebroso!*) and an aria ('And thou, O wall') that ends as most nineteenth-century Italian arias do, *con espansione*. The heroine's first appearance is accompanied, predictably, by harp and flute in a prim *allegretto grazioso*. Seconds later, love is naturally being plighted in an *allegro brillante*.

Shortly afterward, Snug presents his Lion and, fearful that genuine fright might sweep through his audience, sings his part at first *leggiero*, then *dolce* and *intimo*. Still, Britten gives him a *presto feroce* to drive Thisby offstage. At this point the audience is in a very generous mood; even Starveling's Moon gets a bravo ('Well shone, Moon!' says Hippolyta). The catastrophe comes with admirable haste; Bottom spies Thisby's bloody mantle and dispatches himself: 'Thus die I, thus, thus, thus, thus, thus.' But, like certain operatic heroes and heroines, he rises for one last repetitive lyric outburst that milks the passionate moment for all it is worth:

> Now am I dead,
> Now am I fled,
> My soul is in the sky,
> Tongue lose thy light!
> Moon take thy flight!
> Now die, die, die, die, die.

Thisby soon appears to converse, as Donizetti's Lucia does, with an imitative flute, then shifts into an *adagio lamentoso* for the aria that brings her to stab herself and end the opera: 'Thus Thisby ends, Adieu, adieu, adieu . . .' In lieu of an epilogue comes a ballet divertissement in the form of bergomask dances. It is telling that Britten uses every part of

Shakespeare's parody of his own style and dramaturgy to parody the methods of composers from the heyday of grand opera.

GARY SCHMIDGALL, Shakespeare & Opera, 1990

The recording of Ellington's Shakespearean Suite called *Such Sweet Thunder* [1957] climaxed several weeks during which Duke and Billy read Shakespeare. I never quite discovered how they read it, for Duke's summaries of the plays and characters were unlike any I had heard before. Ellington gathered together a series of short pieces descriptive of various impressions he had received from his quick course in the Bard and we recorded them under such temporary titles as 'Cleo,' 'Puck,' and 'Hamlet.' We all searched later for the final titles, and I found 'Such Sweet Thunder'° in Bartlett's Quotations. To appreciate the Suite in its final form, one must listen to the music as a statement of what Duke got out of Shakespeare, a uniquely personal, yet deeply perceptive encounter. To overlay someone else's concept of the characters described in *Thunder* is deceptive and unfair. Duke likes Lady Macbeth, whether you're supposed to like her or not, and he treats her right.

IRVING TOWNSEND, 'When Duke Records', 1960

Irving Townsend produced a number of Duke Ellington's records for Columbia in the 1950s and 1960s. 'Billy' was Ellington's co-composer, Billy Strayhorn.

Of the thirteen pieces that comprise *Such Sweet Thunder*, the four 'sonnets' are different in mood, orchestration, and rhythm, but have in common, as Ellington scholar Bill Dobbins points out, fourteen phrases of ten notes each, musically mirroring the fourteen lines of iambic pentameter (ten syllables) that make up the literary sonnet Shakespeare favored. Throughout, there are witty and dramatic, melancholy and romantic sections, some combining aspects of various works for poetic fusions of material, such as 'The Telecasters,' which combines the three witches (the trombones) from *Macbeth* with Iago from *Othello* (the baritone), or the concluding section, 'Circle of Fourths,' 'inspired,' as Irving Townsend wrote in the original notes for the album, 'by Shakespeare

---

'Such Sweet Thunder'] the phrase comes from *A Midsummer Night's Dream*: 'I never heard | So musical a discord, such sweet thunder'

himself and the four major parts of his artistic contribution: tragedy, comedy, history, and the sonnets.'

STANLEY CROUCH, programme notes for a concert at Lincoln Center, 1988

In 1964 Philip Larkin reviewed Johnny Dankworth's recording Shakespeare and All That Jazz, *'settings of Shakespearean or pseudo-Shakespearean word-pieces featuring Cleo Laine'. For the most part Larkin was disappointed; he rated the work well below Dankworth's Dickens suite of the previous year. But it had its virtues, even so:*

Cleo Laine's sultry, slightly-adenoidal contralto is in good form, and one or two pieces succeed—the Minnie-the-Moocher-like 'Dunsinane Blues', for instance, or Dankworth's own 'Shall I Compare Thee to a Summer's Day', in which by a subtle extension of the metre the line 'By chance, or nature's changing course untrimm'd' comes over with devastating poignance.

★　★　★

In *Henry V* more than any other play, Shakespeare moans about the confines of his Globe Theatre—'or may we cram | Within this wooden O the very casques | That did affright the air at Agincourt?'—and all those short battle scenes, in a lot of his plays, are frustrated cinema.

LAURENCE OLIVIER, *On Acting*, 1986

The following scene is the one corresponding to the murder of Duncan in Throne of Blood, *Akira Kurosawa's 1957 film adaptation of* Macbeth. *(Taketoki Washizu is the Macbeth figure, Asaji is his wife.)*

The scene in the Unopened Chamber—Taketoki Washizu is sitting alone in the centre of the room. Each time the flame of the candle stirs, the shadow of Taketoki moves. There is an air of gloom—Taketoki's glaring, bloodshot eyes stare.

The dark-coloured traces of bloodshed upon the wainscot—Taketoki turns his eyes away, yet on the very wood of the floor from which he averted his eyes the outline is suggested of a strange figure which the blood has drawn. Suddenly Taketoki rises impatiently to his feet; but he remains standing motionless, looking to the side. Asaji, with a spear in her hands, enters quietly. Taketoki is staring at Asaji lost in a trance. Asaji, approaching Taketoki, forces him to take hold of the spear. At the same time, the two stare at each other, pale.

The sky—an owl with its sharp cry flies across the crescent moon, which looks like a sickle.

In the Unopened Chamber—Taketoki looks up to the sky, and staring for an instant at Asaji with a strange smile, walks from the room uncertainly.

Asaji—seeing him go, sits down quietly, and keeps quite still in the same pose.

—A long interval—

Taketoki comes back with a ghastly look; splashed with blood, he stands with the spear like a stick, and sits down. Asaji wrests the spear from Taketoki's hands and goes out.

In front of the Chamber—Asaji appears, and eases the blood-smeared spear into the hands of the sleeping warrior.

From the script of the film, quoted in ROGER MANVELL,
Shakespeare and the Film, 1971

The play begins with the theatrical—fine dress, pretence, props (the map, coats of arms) contrived speeches and assumed poses. The end of the play has stepped into the real world, on to the dirty blood-soaked earth. The wind has long ago torn the theatrical costumes; the rain has washed the make-up from the actors' faces.

*

The advantage of the cinema over the theatre is not that you can even have horses, but that you can stare closer into a man's eyes; otherwise it is pointless to set up a cine camera for Shakespeare.

*

How difficult it is to take the starch out of these figures. They stick in one's memory—straight, rigid, and speaking in beautiful, contrived voices.

One must get Goneril moving and ruffle her hair. She slops about the house in a rumpled evil-smelling gown. In an odious and imperious voice she sets Oswald at her father.

Her entrance into supper does not look like a duchess's in any way. She rebukes a servant on the way, takes a spoonful of soup, blows on it, and frowns.

At home she is slovenly and sullen. She carves fatty meat.

When *Hamlet* was being discussed at the Leningrad Institute of Theatre and Music I came under a lot of fire for the hens which cackled around the courtyard at Elsinore. In the opinion of the drama experts hens lowered the tone of the tragedy. Alas, I did not admit my mistake. Let hens have their cackle during famous soliloquies.

Long live hens and down with pathos!

★

Shakespeare saw a black cloud encroaching on history, a black death threatening to annihilate history, to return it to primeval horror. And he expressed it with all the demonic power of tragedy. But he also wrote of how Cordelia found within herself the strength to say 'no', and of Edgar's brave behaviour, and, first and foremost, of the fearlessness of Lear's thoughts. 'I must be cruel' said Hamlet, however this is only the beginning of the sentence. 'I must be cruel only to be kind.'

GRIGORI KOZINTSEV, *King Lear: The Space of Tragedy*, 1973, tr. Mary Mackintosh

Kozintsev's film of Hamlet *was first shown in 1964 and his film of* King Lear *in 1972.*

IN THE MARGIN

I have heard of the Wife of Bath, I think in Shakespeare.

JONATHAN SWIFT, letter to John Gay, November 1729

According to the editor of Swift's letters, Harold Williams, this is 'presumably a jesting remark'.

    Immortal! William Shakespeare, there's none can you excel,
    You have drawn out your characters remarkably well.

WILLIAM McGONAGALL, 'An Address to Shakespeare', 1878

In 1910 Bernard Shaw wrote a sketch in which a bust of Shakespeare addresses a group of guests assembled at a fancy-dress party, one of them got up as Lady Macbeth:

'You are another of my failures. I meant Lady Mac to be something really awful; but she turned into my wife. . . .'

    'Your wife! Anne Hathaway!! Was she like Lady Macbeth?'

    'Very,' said Shakespeare, with conviction. 'If you notice, Lady Macbeth has only one consistent characteristic, which is, that she thinks everything her husband does is wrong and that she can do it better. If I'd ever murdered anybody she'd have bullied me for making a mess of it and gone upstairs to improve on it herself. Whenever we gave a party she apologized to the company for my behavior.'

Imitation

Hen.   Therefore do thou, stiff-set Northumberland,
        Retire to Chester, and my cousin here,
        The noble Bedford, hie to Glo'ster straight
        And give our Royal ordinance and word
        That in this fit and strife of empery

No loss shall stand account. To this compulsion
I pledge my sword, my person and my honour
On the Great Seal of England: so farewell.
Swift to your charges: nought was ever done
Unless at some time it were first begun.

HILAIRE BELLOC

The devil damn thee black, thou cream-faced loon—
Whom we invite to see us crowned at Scone.

PAUL DEHN, 'Potted Swan' (a condensed version of some
of Shakespeare's more celebrated scenes), 1956

O saucy Worcester, dost thou lie so low?

Shakespeare parody, *Beyond the Fringe*, 1960

The Seven Ages of Man

Seven ages, first puking and mewling,
Then very pissed off with one's schooling,
Then fucks, and then fights,
Then judging chap's rights;
Then sitting in slippers; then drooling.

VICTOR GRAY

FRB [Frank Benson] played Caliban, one of his favourite performances. He spent many hours watching monkeys and baboons in the zoo, in order to get the movements and postures in keeping with his 'make-up'.

His old nurse saw him one night, dressed in this curious costume, and exclaimed, 'Oh, Mr Frank, you are the image of your sister in that dress.'

CONSTANCE BENSON, *Mainly Players*, 1926

My Rosencrantz was not up to much, but my Guildenstern was tremendous.

GORDON BROWNE, Edwardian actor

(He was the husband of the actress Dame Marie Tempest.)

from Shakespeare and Christmas, *by Fr*nk H*rr*s*

That Shakespeare hated Christmas—hated it with a venom utterly alien
to the gentle heart in him—I take to be a proposition that establishes
itself automatically. If there is one thing lucid-obvious in the Plays and
Sonnets, it is Shakespeare's unconquerable loathing of Christmas. The
Professors deny it, however, or deny that it is proven. With these
gentlemen I will deal faithfully. I will meet them on their own parched
ground, making them fertilise it by shedding there the last drop of the
water that flows through their veins.

If you find, in the works of a poet whose instinct is to write about
everything under the sun, one obvious theme untouched, or touched
hardly at all, then it is at least presumable that there was some good
reason for that abstinence. Such a poet was Shakespeare. It was one of
the divine frailties of his genius that he must be ever flying off at a
tangent from his main theme to unpack his heart in words about some
frivolous-small irrelevance that had come into his head. If it could be
shown that he never mentioned Christmas, we should have proof pre-
sumptive that he consciously avoided doing so. But if the fact is that he
did mention it now and again, but in grudging fashion, without one
spark of illumination—he, the arch-illuminator of all things—then we
have proof positive that he detested it.

I see Dryasdust thumbing his Concordance. Let my memory save him
the trouble. I will reel him off the one passage in which Shakespeare
spoke of Christmas in words that rise to the level of mediocrity.

> Some say that ever 'gainst that season comes
> Wherein our Saviour's birth is celebrated,
> The bird of dawning singeth all night long:
> And then, they say, no spirit dare stir abroad;
> The nights are wholesome; then no planets strike,
> No fairy takes, nor witch hath power to charm,
> So hallowed and so gracious is the time.

So says Marcellus at Elsinore. This is the best our Shakespeare can
vamp up for the birthday of the Man with whom he of all men had
the most in common. And Dryasdust, eternally unable to distinguish
chalk from cheese, throws up his hands in admiration of the marvellous poetry. If Dryasdust had written it, it would more than pass

muster. But as coming from Shakespeare, how feeble-cold—aye, and sulky-sinister! The greatest praiser the world will ever know!—and all he can find in his heart to sing of Christmas is a stringing-together of old women's superstitions! Again and again he has painted Winter for us as it never has been painted since—never by Goethe even, though Goethe in more than one of the *Winter-Lieder* touched the hem of his garment. There was every external reason why he should sing, as only he could have sung, of Christmas. The Queen set great store by it. She and her courtiers celebrated it year by year with lusty-pious unction. And thus the ineradicable snob in Shakespeare had the most potent of all inducements to honour the feast with the full power that was in him. But he did not, because he would not. What is the key to the enigma?

For many years I hunted it vainly. The second time that I met Carlyle I tried to enlist his sympathy and aid. He sat pensive for a while and then said that it seemed to him 'a goose-quest.' I replied, 'You have always a phrase for everything, Tom, but always the wrong one.' He covered his face, and presently, peering at me through his gnarled fingers, said 'Mon, ye're recht.' I discussed the problem with Renan, with Emerson, with Disraeli, also with Cetewayo—poor Cetewayo, best and bravest of men, but intellectually a Professor, like the rest of them. It was borne in on me that if I were to win to the heart of the mystery I must win alone.

The solution, when suddenly it dawned on me, was so simple-stark that I was ashamed of the ingenious-clever ways I had been following. (I learned then—and perhaps it is the one lesson worth the learning of any man—that truth may be approached only through the logic of the heart. For the heart is eye and ear, and all excellent understanding abides there.) On Christmas Day, assuredly, Anne Hathaway was born . . .

MAX BEERBOHM, *A Christmas Garland*, 1912

In The Man Shakespeare *(1909) Frank Harris portrays Anne Hathaway as a scold who embitters Shakespeare's existence.*

Sometimes we hav to recite which is girly in the extreme and there is no chance to read famous CRIB which you copied out in prep.

when i recite it is something like this:

Tomow and tomow and tomow
Um ah um ah
Tomow and tomow and tomow
Um—ah creeps creeps in the last syll—
No!
Tomowandtomowandtomow
Creeps in this um um
Out!
OUT!
brief candle
Yes i kno sir half a mo sir
Yes
fie
O fie!
Um um tis an unweeded syllable an un—
No!
Tomowandtomowandtomow etc. . . .

In other words quite frankly i just don't kno it.
Also quite frankly
I COULDN'T CARE LESS
What use will *that* be to me in the new atomic age?
Occasionally english masters chide me for this point of view o moles-worth one you must learn the value of spiritual things until i spray them with 200 rounds from my backterial gun. i then plant the british flag in the masters inkwell and declare a whole holiday for the skool. boo to shakespeare.
So much for english masters.

GEOFFREY WILLANS, *Down with Skool!*, 1953

'Remember what the poet Shakespeare said, Jeeves.'
    'What was that, sir?'
    ' "Exit hurriedly, pursued by a bear." You'll find it in one of his plays. I remember drawing a picture of it on the side of the page, when I was at school.'

P. G. WODEHOUSE, *Very Good, Jeeves!*, 1930

The Immortal Bard

'Oh, yes,' said Dr Phineas Welch, 'I can bring back the spirits of the illustrious dead.'

He was a little drunk, or maybe he wouldn't have said it. Of course, it was perfectly all right to get a little drunk at the annual Christmas party.

Scott Robertson, the school's young English instructor, adjusted his glasses and looked to right and left to see if they were overheard. 'Really, Dr Welch.'

'I mean it. And not just the spirits. I bring back the bodies, too.'

'I wouldn't have said it were possible,' said Robertson primly.

'Why not? A simple matter of temporal transference.'

'You mean time travel? But that's quite—uh—unusual.'

'Not if you know how.'

'Well, how, Dr Welch?'

'Think I'm going to tell you?' asked the physicist gravely. He looked vaguely about for another drink and didn't find any. He said, 'I brought quite a few back. Archimedes, Newton, Galileo. Poor fellows.'

'Didn't they like it here? I should think they'd have been fascinated by our modern science,' said Robertson. He was beginning to enjoy the conversation.

'Oh, they were. They were. Especially Archimedes. I thought he'd go mad with joy at first after I explained a little of it in some Greek I'd boned up on, but no—no——'

'What was wrong?'

'Just a different culture. They couldn't get used to our way of life. They got terribly lonely and frightened. I had to send them back.'

'That's too bad.'

'Yes. Great minds, but not flexible minds. Not universal. So I tried Shakespeare.'

'*What!*' yelled Robertson. This was getting closer to home.

'Don't yell, my boy,' said Welch. 'It's bad manners.'

'Did you say you brought back Shakespeare?'

'I did. I needed someone with a universal mind; someone who knew people well enough to be able to live with them centuries away from his own time. Shakespeare was the man. I've got his signature. As a memento, you know.'

'On you?' asked Robertson, eyes bugging.

'Right here.' Welch fumbled in one vest pocket after another. 'Ah, here it is.'

A little piece of pasteboard was passed to the instructor. On one side it said: 'L. Klein & Sons, Wholesale Hardware.' On the other side, in straggly script, was written, 'Willm Shakesper.'

A wild surmise filled Robertson. 'What did he look like?'

'Not like his pictures. Bald and an ugly mustache. He spoke in a thick brogue. Of course, I did my best to please him with our times. I told him we thought highly of his plays and still put them on the boards. In fact, I said we thought they were the greatest pieces of literature in the English language, maybe in any language.'

'Good. Good,' said Robertson breathlessly.

'I said people had written volumes of commentaries on his plays. Naturally he wanted to see one and I got one for him from the library.'

'And?'

'Oh, he was fascinated. Of course, he had trouble with the current idioms and references to events since 1600, but I helped out. Poor fellow. I don't think he ever expected such treatment. He kept saying, "God ha' mercy! What cannot be racked from words in five centuries? One could wring, methinks, a flood from a damp clout!"'

'He wouldn't say that.'

'Why not? He wrote his plays as quickly as he could. He said he had to on account of the deadlines. He wrote *Hamlet* in less than six months. The plot was an old one. He just polished it up.'

'That's all they do to a telescope mirror. Just polish it up,' said the English instructor indignantly.

The physicist disregarded him. He made out an untouched cocktail on the bar some feet away and sidled toward it. 'I told the immortal bard that we even gave college courses in Shakespeare.'

'*I* give one.'

'I know. I enrolled him in your evening extension course. I never saw a man so eager to find out what posterity thought of him as poor Bill was. He worked hard at it.'

'You enrolled William Shakespeare in my course?' mumbled Robertson. Even as an alcoholic fantasy, the thought staggered him. And *was* it an alcoholic fantasy? He was beginning to recall a bald man with a queer way of talking. . . .

'Not under his real name, of course,' said Dr Welch. 'Never mind what he went under. It was a mistake, that's all. A big mistake. Poor fellow.' He had the cocktail now and shook his head at it.

'Why was it a mistake? What happened?'

'I had to send him back to 1600,' roared Welch indignantly. 'How much humiliation do you think a man can stand?'

'What humiliation are you talking about?'

Dr Welch tossed off the cocktail. 'Why, you poor simpleton, you *flunked* him.'

ISAAC ASIMOV, 1953

I dreamt last night that Shakespeare's ghost
Sat for a Civil Service post;
The English paper for the year
Had several questions on *King Lear*
Which Shakespeare answered very badly
Because he hadn't read his Bradley.

GUY BOAS, *Lays of Learning*, 1926

In his Journey from This World to the Next *(1743) Henry Fielding satirizes the freedom with which Shakespeare's editors indulged in conjecture and emendation. The narrator encounters the poet during his journey through Hades, in the company of the actors Thomas Betterton and Barton Booth:*

I then observed *Shakespeare* standing between *Betterton* and *Booth*, and deciding a Difference between those two great Actors, concerning the placing an Accent in one of his Lines: this was disputed on both sides with a Warmth which surprized me in *Elysium*, till I discovered by Intuition, that every Soul retained its principal Characteristic, being, indeed, its very Essence. The Line was that celebrated one in *Othello*;

> *Put out the Light, and then put out the Light,*

according to *Betterton*. Mr. *Booth* contended to have it thus;

> *Put out the Light, and then put out* the *Light.*

I could not help offering my Conjecture on this Occasion, and suggested it might perhaps be,

> *Put out the Light, and then put out* thy *Light.*

Another hinted a Reading very *sophisticated* in my Opinion,

> *Put out the Light, and then put out* thee, *Light;*

making Light to be the vocative Case. Another would have altered the last Word, and read,

> Put out thy Light, and then put out thy Sight.

But *Betterton* said, if the Text was to be *disturbed*, he saw no reason why a Word might not be changed as well as a Letter, and instead of *put out thy* Light, you might read *put out thy* Eyes. At last it was agreed on all sides, to refer the matter to the Decision of *Shakespeare* himself, who delivered his Sentiments as follows: 'Faith, Gentlemen, it is so long since I wrote the Line, I have forgot my Meaning. This I know, could I have dreamt so much Nonsense would have been talked & writ about it, I would have blotted it out of my Works: for I am sure, if any of these be my Meaning, it doth me very little Honour.'

Henry IV Part Two, i. i. 1

and an accompanying note in the Arden edition (1923):

Text
LORD BARDOLPH: Who keeps the gate here, ho!
Footnote
1. *Who* . . . here, ho!] 'Who' is here, I think, the indefinite ('He who'), and not the interrogative pronoun, as is implied, for instance, by the punctuation, 'Who keeps the gate here? ho!' (*Oxford Shakespeare*), and 'Who keeps the gate here, ho?' (*Cambridge Shakespeare*). 'Who keeps the gate' is a periphrasis (= 'Porter') of a kind usual in calling to servants or others, in attendance but out of sight. Cf. 2 *Henry VI*.i.iv.82: 'York . . . Who's within there, ho! *Enter a Serving-man.*' (*Oxford Shakespeare*); *Henry VIII*, v.ii.2, 3: 'Cran. . . . Ho! Who waits there! ('there?' *Oxford Shakespeare*). *Enter Keeper.*' Massinger, *The Roman Actor*, iii.ii: 'Iphis. . . . I must . . . knock . . . Within there, ho! something divine come forth. . . . (*Enter* Latinus *as a Porter*)'; Jonson, *Every Man in his Humour*, iv.viii; R. Steele, *The Funeral* (1701), ii.iii: 'Fardingale. No—who waits there—pray bring my lute out of the next room. *Enter* Servant, *with a Lute*.' In *Henry VIII*. v.iii.4, the 'Keeper at the door' is doubtful whether Norfolk's question, 'Who waits there?' is or is not the conventional call to the Doorkeeper, *viz.* 'Who waits there!': '*Nor.* Who waits there? *Keeper at the door.* Without, my noble lords? *Gar.* Yes. *Keep.* My lord archbishop: And has done half-an-hour, to know your pleasures.' Cf. also Beaumont and Fletcher, *Maid's Tragedy*, v.iii: '*Lys.* . . . Summon him, Lord Cleon. *Cleon.* Ho, from

the walls there!'; and *Jack Straw* (Hazlitt's *Dodsley*, v. 396): 'Neighbours, you that keep the gates.'

This footnote was included by Stephen Potter, not without reason, in his anthology of comic writing Sense of Humour *(1954).*

Whaur's your Wullie Shakespeare noo?

> A supposed cry from a member of the audience at the first night of John Home's tragedy *Douglas*, 1756

Fresh arrivals were expected and the party was keeping together to welcome them. The Duchess contrived to establish one large circle and start a general discussion of the play. For a time it ran on practical lines: dresses, make-up, the next day's rehearsals. Then it took a historical turn and the talk narrowed to those with special knowledge: Gott, the slightly uncomfortable specialist; Lord Auldearn, with rather more than a smattering of everything; Melville Clay, genuinely learned in the histories of all Hamlets that had ever been; and the Duchess, fresh from intensive reading. Garrick's trick chair that overturned automatically on his starting up in the closet scene, the performance on board the *Dragon* at Sierra Leone in 1607, Mrs Siddons and other female Hamlets, the tradition that Shakespeare's own best performance was as the ghost: the talk ran easily on. Mrs Terborg gave a formidably perceptive account of Walter Hampden's celebrated Hamlet in New York in 1918. Elizabeth remembered how Pepys had once spent an afternoon getting 'To be, or not to be' by heart. And this gave the Duchess her chance. She immediately turned Clay to presenting Mr Pepys delivering the soliloquy to Mrs Pepys. Anything that Anne Dillon had once been used to impose on obscure young men at Hampstead she would never hesitate to impose on the great and the famous at Scamnum.

There can be nothing more trying to an actor than being required to extemporise before a drawing-room—even a drawing-room of quick and sympathetic spirits. But Clay showed no trace of annoyance; the difficulty of the odd task had wholly possessed and absorbed him in a moment. He stood with knitted brows for perhaps twenty seconds, and then—suddenly—Pepys was in the room. And Gott, with no great opinion of the wits of actors, had the feeling that this two minutes' *tour de force*—for it lasted no longer—was one of the most remarkable things he had ever seen. Anyone might know his Pepys and his Hamlet, but instantly to

produce the sheer and subtle imaginative truth that was Clay's picture of
Pepys *as* Hamlet was a miniature but authentic intellectual triumph.

MICHAEL INNES, *Hamlet, Revenge!*, 1937

*The suspects, or some of them, gather in one of the finest of 'literary' detective-
stories, a whodunit which makes witty and subtle use of Shakespearian motifs.*

   *'Michael Innes' was the pseudonym adopted by the scholar and critic J. I. M.
Stewart for his crime fiction. The works which he published under his own
name include* Character and Motive in Shakespeare, *an unusually sprightly
critical study;* The Hawk and the Handsaw, *a radio play in which Hamlet is
confronted with a Freudian explanation of his condition; and* The Mysterious
Affair at Elsinore, *a jeu d'esprit in which the mysteries of* Hamlet *are explored
in the spirit (though not the style) of Agatha Christie.*

   Many crime stories feature a Shakespearian element, ranging from titles—
Poison in Jest, Let's Choose Executors, Bloody Instructions *(set in a
solicitor's office),* Kill Claudio!, Deed without a Name, Double, Double*—
to full-blown themes. Edmund Crispin's* Love Lies Bleeding *(1948) turns on
the discovery of the lost manuscript of* Love's Labour's Won.

Brush Up your Shakespeare

> The girls today in society
> Go for classical poetry
> So to win their hearts one must quote with ease
> Aeschylus and Euripides.
> One must know Homer and, b'lieve me, bo,
> Sophocles, also Sappho-ho.
> Unless you know Shelley and Keats and Pope,
> Dainty debbies will call you a dope.
> But the poet of them all
> Who will start 'em simply ravin'
> Is the poet people call
> 'The bard of Stratford-on-Avon.'
>
> Brush up your Shakespeare,
> Start quoting him now,
> Brush up your Shakespeare
> And the women you will wow.
> Just declaim a few lines from 'Othella'
> And they'll think you're a helluva fella,

If your blonde won't respond when you flatter'er
Tell her what Tony told Cleopaterer,
If she fights when her clothes you are mussing,
What are clothes? 'Much Ado About Nussing.'
Brush up your Shakespeare
And they'll all kowtow.

Brush up your Shakespeare,
Start quoting him now,
Brush up your Shakespeare
And the women you will wow.
With the wife of the British embessida
Try a crack out of 'Troilus and Cressida,'
If she says she won't buy it or tike it
Make her tike it, what's more, 'As You Like It.'
If she says your behavior is heinous
Kick her right in the 'Coriolanus,'
Brush up your Shakespeare
And they'll all kowtow.

Brush up your Shakespeare,
Start quoting him now,
Brush up your Shakespeare
And the women you will wow.
If you can't be a ham and do 'Hamlet'
They will not give a damn or a damnlet,
Just recite an occasional sonnet
And your lap'll have 'Honey' upon it,
When your baby is pleading for pleasure
Let her sample your 'Measure for Measure,'
Brush up your Shakespeare
And they'll all kowtow.

Brush up your Shakespeare,
Start quoting him now,
Brush up your Shakespeare
And the women you will wow.
Better mention 'The Merchant of Venice'
When her sweet pound o' flesh you would menace,
If her virtue, at first, she defends—well,
Just remind her that 'All's Well That Ends Well,'

And if still she won't give you a bonus
You know what Venus got from Adonis!
Brush up your Shakespeare
And they'll all kowtow.

Brush up your Shakespeare
Start quoting him now,
Brush up your Shakespeare
And the women you will wow.
If your goil is a Washington Heights dream
Treat the kid to 'A Midsummer Night's Dream,'
If she then wants an all-by-herself night
Let her rest ev'ry 'leventh or 'Twelfth Night,'
If because of your heat she gets huffy
Simply play on and 'Lay on, Macduffy!'
Brush up your Shakespeare
And they'll all kowtow.

Brush up your Shakespeare,
Start quoting him now,
Brush up your Shakespeare
And the women you will wow.
So tonight just recite to your Katey
'Kiss me, Kate, Kiss me, Kate, Kiss me, Katey,'
Brush up your Shakespeare
And they'll all kowtow.

COLE PORTER, from *Kiss Me, Kate*, 1948

1601

or *Conversation as it was by the Social Fireside in the Time of the Tudors*

[Mem.—the following is supposed to be an extract from the diary of the Pepys of that day, the same being cup-bearer to Queen Elizabeth. It is supposed that he is of ancient and noble lineage; that he despises these literary *canaille*; that his soul consumes with wrath to see the Queen stooping to talk with such; and that the old man feels his nobility defiled by contact with Shakspere, etc., and yet he has *got* to stay there till Her Majesty chooses to dismiss him.]

Yesternight toke her maiste ye queene a fantasie such as she sometimes hath, and hadde to her closet certain that doe write playes, bokes, and such like, these being my lord Bacon, his worship Sr Walter Ralegh, Mr Ben Jonson, and ye childe Francis Beaumonte, which being but sixteen, hath yet turned his hande to ye doing of ye Lattin masters into our Englishe tong, wh grete discretion and much applaus. Also came wh these ye famous Shaxpur. A righte straunge mixing truly of mightie blode wh mean, ye more in especial since ye queenes grace was present, as likewise these following, to wit: Ye Duchess of Bilgewater, twenty-two yeres of age; ye Countesse of Granby, twenty-six; her doter, ye Lady Helen, fifteen; as also these two maides of honour, to wit: ye Lady Margery Boothy, sixty-five, and ye Lady Alice Dilberry, turned seventy, she being two yeres ye queenes graces elder.

I being her maistes cup-bearer, hadde no choice but to remaine and beholde rank forgot, and ye high holde converse wh ye low as uppon equal termes, a grete scandal did ye world heare therof.

In ye heat of ye talk it befel yt one did breake wynde, yielding an exceding mightie and distresful stink, wherat all did laffe full sore, and then—

Ye Queene.—Verily in mine eight and sixty yeres have I not heard the fellow to this fart. Meseemeth, by ye grete sounde and clamour of it, it was male; yet ye belly it did lurk behinde shoulde now fall leane and flat against ye spine of him yt hath bene delivered of so stately and so vaste a bulk, wheras ye guts of them yt doe quiff-splitters beare, stande comely still and rounde. Prithee let ye author confes ye offspring. Will my Lady Alice testify?

Lady Alice.—Good your grace, an' I hadde room for such a thunder-bust within mine ancient bowels, 'tis not in reason I coulde discharge ye same and live to thank God for yt He did choose handmaide so humble wherby to shew his power. Nay, 'tis not I yt have broughte forth this rich o'ermastering fog, this fragrant bloom, so pray ye seeke ye further.

Ye Queene.—Mayhap ye Lady Margery hath done ye companie this favour?

Lady Margery.—So please ye madam, my limbs are feeble wh ye weighte and drouth of five and sixty winters, and it behoveth yt I be tender unto them. In ye good providence of God, an' I hadde contained this wonder, forsoothe wolde I have gi'en ye whole evening of my sinking life to ye dribbling of it forth, wh trembling and uneasy soul, not launched it sudden in its matchless might, taking mine own life wh violence, rending my weak frame like rotten rags. It was not I, your maiste.

Ye Queene.—O' God's name who hath favoured us? Hath it come to pass yt a fart shall fart *itself*? Not such a one as this, I trow. Young Master Beaumonte—but no; 'twolde have wafted him to heav'n like downe of gooses boddy. 'Twas not ye little Lady Helen—nay, ne'er blush, my childe; thoul't tickle thy tender maidenhedde with many a mousie-squeak before thou learnest to blow a harricane like this. Was't you, my learned and ingenious Jonson?

Jonson.—So fell a blast hath ne'er mine ears saluted, nor yet a stench so all-pervading and immortal. 'Twas not a novice did it, good your maiste, but one of veteran experience—else hadde he failed of confidence. In soothe it was not I.

Ye Queene.—My lord Bacon?

Lord Bacon.—Not from mine leane entrailes hath this prodigie burst forth, so pleas your grace. Naught doth so befit ye grete as grete performance; and haply shall ye finde yt 'tis not from mediocrity this miracle hath issued.

[Tho' ye subject be but a fart, yet will this tedious sink of learning pondrously phillosophize. Meantime did the foul and deadly stink pervade all places to that degree, yt never smelt I ye like, yet dare I not to leave ye presence, albeit I was like to suffocate.]

Ye Queene.—What saith ye worshipful Master Shaxpur?

Shaxpur.—In the grete hand of God I stande and so proclaim mine innocence. Though ye sinless hosts of heav'n hadde foretolde ye coming of this most desolating breath, proclaiming it a work of uninspired man, its quaking thunders, its firmament-clogging rottenness, its own achievement in due course of nature, yet hadde not I believed it; but hadde said the pit itself hath furnished forth the stink, and heav'ns artillery hath shook the globe in admiration of it.

[Then there was a silence, and each did turn him toward the worshipful Sr Walter Ralegh that browned, embattled, bloody swashbuckler, who rising up did smile, and simpering say]

Sr W.—Most gracious maiste, 'twas I that did it, but indeed it was so poor and frail a note, compared wh such as I am wont to furnish, yt in sooth I was ashamed to call the weakling mine in so august a presence. It was nothing—less than nothing, madam—I did it but to clear my nether throat; but hadde I come prepared, then hadde I delivered something worthie. Bear wh me, pleas your grace, till I can make amends.

[Then delivered he himself of such a godless and rock-shivering blast that all were fain to stoppe their ears, and following it did come so dense and foul a stink that yt which went before did seem a poor and trifling thing beside it. Then saith he, feigning that he blushed and was confused, *I perceive that I am weak to-day, and cannot justice do unto my powers:* and sat him down as who shoulde say, *There it is not much; yet he yt hath an arse to spare, let him fellow yt, an think he can.* By God, an I were ye Queene, I wolde e'en tip this swaggering braggart out o' the court, and let him air his grandeurs and break his intolerable wynde before ye deaf and such as suffocation pleaseth.]

Then felle they to talk about ye manners and customs of many peoples, and Master Shaxpur spake of ye boke of ye sieur Michael de Montaine, wherein was mention of ye customs of widows of Perigord to wear uppon ye headdress, in signe of widowhood, a jewel in ye similitude of a man's member wilted and limber, wherat ye queene did laffe and say, *Widows in England doe wear prickes too, but betwixt the thighs, and not wilted neither, till coition hath done that office for them.* Master Shaxpur did likewise observe how yt ye sieur de Montaine hath also spoken of a certain emperor of such mightie prowess yt he did take ten maidenheddes in ye compass of a single night, ye while his empress did entertain two and twenty lusty knights between her sheetes, yet was not satisfied; wherat ye merrie Countesse Granby saith a ram is yet ye emperor's superior, sith he will tup a hundred yewes 'twixt sun and sun; and after, if he can have none more to shag, will masturbate until he hath enrich'd whole acres wh his seed . . .

. . . Then conversed they of religion, and ye mightie work ye olde dead Luther did doe by ye grace of God. Then next about poetry, and Master Shaxpur did rede a part of his King Henry IV, ye which, it seemeth unto me, is not of the value of an arseful of ashes, yet they praised it bravely, one and all.

Ye same did rede a portion of his 'Venus and Adonis' to their prodigious admiration, wheras I, being sleepy and fatigued withal, did deme it but paltrie stuff, and was the more discomfited in yt ye blodie bucanier hadde got his secconde wynde, and did turn his mind to farting wh such villain zeal that presently I was like to choke once more. God damn this wyndie ruffian and all his breed. I wolde yt hell mighte get him. . . .

MARK TWAIN, 1876 (first published privately, 1882)

Versions of Love

'My love for you has faded'—thus the Bad
Quarto, the earliest text, whose midget page
Derived from the imperfect memories
Of red-nosed, small-part actors
Or the atrocious shorthand of the age.

However, the far superior Folio had
'My love for you was fated'—thus implying
Illicit passion, a tragic final act.
And this was printed from the poet's own
Foul papers, it was reckoned;
Supported by the reading of the Second
Quarto, which had those sombre words exact.

Such evidence was shaken when collation
Showed that the Folio copied slavishly
The literals of that supposedly
Independent Quarto. Thus one had to go
Back to the first text of all.

'My love for you has faded'—quite impossible.
Scholars produced at last the emendation:
'My love for you fast endured.'
Our author's ancient hand that must have been
Ambiguous and intellectual
Foxed the compositors of a certainty.
And so the critical editions gave
Love the sound status that she ought to have
In poetry so revered.

But this conjecture cannot quite destroy
The question of what the poet really wrote
In the glum middle reaches of his life:
Too sage, too bald, too fearful of fiasco
To hope beyond his wife,
Yet aching almost as promptly as a boy.

ROY FULLER, c.1960

Exit the Players

It is over. Self-mortifying Hamlet
gets up and puts his sword back on the shelf;
Laertes, unbloody, shuts his manila folder;

the Queen, who moved two separate amendments,
thinks Yorick played the fool offensively;
Horatio had the numbers this afternoon

and buffaloed through a policy decision
the Ghost would not have stomached;
Denmark is feeling just a wee bit whacked.

Ophelia's hair is dry: she didn't say much
but wouldn't mind slipping over to the pub
with Rosencrantz—why does he have to keep nattering

to the King? It's drinking time. Stiff Guildenstern
will not forgive Polonius and, to boot,
has lost his biro somewhere round the place.

It could have been worse. The dead all kept their tempers,
Gertrude cracked several, Hamlet one good joke
and they got through the whole agenda, perhaps because

Fortinbras is still on sabbatical leave.

CHRIS WALLACE-CRABBE

'From time to time I detect signs of fellow-travelling. Then I think I'm on the wrong tack entirely, he's positively Right Wing Labour. Again, you find him stringing along with the far, but anti-Communist, Left. You can't help admiring the way he conceals his hand. My guess is he's playing ball with the Comrades on the quiet for whatever he can get out of it, but trying to avoid the appearance of doing so. He doesn't want to prejudice his chances of a good job in the Government when the moment comes.'

'Was that the game Hamlet was playing when he said:

> The undiscovered country from whose bourn
> No fellow-traveller returns, puzzles the will?'

'There was something fishy about Hamlet's politics, I agree,' said

Bagshaw. 'But the only fellow-travellers we can be certain about were Rosencrantz and Guildenstern.'

ANTHONY POWELL, *Books Do Furnish a Room*, 1971

The acquaintance being discussed is Widmerpool.

In Anthony Burgess's Enderby's Dark Lady, *Shakespeare, who has learned the details of the Gunpowder Plot, is granted an interview with King James's chief minister:*

Robert Cecil, Earl of Salisbury, big-headed and dwarf-bodied, stood with his hunchback turned to the great seacoal fire. Papers, papers everywhere. He said:
    'I am glad, albeit it be brief, to make acquaintance of the man. The plays I know. Your *Amblet* was a fine comedy. What is this story?'

Shakespeare reports on what he has heard, and Cecil is duly grateful—

'. . . So, I thank you for your loyal work—'
    'A tragedy, good my lord.'
    'It might well have been so.'
    'No, no, my play, which some call *Hamlet*.'
    'Was it so? I remember laughing . . . '

ANTHONY BURGESS, *Enderby's Dark Lady*, 1984

Will. Follow that boat!
Boatman. Right you are, governor!
Will sits in the stern of the boat and the Boatman sits facing him, rowing lustily.
Boatman (Cont'd). I know your face. Are you an actor?
Will (oh God, here we go again). Yes.
Boatman. Yes, I've seen you in something. That one about a king.
Will. Really?
Boatman. I had that Christopher Marlowe in my boat once.

From *Shakespeare in Love*, a screenplay by MARC NORMAN and TOM STOPPARD, 1999

To characterize Hamlet as a thorough-going weakling, Shakespeare allows him to appear, in his conversation with the players, as a good theatre critic.

HEINRICH HEINE, *The Romantic School*, 1836, tr. S. S. Prawer

Some titles taken or adapted from Shakespeare:

All Our Yesterdays (novel, H. M. Tomlinson; from *Macbeth*)
Ape and Essence (novel, Aldous Huxley; from *Measure for Measure*)
Benefits Forgot (memoir, John Masefield; from *As You Like It*)
Brave New World (novel, Aldous Huxley; from *The Tempest*)
Brief Candles (short stories, Aldous Huxley; from *Macbeth*)
Cakes and Ale (novel, Somerset Maugham; from *Twelfth Night*)
The Darling Buds of May (stories, H. E. Bates; from Sonnet xviii)
Dear Brutus (play, J. M. Barrie; from *Julius Caesar*)
The Demi-Paradise (film, directed by Anthony Asquith; from *Richard II*)
'Down, Wanton, Down!' (poem, Robert Graves; from *King Lear*)
The Dyer's Hand (essays, W. H. Auden; from Sonnet cxi)
The Enchafed Flood (criticism, W. H. Auden; from *Othello*)
Following Darkness (novel, Forrest Reid; from *A Midsummer Night's Dream*)
A Giant's Strength (novel, Upton Sinclair; from *Measure for Measure*)
The Glimpses of the Moon (novel, Edith Wharton; from *Hamlet*)
A Hazard of New Fortunes (novel, William Dean Howells; from *King John*)
He Should Have Died Hereafter (mystery story, Cyril Hare; from *Macbeth*)
Household Words (periodical, founded by Charles Dickens; from *Henry V*)
It Was the Nightingale (memoir, Ford Madox Ford; from *Romeo and Juliet*)
Let It Come Down (novel, Paul Bowles; from *Macbeth*)
The Long Divorce (mystery story, Edmund Crispin; from *Henry VIII*)
'Millions of Strange Shadows' (poem, Anthony Hecht; from Sonnet liii)
The Moon is Down (novel, John Steinbeck; from *Macbeth*)
Mortal Coils (stories, Aldous Huxley; from *Hamlet*)
Music Ho! (music criticism, Constant Lambert; from *Antony and Cleopatra*)
My Sad Captains (collection of poems, Thom Gunn; from *Antony and Cleopatra*)
O, How the Wheel Becomes It! (novella, Anthony Powell; from *Hamlet*)
Old Men Forget (memoir, Duff Cooper; from *Henry V*)
'Out, Out—' (poem, Robert Frost; from *Macbeth*)
Pale Fire (novel, Vladimir Nabokov; from *Timon of Athens*)
Perchance to Dream (musical, Ivor Novello; from *Hamlet*)
Present Laughter (play, Noel Coward; from *Twelfth Night*)
Remembrance of Things Past (novel, Marcel Proust, tr. C. K. Scott Moncrieff; from Sonnet xxx)
Sad Cypress (mystery story, Agatha Christie; from *Twelfth Night*)
Salad Days (musical, Julian Slade; from *Antony and Cleopatra*)

Sigh No More (revue, Noel Coward; from *Much Ado about Nothing*)

The Sound and the Fury (novel, William Faulkner; from *Macbeth*)

A Star Danced (memoir, Gertrude Lawrence; from *Much Ado About Nothing*)

The Strings are False (memoir, Louis MacNeice; from *Julius Caesar*)

Taken at the Flood (mystery story, Agatha Christie; from *Julius Caesar*; title changed to *There is a Tide* in the USA)

A Thirsty Evil (stories, Gore Vidal; from *Measure for Measure*)

This Happy Breed (play, Noel Coward; from *Richard II*)

Time Must Have a Stop (novel, Aldous Huxley; from *Henry IV Part One*)

To Be or Not To Be (film, directed by Ernst Lubitsch; from *Hamlet*)

Told By an Idiot (novel, Rose Macaulay; from *Macbeth*)

Who Is Sylvia? (play, Terence Rattigan; from *The Two Gentlemen of Verona*)

With a Bare Bodkin (mystery story, Cyril Hare; from *Hamlet*)

Without My Cloak (novel, Kate O'Brien; from Sonnet xxxiv)

The most oblique of these borrowings is Forrest Reid's Following Darkness. *It comes from Puck's line about the fairies 'following darkness like a dream'.*

BY WAY OF AN AFTERWORD

Shakespeare has surface beneath surface, to an immeasurable depth, adapted to the plummet-line of every reader; his works present many phases of truth, each with scope large enough to fill a contemplative mind. Whatever you seek in him you will surely discover, provided you seek truth. There is no exhausting the various interpretation of his symbols; and a thousand years hence, a world of new readers will possess a whole library of new books, as we ourselves do, in these volumes old already.

NATHANIEL HAWTHORNE, Our Old Home, 1863

It is just because Shakespeare insists on leaving matters in the mist in which they are born that his thought endures. Persons who schematize the Unknowable codify themselves, and pass by with the age they live in.

JOHN JAY CHAPMAN, Greek Genius and Other Essays, 1915

the great, ever-living dead man . . .

COLERIDGE, Biographia Literaria, 1817

It takes a bold man to presume that Newton and Shakespeare will still be familiar names ten thousand, to say nothing of ten million, years hence.

JOHN PASSMORE, The Perfectibility of Man, 1970

To Shakespeare

After Three Hundred Years

Bright baffling Soul, least capturable of themes,
Thou, who display'dst a life of commonplace,
Leaving no intimate word or personal trace
Of high design outside the artistry
Of thy penned dreams,
Still shalt remain at heart unread eternally.

Through human orbits thy discourse to-day,
   Despite thy formal pilgrimage, throbs on
   In harmonies that cow Oblivion,
   And, like the wind, with all-uncared effect
      Maintain a sway
Not fore-desired, in tracks unchosen and unchecked.

   And yet, at thy last breath, with mindless note
   The borough clocks but samely tongued the hour
   The Avon just as always glassed the tower,
   Thy age was published on thy passing-bell
      But in due rote
With other dwellers' deaths accorded a like knell.

   And at the strokes some townsman (met, maybe,
   And thereon queried by some squire's good dame
   Driving in shopward) may have given thy name,
   With, 'Yes, a worthy man and well-to-do;
      Though, as for me,
I knew him but by just a neighbour's nod, 'tis true.

   'I' faith, few knew him much here, save by word,
   He having elsewhere led his busier life;
   Though to be sure he left with us his wife.'
   —'Ah, one of the tradesmen's sons, I now recall . . .
      Witty, I've heard . . .
We did not know him. . . . Well, good-day. Death comes to all.'

   So, like a strange bright bird we sometimes find
   To mingle with the barn-door brood awhile,
   Then vanish from their homely domicile—
   Into man's poesy, we wot not whence,
      Flew thy strange mind,
Lodged there a radiant guest, and sped for ever thence.

THOMAS HARDY, 1916

ACKNOWLEDGEMENTS

The editor and publisher gratefully acknowledge permission to include the following copyright material:

Anna Akhmatova: 'To the Londoners' from *Second Thoughts* tr. D. M. Thomas (Secker & Warburg, 1985), by permission of The Random House Group Ltd.

Isaac Asimov: '*The Immortal Bard*', copyright © 1953 by Palmer Publications, Inc., from *Earth is Room Enough* (1957), by permission of the publisher, Doubleday, a division of Random House, Inc.

W. H. Auden: extract from 'Shakespeare's Sonnets' (1964) from *Forewords and Afterwords* (1973) and 'Trinculo' from 'The Sea and the Mirror' (1944), copyright 1944 by W. H. Auden, from *Collected Poems* (1976), by permission of the publishers, Faber & Faber Ltd. and Random House, Inc.

Ingeborg Bachmann: 'Bohemia Lies by the Sea' from *In the Storm of Roses* tr. Mark Anderson (Princeton University Press, 1986).

Charles Baudelaire: extracts from 'Eugène Delacroix' (1855) from *The Mirror of Art* tr. Jonathan Mayne (Phaidon Press, 1955), copyright © Phaidon Press Ltd. 1955, by permission of the publishers.

Samuel Beckett: lines from 'Love and Lethe' (1934) in *More Pricks than Kicks* (Calder & Boyars, 1970), by permission of Calder Publications Ltd.

Max Beerbohm: extract from *Around Theatres* (Hart Davis, 1953), copyright © the Estate of Max Beerbohm, by permission of London Management.

Hilaire Belloc: 'Imitation' from *Complete Verse* (Pimlico, 1991), by permission of PFD on behalf of the Estate of Hilaire Belloc.

Saul Bellow: extract from *Seize the Day* (Weidenfeld & Nicolson, 1956), by permission of The Orion Publishing Group Ltd.

Walter Benjamin: extract from 'Karl Kraus' (1931) from *Reflections: Essays, Aphorisms, Autobiographical Writings*, tr. Edmund Jephcott, translation copyright © 1978 by Harcourt, Inc., by permission of the publisher, taken from *Selected Writings of Walter Benjamin*, vol. ii *1927–1934* ed. Michael W. Jennings, Howard Eiland, and Gary Smith (The Belknap Press of Harvard University Press, 1999), copyright © by the President and Fellows of Harvard College, by permission of the publisher.

John Berryman: extract from 'On Macbeth' from *Berryman's Shakespeare* ed. John Haffenden (Farrar, Straus, & Giroux, 1960), copyright © 1999 by Kate Donahue Berryman; lines from *Love and Fame, Part One* (Faber, 1971), copyright © 1970 by John Berryman and © 1972 by the Estate of John Berryman, by permission of the publishers, Faber & Faber Ltd. and Farrar, Straus, & Giroux, LLC.

Guy Boas: 'I dreamt last night of Shakespeare' first published in *Punch*, February 1926, by permission of Punch Library.

Edward Bond: extract from the Preface to *Bingo: Scenes of Money and Death* (Eyre Methuen, 1974), copyright © Edward Bond 1974, by permission of Methuen Publishing Ltd. and Casarotto Ramsay & Associates Ltd.

Jorge Luis Borges: extract from 'Everything and Nothing' tr. Kenneth Krabbenhoft from *The Maker* (1960) in *Selected Poems* ed. Alexander Coleman (Allen Lane, The Penguin Press, 1999), copyright © Maria Kodama 1999, translation copyright © Kenneth Krabbenhoft 1999; and 'Shakespeare's Memory' (1980) from *Collected Fictions* tr. Andrew Hurley (Viking, 1998), copyright © Maria Kodama 1998, translation copyright © Penguin Putnam Inc. 1998; both by permission of Penguin Books Ltd. and Viking Penguin, a division of Penguin Putnam, Inc.

Ulrich Bräker: extracts from *A Few Words About Shakespeare's Plays* tr. Derek Bowman (Oswald Wolff, 1979), by permission of Berg Publishers.

Bertolt Brecht: 'On Shakespeare's Play *Hamlet*' tr. John Willett from *Bertolt Brecht's Poems 1913–1956* ed. John Willett and Ralph Manheim (Eyre Methuen, 1976), by permission of Methuen Publishing Ltd. and Suhrkamp Verlag.

Anthony Burgess: extract from *Nothing Like the Sun: A Story of Shakespeare's Love-Life* (Penguin, 1966), copyright © The Estate of Anthony Burgess 1964, and extracts from *Enderby's Dark Lady, or No End to Enderby* (Hutchinsons, 1984), copyright © The Estate of Anthony Burgess 1984, by permission of Artellus Ltd.

Michael Burns: extract from *Dreyfus: A Family Affair* (Chatto & Windus, 1992), by permission of David Higham Associates Ltd.

David Cairns: extracts from *Berlioz: The Making of an Artist* (Allen Lane, 1999), copyright © David Cairns 1999, 2000, and extracts from *Berlioz: Servitude and Greatness 1832–1869*: vol. 2 (Allen Lane, The Penguin Press, 1999), copyright © David Cairns 1999, 2000, by permission of Penguin Books Ltd. and the University of California Press.

David Campbell: lines from 'Winter' from *Speak with the Sun* (Chatto & Windus, 1949), by permission of The Random House Group Ltd.

C. P. Cavafy: 'King Claudius' from *The Complete Poems* tr. Rae Dalven (Hogarth Press/Harcourt Brace, 1961), copyright © 1961 and renewed 1989 by Rae Dalven, by permission of The Random House Group Ltd. and Harcourt, Inc.

Nirad C. Chaudhuri: extracts from *The Autobiography of an Unknown Indian* (Macmillan, 1951), by permission of Macmillan, London, UK.

G. K. Chesterton: extract from 'A Midsummer Night's Dream' in *The Common Man* (Sheed & Ward, 1950), and extract from 'The Tragedy of King Lear' in *The Spice of Life* (Darwen Finlayson, 1964), by permission of A. P. Watt Ltd. on behalf of The Royal Literary Fund.

Eugène Delacroix: extracts from *Journals of Eugène Delacroix* tr. Walter Pach (Crown Publishers, 1948), by permission of Random House, Inc.

Emily Dickinson: 'The Humming-Bird', poem 1463 (*c*.1879), from *The Poems of Emily Dickinson* ed. Thomas H. Johnson (The Belknap Press of Harvard University Press), copyright © 1951, 1955, 1979 by the President and Fellows of Harvard College, by permission of the publishers and the Trustees of Amherst College.

Fyodor Dostoevsky: extracts from *The Devils* (1871) also known as *The Possessed* tr. David Magarshack (Penguin Classics, 1953, 2e 1971), copyright © David Magarshack 1953, 1971; extracts from *The Brothers Karamazov* (1880) tr. David McDuff (Penguin Classics, 1993), copyright © David McDuff 1993; and extracts from *Notes from Underground* (1864) tr. Jessie Coulson (Penguin Classics, 1972), copyright © Jessie Coulson 1972; all by permission of Penguin Books Ltd.

T. S. Eliot: 'Lines to a Yorkshire Terrier' from 'Five Finger Exercises' from *Collected Poems 1909–1962* (1963), copyright © 1936 by Harcourt Inc., copyright © 1964, 1963 by T. S. Eliot, by permission of the publishers, Faber & Faber Ltd. and Harcourt, Inc.

William Empson: extract from *Seven Types of Ambiguity* (Hogarth Press, 1930), and lines from 'To an Old Lady' (1928) from *Collected Poems* (Chatto & Windus, 1935), copyright 1949 and renewed 1977 by William Empson, both by permission of Lady Empson, The Random House Group Ltd. and Harcourt, Inc.

D. J. Enright: 'All's Well That Ends or, Shakespeare Unmasked' (1973) from *Collected Poems* (Carcanet, 2000) reprinted by permission of Carcanet Press Ltd.; and extract from *Shakespeare and the Students* (Chatto & Windus, 1970), by permission of Watson, Little Ltd. on behalf of the author.

Gavin Ewart: 'Sonnet: Tidying Up' (1976) and 'Sonnet: Shakespeare's Universality' (1977) from *The Collected Ewart 1933–1980* (Hutchinson, 1980), by permission of Margo Ewart.

Frank Field: extract from *Last Days of Mankind: Karl Kraus and His Vienna* (Macmillan, 1967): copyright holder not traced.

Gustave Flaubert: extracts from *The Letters of Gustave Flaubert 1830–1857* selected and tr. Francis Steegmuller, vol. 1 (Harvard University Press, 1980), copyright © 1977 by the President and Fellows of Harvard College, by permission of the publisher.

Sigmund Freud: extract from *The Origins of Psychoanalysis (Correspondence with Wilhelm Fliess)* tr. Eric Mosbacher and James Strachey (Imago, 1954), by permission of Sigmund Freud Copyrights at Mark Paterson & Associates.

Robert Frost: lines from 'Mowing' from *The Complete Poems of Robert Frost* ed. Edward Connery Lathem (Jonathan Cape, 1951), copyright © 1969 by Henry Holt & Co., by permission of the Estate of Robert Frost, The Random House Group Ltd., and Henry Holt & Co., LLC.

Roy Fuller: 'Versions of Love' from *New and Collected Poems* (Secker & Warburg, 1985), by permission of John Fuller.

Pieter Geyl: extracts from 'Shakespeare as an Historian: a Fragment' in *Encounters in History* (Collins, 1963); copyright holder not traced.

André Gide: extract from *Journals* tr. Justin O'Brien (Martin, Secker & Warburg), by permission of the publishers, The Random House Group Ltd. and Alfred A. Knopf, a division of Random House, Inc.

Sir W. S. Gilbert: extract from burlesque 'Rosencrantz and Guildenstern', first published in the magazine *Fun* in 1874, reprinted from the *Original Plays, Third Series* version (Chatto & Windus, 1893, reprinted 1923), by permission of The Royal Theatrical Fund of 11 Garrick Street London WC2E 9AR.

Johann Wolfgang von Goethe: extracts from *Wilhelm Meister's Years of Apprenticeship* tr. H. M. Waidson (John Calder, 1977–8), by permission of Calder Publications Ltd.

Alethea Hayter: extract from *Horatio's Version* (1972), by permission of the publishers, Faber & Faber Ltd.

Seamus Heaney: lines from 'Traditions' from *Wintering Out* (1973) also from *Poems 1965–1975*, copyright © 1980 Seamus Heaney, by permission of the publishers, Faber & Faber Ltd. and Farrar, Straus, & Giroux, Inc.

Heinrich Heine: extracts from 'Shakespeare's Girls and Women' (1938) in *Frankenstein's Island* tr. S. S. Prawer (Cambridge, 1986), by permission of Cambridge University Press; extract from 'Shakespeare's Girls and Women' (1938) tr. E. B. Ashton in *Heinrich Heine: Works of Prose* ed. Herman Kesten (L. B. Fischer, 1943), copyright holder not traced; and extract from *Heine's Jewish Comedy* tr. S. S. Prawer (OUP, 1983), by permission of Oxford University Press.

Zbigniew Herbert: 'Elegy of Fortinbras' from *Zbigniew Herbert: Selected Poems* tr. Czesław Milosz and Peter Dale Scott (Penguin, 1968), translation copyright © Czesław Milosz and Peter Dale Scott 1968, by permission of Penguin Books Ltd.

Alexander Herzen: extracts from *My Past and Thoughts* (1861–6), vol. iii, tr. Constance Garnett, revised by Humphrey Higgens (Chatto & Windus, 1968), by permission of A. P. Watt Ltd. on behalf of the Estate of Constance Garnett.

Miroslav Holub: 'Polonius' from *Poems Before and After: Collected English Translations* tr. from the Czech by Ian Milner (Bloodaxe Books, 1990), by permission of the publishers.

A. E. Housman: 'A Shropshire Lad XLIII', 'A Shropshire Lad XLIV', 'Last Poems II', and 'Last Poems XXXVII' from *The Collected Poems of A. E. Housman*, copyright © 1965 by Henry Holt & Co., by permission of Henry Holt & Co., LLC and The Society of Authors as the Literary Representative of the Estate of A. E. Housman.

Ted Hughes: 'Prospero and Sycorax' from *Selected Poems 1957–1981* (1982), by permission of the publishers, Faber & Faber Ltd.

Aldous Huxley: extracts from *Brave New World* (Chatto & Windus, 1932) and extract from 'Shakespeare and Religion' first published in *Aldous Huxley: A Memorial Volume* ed. Julian Huxley (Chatto & Windus, 1965), by permission of the Reece Halsey Agency on behalf of the Huxley Estate.

Douglas Hyde: lines from 'How it fared with a Gael at Stratford-on-Avon' translated from the Gaelic, in *A Book in Homage to Shakespeare* ed. Sir Israel Gollancz (OUP, 1916), by permission of Oxford University Press.

Michael Innes: extract from *Hamlet, Revenge!* (Gollancz, 1937), by permission of A. P. Watt Ltd. on behalf of the author.

Eugene Ionesco: from *Macbett* tr. Donald Watson in *Plays* vol. ix (Calder & Boyars, 1973), by permission of Calder Publications Ltd.

David Jones: extracts from *In Parenthesis* (1937), by permission of the publishers, Faber & Faber Ltd.

Gabriel Josipovici: 'A Changeable Report' from *Shakespeare Stories* ed. Giles Gordon (Hamish Hamilton, 1982), by permission of the author.

James Joyce: extracts from *Finnegans Wake* (1939); and extracts from *Ulysses* (1922), copyright © Estate of James Joyce, reprinted by permission of the Estate of James Joyce.

John Maynard Keynes: extract from *A Treatise on Money* (1930) in *Collected Writings*, vol. vi (Macmillan, 1971); copyright holder not traced.

Søren Kierkegaard: extracts from the draft of *The Sickness Unto Death* (1849) tr. Howard V. Kong and Edna H. Kong (Princeton, 1980), copyright © Princeton University Press 1980, by permission of the publishers.

Rudyard Kipling: 'The Craftsmen' (1919) and 'Proofs of Holy Writ' (1934) from *The Definitive Kipling* (1940), by permission of A. P. Watt Ltd on behalf of The National Trust for Places of Historical Interest or Natural Beauty.

Grigori Kosintsev: extracts from *King Lear: The Space of Tragedy* tr. by Mary Mackintosh (Heinemann, 1973), by permission of the Russian Author's Society (RAO).

Jules Laforgue: extract from 'Hamlet, or the consequence of Filial Pity' from *Moral Tales* tr. William Jay Smith (New Directions, 1985), English translation copyright © William Jay Smith 1956, 1957, 1964, 1974, 1984, 1985, by permission of New Directions Publishing Corporation and the JCA Literary Agency.

Giuseppe Tomasi di Lampedusa: extract from *The Siren and Collected Writings* tr. David Gilmour (first published in Great Britain by The Harvill Press, 1995), copyright © Sellerio Editore 1977, English translation copyright © The Harvill Press 1995, by permission of The Harvill Press.

Philip Larkin: extract from *All What Jazz* (1970), by permission of the publishers, Faber & Faber Ltd.

Percy Lubbock: extract from *Mary Cholmondeley* (Jonathan Cape, 1928), copyright © Percy Lubbock 1928, by permission of the Estate and the Sayle Agency.

Louis MacNeice: 'Autolycus' (1945) from *Collected Poems* (Faber, 1966), by permission of David Higham Associates Ltd.

Nadezhda Mandelstam: extract from *Hope Abandoned* tr. Max Hayward (first published in Great Britain by The Harvill Press, 1974), copyright © Atheneum Publishers, 1972, English translation copyright © Atheneum Publishers, New York and Harvill, London, by permission of The Harvill Press.

Don Marquis: 'archy confesses' from *Archy and Mehitabel*, copyright © 1927 by Doubleday, a division of Random House, Inc., by permission of Doubleday.

François Mauriac: extract from *Second Thoughts* (1940) tr. Adrienne Foulke (Darwen Finlayson, 1961), by permission of the publishers, Phillimore & Co., Ltd., Shopwyke Manor Barn, Chichester, West Sussex.

Lord Moran (Charles McMoran Wilson): extract from *Winston Churchill: The Struggle for Survival 1940–1965*: taken from the diaries of Lord Moran (Constable, 1966), by permission of Constable Publishers.

Alexander Moszkowski: extract from *Conversations with Einstein* tr. Henry Brose (Sidgwick & Jackson, 1921): copyright holder not traced.

Iris Murdoch: extracts from *Existentialists and Mystics* (Chatto & Windus, 1997), copyright 1950–2, © 1956–9, 1961–2, 1966, 1969–70, 1972, 1977, 1978, 1986, 1997 by Iris Murdoch, by permission of The Random House Group Ltd. and Penguin, a division of Penguin Putnam Inc.

Vladimir Nabokov: extracts from *Bend Sinister* (1947), from *Strong Opinions* (1973), and from *Pale Fire* (1962), by permission of Random House, Inc.

R. K. Narayan: extract from *The English Teacher* (Eyre & Spottiswoode, 1945/ University of Chicago Press, 1980), copyright 1945 by R. K. Narayan, by permission of The Random House Group Ltd. and The Wallace Literary Agency.

Friedrich Nietzsche: extract from *The Gay Science* (1882) tr. and ed. with commentary by Walter Kaufmann (Random House, 1974), copyright © Random House, Inc. 1974, by permission of Random House, Inc.

Robert Nye: extract from *Mrs Shakespeare: The Complete Works* (Sinclair-Stevenson, 1993), by permission of Sheil Land Associates on behalf of the author.

Ben Okri: extract from 'Leaping Out of Shakespeare's Terror—Five Meditations on Othello' in *A Way of Being Free* (Phoenix House, 1997), by permission of David Godwin Associates on behalf of the author.

Laurence Olivier: extract from *On Acting* (Weidenfeld & Nicolson, 1986), copyright © 1986 Wheelshare Ltd., by permission of The Orion Publishing Group Ltd. and Simon & Schuster, Inc.

Eugene O'Neill: extract from *Long Day's Journey Into Night* (Jonathan Cape, 1956), by permission of The Random House Group Ltd. and Random House, Inc.

Charles Osborne: extracts from *Verdi: A Life in the Theatre* (Knopf, 1987), by permission of Random House, Inc.

John Osborne: extract from *A Place Calling Itself Rome* (Faber, 1973), by permission of David Higham Associates Ltd.

John Passmore: extract from *The Perfectibility of Man* (Gerald Duckworth & Co., 1970), reprinted by permission of the publisher.

Boris Pasternak: 'Hamlet' (1946) from *Selected Poems* tr. Jon Stallworthy and Peter France (Allen Lane, 1983), copyright © Jon Stallworthy and Peter France 1983, by permission of Penguin Books Ltd.; 'Shakespeare' from *Pasternak: Poems* tr. Eugene M. Kayden (University of Michigan Press, 1959), copyright © Eugene M. Kayden 1959, by permission of the publishers; extracts from 'Observations on Translating Shakespeare' (1939–46) from *People and Propositions* tr. Ann Pasternak Slater, ed. Christopher Barnes (Polygon, 1990), by permission of Polygon Press.

Samuel Pepys: extracts from *The Diary of Samuel Pepys* ed. Robert Latham and William Matthews, copyright © The Master, Fellows and Scholars of Magdalene College, Cambridge, Robert Latham and William Matthews 1983, by permission of PFD on behalf of The Master, Fellows and Scholars of Magdalene College, Cambridge and the Estates of Robert Latham and William Matthews.

Peter Porter: 'Reading M. N. D. in Form 4B' from *Poems Ancient and Modern* (1964), by permission of the author.

Richard Posner: extract from 'Law and Literature' in *The Federal Courts: Challenge and Reform* (Harvard University Press, 1985), copyright (Harvard, 1988).

Cole Porter: 'Brush Up Your Shakespeare' from *Kiss Me, Kate* (1948), words and music by Cole Porter, copyright © 1949 Cole Porter and Buxton Hill Music Corporation USA, Chappell Music Ltd., London W6 8BS, by permission of The Cole Porter Musical and Literary Property Trusts and International Music Publications Ltd. All rights reserved.

Anthony Powell: extract from *The Military Philosophers* (Heinemann, 1968) and extract from *Books Do Furnish a Room* (Heinemann, 1971), by permission of David Higham Associates Ltd.

Marcel Proust: extract from *Swann's Way* (1914) from *In Search of Lost Time*, tr. C. K. Scott Moncrieff and Terence Kilmartin, revised by D. J. Enright (Chatto & Windus, 1992), by permission of The Random House Group Ltd. and Random House, Inc.

Alexander Pushkin: extracts from 'Table Talk' in *Pushkin on Literature* ed. and tr. Tatiana Wolff (Methuen, 1971), by permission of Tatiana Wolff.

Jonathan Rose: extracts from *The Intellectual Life of the British Working Classes* (Yale, 2001), by permission of Yale University Press.

Tadeusz Różewicz: 'Nothing in Prospero's Cloak' from *They Came to See a Poet* tr. from the Polish by Adam Czerniawski (Anvil, 1991), by permission of Anvil Press Poetry Ltd.

John Ruskin: extracts from *The Brantwood Diary of John Ruskin* ed. Helen Viljoen (Yale, 1971), by permission of Yale University Press.

Bertrand Russell: extracts from *Nightmares of Eminent Persons* (Bodley Head, 1954), copyright © The Bertrand Russell Peace Foundation, by permission of the Bertrand Russell Peace Foundation Ltd.

Anthony Sampson: extract from *Mandela* (HarperCollins, 1999), by permission of the publishers.

George Santayana: extract from *Interpretations of Poetry and Religion* (A. & C. Black, 1900); copyright holder not traced.

Jean-Paul Sartre: extract from *The Family Idiot* tr. Carol Cosman, vol. iv (Chicago, 1991) by permission of The University of Chicago Press.

Gary Schmidgall: extracts from *Shakespeare and Opera* (OUP, 1990), copyright © 1990 Oxford University Press, Inc., by permission of Oxford University Press, New York.

Bernard Shaw: extracts from article in *The Star*, 1890 ; from Preface to *The Quintessence of Ibsenism*, 1891; from Review of *The Man Shakespeare* by Frank Harris, 1910; from a sketch written in 1910; from Preface to *Geneva*, 1938; from Foreword to *Cymbeline Refinished*, 1945; from *Shakes versus Shav*, 1949; and from *Shaw on Shakespeare* ed. Edwin Wilson (Cassell, 1962); all by permission of The Society of Authors on behalf of the Bernard Shaw Estate.

Logan Pearsall Smith: extract from *On Reading Shakespeare* (Constable, 1933), by permission of Constable Publishers.

Denis Mack Smith: extract from *Cavour* (Weidenfeld & Nicolson, 1985), by permission of The Orion Publishing Group Ltd.

Stevie Smith: extract from *Novel on Yellow Paper* (Jonathan Cape, 1936), by permission of the Estate of James MacGibbon.

Wole Soyinka: extract from 'Shakespeare and the Living Dramatist' first published in *Shakespeare Survey* 36 ed. Stanley Wells (Cambridge University Press, 1983), by permission of Morton L. Leavy on behalf of the author.

Enid Starkie: extract from *Baudelaire* (1957), by permission of the publishers, Faber & Faber Ltd.

Tom Stoppard: extract from *Rosencrantz and Guildenstern are Dead* (Faber, 1966), copyright © Tom Stoppard 1996, 1997, by permission of the publishers, Faber & Faber Ltd and Grove/Atlantic, Inc.; extract from 'Dog's Hamlet, Cahoot's Macbeth' from *The Real Inspector Hound and Other Plays* (Faber, 1980), copyright © Tom Stoppard 1980, by permission of the publishers, Faber & Faber Ltd. and Grove/Atlantic, Inc.

Tom Stoppard with Marc Norman: extract from *Shakespeare in Love* (Faber, 1999), by permission of the publishers, Faber & Faber Ltd. and Hyperion.

Zdenek Stribny: extract from *Shakespeare and Eastern Europe* (OUP, 2000), by permission of Oxford University Press.

August Strindberg: extracts from *Strindberg's Letters* tr. Michael Robinson (Athlone Press, 1992), by permission of Continuum Publishing; extract from *The*

Father (1887) in *Three Plays* tr. Peter Watts (Penguin Classics, 1958), copyright © Peter Watts 1958, by permission of Penguin Books Ltd.

Gerwyn Strobl: extract from 'Shakespeare and the Nazis' first published in *History Today* magazine, May 1997, by permission of *History Today*.

Leo Tolstoy: extract from *Recollections and Essays* tr. Aylmer Maude (Oxford Centenary Edition, 1937), by permission of Oxford University Press.

Leon Trotsky: extract from *Literature and Revolution* (1923) tr. Rose Strunsky (Allen & Unwin, 1925); copyright holder not traced.

Marina Tsvetayeva: 'Ophelia: in Defence of the Queen' (1923) from *Selected Poems* tr. Elaine Feinstein (Carcanet, 2000), by permission of Carcanet Press Ltd.

Ivan Turgenev: extract from *Turgenev's Letters*, selected, tr. and ed. A. V. Knowles (Athlone Press, 1983), by permission of Continuum Publishing; extract from *Hamlet and Don Quixote* (1860) tr. Robert Nichols (Hendersons, 1930), by permission of the literary executor for Robert Nichols.

Giuseppe Ungaretti: extract from 'Notes on Shakespeare's Art of Poetry' (1945) tr. Alfred Triolo, quoted in *Shakespeare in Europe* ed. Oswald Lewinter (Penguin, 1970); copyright holder not traced.

John Updike: extracts from *Gertrude and Claudius* (Hamish Hamilton, 2000), copyright © John Updike 2000, by permission of Penguin Books Ltd. and Alfred A. Knopf, a division of Random House, Inc.

Paul Valéry: extract from 'The Intellectual Crisis' (1919) from *Paul Valéry: Selected Writings* tr. Malcolm Cowley (New Directions, 1950), English translation copyright © 1950 by New Directions Publishing Corporation, by permission of the publishers.

Vincent Van Gogh: extract from *Complete Letters of Vincent Van Gogh* vol. ii (Thames & Hudson, 1978), by permission of the publishers.

Ralph Vaughan Williams: extract from 'A Minim's Rest' (1947) from *National Music and Other Essays* (OUP, 1963), by permission of Mrs Vaughan Williams and RVW Ltd.

Jules Verne: extract from *Journey Backwards to England and Scotland (Voyage à reculons en Angleterre et en Écosse)* tr. Janice Valls-Russell (Chambers Harrap, 1992), by permission of the publishers.

Chris Wallace-Crabbe: 'Exit the Players' from *Selected Poems*, by permission of Carcanet Press Ltd.

Derek Walcott: 'Goats and Monkeys' (1964) from *Collected Poems 1948–1984* (1986) copyright © 1986 by Derek Walcott, by permission of the publishers, Faber & Faber Ltd. and Farrar, Straus, & Giroux, Inc.

Simone Weil: extract from *Simone Weil: Seventy Letters* tr. Richard Rees (OUP, 1975), by permission of Éditions Gallimard and the author's Estate.

Rebecca West: extract from *The Court and the Castle* (Macmillan, 1958), copyright © Rebecca West 1957, by permission of PFD on behalf of the Estate of Rebecca West.

Geoffrey Willans: extract from *Down With Skool! A Guide to School Life for Tiny*

Pupils and their Parents (Max Parrish, 1953/Pavilion, 1992), by permission of the author and the Sayle Agency.

John Dover Wilson: extract from *Milestones on the Dover Road* (1969), by permission of the publishers, Faber & Faber Ltd.

Ludwig Wittgenstein: extracts from *Culture and Value* tr. Peter Winch (Blackwell, 1998), by permission of the publishers.

P. G. Wodehouse: extracts from *Jeeves in the Offing* (1960) and *Very Good, Jeeves!* (1930), by permission of The Random House Group Ltd. and A. P. Watt Ltd. on behalf of The Trustees of the Wodehouse Estate.

Virginia Woolf: extracts from *The Diaries of Virginia Woolf* Vol. III 1925–30, copyright © 1980 by Quentin Bell and Angelica Garnett, and Vol. IV, 1931–35, copyright © 1982 by Quentin Bell and Angelica Garnett, ed. Anne Olivier Bell (The Hogarth Press, 1977–84), by permission of The Random House Group Ltd. and Harcourt, Inc.; extract from *A Room of One's Own* (The Hogarth Press/Harcourt Brace, 1929), copyright 1929 by Harcourt, Inc. and renewed 1957 by Leonard Woolf, by permission of The Society of Authors as the Literary Representative of the Estate of Virginia Woolf, and Harcourt, Inc.

J. B. Yeats: extracts from *Letters to His Son W. B. Yeats* ed. Joseph Hone (Secker & Warburg, 1983), by permission of A. P. Watt Ltd. on behalf of Michael B. Yeats.

W. B. Yeats: extract from 'At Stratford-on-Avon' (1901) from *Essays and Introductions*, copyright © 1961 by Mrs W. B. Yeats, by permission of A. P. Watt Ltd. on behalf of Michael B. Yeats, and Scribner, a division of Simon & Schuster, Inc.

Extract from film script of *Throne of Blood*, Akira Kurosawa's 1957 film adaptation of *Macbeth* quoted in Roger Manvell, *Shakespeare and the Film* (Dent, 1971); copyright holder not traced.

Extracts from *The Duke Ellington Reader* (Oxford University Press, 1993), Irving Townsend 'When Duke Records' (1960) and Stanley Crouch: programme notes; copyright holders not traced.

Although every effort has been made to trace and contact copyright holders, this has not been possible in all cases. If notified, the publishers will be pleased to rectify any errors or omissions at the earliest opportunity.

INDEX OF PLAYS AND CHARACTERS

INDEX OF AUTHORS